D0296060

The Shifts and the Shocks

MARTIN WOLF

The Shifts and the Shocks

What we've learned – and have still to learn – from the financial crisis

ALLEN LANE
an imprint of
PENGUIN BOOKS

ALLEN LANE

Published by the Penguin Group
Penguin Books Ltd, 80 Strand, London WC2R ORL, England
Penguin Group (USA) Inc., 375 Hudson Street, New York, New York 10014, USA
Penguin Group (Canada), 90 Eglinton Avenue East, Suite 700, Toronto, Ontario, Canada M4P 2Y3
(a division of Pearson Canada Inc.)
Penguin Ireland, 25 St Stephen's Green, Dublin 2, Ireland (a division of Penguin Books Ltd)
Penguin Group (Australia), 707 Collins Street, Melbourne, Victoria 3008, Australia
(a division of Pearson Australia Group Pty Ltd)
Penguin Books India Pvt Ltd, 11 Community Centre, Panchsheel Park, New Delhi – 110 017, India
Penguin Group (NZ), 67 Apollo Drive, Rosedale, Auckland 0632, New Zealand
(a division of Pearson New Zealand Ltd)
Penguin Books (South Africa) (Pty) Ltd, Block D, Rosebank Office Park,
181 Jan Smuts Avenue, Parktown North, Gauteng 2193, South Africa

Penguin Books Ltd, Registered Offices: 80 Strand, London WC2R ORL, England

www.penguin.com

First published 2014
002

Copyright © Martin Wolf, 2014

The moral right of the author has been asserted

Set in 10.5/14 pt Sabon LT Std
Typeset by Jouve (UK), Milton Keynes
Printed in Great Britain by Clays Ltd, St Ives plc

ISBN: 978-1-846-14697-8

MIX
Paper from
responsible sources
FSC
www.fsc.org   FSC™ C018179

www.greenpenguin.co.uk

Penguin Books is committed to a sustainable
future for our business, our readers and our planet.
This book is made from Forest Stewardship
Council™ certified paper.

For Jonathan, Benjamin and Rachel,
without whom my life would have been empty

Contents

CONTENTS

Acknowledgements

In writing a book one accumulates many debts. Here I acknowledge just a few of them.

I have to start with thanking Andrew Wylie, my agent, whose boundless energy and enthusiasm made this book happen. I want to thank John Makinson, chairman and chief executive of Penguin, who decided to publish it. I also acknowledge the invaluable contributions of Scott Moyers and Stuart Proffitt, my editors at Penguin, whose care and attention to detail have made the book immeasurably better and clearer than it would otherwise have been. Stuart in particular was inexorable. I recognize the immense importance of his contribution and greatly appreciate the time he took and the attention he bestowed on this book. I also want to note their patience with the delays in completing a book whose writing had to fit in with my normal duties. In addition, I extend my thanks to Richard Duguid and Donald Futers on the Penguin production team, and to Richard Mason for his very helpful editorial input.

I would also like to thank Lionel Barber, the editor of the *Financial Times*, for accommodating the needs of the book. I have taken off a substantial amount of time in order to write it, more than I had hoped, in fact. I appreciate enormously the way the FT has accommodated this and promise not to do it again in the near future. I also want to thank colleagues at the FT from whom I have learned so much. Particular thanks for contributions to ideas in this book go to Chris Giles, Ferdinando Giugliano, my former colleague Krishna Guha, Robin Harding, Martin Sandbu and Gillian Tett.

I owe thanks to an immense number of thinkers and policymakers from whose writings I have been privileged to learn over many years.

I recognize most of these debts via citations in the text, endnotes and references. I would like to record particular thanks to three individuals. The first is Max Corden, who taught me at Oxford and whose remarkable combination of clarity, rigour and good sense has marked me for life. I have aspired, not always successfully, to match these qualities in my professional activities. It was a great honour and still greater pleasure to deliver a lecture, named after him, in his home town of Melbourne in October 2012.[1] The second person is Adair Turner, former chairman of the Financial Services Authority. Adair was kind enough to read the third part of the book and the concluding chapter. I have greatly appreciated his wisdom and support, and learned immensely from his writing on the crisis and its aftermath. The final person is Mervyn King, former governor of the Bank of England and a friend for more than two decades. Despite inevitable professional disagreements, I have always greatly admired his intelligence and integrity. I am grateful to Mervyn for reading the book in draft and giving me supportive and helpful comments. He encouraged me to be even more radical than I had intended to be.

Others to whom I owe gratitude for conversations on the topics of this book include Anat Admati of Stanford University, C. Fred Bergsten of the Peterson Institute for International Economics, Ben Bernanke, former Chairman of the Federal Reserve, Olivier Blanchard of the International Monetary Fund, Claudio Borio of the Bank for International Settlements, Paul de Grauwe of the London School of Economics, my former colleague Chrystia Freeland, Member of the Canadian Parliament, Andy Haldane of the Bank of England, Robert Johnson of the Institute for New Economic Thinking, Paul Krugman of Princeton University, Philippe Legrain, former adviser to the president of the European Commission, Michael Pettis of Peking University, Adam Posen of the Peterson Institute for International Economics, Raghuram Rajan, governor of the Reserve Bank of India, Carmen Reinhart of Harvard University, Kenneth Rogoff of Harvard University, Jeffrey Sachs of Columbia University, Hans-Werner Sinn of CESifo, George Soros, Joseph Stiglitz of Columbia University, Andrew Smithers of Smithers & Co., Lawrence Summers of Harvard University, Alan Taylor of the University of California, Paul Tucker, formerly of the Bank of England, David Vines of Oxford University,

William White, formerly of the Bank for International Settlements, and Malcolm Wiener. I wish also to offer thanks to John Vickers, Claire Spottiswoode, Martin Taylor and William (Bill) Winters, with whom I had the pleasure to serve on the UK government's Independent Commission on Banking in 2010–11, as well as to the members of its admirable secretariat. I apologize to all who might feel slighted by omission from this list. It is far from exhaustive. Needless to say, none of the people I have listed bears any responsibility for what appears in this book.

I also want to give my special thanks to Douglas Irwin of Dartmouth University and Kevin O'Rourke of Oxford University for permission to use the title *The Shifts and the Shocks*, which I have drawn from their interesting paper, 'Coping with Shocks and Shifts'.[2] This phrase captured my theme perfectly.

Finally, and far above all, I must offer my deepest thanks to Alison, my wife of more years than she would like to admit. She has given me everything that could make a man's life happy, including the three children to whom this book is dedicated. Beyond that, I thank her for her encouragement and support in writing this book, which was far from an easy process. Without her, I am sure it would not have been finished. I must thank her, not least, for reading all of the draft and giving me comments that were both sensible and to the point, as she has always done. Above all, she forced me to explain what I mean to a highly intelligent reader who does not live in the world of international macroeconomics and global finance. The value of such a reader is and has always been beyond measure.

List of Figures

Preface: Why I Wrote this Book

Can 'It' – a Great Depression – happen again? And if 'It' can happen why didn't 'It' occur in the years since World War II? These are questions that naturally follow from both the historical record and the comparative success of the past thirty-five years. To answer these questions it is necessary to have an economic theory which makes great depressions one of the possible states in which our type of capitalist economy can find itself.

Hyman Minsky, 1982[1]

This book is about the way in which the financial and economic crises that hit the high-income countries after August 2007 have altered our world. But its analysis is rooted in how these shocks originated in prior shifts – the interactions between changes in the global economy and the financial system. It asks how these disturbing events will – and should – change the ways we think about economics. It also asks how they will – and should – change the policies followed by the affected countries and the rest of the world.

The book is an exploration of an altered landscape. I must start by being honest with myself and with the reader: although I spend my professional life analysing the world economy and have seen many financial crises, I did not foresee a crisis of such a magnitude in the high-income countries. This was not because I was unaware of the unsustainable trends of the pre-crisis era. My previous book, *Fixing Global Finance*, published in 2008 but based on lectures delivered in 2006, discussed the fragility of finance and the frequency of financial crises since the early 1980s. It also examined the worrying growth of huge current-account surpluses and deficits – the so-called 'global imbalances' – after the emerging market crises of 1997–99. It focused particularly on the implications of the linked phenomena of the yawning US current-account deficits, the accumulations of foreign-currency reserves by emerging economies, and the imbalances within the Eurozone.[2] That discussion arose naturally from the consideration of finance in my earlier book, *Why Globalization Works*, published in 2004.[3] That book, while arguing strongly in favour of globalization, stressed the heavy costs of financial crises. Nevertheless, I did not expect these trends to end in so enormous a financial crisis, so comprehensive a rescue, or so huge a turmoil within the Eurozone.

My failure was not because I was unaware that what economists called the 'great moderation' – a period of lower volatility of output in the US, in particular, between the late 1980s and 2007 – had coincided with large and potentially destabilizing rises in asset prices and debt.[4] It was rather because I lacked the imagination to anticipate a meltdown of the Western financial system. I was guilty of working with a mental model of the economy that did not allow for the possibility of another Great Depression or even a 'Great Recession' in the world's most advanced economies. I believed that such an event was possible only as a consequence of inconceivably huge errors by bankers and regulators. My personal perspective on economics had failed the test set by the late and almost universally ignored Hyman Minsky.

This book aims to learn from that mistake. One of its goals is to ask whether Minsky's demand for a theory that generates the possibility of great depressions is reasonable and, if so, how economists should respond. I believe it is quite reasonable. Many mainstream economists react by arguing that crises are impossible to forecast: if they were not, they would either already have happened or been forestalled by rational agents. That is certainly a satisfying doctrine, since few mainstream economists foresaw the crisis, or even the possibility of one. For the dominant school of neoclassical economics, depressions are a result of some external (or, as economists say, 'exogenous') shock, not of forces generated within the system.

The opposite and, in my view, vastly more plausible possibility is that the crisis happened partly *because* the economic models of the mainstream rendered that outcome ostensibly so unlikely in theory that they ended up making it far more likely in practice. The insouciance encouraged by the rational-expectations and efficient-market hypotheses made regulators and investors careless. As Minsky argued, stability destabilizes. This is an aspect of what George Soros, the successful speculator and innovative economic thinker, calls 'reflexivity': the way human beings think determines the reality in which they live.[5] Naive economics helps cause unstable economies. Meanwhile, less conventional analysts would argue that crises are inevitable in our present economic system. Despite their huge differences, the 'post-Keynesian' school, with its suspicion of free markets, and the 'Austrian' school, with its fervent belief in them, would agree on that last point, though they would disagree on what causes crises and what to do about them when they happen.[6]

Minsky's view that economics should include the possibility of severe crises, not as the result of external shocks, but as events that emerge from within the system, is methodologically sound. Crises, after all, are economic phenomena. Moreover, they have proved a persistent feature of capitalist economies. As Nouriel Roubini and Stephen Mihm argue in their book *Crisis Economics*, crises and subsequent depressions are, in the now celebrated terminology of Nassim Nicholas Taleb, not 'black swans' – rare and unpredictable events – but 'white swans' – normal, if relatively infrequent, events that even follow a predictable pattern.[7] Depressions are indeed one of the states a capitalist economy can fall into. An economic theory that does not incorporate that possibility is as relevant as a theory of biology that excludes the risk of extinctions, a theory of the body that excludes the risk of heart attacks, or a theory of bridge-building that excludes the risk of collapse.

I would also agree with Minsky that governments have to respond when depressions happen, this being the point on which the views of the post-Keynesian and Austrian schools diverge – the former rooted in the equilibrium unemployment theories of John Maynard Keynes and the latter in the free-market perspectives of Ludwig von Mises and Friedrich Hayek. Minsky himself put his faith in 'big government' – a government able to finance the private sector by running fiscal deficits – and a 'big bank' – a central bank able to support lending when the financial system is no longer able to do so.[8] Indeed, dealing with such threatening events is a big part of the purpose of modern governments and central banks. In addition to tackling crises, as and when they arise, policymakers also need to consider how to reduce vulnerability to such events. Needless to say, every part of these views on the fragility of the market economy and the responsibilities of government is controversial.

These events have not been the first to change my views on economics since I started studying the subject at Oxford University in 1967.[9] Over the subsequent forty-five years I have learned a great deal and, unsurprisingly, changed my mind from time to time. In the late 1960s and early 1970s, for example, I came to the view that a bigger role for markets and a macroeconomic policy dedicated to monetary stability were essential, in both high-income and developing countries. I participated, therefore, in the move towards more market-oriented economic perspectives that took place at that time. I was particularly impressed with the Austrian view of the market economy as a system for encouraging the search for profitable opportunities, in contrast to the neoclassical fixation with equilibrium: the writings of Joseph Schumpeter and Hayek were (and remain) powerful influences. The present crisis has underlined my scepticism about equilibrium, but has also restored a strong and admiring interest in the work of Keynes, which had begun when I was at Oxford.

After a passage of eighty years, Keynes's concerns of the 1930s have again become ours. Those who fail to learn from history are, we have been reminded, condemned to repeat it. Thus, the crisis has altered the way I think about finance, macroeconomics and the links between them, and so, inevitably, also about financial and monetary systems. In some ways, I find, the views that animate this book bring me closer to my attitudes of forty-five years ago.

It is helpful to separate my opinions about how the world works, which do change, from my values, which have remained unaltered. I acquired these values from my parents, particularly from my late father, Edmund Wolf, a Jewish refugee from 1930s Austria. He was a passionate supporter of liberal democracy. He opposed utopians and fanatics of both the left and the right. He believed in enlightenment values, tempered by appreciation of the frailties of humanity. The

latter had its roots in his talent (and career) as a playwright and journalist. He accepted people as they are. He opposed those who sought
to transform them into what they could not be. These values made
him, and later me, staunchly anti-communist during the Cold War.

I have remained attached to these values throughout my life. My
views on the economy have altered over time, however. As economic
turbulence hit the Western world during the 1970s, I became concerned that this might undermine both prosperity and political
stability. When UK retail price inflation hit 27 per cent in August
1975, I even wondered whether my country would go the way of
Argentina. I was happy to see Margaret Thatcher seek to defeat inflation, restrict the unnecessary extensions of state intervention in the
economy, curb the unbridled power of the trades unions, and liberal-
ize markets. These were, I thought, essential reforms. Similarly, it
seemed to me that the US needed at least some of what Ronald Reagan offered. In the context of the ongoing Cold War, a restored and
reinvigorated West appeared necessary and right. I believed that the
moves away from what was then an overstretched and unaccountable
state towards a more limited and accountable one were in the right
direction if the right balance between society and the state was to be
restored. In the 1970s, I concluded, the state had become weak
because overextended, notably in the UK: three-day weeks, soaring
inflation, collapsed profits and labour unrest all indicated that the
state was decreasingly able to perform its basic functions. The US and
the UK needed to have more limited and more effective states together
with more self-reliant and more vigorous civil societies.

No less necessary, I concluded from what I learned as a postgradu-
ate at Nuffield College, Oxford, and subsequently during my ten years
at the World Bank, was reform and liberalization of the economies of
developing countries. The results have largely been positive over the
past three decades, though there, too, the threat of financial instability
was never far away, as became evident from August 1982, the month
when the Latin American debt crisis of the 1980s broke upon the
world. The era of market liberalization has also been the era of financial crises, culminating in the biggest and most important of them,
which began in 2007.[10]

Between 1989 and 1991 the Cold War suddenly ended. I delighted in the collapse of Soviet communism and the triumph of liberal democracy. I thought a period of peace and stable prosperity would be on offer. The period since then has indeed been a time of extraordinary economic progress in much of the developing world, above all in China and then India, countries accounting for almost 40 per cent of the world's population. No less encouraging has been the spread of democracy in important parts of the world, notably Latin America, sub-Saharan Africa and, of course, post-Soviet Europe. Today, it is possible to identify at least the spread of democratic ideals, if not working democratic practices, in parts of the Arab and wider Muslim world. What is emerging is, of course, not only imperfect and corrupt but often marred by violence and oppression. But it is impossible to look back at the developments of the past three decades without concluding that, notwithstanding the failures and disappointments, the general direction has been towards more accountable governments, more market-oriented economies, and so towards more cooperative and positive-sum relations among states.[11] The creation of the World Trade Organization in 1996 is just one, albeit particularly important, sign of these fundamentally hopeful developments.

Yet much has also gone wrong. During the 1990s, and particularly during the Asian financial crisis of 1997–98, I became concerned that the liberalization of the 1980s and 1990s had brought forth a monster: a financial sector able to devour economies from within. I expressed those concerns in columns for the *Financial Times* written in response. This suspicion has hardened into something close to a certainty since 2007. Connected to this is concern about the implications of ever-rising levels of debt, particularly in the private sector, and, beyond that, what is beginning to look like chronically weak demand, at the global level.

Faith in unfettered financial markets and the benefits of ever-rising private debt was not the only dangerous form of economic hubris on offer. Another was the creation of the euro. Indeed, in a column written in 1991, as the negotiation of the Maastricht Treaty was completed, I had already judged this risky venture in words used by the ancient Greeks of the path taken by a tragic play: *hubris* (arrogance); *atē* (folly); *nemesis* (retribution).[12] In addition, we have seen a marked rise in inequality in many of the world's economies, particularly in the more market-oriented high-income countries. Rising inequality has many adverse effects – declining social mobility, for example. Among these adverse effects is a link with financial instability, as people feel forced to borrow in order to make up for stagnant or even declining real incomes.[13]

The solutions of three decades ago have morphed into the problems of today. That is hardly a new experience in human history. Yet it is particularly likely when a philosophy is taken to its extreme. Liberal democracy is, I believe, now as threatened by financial instability and rising inequality as it was by the high inflation and squeezed profits of the 1970s. In learning lessons from that era, we have, perhaps inevitably, made mistakes in this one.

'Liberal democracy' contains two words that correspond to two related, but distinct, concepts of liberalism. Both have deep roots. One concept is freedom of the individual under the law. This form of freedom – personal autonomy – represents what the late Isaiah Berlin, in his classic essay 'Two Concepts of Liberty', called 'negative freedom'.[14] The other concept is not quite that of 'positive freedom', as Berlin defined it, though it bears some relation to that concept. It is rather of the individual as citizen.

As the late Albert Hirschmann argued, 'voice' – the ability to have a say in collective decisions that affect one – is just as important as 'exit' – the ability of the individual to choose alternatives, not just as a consumer and producer, but as a citizen.[15] Whereas the first concept of liberty is quintessentially English, the second goes back to the ancient world.[16] For Athenians, the separated individual who took no place in public life was an *idiōtēs* – the word from which our word 'idiot' is derived. Such a person was an inadequate human being because he (for the Greeks, it was always 'he') focused only on his private concerns rather than on those of his *polis*, or city state, the collective that succoured him and to which he owed not just his loyalty, but also his energy.

The ideal of a liberal democracy derives from the marriage of these two ideas – freedom and citizenship. It is based on the belief that we are not only individuals with rights to choose for ourselves, subject to the law; we are also, as Aristotle put it, 'political animals'. As such, we have both a need and a right to participate in public life. Citizenship translates the idea of individual self-worth to the political level. As citizens, we can and should do things together. Many of these things are, in turn, the foundation stones of Berlin's 'positive liberty', or individual agency.

Obvious examples of socially provided public and semi-public goods, beyond the classic public goods of defence and justice, are environmental protection, funding of basic scientific research, support for technical innovation and provision of medical care, education and a social safety net. Making choices, together, about the provision of such goods does not represent a violation of freedom, but is rather both an expression and a facilitator of that fundamental value.

Today, then, the threats to liberal democracy, as I define it, come not from communism, socialism, labour militancy, soaring inflation, or a collapse in business profitability, as was the case in the 1970s, but from financial and economic instability, high unemployment and soaring inequality. The balance needs to be shifted again. Recognizing that need does not change my view that markets and competition are the most powerful forces for economic dynamism. Nor has it changed my view that a market economy is both a reflection of personal liberty and a precondition for its survival.[17] Only if people are free in their means can they be free in their ends.[18] Democracy, too, will not function in the long run without a citizenry that is, to a substantial degree, economically independent of the state. But the financially driven capitalism that emerged after the market-oriented counter-revolution has proved too much of a good thing. That is what I have learned from the crisis. This book bears witness to this perspective and attempts to make sense of how it has changed the way I think about our world.

Introduction: 'We're not in Kansas any more'[1]

*No longer the boom-bust economy, Britain has had the lowest
interest rates for forty years.*

 *And no longer the stop-go economy, Britain is now enjoying
the longest period of sustained economic growth for 200 years.*
Gordon Brown, 2004[2]

*My view is that improvements in monetary policy, though cer-
tainly not the only factor, have probably been an important
source of the Great Moderation. In particular, I am not con-
vinced that the decline in macroeconomic volatility of the past
two decades was primarily the result of good luck, as some
have argued, though I am sure good luck had its part to play
as well.*

Ben Bernanke, Governor of the
Federal Reserve Board, 2004[3]

The past is a foreign country. Even the quite recent past is a foreign
country. That is certainly true of the views of leading policymakers.
The crisis that broke upon the world in August 2007, and then morphed
into a widening economic malaise in the high-income countries and
huge turmoil in the Eurozone, has put not just these countries but the
world into a state previously unimagined even by intelligent and
well-informed policymakers.

 Gordon Brown was, after all, a politician, not a professional economist. Hubris was not, in his case, so surprising. But Ben Bernanke
is an exceptionally competent economist. His mistakes were, alas,

representative of the profession. In a celebrated speech from February 2004 on what economists called the 'great moderation', Mr Bernanke talked about what now seems an altogether different planet – a world not of financial crisis and long-term economic malaise, but one of outstanding stability and superlative monetary policy.[4] Moreover, claimed Mr Bernanke, 'improved monetary policy has likely made an important contribution not only to the reduced volatility of inflation (which is not particularly controversial) but to the reduced volatility of output as well'.[5]

This now seems quaint. The economics establishment failed. It failed to understand how the economy worked, at the macroeconomic level, because it failed to appreciate the role of financial risks; and it failed to understand the role of financial risks partly because it failed to understand how the economy worked at the macroeconomic level. The work of economists who did understand these sources of fragility was ignored because it did not fit into the imagined world of rational agents, efficient markets and general equilibrium that these professors Pangloss had made up.[6]

The subsequent economic turmoil has done more than make the economics of even a few years ago look as dead as the dodo. It has (or should have) changed the world. That is the subject of this book. It does not offer a detailed history of the crisis. It is, instead, an attempt to analyse what the crisis tells us about the economy and economics. Only by analysing this event in some detail is it possible to discuss what needs to be done and then set that against what has been – and is being – done. Are we now on a sustainable course? The answer, I will argue, is no.

OUTLINE OF THE ANALYSIS

Part I – 'The Shocks' – looks at how the financial crises that hit the advanced economies after 2007 made the world what it was in early 2014. Yes, globalization is continuing. But the latest and most dangerous financial crises of the post-war era have made the world economy fragile and the economies of the high-income countries weak.

Chapter One, the first chapter in Part I, looks at the global financial crisis and its aftermath, focusing on where the high-income economies now are. Economic orthodoxy treated such huge financial crises as more or less inconceivable. Nevertheless, they happened. The wave of financial crises and the policy measures used to combat them – the bailout of the banking system, the unprecedented monetary expansion and the huge fiscal deficits – were extraordinary. While such heroic measures halted the move into another Great Depression, they failed to return the high-income countries to a state of good health. Governments have been struggling with an aftermath of high unemployment, low productivity growth, de-leveraging, and rising concerns about fiscal solvency. The spectre of a Japanese malaise has loomed.

Chapter Two then turns to the crisis in the Eurozone. Once the credit flows stopped in 2008, the structural weaknesses of the Eurozone became evident. Subsequently, a host of inadequate policy interventions barely staved off a meltdown. Despite some progress in tackling the crisis, the post-war European project remains at risk, since it is impossible to go forward to a far stronger union or back to monetary independence.

Chapter Three, the last in Part I, looks at the consequences of the crises for the emerging economies. In general, economic growth in emerging markets remained rapid, despite weaknesses in high-income economies. But there, too, including in China and India, concerns have grown about excessive private or public sector debts and asset bubbles. In addition, the exceptional monetary policies of advanced countries and huge private outflows of capital from them, seeking higher yields, also created severe dilemmas for policymakers in emerging countries: should they accept higher exchange rates and reduced external competitiveness or resist them, perhaps by intervening in currency markets, so risking a loss of monetary control, excessive credit growth, inflation and financial disorder? Finally, evidence of slowing underlying growth has emerged. Further structural reforms are needed.

Part II – 'The Shifts' – examines how the world economy got here. What created the fragility that finally turned into such huge financial and economic shocks? If we are to do better in future, we have to understand the roots of what went wrong.

Chapter Four, the first chapter in Part II, focuses on financial fragility. Why did core parts of the financial system disintegrate? Was this because of inherent weaknesses in the financial system? Was it because of specific policy errors, before and during the crisis? Were the mistakes in handling the crisis, as some argue, even more important than those made before the crisis? All these views turn out to be partially correct.

The chapter will analyse what makes financial systems inherently fragile. It will then look closely at what made the financial system particularly fragile, prior to 2007. It will examine the growth of 'shadow banking', the increase in financial complexity and interconnectedness, the role of 'moral hazard', and the responsibilities of governments in handling crises. It will also argue that important mistakes were made in understanding the limitations of inflation targeting in managing economies.

Yet – Chapter Five will add – the vulnerability to crisis was not due to what happened inside the financial system alone. Underneath it were global economic events, notably the emergence of a 'global savings glut' and the associated credit bubble, partly due to a number of interlinked economic shifts. A crucial aspect of this was the rise of the global imbalances, with emerging economies deciding to export capital to advanced countries that the latter proved unable to use effectively. After the Asian crisis, global real interest rates fell to exceptionally low levels. This triggered an asset-price boom that then turned into a bubble. But also important in forming the savings glut was the changing distribution of income between capital and labour and among workers. The chapter will argue that popular alternative explanations of the macroeconomic causes of the crisis – loose monetary policy, in particular – confuse results with causes. Behind the rising imbalances and the associated savings glut lay fundamental shifts in the world economy driven by liberalization, technology and ageing, and revealed in globalization, rising inequality and weak investment in high-income economies.

Chapter Five will also look at how the combination of the credit bubble with the savings glut and the underlying design flaws drove the Eurozone into such a deep crisis. It will argue that one must understand the interaction of five elements: errors in design; errors in policymaking among creditor and debtor countries prior to the crisis; the fragility of finance, notably the banking system in Eurozone countries; mistakes of monetary policy; and failures to work out effective ways of dealing with the crisis when it hit. As a result, the risks of breakdown remain significant, with devastating potential effects on the economic stability of the continent.

Part III – 'The Solutions' – then looks at where we *should* be going. The salient characteristic of the response to the crisis was to do barely the minimum needed to 'put the show back on the road'. This is true of macroeconomic policy. It is true of financial sector reform. And it is also true of reform of the Eurozone. All this is understandable. But it is not good enough. It makes it almost certain that the recovery will be too weak and unbalanced and that still bigger crises will emerge in future.

Chapter Six, the first chapter in Part III, will take up the search for better economic ideas. The crisis has revealed deep misunderstandings of the way the modern economy works that resulted in huge policy mistakes, both before and, in the case of fiscal policy, also after the crisis. It is necessary to ask how much of the orthodox economics of the past few decades holds up in the light of events. Were the Austrian economists or the post-Keynesians closer to the truth than orthodox economists who ran central banks and advised treasuries? The answer will be that the heterodox economists were indeed more right than the orthodox. The challenge for economics is large and the need for experimentation strong. Some argue that we need to move back to the gold standard. The chapter will show that this is a fantasy. But the issue of the link between money and finance is central and must be addressed.

Chapter Seven will look at how to achieve a better financial system. It will start from the reforms that are now being undertaken and ask whether they will be sufficient to generate a secure future. The discussion will then look at further possible reforms, including much higher capital requirements and proposals to eliminate 'fractional reserve banking' altogether. The discussion will conclude by arguing that further radical reform is essential, because the current financial system is inherently dependent on the state. That creates dangerous incentives, ultimately quite likely to destroy the solvency of states. A particularly important aspect of the frailty of finance is its role in generating property bubbles. The leveraging up of the stock of land is a consistently destabilizing phenomenon.

Chapter Eight will then turn to the search for a better economy, both domestic and global. The starting point must be how to achieve a more vigorous and better-balanced recovery. There should have been much stronger monetary and, particularly, fiscal support for the recovery. The failure to do this will cast a long shadow over economic prospects. Policymakers made a big mistake in 2010 when they embraced austerity prematurely. But there are important longer-term constraints on achieving a return to pre-crisis rates of growth and balancing demand and supply without resort to another destabilizing credit and asset-price bubble. The obvious solutions are a big expansion of investment and net exports. Yet there are obstacles to both. The world economy needs to be sustainably rebalanced, with capital flowing from developed to emerging countries on a large scale. The chapter will explain how this might be done and why it will be so difficult. It will require reforms of the global monetary system. Among other things, there is a strong case for generating a new reserve asset that would make far less necessary the mercantilist policies of emerging economies. But if that is impossible, as seems likely, and the high-income countries are unable to generate an investment boom, the latter may have to consider radical reforms of monetary arrangements, including direct monetary financing of budget deficits.

Chapter Nine, the last in Part III, will examine the search for a reformed Eurozone. Today, the Eurozone confronts an existential challenge. It has to decide either to break up, in whole or in part, or to create a minimum set of institutions and policies that would make it work much better. Dismantling the Eurozone is conceivable, but it would create a huge financial, economic and political mess in at least the short to medium term. The mess would stretch into the far distant future if dismantling the Eurozone led to the unravelling of the entire project for European integration. The alternative reforms will have to include more effective support for countries in temporary difficulties, a degree of fiscal federalism, greater financial integration, a more supportive central bank and mechanisms for ensuring symmetrical adjustment of competitiveness. Without such changes the Eurozone will never work well, and even with them it may still not survive in the long term.

Finally, the Conclusion will return to what this crisis means for the world. It will argue that this is a turning point. Fundamental reforms are needed if we are to achieve greater stability. We will need both more globalization and less – more global regulation and cooperation, and more freedom for individual countries to craft their own responses to the pressures of a globalizing world. There are huge long-term tasks in maintaining the supply of global public goods – a stable world economy, peace and, above all, management of huge global environment challenges – as the world integrates and develops. Yet these challenges will not be met if we do not first overcome the legacy of the crisis. Moreover, all this must be managed at a time of transition in global power and responsibility from a world dominated by Western powers to one in which new powers have arisen.

WHY THE SHOCKS MATTER

What makes this analysis important? The answer is that the financial and economic crises of the West have changed the world. They change what is happening, how we should think about what is happening, and what we should do about it.

Let's start with the obvious point. The world economy turned out to be very different from what most people imagined in 2007. Economies that were deemed vigorous have turned out to be sickly. In all the important high-income countries, output had remained far below previous trends and the rate of growth is mostly well below what had previously been considered its potential. Levels of activity were still below pre-crisis peaks in a number of important countries in 2013, notably France, Italy, Japan and the UK. Moreover, unemployment rates were elevated and persistent. The concern that something similar to the lengthy Japanese economic malaise was about to hit a number of high-income countries had, alas, grown more credible. Maybe the outcome would be even worse than in Japan: on balance, it has been, so far.

Meanwhile, emerging countries mostly recovered vigorously. They did so, in part, by replacing the external demand they had lost with domestic stimulus. This worked in the short run, remarkably so in China. But such action could leave a difficult legacy in the form of low-quality investments, asset-price bubbles and bad debts, and might, for such reasons, prove unsustainable. At the same time, the emerging countries could not return to the strategies of export-led growth-cum-reserve accumulation followed by many of the most successful among them prior to the crisis. The weakness of private demand within high-income countries has precluded that and, in particular, the loss of creditworthiness by many households. In all, the legacy of the crises includes deep practical challenges to policymaking almost everywhere.

As a result of these unexpected economic developments, crisis-hit countries have been forced to struggle with worse fiscal positions than they had previously imagined. As the work of Carmen Reinhart and Kenneth Rogoff, both now at Harvard University, has shown, fiscal crises are a natural concomitant of financial crises, largely because of the impact on government revenue and spending of declining profits and economic activity, together with rising unemployment. These come on top of the direct fiscal costs of bank bailouts.[7] As was to be predicted, in the current crisis the biggest adverse fiscal effects were felt in countries that suffered a direct hit from the financial crises, such as the US, the UK, Ireland and Spain, rather than in countries that suffered an indirect hit, via trade. Worse still, the longer-term fiscal position of the crisis-hit countries was always likely to be difficult, because of population ageing. Now, the legacy of the crisis has sharply curtailed the room for manoeuvre.

Along with the fiscal impact has come a huge monetary upheaval. In today's credit-based system, the supply of money is a by-product of the private creation of credit. The central banks regulate the price of money, while the central bank and government in concert ensure the convertibility of deposit money into government money, at par, by acting as a lender of last resort (in the case of the central bank) and provider of overt or covert insurance of liabilities (in the case of the government). However, because this financial crisis has been so severe, central banks went far beyond standard operations. They not only lowered their official intervention rates to the lowest levels ever seen, but enormously expanded their balance sheets, with controversial long-term effects.

The most obvious of all the changes is the transformed position of the financial system. The crisis established the dependence of the world's most significant institutions on government support. It under-lined the existence of institutions that are too big and interconnected to fail. It confirmed the notion that the financial system is a ward of the state, rather than a part of the market economy. It demonstrated the fragility of the financial system. As a result of all this, the crisis inflicted huge damage on the credibility of the market-oriented global financial system and so also on the credibility of what is often called 'Anglo-Saxon financial capitalism' – the system in which financial markets determine not only the allocation of resources but also the ownership and governance of companies. One consequence is that the financial system has been forced through substantial reform. Another is that a debate about the proper role and structure of the financial industry became inescapable. Yet another is that the willingness of emerging economies to integrate into the global financial system was reduced.

As a result of the crises, the established high-income countries suffered a huge loss of prestige. These countries, above all the US, though counting for a steadily smaller share of the world's population, remained economically and politically dominant throughout the post-Second World War era. This was partly because they had the largest economies and so dominated global finance and trade. It was also because they controlled global economic institutions. However much the rest of the world resented the power and arrogance of the high-income countries, it accepted that, by and large, the latter knew what they were doing, at least in economic policy. The financial crisis and subsequent malaise destroyed that confidence. Worse, because of the relative success of China's state capitalism, the blow to the prestige of Western financial capitalism has carried with it a parallel blow to the credibility of Western democracy.

These crises also accelerated a transition in economic power and influence that was already under way. Between 2007 and 2012, the gross domestic product of the high-income countries, in aggregate, rose by 2.4 per cent, in real terms, according to the International Monetary Fund, with that of the US rising by 2.9 per cent and that of the Eurozone falling by 1.3 per cent. Over the same period, the real GDP of the emerging countries grew by 31 per cent and those of India and China by 39 and 56 per cent respectively. Such a speedy transformation in relative economic weight among important countries has no precedent. It is plausible that China's economy already is the biggest in the world, at purchasing power parity, in the middle of this decade, and will be the biggest in market prices by the early part of the next decade. The crisis has accelerated the world economy towards this profound transition.

The coincidence of a huge financial and economic crisis with a prior transformation in relative economic power also occurred in the 1930s. The rise of the US as a great economic power in the early twentieth century and the overwhelming strength of its balance of payments after the First World War helped cause both the scale of the global economic crisis and the ineffectiveness of the response in the 1930s. This time, between 2007 and 2012, the rise of China, a new economic superpower, was among the explanations for the global imbalances that helped cause the crises. Fortunately, this did not thwart an effective response. In future, the world may not be so fortunate. Transitions in global power are always fraught with geo-political and geo-economic peril because the incumbent ceases to be able to provide the necessary political and economic order and the rising power does not see the need to do so.

The crises have generated, in addition, fundamental challenges to the operation of the global economy. Among the most important features of the pre-crisis global economy – indeed, one of the causes of the crisis itself – were huge net flows of capital from emerging economies into supposedly safe assets in high-income countries. The governments of emerging countries organized these flows, largely as a result of intervention in currency markets and the consequent accumulations of foreign-currency reserves, which reached $11.4tn at the end of September 2013, quite apart from over $6tn in sovereign wealth funds.[8] The recycling of current-account surpluses and private-capital inflows into official capital outflows – described by some as a 'savings glut' and by others as a 'money glut' – was one of the causes of the crisis. These flows are certainly unsustainable, because high-income countries have proved demonstrably unable to use the money effectively. The crisis has, in this way, too, changed the world: what was destabilizing before the crisis became unsustainable after it.[9]

Furthermore, the globalization of finance is also under threat. The reality is that economies have become more integrated, but political order still rests on states. In the case of finance, taxpayers bailed out institutions whose business was heavily abroad. Similarly, they were forced to protect financial businesses from developments abroad, including those caused by regulatory incompetence and malfeasance. This is politically unacceptable. Broadly, two outcomes seem possible: less globalized finance or more globalized regulation. This dilemma is particularly marked inside the Eurozone, as Adair (Lord) Turner, chairman of the UK's Financial Services Authority, has noted. This is because financial markets are more integrated and the autonomy of national policy is more limited than elsewhere.[10] In practice, the outcome in Europe is likely to be some mixture of the two. The same is also true for the world as a whole, where tension arises between a desire to agree at least a minimum level of common regulatory standards and a parallel desire to preserve domestic regulatory autonomy.[11] Such pressure for 'de-globalization' may not be limited to finance. The combination of slow growth with widening inequality, higher unemployment, financial instability, so-called 'currency wars' and fiscal defaults may yet undermine the political legitimacy of globalization in many other respects.

Inevitably, the legacy of the crises includes large-scale institutional changes in many areas of policy, at national, regional and global levels. The obvious areas for reform are financial regulation, the functioning of monetary systems, global governance and global economic institutions. Reforms are under way. But big questions remain unaddressed and unresolved, notably over global monetary and exchange rate regimes. A revealing step, taken early in the crisis, was the shift from the group of seven leading high-income countries as the focus for informal global decision-making to the group of twenty – a shift that brought with it an increase in relevance at the price of a reduction in effectiveness. This is just one aspect of the complications created by the need to take account of the views and interests of more players than ever before.

Whatever happens at the global level, the crises created an existential challenge for the Eurozone and so for the post-Second World War European 'project'. The Eurozone might still lose members, though the chances of that have much reduced since the worst of the crisis.

Such a reversal would imperil the single market and the European Union itself. It would mark the first time that the European project had gone backwards, with devastating consequences for the prestige and credibility of this idea. Worst of all, such a breakdown would reflect – and exacerbate – a breakdown in trust among the peoples and countries of Europe, with dire effects on their ability to sustain a cooperative approach to the problems of Europe and act effectively in the wider world. Fortunately, policymakers understand these risks. Yet even if everything is resolved, as seems likely, Europe will remain inward-looking for many years. If everything were not resolved, the collapse of the European model of integration would shatter the credibility of what was, for all its faults, the most promising system of peaceful international integration there has ever been.

Yet perhaps the biggest way in which the crises have changed the world is – or at least should be – intellectual. They have shown that established views of how (and how well) the world's most sophisticated economies and financial systems work were nonsense. This poses an uncomfortable challenge for economics and a parallel challenge for economic policymakers – central bankers, financial regulators, officials of finance ministries and ministers. It is, in the last resort, ideas that matter, as Keynes knew well. Both economists and policymakers need to rethink their understanding of the world in important respects. The pre-crisis conventional wisdom, aptly captured in Mr Bernanke's speech about the contribution of improved monetary policy to the 'great moderation', stands revealed as complacent, indeed vainglorious. The world has indeed changed. The result is a ferment of ideas, with many heterodox schools exerting much greater influence and splits within the neoclassical orthodoxy. This upheaval is reminiscent of the 1930s and 1940s and, again, of the 1970s. The opportunity of securing a more prosperous and integrated global economy surely remains. But the challenge of achieving it now seems more intractable than most analysts imagined. In the 1930s, the world failed. Will it do better this time? I fervently hope so. But the story is not yet over. As Dorothy says in *The Wizard of Oz*, 'Toto, I've a feeling we're not in Kansas any more.'

PART ONE

The Shocks

Prologue

The financial and economic crises of the Western world became visible in the summer of 2007 and reached their apogee in the autumn of 2008. The response was an unprecedented government-led rescue operation. That, in turn, triggered an economic turn-around in the course of 2009. But the recovery of the high-income countries was, in general, disappointing: output remained depressed, unemployment stayed elevated, fiscal deficits remained high, and monetary policy seemed, by conventional measures, unprecedentedly loose. This is beginning to look like a Western version of Japan's prolonged post-bubble malaise.

One reason for persistent disappointment is that the Western crisis became, from 2010 onwards, also a deep crisis of the Eurozone. Crisis dynamics engulfed Greece, Ireland, Portugal, Spain and even Italy. All these countries were pushed into deep recessions, if not depressions.[1] The price of credit remained high for a long time. By early 2013, the sense of crisis had abated. But chronic economic malaise continued, with no certainty of a strong recovery or even of enduring stability.

Meanwhile, emerging economies, in general, thrived. The worst hit among them were the countries of Central and Eastern Europe, many of which had run huge current-account deficits before the crisis. Like the members of the Eurozone in Southern Europe, these were then devastated by a series of 'sudden stops' in capital inflows. Other emerging and developing countries proved far more resilient. This was the result of a big improvement in policy over the previous decades. Particularly important was the move towards stronger external positions, including a massive accumulation of foreign-exchange reserves, particularly by Asian emerging countries, notably including China. This gave them the room to expand domestic demand and so return swiftly to prosperity, despite the crisis. Those emerging and developing countries that could not expand demand themselves were often able to piggyback on the stimuli of others, particularly China. That was particularly true of the commodity exporters. This represents an important – and probably enduring – shift in the world economy: the old core is becoming more peripheral. But the sustainability of the expansionary policies adopted by emerging economies, and so their ability to thrive while high-income countries continue to be weak, is in doubt. Particularly important is the risk of a sharp slowdown in the Chinese economy and the likely associated weakness of commodity prices.

I

From Crisis to Austerity

The central problem of depression-prevention [has] been solved, for all practical purposes, and has in fact been solved for many decades.

Robert E. Lucas, 2003[1]

When I became Treasury secretary in July 2006, financial crises weren't new to me, nor were the failures of major financial institutions. I had witnessed serious market disturbances and the collapses or near collapses of Continental Illinois Bank, Drexel Burnham Lambert, and Salomon Brothers, among others. With the exception of the savings and loan debacle, these disruptions generally focused on a single organization, such as the hedge fund Long-Term Capital Management in 1998.

The crisis that began in 2007 was far more severe, and the risks to the economy and the American people much greater. Between March and September 2008, eight major US financial institutions failed – Bear Stearns, IndyMac, Fannie Mae, Freddie Mac, Lehman Brothers, AIG, Washington Mutual, and Wachovia – six of them in September alone. And the damage was not limited to the US. More than 20 European banks, across 10 countries, were rescued from July 2007 through February 2009. This, the most wrenching financial crisis since the Great Depression, caused a terrible recession in the US and severe harm around the world. Yet it could have been so much worse. Had it not been for unprecedented interventions by the US and other governments, many more financial

*institutions would have gone under – and the economic dam-
age would have been far greater and longer lasting.*

Hank Paulson, On the Brink *(2010)²*

Hank Paulson is a controversial figure. For many Americans, he is the man who bailed out Wall Street too generously. For others, he is the man who failed to bail out Wall Street generously enough. In his thought-provoking book, *Capitalism 4.0*, the British journalist Ana-tole Kaletsky blames him for the disaster, writing that 'the domino-style failure of US financial institutions that autumn [of 2008] was not due to any worsening of economic conditions – it was simply a conse-quence of the US Treasury's unpredictable and reckless handling first of Fannie and Freddie, then of Lehman, and finally of AIG.'³

Whatever we may think of Mr Paulson's culpability, we cannot deny his outline of what actually happened in 2007 and 2008. In this chapter, I will not attempt a detailed account of how the crisis that hit the core high-income countries in those years unfolded. That has been done in other publications.⁴ My aim here is rather to demonstrate its scale, the extraordinary policy response and the economic aftermath. I will postpone detailed discussion of the economic and financial ori-gins of the crisis to Part II of the book and analysis of the very different impact upon emerging and developing countries to Chapter Four. By focusing on the high-income countries, I want to show that this was no ordinary economic event. To pretend that one can return to the intellectual and policymaking *status quo ante* is profoundly mistaken.

THE SCALE OF THE CRISIS

The world economy of the 2000s showed four widely noticed and, as we shall see, closely related characteristics: huge balance-of-payments imbalances; a surge in house prices and house building in a number of high-income countries, notably including the US; rapid growth in the scale and profitability of a liberalized financial sector; and soar-ing private debt in a number of high-income countries, notably the US, but also the UK and Spain. Many observers doubted whether this combination could continue indefinitely. The questions were: when would it end, and would it do so smoothly, bumpily or disastrously?

The answers, it turned out, were: in 2007 and 2008, and disastrously. Already in March 2008, I assessed the unfolding crisis as follows:

> What makes this crisis so significant? It tests the most evolved financial system we have. It emanates from the core of the world's most advanced financial system and from transactions entered into by the most sophisticated financial institutions, which use the cleverest tools of securitisation and rely on the most sophisticated risk management. Even so, the financial system blew up: both the commercial paper and inter-bank markets froze for months; the securitized paper turned out to be radioactive and the ratings proffered by ratings agencies to be fantasy; central banks had to pump in vast quantities of liquidity; and the panic-stricken Federal Reserve was forced to make unprecedented cuts in interest rates.[5]

Far worse was to follow in the course of 2008.

This crisis had become visible to many observers on 9 August 2007, when the European Central Bank injected €94.8bn into the markets, partly in response to an announcement from BNP Paribas that it could no longer give investors in three of its investment funds their money back.[6] This event made it clear that the crisis would not be restricted to the US: in the globalized financial system, 'toxic paper' – marketed debt of doubtful value – had been distributed widely across borders. Worse, contrary to what proponents of the new market-based financial system had long and, alas, all too persuasively argued, risk had been distributed not to those best able to bear it, but to those least able to understand it.[7] Examples turned out to include IKB, an ill-managed German Landesbank, and no fewer than eight Norwegian municipalities.[8] These plucked chickens duly panicked when it became clear what, in their folly, they had been persuaded to buy.

On 13 September 2007, Northern Rock, a specialized UK mortgage-lender, which had been offering home loans of up to 125 per cent of the value of property and 60 per cent of whose total lending was financed by short-term borrowing, suffered the first large depositor 'run' on a British bank since the nineteenth century.[9] Ultimately, the Labour government nationalized Northern Rock – paradoxically, very much contrary to the company's wishes. Reliance on short-term loans from financial markets, rather than deposits, for funding of long-term illiquid assets had, it soon turned out, become widespread. This was also a dangerous source of vulnerability, since explicit and implicit insurance had made deposits relatively less likely to run than market-based finance. That lesson proved of particular importance for the US, because of the scale of market-based lending in the funding of mortgages. As managing director of the huge California-based fund manager PIMCO (the Pacific Investment Management Company), Paul McCulley in 2007 labelled this the 'Shadow Banking System' when he spoke in Jackson Hole, Wyoming, at the annual economic symposium of the Federal Reserve Bank of Kansas City. The label stuck.[10] Both these lessons – the widespread distribution of opaque securitized assets (the bundling of debts into marketable securities) and the reliance of so many intermediaries on funding from wholesale markets – turned out to have great relevance as the crisis worsened in 2008.

Then, on 16 March 2008, the *Financial Times* reported: 'JP Morgan Buys Bear Stearns for $2 a Share'.[11] The Federal Reserve provided backup funding of $30bn for this operation, taking some of the credit risk in the process. Just a year before that calamity the *Financial Times* had reported: 'Bear Stearns yesterday became the latest Wall Street bank to report strong earnings and insist that it does not see much lasting impact from the crisis in the subprime mortgage market.'[12] It would say that, wouldn't it? But the likelihood is that its management, along with almost everybody else, did not imagine the horrors to come. They were probably more fools than knaves.

The rescue prompted me to write in the *Financial Times* of 25 March 2008:

> Remember Friday March 14 2008: it was the day the dream of global free-market capitalism died. For three decades we have moved towards market-driven financial systems. By its decision to rescue Bear Stearns, the Federal Reserve, the institution responsible for monetary policy in the US, chief protagonist of free-market capitalism, declared this era over. It showed in deeds its agreement with the remark by Joseph

Ackermann, chief executive of Deutsche Bank, that 'I no longer believe in the market's self-healing power'. Deregulation has reached its limits.[13]

The US government took the two government-sponsored enterprises, Fannie Mae and Freddie Mac, which then guaranteed three-quarters of US mortgages, into 'conservatorship' on 7 September. This proved what investors (and critics) had long believed, namely, that the US government stood behind the vast borrowings of these allegedly private companies ($5,400bn in outstanding liabilities at the time of the rescue).[14] Yet it then, controversially, allowed (or felt obliged to allow) Lehman Brothers to go bankrupt on 15 September.[15] Merrill Lynch was sold to Bank of America for $50bn, or $29 a share, on the same day – a big premium above its share price of $17, but a reduction of 61 per cent on its share price of $75 a year before and 70 per cent from its pre-crisis peak.[16] Then, promptly after refusing to rescue Lehman, the US government saved the insurance giant, AIG, taking a 79.9 per cent equity stake and lending it $85bn on 16 September.[17] In his book, Mr Paulson argues that the decisions were not inconsistent, because, 'Unlike with Lehman, the Fed felt it could make a loan to help AIG because we were dealing with a liquidity, not a capital, problem.'[18] If the Fed really believed that, it was soon proved wrong. A more likely reason is that Mr Paulson believed (wrongly, as it turned out) that the markets would take Lehman's failure in their stride, but was sure the same would not be true for AIG, given its role as a seller of 'credit default swaps' – insurance contracts on bonds, including the securitized assets that had become increasingly toxic.

Then, on 17 September, one of the money-market funds managed by Reserve Management Corporation (a manager of mutual funds) 'broke the buck' – that is, could no longer promise to redeem money invested in the fund at par (or dollar for dollar) – because of its exposure to loss-making loans to Lehman. That threatened a tsunami of redemptions from the $3.5tn invested in money-market funds, a crucial element in funding McCulley's 'Shadow Banking System'.[19]

PriceWaterhouseCoopers, the UK's bankruptcy administrator for Lehman, seized the failed company's assets in the UK, including the collateral of those who traded with it.[20] This came as a shock to many hedge funds and US policymakers. The fact that bankruptcy regimes were different in different countries – obvious, one would have thought – turned out to be a significant problem in dealing with the aftermath of Lehman's failure. As Mervyn (later Lord) King, governor of the Bank of England, famously quipped: banks were 'international in life, but national in death'.[21] Funding for Morgan Stanley and Goldman Sachs, the two surviving broker-dealers, dried up.[22] On 21 September these two institutions turned themselves into bank holding companies, a change that gave them access to funds from the Federal Reserve.[23] On 25 September the Federal Deposit Insurance Corporation took over Washington Mutual, the sixth largest bank in the US.[24] Not long afterwards, on 9 October, Wells Fargo, the country's fifth largest commercial bank, agreed to a takeover of Wachovia, the country's fourth largest.[25]

The mayhem was not restricted to the US. On the weekend before the Lehman bankruptcy, the UK government refused to support the takeover mooted by Barclays. As Alistair Darling, then chancellor of the exchequer, claims in his memoir, 'we could not stand behind a US bank that was clearly in trouble'. Why, indeed, should the UK government provide guarantees that the US government had rejected? Moreover, he adds, 'I was determined that UK taxpayers would not end up having to bail out a US bank.'[26] On 17 September, with government encouragement, Lloyds TSB announced a £12.2bn takeover of Halifax Bank of Scotland (HBOS). The government argued that the public interest justified clearing the deal, despite concerns over its adverse impact on competition, in order to 'ensure the stability of the UK financial system'.[27] On 29 September the government decided to nationalize Bradford & Bingley, the biggest lender in the UK's 'buy-to-let' market, while its branch network was subsequently sold to Santander.[28] Worse, it was becoming obvious that HBOS was too bad a bank for Lloyds to support unaided. Furthermore, the Royal Bank of Scotland (RBS), which had become the biggest bank in the world by assets, partly as a result of ill-considered takeovers, notably of ABN-Amro, was also in terrible trouble.

The crisis went far beyond the US and the UK, affecting Iceland, Ireland and much of continental Europe. As the panic worsened, credit markets froze and assets were dumped, causing a vicious spiral of shrinking availability of credit to speculators and so further forced sales.[29] The *economic* consequences turned out to be less severe than those of the Great Depression of the 1930s, but the *financial* crisis was even worse. The earlier crisis brought down banks on the periphery of the world economy (a huge number of smaller US banks and banks in vulnerable European countries, such as Austria and Germany) more than those at the core. The more recent crisis, however, tore apart the heart of the financial system: the networks connecting the big financial institutions that dominate activity in the world's two most important financial centres, New York and London. The private sector also ceased to trust almost all counterparties other than the governments and central banks of the most important and most unimpeachably creditworthy Western economies, first and foremost the US.

This, then, was what Latin American economists call a 'sudden stop' in capital markets. It affected not just a range of private borrowers, but also sovereign governments whose banks had borrowed heavily in foreign currency:[30] Iceland was quickly revealed as a salient example, but the same would soon prove to be true of weaker members of the Eurozone, who were, it soon became clear, borrowing something that had many of the characteristics of a foreign currency.[31] One of the paradoxical features of the crisis was that the frightened money of the world flowed into US Treasury bonds and bills (shorter-term securities), even though, at least initially, the crisis had its epicentre in that country. That, of course, gave the US government an enormous margin of manoeuvre.

John Taylor, a conservative economist and former member of the administration of George W. Bush as undersecretary of the treasury for international affairs, argues that it was not the decision to let Lehman fail that triggered this stop, but the decision by Chairman Bernanke and Secretary Paulson to approach Congress for a rescue package a week later.[32] This is quite unpersuasive. As Thomas Ferguson of the University of Massachusetts and Robert Johnson, former chief economist of the US Senate banking committee, note, 'the evidence that the Lehman bankruptcy sundered world markets is overwhelming'.[33]

A fundamental indicator is the spread between three-month Libor

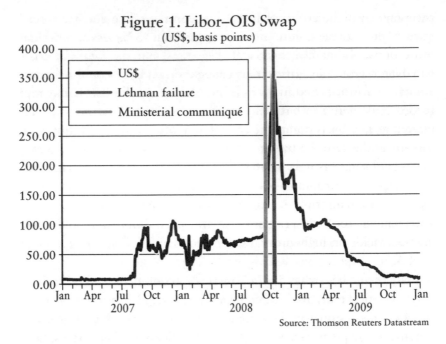

Figure 1. Libor–OIS Swap
(US$, basis points)

Source: Thomson Reuters Datastream

(the rate at which banks can borrow from one another) and the Overnight Indexed Swap rate (the implied central-bank rate over the same three-month period). While traders at certain banks have distorted the measurement of Libor, no reason exists to doubt the scale of the rise in spread shown in Figure 1. This is a measure of the credit risk – the risk of default, in other words – on unsecured interbank lending (the process by which banks make short-term loans to one another out of surplus funds).[34] In normal times, the spread between the two rates had been just a few basis points (hundredths of a percentage point). The spread on dollar lending had already reached 78 basis points by the end of August 2008, as worries about the solvency of counterparties rose. It rose by another 40 basis points between the Friday before Lehman's bankruptcy (12 September) and the following Friday – so *before* the US government's rescue package was officially launched, let alone ratified. But it did take a while for investors to realize some of the least obvious implications of Lehman's failure, including implications for AIG and so other financial institutions.

The spread reached a peak of 364 basis points on 10 October 2008, precisely when the group of seven finance ministers made a commitment to prevent the failure of further systemically significant financial institutions. Ultimately, therefore, only decisive and globally coordinated intervention by governments and central banks halted the panic. Similar jumps occurred in spreads in other currencies. In sterling, the spread peaked at 299 basis points on 6 November 2008. In euros, it peaked at 189 basis points on 27 October 2008. Even these jumps in spreads understate the panic: the market for interbank lending dried up, as banks increasingly lent to one another via central banks instead.

Spreads on corporate bonds over yields on US treasuries also exploded. Even on triple-A securities they rose from 181 basis points on 1 September 2008 to 414 basis points on 10 October. The spreads between yields on high-grade commercial paper (the marketed debt of top-quality corporations, such as General Electric) issued by non-financial companies and US Treasury bills rose from little more than a percentage point in August to over 6 percentage points in mid-October, partly because the rates on T-bills collapsed. This was a flight to safety, indeed.

Moreover, as is usually the case, such jumps in the cost of borrowing masked a grimmer reality – a freezing of supply. Mr Paulson reports a conversation he had on 8 September with Jeff Immelt, Chief Executive Office of GE, who told him that even his company, with its rare triple-A rating, 'was having problems selling commercial paper' (that is, borrowing):[35] interest rates did not go still higher because so many borrowers were rationed out of the market, just as happened in the market for unsecured interbank lending. Particularly revealing, then, is the permanent shrinkage of the commercial paper market, even though rates of interest did fall back to very low levels in the course of 2009. The seasonally adjusted value of commercial paper outstanding in the US was $2,150bn at the end of June 2007.[36] A year later, this had shrunk to $1,741bn. A year after that, in June 2009, it was down to $1,229bn. It had still not recovered in June 2013, when the outstanding amount was just $998bn. Asset-backed commercial paper, which is used to finance mortgages, shrank even more dramatically, from $1,200bn in June 2007, to $523bn two years later and a mere $276bn in June 2013. An important source of funding had disappeared. While this shrinkage was surely inevitable, it forced government agencies – Fannie Mae, Freddie Mac (both now under government control) and the Federal Reserve itself – to become the overwhelmingly dominant source of US mortgages. In a country supposedly dedicated to the ideals of market economics, arguably the most important social function of finance – lending for home purchase – had become almost completely nationalized.

CRISIS AND RESCUE IN HIGH-INCOME COUNTRIES

The Irish government guaranteed all the money in Irish banks on the morning of 30 September 2008 – a decision that turned out to be ruinous for Irish taxpayers and the Irish economy, but also triggered interventions elsewhere. On 8 October 2010 the British government, under Chancellor of the Exchequer Darling and Prime Minister Gordon Brown, announced a £500bn rescue programme for the UK banks – up to £50bn for purchases of equity, an increase in the Bank of England's 'special liquidity scheme' from £100bn to £200bn, and £250bn in credit guarantees.[37] Ultimately, the equity went only to the Royal Bank of Scotland (in which the government ended up owning 82 per cent of the equity) and Lloyds HBOS (in which it ended up owning 43 per cent). Persuading the banks to cooperate was not, claims Mr Darling, at all easy. He states that, in the discussions on the evening of 7 October, 'It crossed my mind not only that the banks had failed to appreciate that there could be no negotiation, but also that they might be daft enough to take up the option of suicide – and I simply couldn't afford a row of dead banks in the morning.'[38]

Rightly or wrongly (rightly, in my view, since allowing the banks to fail was unthinkable, though some still believe it should have been done, regardless of the consequences), such direct infusions of equity became the central element in the solutions chosen elsewhere. The US reached a similar destination, though the complexities of US politics made the journey rather more difficult. US policymakers first discussed what became the Troubled Assets Relief Program (TARP) with legislators on 19 September 2008. The president ratified it on 3 October 2010, though only after initial defeat in the House of Representatives.[39] But the collapse of the equity markets concentrated the minds of legislators wonderfully, to paraphrase Samuel Johnson. Initially presented as a plan to purchase 'toxic assets', it was soon turned into one of injecting capital directly into banks.[40]

The turning point came at the meeting of the group of seven finance ministers during the annual meetings of the International Monetary Fund and World Bank, in Washington DC on 10 October 2008. I well remember the hysteria. One US-based fund manager told me he had advised his wife to take enough cash from their bank to last weeks. This was the environment in which the ministers met. Their crucial decision – taken at the suggestion of Mr Paulson, to his credit – was to scrap the draft communiqué, which had taken no account of the scale of the crisis they confronted, and agree to a new one instead.[41] What they then produced was among the most important pieces of global economic policymaking since the Second World War:

> The G-7 agrees today that the current situation calls for urgent and exceptional action. We commit to continue working together to stabilize financial markets and restore the flow of credit, to support global economic growth. We agree to:
>
> Take decisive action and use all available tools to support systemically important financial institutions *and prevent their failure* [my emphasis].
>
> Take all necessary steps to unfreeze credit and money markets and ensure that banks and other financial institutions have broad access to liquidity and funding.
>
> Ensure that our banks and other major financial intermediaries, as needed, can raise capital from public, as well as private sources, in sufficient amounts to re-establish confidence and permit them to continue lending to households and businesses.
>
> Ensure that our respective national deposit insurance and guarantee programs are robust and consistent so that our retail depositors will continue to have confidence in the safety of their deposits.
>
> Take action, where appropriate, to restart the secondary markets for mortgages and other securitized assets. Accurate valuation and transparent disclosure of assets and consistent implementation of high-quality accounting standards are necessary.

In essence, then, the ministers said three things: first, responsibility for solving the financial crisis rested on the states they represented;

second, the G-7 states would do whatever it took to save the financial system; and, third, they would prevent any more failures of institutions deemed systemic. In brief, no more Lehmans. Governments had socialized the liabilities of the core institutions of the global financial system. These businesses were now wards of the state.

This had to be a turning point, not just in the crisis, but also in the broader relationship between states and markets. Morally, at least, and in all probability practically, the era of financial liberalization was over. The question was only how far backwards policymakers would go. For how could taxpayers be dragooned into rescuing this industry from the consequences of its incompetence, without stronger regulation? Beyond these longer-term implications, immediate questions arose: would the world economy avoid a depression? If it did, what sort of recovery could it enjoy?

Policymakers put the full resources of their states behind the financial system. Bankers had proved to be, in effect, merely exceptionally highly paid civil servants. In brief, the world soon saw huge fiscal deficits, far and away the most expansionary policies in the history of the developed countries, unlimited support for the liquidity and solvency of important financial institutions and, where that was insufficient to revive lending, direct state-funding of core financial functions, notably mortgage lending. This dependence of a supposedly free-market financial system on the state can be neither forgotten nor ignored.

Policymakers lived up to their promise to support what were judged systemically significant financial institutions, by injecting capital, providing liquidity and guaranteeing liabilities. Piergiorgio Alessandri and Andrew Haldane of the Bank of England have estimated that the total value of the support offered to the crisis-hit financial system by the relevant central banks and governments, as of mid- to late-2009, was 18 per cent of Eurozone GDP, 73 per cent of US GDP, 74 per cent of UK GDP and, taken together, 25 per cent of world GDP. The support was extremely heterogeneous in nature, consisting of direct capital infusions, money creation, used to purchase a wide range of different assets, guarantees and insurance.[42] According to the International Monetary Fund, the direct impact on gross public debt of post-crisis support for the financial sector up to early 2012 was 38.5 per cent of GDP for Ireland, 6.7 per cent for Belgium, 5.7 per cent for the UK,

4.9 per cent for the Netherlands and 3.2 per cent for the US.[43] Yet it is impossible to measure the scale of the measures either by the sums promised or by the far smaller sums used. The full faith and credit of governments were put behind their financial systems. The only constraint was loss of creditworthiness by the governments themselves.

The central banks also slashed their interest rates to unprecedentedly low levels. The Federal Reserve lowered its 'federal funds target rate' (the 'Fed Funds' rate) from 5.25 per cent in September 2007 to 0.25 per cent in December 2008. The European Central Bank (ECB), convinced for far too long that the crisis was largely an 'Anglo-Saxon' affair, lowered its intervention rate (refinancing rate) from 4.25 per cent in October 2008 to 1 per cent by May 2009. It then, in an action of astonishing myopia, raised rates back to 1.5 per cent in 2011, before lowering them, in five quarter-point reductions, to 0.25 per cent in November 2013 and then to 0.15 per cent in June 2014. The Bank of England lowered its intervention rate (base rate) from 5.75 per cent in December 2007 to 0.5 per cent in March 2009. To put this in context, prior to this the lowest rate offered by the Bank of England in more than three centuries of history had been 2 per cent. Meanwhile, the Bank of Japan stuck with the close-to-zero interest rates it had established in the 1990s.

In essence, then, the developed countries' most important central banks offered free or nearly free money to their banks from 2009 or, in some cases, from slightly earlier than that. It was little surprise that this official largesse to banks, not matched by comparable largesse from banks to their own borrowers – indeed accompanied by foreclosures on a grand scale in some countries – became a source of significant popular resentment. In addition, central banks adopted a wide range of 'unconventional' policies, including, notably, the policy known as 'quantitative easing' – expansion of the monetary base and central-bank purchases of longer-term assets.[44] Such unconventional policies were aimed at financing banks, lowering yields on government bonds, increasing the money supply and easing credit supply. In domestic currency, the balance sheet of the ECB increased roughly threefold between 2007 and mid-2012, before shrinking modestly, while that of the Federal Reserve rose three and a half times and that of the Bank of England more than fourfold between 2007 and early 2013.[45] To take the most important example, the US monetary base rose by $2.8tn between August 2008 and November 2013 – a sum equal to 17 per cent of annualized US gross domestic product in the third quarter of 2013.

Finally, consider the fiscal support. Fiscal deficits of a number of significant high-income countries rose to unprecedented peacetime levels when the crisis hit. Among the six largest high-income countries (US, Japan, Germany, France, UK and Italy), these increases were particularly big for Japan, the UK and the US (see Figure 2). In the case of the US, the general government fiscal deficit soared from 2.7 per cent of GDP in 2007 to 13 per cent in 2009 – an astounding rise.[46] A number of countries ran fiscal deficits at levels previously experienced only in world wars. In the case of the UK, for which excellent historical records exist, this event will deliver the fourth biggest cumulative rise in public debt relative to GDP since 1700, behind only the Napoleonic Wars and the First and Second World Wars. In the US, too, the fiscal costs of this event rival only those of the Second World War.

What explains this huge increase in deficits? The answer, contrary to conventional wisdom on the political right in the US and the UK, is not, to any great extent, discretionary fiscal 'stimuli' (increases in

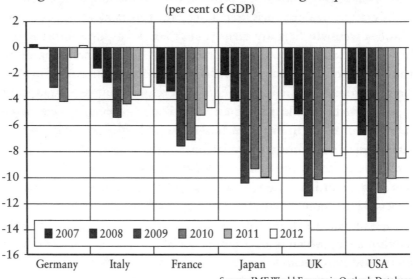

Figure 2. General Government Borrowing Requirement
(per cent of GDP)

Source: IMF World Economic Outlook Database

spending or cuts in taxation designed to increase aggregate demand) –
a term that, quite wrongly, became taboo. According to the IMF's
November 2010 analysis, the cumulative discretionary fiscal stimulus
of these countries between 2009 and 2011 was far smaller than their
actual deficits, with one – probably surprising – exception: Germany.
There, according to the IMF, the discretionary stimulus explained as
much as 66 per cent of the admittedly modest average deficits of
2.8 per cent of GDP.[47] Italy had no stimulus. In other cases, the discretionary stimulus explained at most a fifth of the actual deficits over
these three years. In the UK, the discretionary stimulus, all of it
applied in 2009, explained a mere 6 per cent of the deficits.

The explanation for the explosion in fiscal deficits – an immensely
helpful way to cushion the immediate impact of the collapse in private spending – was simply the unexpected crisis itself. This lowered
GDP far below trend, automatically raised spending on unemployment benefits and similar counter-cyclical income support, and, even
more important, lowered government revenue, as consumer spending,
income and profits collapsed. In 2011, GDP was, quite unexpectedly,
13 per cent below a continuation of its 1980–2007 trend in both the
US and the UK. In fact, it was a pity that a form of 'sticker shock'
over the scale of the unexpected deficits frightened policymakers into
not giving the discretionary fiscal support then needed and, subsequently, as we shall see further below, into premature retrenchment.

Nobody should be surprised by the huge fiscal deterioration that
followed the crisis. In their seminal book, *This Time is Different*, Carmen Reinhart and Kenneth Rogoff argue that: 'Declining revenues
and higher expenditures, owing to a combination of bailout costs and
higher transfer payments and debt service costs, led to a rapid and
marked worsening in the fiscal balance.'[48] In fact, they note from an
analysis of crises in thirteen countries, the cumulative increase in real
public debt was 86 per cent – close to a doubling.[49] What happened
after 2007 is in line with that prior experience. Indeed, with interest
rates close to zero, the discretionary fiscal response needed to be far
stronger: in such a deep crisis, relying almost entirely on the built-in
stabilizers – by which is meant the counter-cyclical effect on the economy of the way fiscal deficits rise automatically in a recession – was
insufficient, as the Nobel laureate Paul Krugman has argued in his

powerful book, *End this Depression Now!*[50] But, together with support for the financial system and the monetary policy response, the willingness to let the fiscal deficit take the strain was effective at least in halting the slide into a depression.

RECOVERY IN THE BIG HIGH-INCOME COUNTRIES

How successfully, then, did the policy interventions of the big high-income countries – the support for the financial system, the monetary loosening and the combination of the built-in fiscal stabilizers with modest discretionary stimulus – rescue the world economy? The answer is: fairly successfully, but not successfully enough, largely because the fiscal stimulus was both too small and prematurely abandoned.

The immediate impact of the crisis was dramatic: global trade, industrial output and gross domestic product all fell off a cliff, as confidence collapsed, demand shrank and credit, including trade credit, froze. World industrial output fell as fast in the first year after its April 2008 peak as during the Great Depression, which began in June 1929, and the volume of world trade and world equity markets initially fell even faster than then. Thus, the volume of world trade fell by close to 20 per cent in the twelve months from April 2008, against around 10 per cent over the twelve months from June 1929.[51] Again, world equity markets fell by around 50 per cent over twelve months this time, against around 20 per cent in 1929–30. Fortunately, this time, strong policy action reversed the slide far sooner.[52]

The British historian Niall Ferguson was quite right to call this the 'Great Recession'.[53] Between the third quarter of 2008 and the first quarter of 2009, the annualized rate of decline in GDP in the six largest high-income countries ranged from 6.4 per cent in France, 7 per cent in the UK and 7.1 per cent in the US, to 10.2 per cent in Italy, 11.7 per cent in Germany and 13.8 per cent in Japan. But, then, in the second quarter of 2009, the world economy started to turn around, diverging sharply from the disastrous experience of the Great Depression, when global output and trade fell for three years. We may, in our folly, have permitted the emergence of a financial crisis rivalling that of the 1930, but at least we did not repeat all the subsequent policy mistakes: the wave of banking collapses; the willingness to allow a collapse of money and credit; the toleration of a destructive deflation; and the determination to balance budgets, at once, 'to strengthen confidence'.

Avoiding a collapse in economic activity comparable to that of the 1930s was a success, but a qualified one. Global industrial output had recovered to about 10 per cent above its pre-crisis peak by December 2011, though the volume of world trade was only modestly above its pre-crisis level. Above all, in the core high-income countries the crisis threw a long shadow over output and employment. (I leave aside the crises in smaller high-income countries to the discussion of the Euro-zone crisis, in Chapter Two.)

The six largest high-income economies all experienced deep recessions, with output reaching a trough in the first or second quarters of 2009 (see Figure 3). After that, the US experienced much the most sustained recovery. By the fourth quarter of 2013, US GDP was 7.2 per cent above its level in the first quarter of 2008. That was

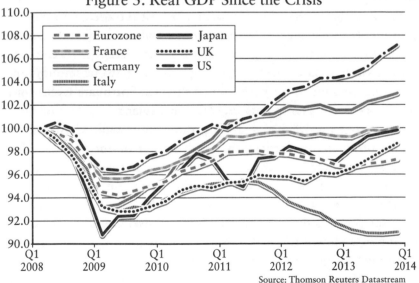

Figure 3. Real GDP Since the Crisis

Source: Thomson Reuters Datastream

THE SHIFTS AND THE SHOCKS

significantly better than Germany's 3 per cent. By then France and Japan were back to pre-crisis levels. The economies of the UK and, far more so, Italy were still smaller than they had been prior to the crisis, as was the Eurozone as a whole. The US economy had managed to grow steadily from 2009, if weakly, by its own historic standards. Germany recovered strongly in 2009 and 2010, but grew weakly again after the middle of 2011, as the Eurozone crisis worsened. German policy bears much responsibility for this outcome, as Chapter Two will show. The French economy stagnated after a relatively mild recession in 2008 and 2009, while Italy's went into a second deep plunge from 2011, as the Eurozone crisis took hold. The UK economy stagnated from the third quarter of 2010 to the beginning of 2013 when recovery started, this hiatus in the recovery being in part due to the coalition government's ill-timed policy of austerity.[54] Finally, the Japanese economy was remarkably volatile.

Another measure of the effectiveness of policy is what happened to employment and unemployment. The data on changes in the ratio of employees to people of working age tells one more than changes in rates of unemployment. When people cannot find work, they often leave the labour force. But the plight of people who no longer even look for work is often worse than that of those who are still searching.

Figure 4 shows that the US experienced a huge decline in the proportion of people aged 15–64 with jobs between 2007 and 2012. In Germany, by contrast, the proportion with jobs actually rose, despite the recession. In 2007 the German employment ratio was nearly three percentage points lower than that of the US. Five years later, it was nearly six percentage points *higher*. The explanation for this divergence is that the US had soaring productivity, while Germany had falling productivity, particularly in the early years of the crisis. This contrast was partly because the US lost many jobs for relatively unskilled men in construction and partly because Germany subsidised short-time working to avoid layoffs.[55] Underlying this contrast has been the rewards that US shareholders give executives for protecting profits in a downturn, at the price of laying off workers. German executives are not rewarded in the same way. Moreover, German corporate culture and institutions are very different from those in

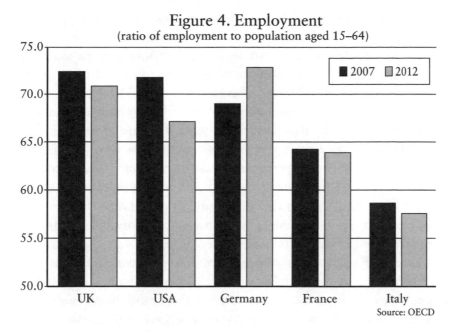

Figure 4. Employment
(ratio of employment to population aged 15–64)

Source: OECD

America. Particularly important is the division between the supervisory board, which includes worker representatives, and the executive board.[56]

How, then, does the outcome in crisis-hit, high-income countries compare with what might have been expected from previous financial calamities? Again, the work of professors Reinhart and Rogoff is illuminating. In *This Time is Different*, they argue 'the aftermath of banking crises is associated with profound declines in output and employment. The unemployment rate rises an average of 7 percentage points during the down phase of the cycle, which lasts on average more than four years. Output falls (from peak to trough) more than 9 per cent on average, although the duration of downturn, averaging roughly two years, is considerably shorter than that of unemployment.'[57]

Against such unhappy comparisons, the big high-income countries did relatively well. Only one, Japan, experienced a fall in GDP as large as the average indicated by Reinhart and Rogoff, at 9.2 per cent. The peak to trough fall of GDP was 4.3 per cent in France, 4.6 per cent in the US, 5.6 per cent in the Eurozone, 6.3 per cent in the UK, 6.8 per cent in Germany and 9.1 per cent in Italy (still falling in the third quarter of 2013). All these were grim statistics. Yet, even so, they were not as bad as the falls suffered, on average, in the earlier crises studied by professors Reinhart and Rogoff. Moreover, the declines were relatively brief. The troughs were reached in four or five quarters, whereupon a turnaround began.

Similarly, the rise in unemployment was also far smaller than the average reported by Reinhart and Rogoff. The rise in the monthly unemployment rate from the pre-crisis trough, by May 2012, was highest in the US, at 5.6 percentage points. It was only 1.6 percentage points in Japan, 2.5 percentage points in France, 3.3 percentage points in the UK, and 4.3 percentage points in Italy. Germany's rise was just 0.9 percentage points in the early months of the crisis, but unemployment then fell to well below the pre-crisis rate.

Even if the post-crisis performance of these economies was not dreadful by previous standards, the crisis proved painful and enfeebling. Why do financial crises do that? And why did the recovery stall or even go into reverse, in some cases? To answer those questions, we need to understand balance-sheet recessions.

THE ECONOMICS OF POST-CRISIS DE-LEVERAGING

Big financial crises cause painful recessions. Big financial crises that follow huge credit booms cause particularly painful recessions and long periods of weak growth. Professor Alan Taylor of the University of Virginia, a well-known economic historian, notes that 'a credit boom and a financial crisis together appear to be a very potent mix that correlates with abnormally severe downward pressures on growth, inflation, credit and investment for long periods'.[58]

At bottom, there are five things going on in post-crisis economies.

First and most important, prior to the crash, unsustainable increases in private debt (the stock), or leverage (the ratio of the stock to wealth and income), had occurred within several economies. (See Figure 5 for the US, which goes up to the third quarter of 2013.) One can debate whether the levels of debt ended up too high, in all cases. One cannot reasonably debate whether the pre-crisis level of borrowing could be sustained: it could not be. It was rising debt – that is, continued net borrowing – that permitted some households and businesses to spend consistently more than their incomes. After the crisis, the debtors could no longer increase their debt: indeed, borrowing became negative, as they started to repay. So erstwhile borrowers were forced to lower their spending dramatically, willy-nilly. Meanwhile, creditors found that their wealth and incomes were lower or less certain (or, usually, both) than they had been before the crisis. So they did not want to spend more either. Bringing debt to sustainable levels is a long-term process: in an important study of post-crisis private-sector de-leveraging, the McKinsey Global Institute notes that this has taken between four and six years in previous cases, such as Finland and Sweden in the early 1990s.[59]

The second reason why the impact of a financial crisis is so prolonged is that the sustained rise in debt and associated spending distorts economies. Asset-price bubbles encourage excessive investment in, for example, housing and commercial property. When the crisis hits and the borrowing dries up, some part of that investment

Figure 5. US Cumulative Private Sector Debt over GDP
(per cent)

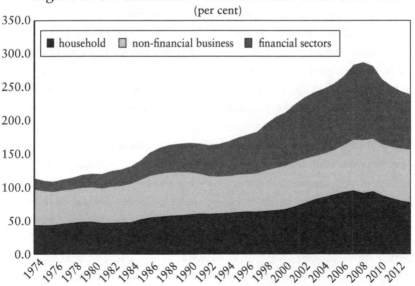

Source: Federal Reserve and Bureau of Economic Analysis

37

will be abandoned and the country's stock of physical capital will shrink. More important, the industries that provided the goods and services demanded by those undertaking the unsustainable spending will shrink, possibly dramatically. The most obvious example is the collapse in spending on construction in some crisis-hit countries. The incomes of bankers, commissions of estate agents (realtors, in American parlance), fees of lawyers, and so on and so forth, will also shrink. Furthermore, the weakness of the economy will itself slow potential growth (that is, the rate at which the capacity to produce itself grows), as investment remains subdued. Analysts have made substantial adjustments in estimates of the level and growth of potential output for many crisis-hit economies. In the UK, for example, in 2011 the Office of Budgetary Responsibility marked down forecast real potential output in 2017 by a massive 18 per cent below its pre-crisis trend.[60]

The third reason why post-crisis economies are so weak is the adverse impact on the financial sector. Overloaded with bad debt and under-capitalized, financial institutions become far more cautious. Regulation tends to encourage such caution. Banks cease to lend. This forces further de-leveraging on the rest of the economy. Moreover, banks automatically create money as a by-product of their normal lending (a point explained in full in Chapter Six below). That is a fundamental characteristic of banks. When they lend, they create a debt from their client to the bank and, simultaneously, a debt from the bank to the client. This is just double-entry bookkeeping. A debt from a bank to a client is a deposit and a deposit is money. So the growth of the stock of money in the hands of the public declines when the growth of bank lending falls.

The fourth reason why post-crisis economies are weak is that inflation may become too low or, worse, deflation may set in. Deflation, or falling prices, creates the danger of what the great American economist Irving Fisher called 'debt deflation' in the 1930s – rising real level of debt and debt service within a collapsing economy.[61] Such debt deflation is already, alas, in progress in parts of the Eurozone. Yet deflation is not only dangerous because of what it does to the real burden of debt; it is also dangerous if it pushes the real rate of interest too high. Equilibrium real interest rates may become strongly negative in a highly leveraged, crisis-hit economy. But with deflation, the real interest rate will be positive even if the nominal rate that the central bank controls is brought down as low as zero. Moreover, longer-term rates will then be higher than short-term rates, because of what Keynes called 'liquidity preference': thus, if short-term and long-term rates were both zero, the owner of bonds would be forgoing the benefits of holding a liquid and riskless asset – money – for no compensating return. As a result, in a deflationary environment, it is even harder to make long-term real rates negative than short-term ones. In these conditions, therefore, deflation or even low inflation may prove highly contractionary for the economy.

Deflation has created notoriously prolonged difficulties for Japan, which suffered a massive post-credit-boom crisis in the 1990s. Japanese consumer prices then fell for more than two decades. As a result, Japan has suffered persistently positive real interest rates, even though the official short-term rate has been either close to zero or actually zero since the mid-1990s, while the long-term rate has been below 2 per cent since 1999 and even below 1 per cent since late 2011. This is why the 'first arrow' of Prime Minister Shinzo Abe's 'Abenomics' has consisted of achieving an inflation target of 2 per cent agreed between the government and the Bank of Japan in early 2013.[62]

Big difficulties may even arise in a low-inflation environment, rather than in a deflationary one if equilibrium real interest rates fall low enough. With inflation at 2 per cent, for example, the real short-term interest rate cannot be less than minus 2 per cent if one ignores the extreme possibility of negative nominal rates (which are feasible up to a point, though tricky to impose). Therefore, some economists, including Olivier Blanchard, chief economist of the International Monetary Fund, have argued that the now customary 2 per cent inflation target turned out to be too low in the crisis: thus, with short-term equilibrium rates possibly as low as minus 3 to minus 5 per cent in badly hit economies, inflation needed to be closer to 4 per cent in normal times.[63]

Finally, economies may end up in a state of sustained malaise. As John Maynard Keynes argued, this paralyses what he called the 'animal spirits' of businesses.[64] That, then, may create a vicious spiral: low investment means weak demand and low economic growth, and so justifies the decision to postpone investment. In the post-crisis world, the reasons for people to feel uncertain and act cautiously are legion. Populist politics is one source of uncertainty, notably in the US with the rise of the Tea Party. More important are weak and volatile demand and continued financial fragility.

The overall impact of such a crisis, therefore, is some weakening of supply, relative to its pre-crisis trend, but, even more, a weakening of demand relative to the weakened supply. The danger is a prolonged period of what Richard Koo of Nomura Research calls 'balance-sheet recession', in which the debt-encumbered private sector either tries, or is forced, to lower its debts – or, at the least, is unwilling or unable to increase them.[65]

What happened after the crisis to US sectoral balances – the balance between income and spending of households, corporations, the government and foreigners – offers a classic picture of an economy going into such a balance-sheet recession. Foreigners have run a surplus with the US for a long time and continued to do so, on a slightly smaller scale, following the crisis. US households ran a growing financial deficit (or excess of spending over income) up to 2005, as they borrowed ever more against the rising value of their houses. But this deficit began to shrink as soon as the house-price bubble popped in 2006. That was predictable. Between the third quarter of 2005 and the second quarter of 2009, the financial balance of US households – the relationship between income and spending – shifted towards a surplus of income over spending by the enormous total of 7.2 per cent of GDP: such a huge reduction in spending, relative to incomes, was quite sufficient to cause a depression on its own. But in the corporate sector, an almost equally large shift, of 6.2 per cent of GDP towards surplus, started in the fourth quarter of 2008 in direct response to the crisis, and ended in the third quarter of 2009.

Sectoral financial balances must sum to zero, by definition: this is saying no more than that one agent's income is another agent's spending. So, if one group of agents is spending less than their income, others must be spending more than theirs. This is simple accounting. In this case, the offset to these shifts towards austerity was the deterioration in the fiscal balance (already discussed above). That finished in the second quarter of 2009, long before any substantial policy action came into effect: the idea that deliberate stimulus caused the huge US fiscal deficits is therefore nonsense. The deterioration in the fiscal balance was an automatic and helpful response to a collapse in private spending and a rise in private saving.

In this case, the fiscal deficit did not crowd out spending by the private sector. On the contrary, the private-sector cutbacks *crowded in* the fiscal deficit via the decline in GDP and consequent rise in spending and fall in revenue: thus, the austerity forced on private individuals and businesses by the financial crisis *caused* rising fiscal deficits, as private spending, output and government revenue fell, while spending on unemployment benefits and other adverse consequences of recessions automatically rose. This is quite distinct from what happens when the fiscal deficit is expanded at full employment. In that case, interest rates rise, as the deficit crowds out private spending. Reliance on the fiscal buffer (the ability to let the fiscal deficit rise in response to a private-sector led recession) was essential this time, because even a strongly expansionary monetary policy was insufficient to prevent the shifts of the household and corporate sectors into surplus. We know it was insufficient because the monetary authorities initiated such a policy. This is a situation in which Keynesian fiscal policy becomes relevant.

This is no more than to say that the economy was in a 'liquidity trap': at the lowest interest rate the central bank could create, the private and foreign sectors would have had a large excess of income over desired spending at full employment (the spending that would have occurred had the economy been at full employment, which, of course, it was not). This could be dealt with in only one of two ways: either by a collapse in income greater than the associated collapse in spending – that is, an outright depression – or by a large fiscal deficit. If the government had refused to run the deficits, by slashing its own spending as the private sector was also doing, the result would have been a depression, possibly one as bad as the Great Depression. Viewing the government's finances as if they are those of a household or even a large company is nonsensical. Government must respond to what is happening in the private sector, above all during a severe crisis.

This need to tolerate – even increase – the large fiscal deficits was widely, if not universally, accepted in the immediate aftermath of the crisis. But, Richard Koo argues, these fiscal deficits have to continue so long as the balance-sheet adjustment in the private sector continues. This is because the attempt by private decision-makers to lower their debts forces them to spend less than their incomes and so generate financial surpluses – excesses of income over spending. By definition, if one ignores the external sector, a private financial surplus entails a fiscal deficit: that is just a matter of arithmetic. People find that argument difficult to accept, even if they understand it. Far too soon, policymakers wanted – or, in the case of vulnerable Eurozone member states, were forced – to cut fiscal deficits again, thereby slowing, or even short-circuiting, recovery.

FROM STIMULUS TO AUSTERITY

The leaders of the G-20 countries embraced the argument for a strong policy response, including the strong fiscal response, at their Washington, London and Pittsburg summits in 2008 and 2009. In Pittsburgh, on 25 September 2009, they stated that 'We pledge today to sustain our strong policy response until a durable recovery is secured. We will act to ensure that when growth returns, jobs do too. We will avoid any premature withdrawal of stimulus.'[66]

In Pittsburgh the leaders also stated, simply and correctly of the package of policies adopted almost a year before, that 'it worked'. Indeed, it did. The frightening economic downturn that had begun in 2008 was halted and reversed in 2009. This was an important achievement of modern policymaking.

Yet not long afterwards, at the Toronto Summit of 26–27 June 2010, the view had changed. The G-20 summit now referred, in a worried tone, to the fact that 'Recent events highlight the importance of sustainable public finances and the need for our countries to put in place credible, properly phased and growth-friendly plans to deliver fiscal sustainability, differentiated for and tailored to national circumstances.'[67]

Furthermore, the leaders continued, 'Advanced countries have committed to fiscal plans that will at least halve deficits by 2013 and stabilize or reduce government debt-to-GDP ratios by 2016.'

In the middle of 2010, therefore, the leaders shifted away from their strong counter-cyclical action towards austerity. They did so, moreover, when their economies were still far from having fully recovered from the crisis (see Figure 3). Nor was the new commitment to austerity mere rhetoric. Fiscal tightening did indeed begin in 2010 or 2011 in all the big countries. That surely helps explain why a promising recovery started to wither. Fiscal austerity proved contractionary, given that post-crisis private demand was so weak and interest rates were very close to zero.

So why did this premature policy reversal occur? Part of the explanation was influential academic research on the limits to public indebtedness and the feasibility of 'expansionary contractions', to which I will turn further in Chapter Eight. Another part was a mistaken belief that the recovery was already entrenched. Yet another was the simplistic and mistaken mantra that 'one cannot get out of debt by increasing it further'. The crucial point, however, is that the new debtors are not the same as the old ones. It is necessary for the creditworthy to borrow when those who are no longer creditworthy cannot. If everybody tries to cut down on borrowing and spending at the same time, the result will be a depression: that is the 'paradox of thrift' – a phrase first popularized by the late Nobel laureate, Paul Samuelson.[68]

Yet another explanation was politics. In the US, for both electoral and ideological reasons, the Republican Party was irrevocably opposed to the idea that the government could do anything useful about the economy except by leaving it alone, and so could not tolerate the possibility that the Obama administration might prove the opposite in the aftermath of the biggest economic crisis for eighty years. It therefore dedicated itself in Congress to preventing the administration from doing anything that might improve economic performance. In the UK, the coalition government that gained power in May 2010 made fiscal austerity its *raison d'être*, to differentiate itself from – and fix the blame for the crisis upon – its predecessor. Yet another and even more important event encouraged this shift towards retrenchment. That was the Eurozone crisis, which turned the Eurozone towards austerity and frightened policymakers elsewhere into following their example. The timid and the orthodox argued that every country with large fiscal deficits, even the US, would end up tomorrow where Greece was today. The Greek crisis, which will be discussed in the next chapter, left a toxic aftermath far greater than the size of the Greek economy or the wider relevance of its plight necessitated.[69] That was a Greek tragedy of a new and modern kind.

CONCLUSION

The financial crisis was a calamity. But from October 2008, the collective response was, for about a year and a half, purposeful and effective. It could have been still bigger. However, what was done halted the immediate panic and then reversed the downswing that was well under way in late 2008 and early 2009. It succeeded in doing so even though the recession was initially as bad as it had been in 1930. Unfortunately, policymakers failed to sustain the policies required to support private-sector de-leveraging and so avoid a prolonged balance-sheet recession. Largely as a result, the recovery proved weak or even withered away altogether in 2011 and 2012. For this unhappy outcome, the Eurozone crisis was partly responsible. It turned out to be the second act of the global financial crisis. It is, accordingly, the subject of the next chapter.

2

The Crisis in the Eurozone

Whatever role the markets have played in catalysing the sovereign debt crisis, it is an indisputable fact that excessive state spending has led to unsustainable levels of debt and deficits that now threaten our economic welfare.
Wolfgang Schäuble, German Finance Minister, 2011[1]

Greece was the Eurozone's Lehman. While the worst of the post-Lehman crisis was both severe and relatively brief, the aftermath of the Greek crisis was less severe but longer lasting. It triggered what turned out to be a long-running crisis, as fundamental weaknesses in the Eurozone's economies and institutional structure were laid bare. Far from bringing Europeans together, the euro caused division, disarray and despair. The Eurozone has turned out to be an unhappy monetary marriage from which divorce is almost unthinkable. Since the Eurozone is the world's second-largest economy after the US, its crisis has also endangered global stability. The existence of this fragile structure helped turn a significant financial crisis into an economic disaster.

THE ROLLING CRISES

The moment of truth for the Eurozone came in October 2009, when George Papandreou, the incoming Socialist prime minister of Greece, told the world – and, above all, his country's long-suffering Eurozone partners – that its budget deficit for that year would be 10 per cent of GDP. This was well above the 6 to 8 per cent of GDP predicted only weeks earlier by the outgoing Conservative government.[2] It was still more dramatically above the draft target for 2009 reported by the European Commission in June 2008, which was for a deficit of only 1.8 per cent of GDP (although that did include 0.75 percentage points in one-off deficit-reducing measures).[3] In response, Jean-Claude Juncker, chairman of the finance ministers of the then sixteen-nation Eurozone group, said: 'The game is over. We need serious statistics.'[4] In the end, the deficit reached 15.6 per cent of GDP.[5]

What made the Greek fiscal position so bad was not that its spending was extraordinarily high by Eurozone standards, but rather that its revenue was so low, given the country's high spending. Thus, in 2009, the ratio of Greek public spending to GDP was 54 per cent, according to the IMF. This put Greece into third position among Eurozone members, after France and Finland. But seven Eurozone members had spending above 50 per cent of GDP. Apart from the three already mentioned, these high-spending countries included Belgium, Austria, Italy and the Netherlands. Out of the seven only two (Greece and Italy) subsequently fell into crises. Yet the ratio of total revenue to GDP in Greece was a mere 38 per cent, ahead only of Spain, Ireland and the Slovak Republic, and far below the ratios achieved by the other high-spending countries: Finland, for example, raised 53 per cent of GDP in revenue and France 49 per cent. It was the gulf between the Greek embrace of high public spending (much of it relatively wasteful) and the country's inability or unwillingness to raise taxes that lay at the root of its fiscal difficulties. This was ultimately a political failure more than an economic one, though a failure that membership of the Eurozone helped.

Until the Greek moment of truth, continental European leaders tended to view the crisis as largely 'Anglo-Saxon', with epicentres in New York and London. Yes, their banks had been sucked into the maelstrom: this was, after all, a global financial system. But it was, they were sure, the sloppy regulation and incompetent responses of others that had caused the meltdown. They confidently criticized the actions of US policymakers in September 2008, particularly the decision to let Lehman fail. They knew that they, too, would be affected by this crisis: how could they not be? They knew very well that they had to respond. But it was, they were sure, not their fault.

46

They did protest too much. True, the ideas that had led to trust in financial liberalization had, as argued by the Nobel laureate Joseph Stiglitz of Columbia University in his book *Freefall*, largely originated in the US and the UK.[6] But European institutions, in both their US and their European activities, had fully shared the misbehaviour by banking institutions. Inside the Eurozone, Ireland and Spain had experienced huge housing bubbles and associated credit booms. Above all, the institutional defects of the Eurozone had nothing to do with the US or the UK. The euro was a continental invention for whose frailties not only the Eurozone but the wider world was about to suffer.

In 2009 and 2010, the epicentre of the crisis moved inside the Eurozone, where it subsequently remained. Prior to the crisis, investors had viewed all Eurozone government bonds as equally risky or, rather, as equally safe. Why anybody should have imagined that Greek and German government debts were equivalent is not easy to comprehend. This was partly another of the follies of private investors. But it was also partly the result of the regulatory rules established by the Basel Committee on Banking Supervision (an international committee of banking supervisors). Basel I, the first of these regulations, was published in 1988.[7] It allowed banks to treat government debt as risk free and therefore to fund such debt with zero equity. The view that government debt should be risk free has a certain validity for countries that borrow only in money they create: at least the risk of outright default is very low in such cases, though not the risk of inflation. But it was certainly inapplicable to countries borrowing in euros created by a central bank over which they had next to no influence. That is something investors started to understand as soon as they became reacquainted with the temporarily forgotten idea of risk during 2007 and 2008. Increases in spreads started to emerge between German 'bunds' (the German word for bonds) and yields on weaker countries' bonds, this being a measure of perceptions of riskiness of the latter. By late January 2009, spreads of Greek government bonds over German bunds had hit 280 basis points (2.8 percentage points). Two years before, they had been less than a tenth of that level (see Figure 6).

Market aversion to Greek debt continued to increase: by early April 2010 spreads over bunds reached close to 4 percentage points.

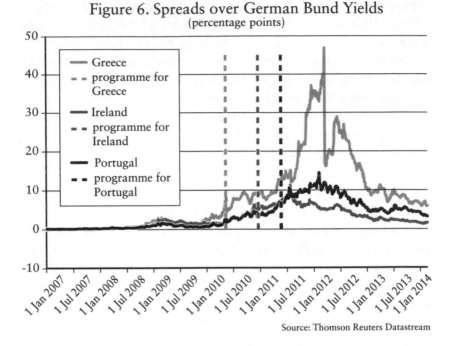

Figure 6. Spreads over German Bund Yields
(percentage points)

Source: Thomson Reuters Datastream

Effectively unable to fund itself in the market, the Greek government then asked for help, including, on the instructions of its Eurozone partners, from the International Monetary Fund.[8] On 9 May 2010 the IMF agreed to provide a €30bn 'stand-by arrangement' (the name for a standard loan from the Fund), while Eurozone members offered another €80bn.[9] In response to the agreement, Dominique Strauss-Kahn, the subsequently disgraced IMF managing director,[10] remarked: 'We are confident that the economy will emerge more dynamic and robust from this crisis – and able to deliver the growth, jobs, and prosperity that the country needs for the future.'[11]

If Mr Strauss-Kahn believed what he said, he was either unreasonably optimistic or the future he was contemplating must have been very distant. Greek spreads remained above – generally, far above – where they had been before the programme was launched up to and including January 2014. This was despite a large restructuring of private-sector loans outstanding in February 2012, whose effects can be seen in Figure 6.[12] Over the period covered in Figure 6, Greek spreads over German bunds remained quite high, though down hugely from their peaks.

Not long after Greece came Ireland, whose economy and public finances were drowning in the bad debt created by the collapse of its property boom. On 16 December 2010 the International Monetary Fund agreed to a three-year lending arrangement worth €22.5bn, part of an international package worth €85bn. The rest came from Ireland's Eurozone partners, via the European Financial Stabilization Mechanism (EFSM) and the European Financial Stability Facility (EFSF), temporary financial facilities that the Eurozone had established in response to the crisis, together with bilateral loans from the UK, Sweden and Denmark, as well as Ireland's own contribution of €17.5bn.[13] As with the programme for Greece, the European Central Bank was involved as provider of liquidity to the bankrupt Irish banking system.[14] This turned out to be a successful programme, from which Ireland exited in December 2013.[15] In early January 2014 its spreads over German bunds were down to 1.5 percentage points.

On 20 May 2011 another programme was agreed, this time with Portugal, with €26bn from the IMF out of total support of €78bn over three years. Portugal, unlike Greece and Ireland, had enjoyed not a boom followed by a bust, but a lengthy period of stagnation, partly because it joined the currency union at an uncompetitive exchange rate. Accordingly, this package, in the words of John Lipsky, at that time the IMF's acting managing director, 'addresses the fundamental problem in Portugal – low growth – with a policy mix based on restoring competitiveness through structural reforms, ensuring a balanced fiscal consolidation path, and stabilizing the financial sector'.[16] Unlike Ireland, Portugal had a long-term lack of competitiveness and growth, in addition to its immediate fiscal and balance-of-payments difficulties.

On 15 May 2013, after intense debate over the terms of the restructuring of its oversized banks, a three-year programme was agreed with Cyprus. The Fund agreed to supply about €1bn under its Extended Fund Facility. This, however, was a small part of a €10bn programme, with the balance coming from the European Stability Mechanism – the newly established permanent Eurozone programme for the rescue of crisis-hit economies, which replaced the EFSM and

EFSF.[17] The need for this programme was partly the result of the prior restructuring of Greek debt, which hit risk-taking Cypriot banks hard. The programme for Cyprus had two significant features: for the first time, it imposed losses on bank creditors, notably including depositors (100 per cent losses on amounts above €100,000 in the now closed Laiki Bank and 60 per cent losses on amounts over €100,000 in the larger Bank of Cyprus), many of whom were, not coincidentally, foreign, particularly Russian; and, no less important, it inflicted controls on transfers of euros outside the country. It became even clearer than before that some euros were more equal than others. A euro deposited in a dodgy bank backed by a weak sovereign was and is not the same as a euro deposited in a solid bank supported by a strong sovereign.[18] This makes the Eurozone structurally vulnerable to bank runs, since it obviously makes sense to move accounts from banks backed by weak sovereigns to banks backed by creditworthy ones, particularly at a time of crisis. It is also why informed observers concluded that some kind of banking union was essential if the Eurozone was to survive in the long run.

In 2011 a far more significant event occurred than this set of crises in small countries. Spain and Italy, two far larger economies, fell into similar financial difficulty, a remarkably dangerous turn of events. The risk of a meltdown of the Spanish or Italian public finances, banking systems and economies was not easily contemplated, let alone managed. The four small countries with programmes generated only 5.7 per cent of Eurozone GDP in 2012. But Spain alone generated 10.8 per cent and Italy as much as 16.5 per cent. Italy is both a member of the G-7 and has the third largest public debt in the world (after the US and Japan). A financial and economic meltdown in Spain and Italy would affect even France. That might prove terminal for the euro itself.

The rising spreads of Italy and Spain began in 2008 (see Figure 7), during the global re-rating of risk. But the dangerous increases in yields occurred in the summer of 2011. From then the spreads in yields on the bonds of these two countries vis-à-vis those of Germany oscillated between three percentage points and over six percentage points. Such spreads had triggered the programmes for Greece, Ireland and Portugal. In June 2012, Madrid did ask for €100bn to assist

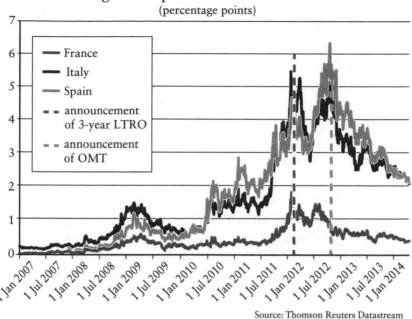

Figure 7. Spreads over Bund Yields
(percentage points)

Source: Thomson Reuters Datastream

with the recapitalization of its ailing banks, which it received as a loan.[19] But external rescue programmes were not launched for Spain and Italy, despite the high spreads on their governments' bonds, partly because the governments of these countries were loath to accept a humiliating loss of independence and partly because the resources required would be too large, particularly in the case of Italy. Nobody knows how costly these rescues would have been. But Italy's public debt is roughly four times as large as the total resources available to the Eurozone emergency rescue funds, much of which were already being used by other member countries. The IMF had less to offer than the European funds themselves. Italy was simply too big to save.

In place of such an external rescue, prime ministers were removed. The Italian government headed by the discredited Silvio Berlusconi was ousted without an election, in favour of one headed by the respected technocrat Mario Monti, in mid-November 2011. Monti ended up being rather less popular with Italians than with the European establishment, as the general election of February 2013 demonstrated. The same thing happened in Greece, in the same month, with the defenestration of the hapless Mr Papandreou in favour of brief rule by Lucas Papademos, former head of the Greek central bank and vice-president of the ECB. After elections in May and June 2012, Antonis Samaras of the New Democracy Party became prime minister, his job being to implement the very programme of austerity and structural reform he had opposed when in opposition. Subsequently, in Italy, Mr Monti's government was succeeded by another coalition, headed this time by the centre-left technocrat, Enrico Letta, himself then overthrown in February 2014 by Matteo Renzi, a centre-left politician.

The personalities changed. The policies did not. In a financial crisis, creditors rule. In the Eurozone crisis, the creditor that mattered was Germany, because it was much the largest. The aims of any plausible German government, and certainly of one headed by Angela Merkel, the country's popular, cautious and self-disciplined chancellor, have been relatively simple to understand: these are to preserve the Eurozone, but on Germany's terms.

Germany wishes to preserve the Eurozone for both political and economic reasons. The economic reasons are that it gives Germany a big home market and a significantly more competitive exchange rate than it would otherwise enjoy. While not every German would accept these are big economic benefits, the dominant view in the business and financial elite is that they are. The political benefits of the Eurozone are that it is the capstone of the European project, to which Germany has been strongly committed since shortly after the Second World War. The German leadership has consistently viewed it as the best solution to the difficulty of managing the relationship between their own relatively powerful country and its many weaker neighbours. Again, not every German would agree with this view and, clearly, the attachment to the European ideal has diminished since German unification in 1990.

The results of the German general election of September 2013 confirmed the overall German orientation towards the EU and the Eurozone. Angela Merkel's Christian Democrats (CDU), supported by the Bavarian Christian Social Union (CSU), won 41.5 per cent of the vote. The pro-euro Social Democratic Party (SPD) won a further 25.7 per cent of the vote. This gave the old pro-European parties a dominant position in the Bundestag and allowed the formation of a grand coalition with an overwhelming majority. In this election a new anti-euro (though not anti-EU) party – Alternative für Deutschland (Alternative for Germany) – entered the fray. But it only won 4.7 per cent of the vote, insufficient to enter the Bundestag. In Germany, extremist single-issue parties have done consistently badly since the Second World War. Arguably, the Greens have been an exception, but they broadened and moderated their views to achieve a relative success. Germans have consistently voted for the established parties and given them the mandate to pursue a pro-European policy on whose benefits a broad national consensus exists. The will towards moderation of an ageing and conservative German electorate is no doubt in part a reaction to what happened in the 1930s and in part a response to the perceived success of this strategy.

Above all, the Eurozone now exists. Unravelling it would create huge economic and political disruption. Exit from the euro is illegal under European law. No legal provisions exist for undertaking it. Quite apart from that, an exit could not possibly be planned without the fact being leaked: this is not the sort of thing that can be done by a few people in secret. Any leak would cause a run on the exiting country's liabilities, including its banks. This would need to be met by exchange controls and controls on withdrawals from banks. The panic would spread to other weaker member countries, creating waves of currency flight and, quite probably, the imposition of protective controls. The euro liabilities of the country or countries about to depart would need to be redenominated. There would be waves of public and private defaults, notably on liabilities contracted outside the country or countries planning to leave. All this would create immense confusion and political stress. In truth, there would be havoc, possibly leading to the break-up of the EU itself. While a unilateral departure by Germany would be less economically traumatic, it, too, would create significant economic and political turmoil.[20] Even if many Germans now think it would have been better never to create the single currency, it is too late for such regrets. Undoing something is not the same as not having done it in the first place.

Yet the cost that Germany is prepared to bear to keep the Eurozone afloat is limited – or at the least German leaders want to make others believe it is limited. Most Germans also strongly believe that the policies being imposed upon recalcitrant deficit countries are in the long-term interests of the latter. The economic ideology of '*Ordoliberalismus*', which had a profound influence upon the 'social market economy' introduced after the Second World War by Ludwig Erhardt, Germany's immensely influential economics minister and subsequent chancellor, also gives German attitudes to economic policy special characteristics.[21] This is a free-market ideology, which emphasizes constitutional rules, as against discretionary policy.[22] It rejected the then highly influential Keynesian idea of discretionary macroeconomic stabilization from its inception, in favour of a central bank dedicated to price stability. While Germans have accepted a welfare state since the nineteenth century, under Erhardt's influence they have also embraced the idea of market competition. One of the main roles of the state, in their view, is to promote competition.

The solution to the Eurozone crisis from the German perspective, then, is to impose these principles throughout the Eurozone. That explains the emphasis on rule-making. It also explains the emphasis on austerity and structural reform. In the German view, this is a long game. Germany believes in tough love. This is also partly because it has been consistently fearful of 'moral hazard' in international lending. The idea of 'moral hazard' is that providing generous and, above all, unconditional insurance against mishap encourages unduly risky behaviour. These concerns about incentives provided by insurance are legitimate: it is why insurance contracts include deductibles payable by the insured. In the end, Germany has shown itself willing to provide conditional and limited support, but only if vulnerable member states are prepared to toe their line: those then are the conditions that accompany the insurance.

Inevitably, Germany, like most creditor nations in history, insists that the difficulties of borrowers are entirely their fault. Its own current-account surpluses have nothing to do with the difficulties of deficit countries: the latter are irresponsible, that is all. This is why it has emphasized fiscal deficits as the main problem, not current-account imbalances, and so has also insisted that this is a fiscal crisis rather than a balance-of-payments-cum-financial crisis in which its own financial institutions and regulators were complicit. Why it should be deemed responsible to lend to people who show gross irresponsibility in their willingness to borrow is a puzzle to which our discussion will return.

Meanwhile, the Franco-German engine of European integration no longer really functions. It is a German engine, with a queasy French passenger. This is partly because France's economic position is weaker than Germany's: it has lost competitiveness since the founding of the Eurozone. Its leaders, since the crisis, have either tagged along behind Germany (as was the case with Nicolas Sarkozy, president until May 2012) or flirted with the idea of opposition to German retrenchment (as was the case with his successor, François Hollande). Neither alternative proved successful. As one senior Eurocrat put it, the partnership merely serves 'to hide the strength of Germany and the weakness of France'.[23]

If Germany felt it faced a head-on clash between its European goals and domestic monetary stability, it would probably choose the latter. Of the members of the Eurozone, it would probably face the smallest adjustment costs if it left the Eurozone. But it would still pay a high economic and political price. In any case, it has not come to that. German policy also assumes it will not come to that: in the end, the Eurozone's members will fall into line and so become worthy of full membership of a more federal Eurozone run on German lines. That, in the predominant German view, is the price they have to pay in return for German willingness to surrender their treasured Deutschmark, the symbol of their country's post-Second World War stability and success.

Thus, once Germany's government lost confidence in leaders of troubled debtor countries, those leaders had to go. But it did not always require a push from outside. Disgusted electorates dismissed the incumbents who had presided over the crisis in Ireland, Portugal and Spain. Ultimately, however, the countries in difficulty had simple choices: accept disorderly default and possibly even departure from the euro; or adopt a combination of fiscal austerity and structural reform. In the end, these countries all chose the latter options.

As the crisis engulfed Spain and Italy in 2011, investors became ever more worried about the destructive nexus between banks and sovereigns: the latter relied on the former for funding, while the former relied on the latter for rescue from crisis. Stressed banks and weak sovereigns behaved like two drunks trying to hold each other up. As doubts about the creditworthiness of sovereigns and fears for the Eurozone economy grew (see Figure 7), so, too, did funding pressures on banks.

In response to these pressures, the ECB announced its three-year long-term refinancing operation (LTRO) in December 2011.[24] This offered €1tn of central-bank credit in secured funding to stressed banks, in two successive tranches.[25] Unfortunately, the LTRO was a Faustian pact. It alleviated funding pressures on banks. But some of the new ECB lending to the banks was recycled by the latter into their government's bonds. That was the collateral the banks often used. In this way, the banks of countries whose sovereigns were under pressure became conduits for medium-term financing of less creditworthy governments by the central bank. This tied banks and sovereigns even more closely together. Moreover, as Figure 7 shows, the impact on the funding costs of governments of even the three-year LTRO did not last.

That led to a far more profound innovation: Outright Monetary Transactions. In a now celebrated speech delivered in London on 26 July 2012, Mario Draghi, president of the European Central Bank, stated baldly that 'Within our mandate, the ECB is ready to do whatever it takes to preserve the euro. And believe me, it will be enough.' He then went on to state that 'Then there's another dimension to this that has to do with the premia that are being charged on sovereign states borrowings. These premia have to do, as I said, with default, with liquidity, but they also have to do more and more with convertibility, with the risk of convertibility.'[26] By 'convertibility' Mr Draghi meant the risk of a break-up. He had found the reason (or, one might argue, the excuse) he needed for offering to buy the sovereign bonds of vulnerable states. The ECB then agreed to the new programme, with the sole, though important, dissent of Jens Weidman, president of the Bundesbank, but, more significantly, the tacit acceptance of the German government.[27]

Mr Draghi's statement that the ECB would do 'whatever it takes' was a bluff, but an astonishingly successful one. It was not a bluff because the ECB could run out of money. A central bank can always create more money. But, for political reasons, the OMT programme offered 'unlimited' but 'conditional' ECB intervention in sovereign bond markets, with the conditions to be set by formal programmes with the governments concerned.[28] The need for conditions arose from the fact that the ECB was the central bank of many countries, not of one. It could not get away with providing unconditional support to a member. Yet the contradiction between the two criteria is evident: conditional support is by definition not unlimited. If a country were to violate the conditions of its agreed programme, ECB support would cease. But this would also be when the market's panic was greatest. Thus, ECB support would be withdrawn when most needed. It is impossible, in any case, to believe the ECB could get away with unlimited intervention even if the conditions were met: the institution would probably fall into a kind of civil war before that happened.

Further increasing the difficulty of actually implementing the OMT, if that were required, was the outcome of the case before the German Constitutional Court in February 2014. In essence, that court judged the OMT to be in violation of the German constitution. True, the German court asked the European Court of Justice to rule on the legality of the OMT in European law. But this increases the doubts about the programme. Furthermore, the German court could well not consider itself bound by any ECJ ruling. Given this situation, the willingness or even ability of any German government to support an EU programme, which would be a necessary condition for implementation of the OMT, is in grave doubt and so, therefore, is the workability of the OMT.[29]

Fortunately, at the time this book went to press these contradictions had not been tested. Not just the announcement but also its tacit acceptance by all member state governments had an extraordinary impact on markets, because it was seen as largely eliminating the tail risk of break-up. As the International Monetary Fund noted in its July 2013 report on the Eurozone: 'The ECB's commitment to do "whatever it takes" – including by establishing the OMT's framework – improved the functioning of monetary policy and safeguarded the viability of the euro.'[30] In particular, as Figures 6 and 7 show, a marked and general decline ensued in spreads on the bonds of riskier sovereigns. The ECB won its victory without firing a shot. Whether the policy would work if its credibility were tested remained uncertain. But, more than a year and a half after it had been launched, it remained untested.

The success of the announcement of the OMT programme appeared to vindicate the arguments of those who had long believed that the soaring spreads reflected panic-induced illiquidity in markets or, more technically, the danger of 'multiple equilibria' in markets. Paul de Grauwe, a distinguished Belgian economist, now at the London School of Economics, had long argued in favour of central-bank intervention, to eliminate the risk of self-fulfilling panics that placed the cost of debt in a bad equilibrium. The success of the OMT supported these arguments.[31] An alternative explanation also exists, however, one with much the same implication for the markets. It is that investors were unable to price these government bonds rationally, because they were faced with a catastrophic and essentially incalculable risk, that of break-up of the Eurozone. They could then take the ECB president's commitment and the launch of the ECB's new programme, with German acquiescence, as indications that the Eurozone's leadership would not allow it to fail. In this way, the OMT made a crucial contribution to (possibly misplaced) confidence in the Eurozone's future and, by lowering the spreads, made that confidence more plausible. It turned a vicious downward spiral of falling confidence into a virtuous upward spiral of rising confidence.

Yet, while the spreads did indeed fall sharply, they remained significant (see Figures 6 and 7). For countries caught in a deflationary trap, these spreads might yet prove unmanageable. Moreover, the debt overhangs, high interest rates, banking-sector weakness and broken mechanisms for transmission of monetary policy, which are characteristic of all financial crises, inevitably led to deep recessions and high unemployment in the crisis-hit Eurozone countries. Furthermore, given their difficulty in borrowing and their lack of access to central-bank financing, the crisis-hit countries could not offset these deep recessions, indeed true depressions, with fiscal or monetary stimulus, at least without external support. That was not to be forthcoming on any significant scale. This was partly because Germany, supported by other creditor countries and the European Commission, argued that necessary structural reforms would not occur without remorseless economic pressure and, for that reason, regarded greater external support as counter-productive. The fiscal and economic hair shirt would, the German government argued, force the guilty to behave better in future. Beyond that, the creditor countries were also unwilling to ask for more money from their own parliaments in support of other governments that their electorates had come to view as contemptible profligates.

Yet the bad economic conditions risked causing a political backlash and so a further bout of financial stress. The Eurozone crisis had become a condition of chronic economic weakness, vulnerable, at any moment, to relapse. Nevertheless, the determination of the governments of crisis-hit countries to persist with austerity was remarkable. There were protests on the streets. There were electoral upheavals, with the overthrow of all the governments that had been in charge during the onset of severe crises. There were protest movements and parties, such as Giuseppe 'Beppe' Grillo's 'Five Star Movement' in Italy and the neo-fascist 'Golden Dawn' and far-left 'Syriza' in Greece. But the Eurozone's orthodox centre held. Whether it would continue to hold was unclear.

UNDERSTANDING THE CRISIS

What caused this rolling crisis in the Eurozone? The proximate cause was very similar to the proximate cause of the global crisis of 2007 and 2008: 'sudden stops' in funding, this time not just of financial institutions, but of countries, though the connection between financial institutions and countries was, as noted, a close one.

The Crisis

Silvia Merler and Jean Pisani-Ferry have traced out the story in a paper for the Bruegel think tank based in Brussels. The authors note laconically that 'the single currency was expected to make balance of payments irrelevant between the euro-area member states. This benign view has been challenged by recent developments.'[32] Indeed, the single most important lesson of the crisis is that the balance of payments continues to matter just as much within a currency union as outside one. Given that currency adjustment has been eliminated, arguably the balance of payments matters even more within a currency union than it does for independent countries with floating currencies and their own central banks. Once a country inside a currency union becomes dependent on large net capital inflows, a sudden turnaround in these flows will cause an economic crisis. Such a crisis will be marked by a financial shock, as external funding is withdrawn, and a deep recession, as the imports on which the economy had come to rely can no longer be financed. The impact of a crisis is also highly asymmetrical: for surplus countries, it is an inconvenience, as the value of their financial claims on deficit countries comes into question; but for deficit countries, it is a matter of economic life or death, as the short-term impact of a sudden withdrawal of external funding devastates the economy.

Thus, before the crisis, huge private-capital flows went into a number of countries in southern Europe and Ireland, mostly from elsewhere in Europe and also mostly in the form of debt, particularly bank debt. These flows came from countries with excess savings and weak demand for credit at home and then flowed to the countries with buoyant demand for credit, which appeared to offer superior returns and at least reasonable safety. Strikingly, as Figures 6 and 7 show, the pre-crisis spreads on sovereign bonds fell to very close to zero: thus, Germany and Greece were, astonishingly, considered equally riskless. This may have been just a mistake by lenders. But it may also have been because the Eurozone was thought to provide a safety net under these flows. As it turned out, this perception was not altogether wrong. In the crisis, lenders to banks got out unscathed and (at least up to early 2014) only the Greek government restructured its debts, though the market value of the debt of other risky sovereigns did for a while fall sharply.

These cross-border flows duly financed large current-account deficits and so, by definition, large excesses of spending over incomes in the deficit countries. Figures 8 and 9 show the scale of the current-account deficits and surpluses in the Eurozone just before the crisis, both in absolute terms and relative to GDP, with the exclusion of a few of the small member countries. The most striking element in this picture is the scale of the German current-account surplus, the second-largest in the world, in absolute terms, after China's. No less striking is the huge Spanish current-account deficit, not just in absolute terms, but also in relation to GDP. Portugal and Greece also had vast deficits relative to GDP, and Ireland an appreciable one. The role of foreign private capital, much of it from within the Eurozone, in funding spending in these deficit countries was, accordingly, enormous. (Why this happened is discussed further in Chapter Five below.) It is also easy to see from Figure 9 that the crisis-hit countries were the ones that had huge current-account deficits, relative to GDP, prior to the crisis.

Proponents of the euro might argue that these flows were exactly what the Eurozone was supposed to achieve: without exchange-rate risk, one would expect huge flows of capital from savings-surplus to savings-deficient countries. But, just as risks in the financial system ended up being concentrated in the hands of those who least understood them, so savings ended up being borrowed by those who proved least able to use them. The Eurozone was poorly equipped to cope

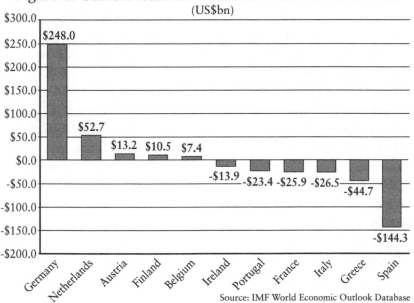

Figure 8. Current Account Balances in the Eurozone 2007
(US$bn)

Source: IMF World Economic Outlook Database

Figure 9. Current Account Balances in the Eurozone 2007
(per cent of GDP)

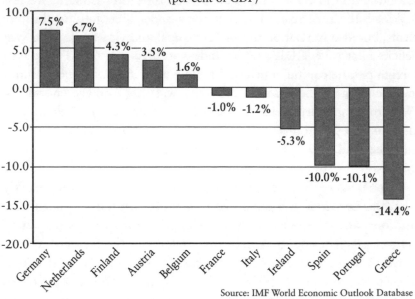

Source: IMF World Economic Outlook Database

with the reversal in financing of deficit countries that occurred in a series of 'sudden stops' (a point to be discussed further below), once providers – endowments, insurance companies, hedge funds, pension funds, private individuals and even government agencies – realized, in the course of the worldwide re-rating of risk after 2007, how big a mistake they had made.

These huge current-account surpluses and deficits can be viewed in three mutually consistent ways.

First, they reflected private-sector capital flows towards what were mistakenly believed to be higher-return opportunities in more dynamic economies, such as construction in Spain. Alas, these higher returns turned out, in many cases, to be illusory, indeed the product of an asset-price bubble. Moreover, by 2011, the net external liability position of several countries had become too large to manage: 103 per cent of GDP for Portugal, 98 per cent of GDP for Ireland, 92 per cent of GDP for Spain and 79 per cent of GDP for Greece.[33] These economies were primed for capital flight, which duly occurred in the succession of crises discussed above.

The second way in which the current-account deficits and surpluses can be viewed is as an excess of income over spending – or a surplus of savings over investment – in surplus countries and the opposite in deficit countries. That is simply what a current-account surplus or deficit means – an excess of income over spending or an excess of spending over income, respectively. The important implication is that the two sides are always, at the level of the world economy as a whole, of equal and opposite sign. The surpluses entail deficits and vice versa. Because they are jointly determined, it is logically impossible to say that countries in deficit are responsible for their plight while those in surplus are guiltless. That is childish moralism.

The third way is that the surpluses and deficits reflected strengthening external competitiveness in surplus countries and declining competitiveness in deficit countries. Real unit labour costs in the former group of countries, especially in Germany, stagnated and real unit labour costs in the latter soared from the beginning of the euro. This was partly because of their strong economies (notably in Spain), which pushed up nominal wages, and partly because their labour markets were relatively inflexible and productivity growth was correspondingly weak (as in Greece, Italy, Portugal and Spain). The most important reason for the relatively inflexible labour markets of southern Europe was legislation, which made it extremely difficult to lay off long-term workers. Particularly large losses in competitiveness occurred in Spain, Italy and Greece (see Figure 10). Ireland, on the other hand, suffered no loss in competitiveness, because of fast productivity growth in its output of tradeable goods and services. Ireland has a flexible labour market and relies for exports on foreign companies, mostly American, with access to state-of-the-art technology. Moreover, these losses of competitiveness were inevitably associated with long-lasting changes in the structure of economies: in surplus countries, industries that produce tradeable goods and services, particularly export-oriented manufacturing, expanded, as in Germany. In countries with external deficits, the opposite happened: businesses oriented to the domestic economy, such as construction and retail, expanded, as in Spain.

The reversal of the excesses requires changes in all three dimensions, changes that are painful and will occur over very different time

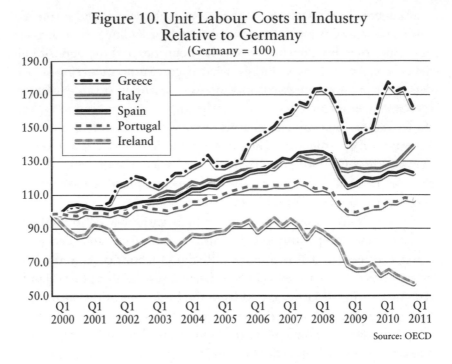

Figure 10. Unit Labour Costs in Industry
Relative to Germany
(Germany = 100)

Source: OECD

periods. Adjustment of the private-capital flows can occur – and did indeed occur – almost overnight when the crises hit. But adjustments in the balance between saving and investment and changes in external competitiveness may take a decade or longer. This makes it impossible for a country to repay huge debts in the short run (or, quite possibly, even in the long run), since that requires it to shift at once into current-account surplus. That requires the structural shifts in the economy explained above, towards increased production of tradeable goods and services. When creditors try to get their money out quickly, one or more of three things must happen, instead of repayment: repricing of assets; default; or refinancing by official sources. In fact, a mixture all of these things happened in the crisis-hit countries.

Post-Crisis Adjustment

Consider the post-crisis reversal of these unsustainable imbalances. The fact that inflation is low throughout the Eurozone and surplus countries also intend to keep it that way has made the external adjustment more painful. Moreover, if some countries are to reduce their deficits, others must reduce their surpluses if the external balance of the Eurozone is not to move towards surplus. If it does move towards surplus, as has been the case, the rest of the world has to adjust via some combination of higher spending and lower output. If it is the latter, the Eurozone crisis is exported.

A clash must also arise, within this low-inflation Eurozone, between improving competitiveness and managing the debt overhang. This is because a rapid restoration in competitiveness of countries like Italy or Spain requires falling wages and prices. But falling wages and prices also raise the real burden of debt. The relatively high interest rates on both private and public debt that characterize these economies make the problem of managing debt even harder. This is 'debt deflation' – a condition in which debtors are forced to save an ever higher share of their incomes in order to pay down debt, because the latter's real value is rising over time. The more countries struggle to restore competitiveness and the weaker their growth, the worse the debt trap into which they will fall. As the IMF's 2013 report on the Eurozone underlines, 'Persistent financial market fragmentation, weak bank balance sheets, low demand, and creeping uncertainty, as well as structural weaknesses, all reinforce each other and contribute to the contraction of real activity.'[34] Not least, a financial crisis starves businesses, on which growth depends, of the credit they need to finance investment. Not surprisingly, a huge shrinkage of the vulnerable economies indeed occurred, making debt management ever harder: between pre-crisis peaks and post-crisis troughs, Greek GDP fell by 23 per cent, Irish GDP by 10 per cent, Italian GDP by 9 per cent and Portuguese and Spanish GDP by 8 per cent. The Irish, Portuguese and Spanish economies appear to have bottomed early in 2013, though none enjoyed a really strong recovery by the third quarter of that year (Spain being the laggard). Italy's GDP was still falling in the third quarter, as was Greek GDP in the first quarter (the last quarter for which data were available, as of January 2014). This is a Red Queen's race: vulnerable countries are forced to run hard to stand still on their debts.

They also have to run hard to improve their competitiveness, because the surplus countries do not stand still. Businesses in such countries are likely to cut their prices, in response to the crisis-driven slowdown in demand for their products. Remember that they built up substantial capacity during the pre-crisis boom in exports. It is in their interests to use this capacity, by cutting their prices and so promoting demand, provided the prices they are able to charge cover the variable costs of production – the labour and purchased inputs needed to create additional output, as well as any extra costs of maintenance of plant and machinery. The long-run fixed costs do not need to be covered in the medium run, since these are just sunk costs. At worst, established exporters may suffer lower than expected profits or need to restructure their debt. More fundamentally, the surplus countries may not develop the higher inflation needed to raise their costs and so facilitate the adjustment in competitiveness needed by deficit ones. Their financial and monetary authorities may, for example, use so-called 'macroprudential policies' (policies directed at financial stability in the economy as a whole) to halt credit expansion at home. If the surplus countries did indeed successfully halt adjustment in this way, the outcome in the Eurozone would be a more prolonged depression in erstwhile deficit countries.

The shadow of managing longer-term adjustments hangs over the Eurozone, a topic to which I will turn in Chapters Five and Nine. But the first of these adjustments – the disruption of private-capital flows across the frontiers of the Eurozone – is no shadow: it is already here. It occurred swiftly, in a series of 'stops'. There were three such episodes: during the global financial crisis of 2008, when the stops particularly affected Greece and Ireland; in spring 2010, which saw contagion from the Greek programme to Ireland and Portugal; and, finally, during the second half of 2011, when the stops reached Spain and Italy.[35]

Imagine that the Eurozone had been not a currency union, but a fixed exchange-rate arrangement, possibly a hardened version of the pre-euro Exchange Rate Mechanism. A halt in the capital inflow would then eliminate the current-account deficit both brutally and quickly: indeed, that is precisely what happened to Bulgaria, Lithuania and Latvia during the crisis. As part of that adjustment, the domestic financial sector, asset prices and spending would collapse and the economy would fall into a depression. The fiscal position would also deteriorate. In the absence of lending from outside, the government would have to cut spending and raise taxes, further weakening the economy.

If the financial and monetary authorities managed to sustain the pegged exchange rate, despite the depression, adjustment would then occur via falling nominal wages and prices (what the Eurozone calls 'internal devaluation'), emigration and a write-down of the bad debt of insolvent banks, non-financial companies, households and possibly even the government. In time, with competitiveness restored and debt restructured, the economy would recover. This used to happen in the nineteenth century. It has happened, more recently, in small open economies, such as Hong Kong after the Asian financial crisis and the Baltic states after the crises that began in in 2007. This is, in effect, the old gold-standard mechanism.

If, however, the authorities let the peg go, the adjustment would be accompanied by a depreciation of the nominal exchange rate. That would obviate debt deflation and the need to cut nominal wages and prices. It is likely, though not certain, that the result would be a swifter and less painful adjustment, without a tidal wave of defaults. All this would have been a big economic mess, but it would not have generated a continent-wide maelstrom. Under such an adjustable-peg exchange-rate system, economic adjustment would have occurred and life would have gone on. It did after crises in the ERM. It did so after devaluations of sterling in 1949 and 1967 and again after sterling's departure from the ERM in 1992.

Consider the opposite possibility – that the currency union was a modern federal state, like the US. In that case, the banking system operates across the union. The federal government finances a large part of government spending directly. Workers move easily across the federation. In this situation, the collapse of even a large property boom in a particular region, in Florida, for example, cannot bring down the banking system there, since the federal government helps ensure its survival. There is also no currency risk in lending to Florida, since the possibility of secession from the dollar area does not arise. The US fought a brutal civil war in the nineteenth century to make it clear that secession was impermissible. There is no capital flight from Florida, for the same reason. Viable companies located there continue to have access to credit. The state government might retrench sharply.

But federal spending is sustained. The combination of ongoing credit, support for the banking system, lower federal taxation and higher federal spending inside Florida sustains economic activity and finances the current-account deficits that nobody bothers to measure. In time, people emigrate, wages fall and new activities emerge. The crisis is painful, but of no enduring moment.

The European currency union lies between these two extremes: indeed, it represents the worst of both worlds. Members are not on their own, as are sovereign countries with fixed exchange rates, while the credibility of the currency arrangement is also greater than that of a unilateral commitment. But members also do not benefit from most of the automatic risk-pooling features of a modern federal state, while their currency union is less credible than one embedded in such a federation.

The currency union does, however, have one functioning federal institution – the central bank. The ECB responded to the sudden stops in capital flows effectively and automatically: as cross-border lenders withdrew funds and asset prices fell, banks in vulnerable countries experienced deteriorating balance sheets and drains on funding. To prevent a chain of collapses, their national central banks acted as lenders of last resort, with the consent of the ECB. These national central banks created new central-bank money (this being the liability side of the central-bank balance sheet) and lent it to their troubled banks, against a wide range of (often doubtful, albeit also discounted) collateral, such as their own government's bonds. Such funds, in turn, allowed the commercial banks to continue to lend to their customers. Indirectly, these activities financed current-account imbalances inside the Eurozone and then emerged as 'Target 2' imbalances within the European System of Central Banks (ESCB), the aggregate of the ECB and national central banks.

By definition, deficit countries also had ongoing excesses of spending over income (that is to say, large current-account deficits). After the crisis, they also suffered substantial capital flight by both non-residents and residents. A settlement imbalance then emerged between Greek, Portuguese, Irish, Spanish and Italian banks on the one hand, and the banks of Germany, the Netherlands and remaining surplus countries on the other.

68

Transfers of balances at central banks are how such imbalances among banks are settled. These settlements show up inside the 'Target 2' settlement system – the interbank payment system owned and operated by the 'Eurosystem', the monetary authority of the Euro-zone, which consists of the ECB and member central banks.[36] This generates large cumulative net claims in the central banks of surplus countries and correspondingly large liabilities in the central banks of deficit countries.[37] In August 2012 the surplus of the German Bundes-bank was €751bn and that of the Dutch central bank €125bn, making a total of €876bn. In the same month the aggregate liability position of the Greek, Irish, Italian, Portuguese and Spanish central banks was €891bn (€429bn for Spain and €289bn for Italy). But by November 2013, as the OMT restored confidence, the surpluses of the Bundes-bank and the Dutch central bank had fallen to €545bn and €59bn, respectively, while those of the five crisis-hit countries had also fallen to €595bn (€254bn for Spain and €216bn for Italy).[38]

Thus, euros created by the national central banks of deficit coun-tries settled the payments shortfalls of their countries. That, in turn, allowed these countries to shrink their large current-account deficits over several years, not at once, despite the collapse of private financ-ing (see Figure 11). In this way, the European System of Central Banks (the ECB plus national central banks; ESCB) provided an essential cushion. By funding the banking system, it also financed payments imbalances. This was an inefficient, because indirect, way of financ-ing external and fiscal deficits in the medium run. But it worked, more or less.

Yet, as Peter Garber of Deutsche Bank warned presciently as far back as 1998, there must be doubts whether the national central bank of a surplus country would be willing to provide unlimited credit to the weak national central banks through the Target system in this way, not least because it would probably suffer large losses in the event of a break-up. The fear of such losses might even precipitate such a break-up, by halting the supply of credit to the weak central bank. In theory, members of the Eurozone would bear these losses in proportion to their shares in the ECB. In practice, it seems unlikely that the deficit countries would pay, particularly if they were con-vinced the break-up was not their fault. Mr Garber concluded that 'As

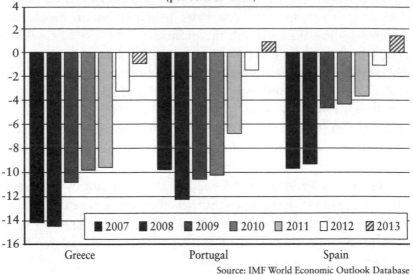

Figure 11. Current Account Balances
(per cent of GDP)

Source: IMF World Economic Outlook Database

long as some doubt remains about the permanence of Stage III exchange rates [i.e. the currency union], the existence of the currently proposed structure of the ECB and Target does not create additional security against the possibility of an attack. Quite the contrary, it creates a perfect mechanism to make an explosive attack on the system.'[39] Such an attack could take the form of a run on banks in a vulnerable country or actions (short-selling of bank stock, for example) that would cause such a run. Thus the creation of gigantic creditor and debtor positions inside the ECB might destroy the credibility of the system.

The actions of the central banks helped countries in difficulty. But they have not provided much, if any, direct support for public debt. Direct financing of deficits was ruled out by the founding treaties of the currency union, because of the concern, particularly in Germany, that this would prove a short route to hyperinflation, as had happened in 1923. As a result, the prices of government bonds fell sharply in deficit countries and rose in surplus ones between 2008 and 2012 (see Figures 6 and 7). With foreigners increasingly concerned about liquidity, solvency, and even the risks of break-up, the funding of vulnerable governments came to depend on their domestic banks, which were themselves heavily dependent on national central banks. Thus the ESCB ended up indirectly funding governments.

That has, in turn, further impaired the availability of credit to the private sector of deficit countries: smaller private businesses in crisis-hit countries found it almost impossible to obtain bank loans. As the IMF noted in July 2012: 'Despite low policy rates, credit conditions vary widely among euro area countries. This was mainly due to starkly diverging perceptions of sovereign and banking risks, as well as drastic decline in interbank activity (as banks reduce cross-border funding, shore up capital and liquidity buffers in their jurisdiction and accumulate overnight deposits at the ECB). As a consequence, financing conditions are now the least supportive in countries where the crisis is most acute.'[40] The IMF made much the same point in 2013, though conditions improved somewhat after the announcement of the OMT.[41]

The explanation for such divergences in monetary conditions is that the currency union – unlike federal unions – is not a banking union. Each country is responsible for its own banks: in countries loath to let banks fail under any circumstances, banks are as strong as the creditworthiness of the governments that back them and whose debt they hold. The emergence of huge divergences in sovereign creditworthiness has inevitably fragmented banking. Thus, as cross-border flows dried up, member countries found themselves in very different fiscal positions and so the risk of break-up rose. In addition, the Eurozone no longer had a single set of monetary conditions, as one would normally expect in a currency union, but distinct national monetary conditions: the IMF has noted that small-business loans became much more expensive in Italy, Spain and Portugal than in Germany.[42]

Meanwhile, the Eurozone provided fiscal support to governments no longer able to borrow in markets, first via temporary facilities – the European Financial Stability Facility and European Financial Stabilization Mechanism – and then via a permanent new arrangement – the European Stability Mechanism, which went into operation in October 2012. The EFSF was created following a decision on 9 May 2010, at the same time as the Greek programme.[43] It had a lending capacity of €440bn, raised in the markets but guaranteed by governments. The

EFSM added a further €60bn borrowed by the European Commission and onlent to members.[44] The ESM is a replacement for the EFSF and the EFSM. It has a lending capacity of €500bn.[45]

That sum is insufficient to take the larger countries, particularly Italy, 'out of the markets' if they lost access. For this reason, some proposed that the ESM be given a banking licence and so be able to borrow, like any other bank, from the ECB. That idea was rejected as far too dangerous: at a leverage ratio of 20 to 1 (normal in banking), it could have lent €10tn, making it much the biggest bank in the world. Instead, as discussed above, the ECB agreed its Outright Monetary Transactions programme – a promise that, as explained above, is to provide 'unlimited', but 'conditional', support to governments that find it difficult to borrow from markets on manageable terms. The purported aim of this programme is to restore a degree of normality to monetary conditions in crisis-hit countries, so making ECB monetary policy effective once again. The ECB is the only institution with the firepower needed to halt a panic in the sovereign debt markets of a country as big as Italy. If that were indeed to happen, the ECB would have to try to make the OMT operational. But the question remains whether it could do so in practice. The ECB has the firepower. But it is not clear that it would be allowed to fire its broadside or that the OMT itself would prove an effective way of doing so, given its internal contradictions.

In addition, the Eurozone already agreed when preparing the Greek programme, probably wisely, to include the IMF and therefore IMF resources and conditionality in its rescue plans. The IMF's engagement also encouraged it to seek additional resources of its own, which it did successfully.[46] The main contribution of the IMF, however, was not financial, but technical and so also political. It is more credibly independent than the European Commission. The ECB has been determined to have the IMF engaged, because it lacks confidence in the Commission, which it views, rightly, as more of a political body captured by national governments than a technocratic organization able to impose its views upon them. The German government has a similar view of the Commission. Yet the IMF's engagement has also been controversial and, in some eyes, particularly those in emerging economies, has tainted its credibility. The Fund's own *ex post* evaluation of the Greek programme of 2010 was, rightly, critical of what never looked to be a credible plan.[47] But the fact that the IMF has been brought in again underlies the fact that the Eurozone is more of a currency arrangement among nation states than a federal union.

In sum, the Eurozone has one strong internal institution, the central bank, but its banking industry has remained largely national, and cross-border fiscal support has remained limited and controversial in the creditor countries. The labour markets of many member countries are highly inflexible. They are also segmented along national lines by language, culture, laws, social institutions and the structure of welfare states (pension arrangements, for example). This structure was unable to handle the financial crisis smoothly. Instead, the members sought to redesign their aircraft while it was crashing.

It proved extremely difficult to convince private decision-makers – investors, bankers, corporate bosses, even ordinary people – that the single currency was irrevocable, largely because the commitment of the member countries to support one another is inevitably circumscribed by domestic political resistance. Indeed, discussion of the possibility of the departure of member states was open and even came from the highest levels. On 11 September 2011, for example, Mark Rutte and Jan Kees de Jager, prime minister and finance minister of the Netherlands, wrote an article in the *Financial Times* in which they declared that 'in future the ultimate sanction can be to force countries to leave the euro'.[48] That was a hedged statement. But if a country were forced or at least encouraged to leave, the consequences for the credibility of the euro could prove devastating. Exit would not affect the exiting country alone. It would have large spillover effects on other countries and, indeed, on the entire system. One would certainly expect some capital flight from other vulnerable countries and, quite probably, devastating financial and economic crises within them. Indeed, it was the realization of this threat that persuaded even Germany's government, in the course of the summer of 2012, that it should keep Greece inside the Eurozone if at all possible.[49]

It is understandable that creditor countries do not want to be chained to those they deem wastrels. But, as they also have realized, as soon as the possibility of break-up becomes real, mayhem threatens. The Eurozone could then no longer be viewed as an irrevocable

THE SHIFTS AND THE SHOCKS

currency union. Once it is no longer seen as irrevocable, some of the principal benefits of the union must vanish: the willingness to make long-term investments will shrink, in both surplus and deficit countries, because of uncertainty about the future; willingness to lend money to financial institutions in vulnerable deficit countries will disappear and, at worst, capital flight will ensue; financial markets will become segmented; and the willingness to lend money to governments of vulnerable countries will evaporate and interest rates of such governments will become elevated.

If all these things were to happen, the chances of full adjustment inside the Eurozone would diminish and the plausibility of break-up would rise. The more credible the possibility of exit, the stronger countervailing commitments need to be. Yet the ultimate assurance – that the system would always stick together, however big the pressure – is just not credible. The willingness to commit much, but not everything, to the project is a permanent invitation to crisis. That is the danger the Eurozone confronts. Whether it can overcome it will be considered in Chapter Nine below.

MISUNDERSTANDING THE CRISIS

The story told above is one of a crisis triggered by huge current-account imbalances followed by a sudden stop in the cross-border private financing that allowed those imbalances to emerge. The central bank responded to the stops, but not by enough to bring order to either monetary conditions or the financing of governments across the Eurozone, and, on its own, it cannot bring about the needed internal adjustments. The currency union has been subject to such huge stresses largely because it is an incomplete and imperfect union. It is unclear whether it can survive. But the greater the loss of credibility the bigger the stresses and so the greater the chances of failure. This is a vicious spiral.

One reason why failure is still possible is that the view advanced above of the proximate causes of the crisis is not universally shared. This view implies that both lenders and borrowers made huge mistakes, that large current-account imbalances are destabilizing, particularly in an imperfect union with limited insurance mechanisms, and that post-crisis adjustment needs to fall on both surplus and deficit countries. There is, however, an alternative view, expressed by Wolfgang Schäuble, the German finance minister, in the quotation that heads this chapter: it is that the crisis is the result of sloppy fiscal policy, that the fault lies with the countries that indulged in such policies, and that the solution is fiscal austerity in the short run and far tighter fiscal rules in the long run. This view is powerful, because the country that believes it holds the purse strings. It is also influential, because the crisis in Greece in 2010 frightened policymakers, even many outside the Eurozone, into believing – or at least saying that they believed – 'there but for the grace of God, go we'. The result was not just a Eurozone shift towards fiscal austerity, but one elsewhere, as well.

This view is not only misleading, but dangerous. That it is held by the Eurozone's strongest country is frightening. As Figure 12 shows, the countries that are now in great difficulty had very divergent fiscal performances before the crisis: Greece did have extremely high average fiscal deficits and Portugal's were at least relatively high, though not that far above the Maastricht Treaty's limit of 3 per cent of GDP. But Italy's average fiscal deficit was only very modestly higher than those of France and Germany, while Ireland and Spain showed a remarkably good fiscal performance. Thus, unlike the current-account position (shown in Figures 8 and 9 above), average fiscal deficits between 2000 and 2007 do not predict whether or not a country fell into a crisis.

Exactly the same is true of the ratio of net public debt to GDP. Greece had the highest ratio, at 105 per cent of GDP in 2007. Italy came second, at 87 per cent. These two countries give support to the view that it was mainly a fiscal problem. But Portugal's net public debt ratio of 64 per cent of GDP was close to the French ratio of 60 per cent. Ireland and Spain had exceptionally low ratios of public debt to GDP, of 11 per cent and 22 per cent of GDP, respectively, far below Germany's 50 per cent. Indeed, if one looked at the fiscal data alone, one would not have concluded that Germany was going to prove the safe haven. Neither its public debt nor its historic deficit performance was in any way exceptionally good. The difference was

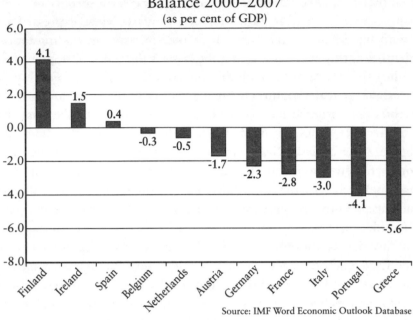

Figure 12. Average General Government Fiscal
Balance 2000–2007
(as per cent of GDP)

Source: IMF Word Economic Outlook Database

that Germany was a surplus country. It was the current account, stupid!

A subtle analyst might respond that, yes, it is true that the Irish and Spanish fiscal position looked very robust at the time. But that was an illusion. The structural deficit was in fact quite large, because the countries were in unsustainable booms. If that had been understood, they should have run much bigger fiscal surpluses than the ones they actually did run. This sounds convincing. Indeed, in an obvious sense, it is true. But it is also highly misleading, on at least two levels.

First, nobody knows what the 'structural' or cyclically adjusted balance is. Worse, it is least knowable precisely when such knowledge is most essential, namely, when the economy is experiencing a boom. The evidence for this is overwhelming. The IMF itself provides the proof. In April 2008 and April 2012 it made wildly divergent estimates of the average structural fiscal balance of Ireland and Spain between 2000 and 2007. It made this huge change because subsequent events – the crises – forced it to reconsider its earlier assessment of the structural position of economies. Note that neither of these was a forecast. They were estimates of what had happened in the past. Unfortunately, in April 2008, almost no economists understood how harsh would be the light that events would shed on what had happened in the recent past.

In the 2008 estimates the IMF declared that Ireland had run a healthy average structural surplus of 1.3 per cent a year between 2000 and 2007. This, it should be stressed, was an estimate intended to take account of the fact that Ireland had enjoyed a huge boom. Spain was believed to have enjoyed an average structural surplus of 0.5 per cent a year over this period. Both countries, in other words, were believed to have had a solid fiscal position that emanated from a long period of disciplined fiscal policy. Then, four years later, the IMF decided that for that very same eight-year period Ireland's average annual structural fiscal balance for 2000–07 was four percentage points worse than it had thought in April 2008: that over that period Ireland had been running an average structural fiscal deficit of 2.7 per cent of GDP. For Spain, the picture was much the same, just not as extreme: the difference between the April 2008 and April 2012 estimate of the 2000–07 average structural fiscal deficit is 1.7 per cent of GDP annually: the earlier surplus has turned into an average structural deficit of 1.2 per cent of GDP. Again, that is a big difference.

Given these huge retrospective revisions, next to no possibility exists of making a reliable estimate of the structural fiscal balance, in real time, particularly during a credit boom. This is one important reason why the Eurozone's new fiscal treaty, which went into effect in January 2013 and is built around achieving a balance in the estimated structural fiscal deficit, is most unlikely to work: Ireland and Spain were both thought to have had structural fiscal surpluses prior to the crisis. So the new rules would not have prevented these disasters.[50]

Second, the fiscal surpluses these countries would have had to run to protect themselves against the calamity that befell them would have been almost unimaginably large and the pre-crisis debt target correspondingly low. Assume, for example, that the aim was to run a pre-crisis fiscal policy so tight that, in the light of what we *now* know, it would have kept gross public debt below the Maastricht Treaty limit of 60 per cent of GDP, at least up to 2013. In Ireland, the gross debt ratio is forecast to rise by 98 per cent of GDP between 2007 and 2013. In Spain, this rise is forecast to be 57 per cent of GDP (see Figure 13). These huge increases in public debt were due to unexpectedly deep recessions and, particularly in the case of Ireland, the fiscal costs of the calamitous decision to bail out all the creditors of its banks. To have avoided going over the Maastricht Treaty ceiling of 60 per cent of GDP in 2013 (with everything else remaining the same), Ireland's gross debt ratio in 2007 would have needed to be minus 38 per cent of GDP, instead of the actual level of 25 per cent. In the case of Spain, the gross debt ratio needed in 2007 to keep the ratio below 60 per cent of GDP in 2013 would have been 3 per cent of GDP, instead of the actual level of 36 per cent. That outcome could have been achieved if the Irish government had accumulated assets after it had expunged its debt. To have gained this position, Ireland's annual fiscal surplus between 2000 and 2007 would have needed to average nearly 8 per cent of GDP more than it did. Spain's fiscal surplus would have needed to average 4 per cent a year more than it did. Of course, these are almost certainly overestimates, since with tighter fiscal policy pre-crisis booms and post-crisis busts would have been smaller. But the direction is clear.

A tighter fiscal policy than the one actually pursued would certainly have been helpful. But the fiscal action needed to protect an economy against a boom and bust of the scale experienced by Ireland and Spain would have been difficult to achieve and hard to justify to electorates prior to the crisis. Instead of putting the blame mainly on fiscal policy, it would make more sense to put the blame on the stupidity of creditors. The great nineteenth-century British journalist, Walter Bagehot, describes what happens perfectly: 'at particular times a great deal of stupid people have a great deal of stupid money ... At intervals ... the money of these people – the blind capital, as we call it, of the country – is particularly large and craving; it seeks for someone to devour it, and there is a "plethora"; it finds someone, and there is "speculation"; it is devoured, and there is "panic".'[51]

As I have noted above, the main feature the deficit countries had in common was the ability to fund large and, in some cases, enormous current-account deficits at very low interest rates. It turned out that it did not make that much difference if the domestic counterpart

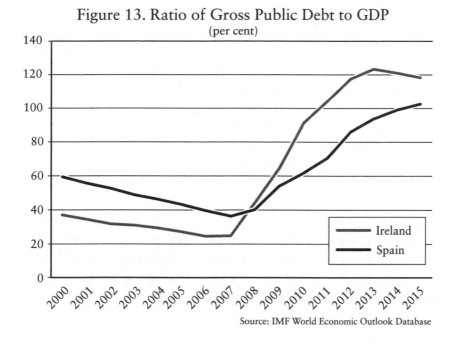

Figure 13. Ratio of Gross Public Debt to GDP
(per cent)

Source: IMF World Economic Outlook Database

of these deficits was entirely a huge private-sector financial deficit (as in Ireland and Spain) or a mixture of private and public deficits (as in Greece and Portugal). Italy did not have large external or fiscal deficits: its problems were mainly due to the scale of the public debt accumulated in the 1980s and 1990s, before it joined the euro. This, in turn, had been the result of prolonged fiscal indiscipline.

It did not make much difference whether, in pre-crisis times, the counterpart of the surplus of the foreign sector – that is, of the flood of capital into the country and the huge consequent current-account deficit – was a private or a fiscal deficit, that is, an excess of spending over incomes in the private or public sectors. The reason is simple, crucial and widely ignored: once the crisis hit, the private-sector financial deficit disappeared swiftly, whereas the fiscal deficit soared. The explanation for the latter is that government revenue fell dramatically, crisis-related government spending automatically rose, and the banks were also rescued, which was particularly costly in Ireland. Moreover, when private spending collapses, as happened in Ireland and Spain, the fiscal deficit always rises more quickly than the external deficit falls provided there continues to be some foreign funding, as there was in the Eurozone, largely via the ECB. That is because the external deficit is dictated in part by the productive structure of the economy, which does not change all that swiftly.

Spain and Ireland, whose private sectors were particularly badly hit by the financial crisis, experienced shifts in the financial balance of the private sector of close to 15 per cent of GDP. The rise in the fiscal deficit is the direct consequence of this crisis-driven leap of the private sector into austerity. Private austerity entails fiscal profligacy: these are two sides of a single coin, given the relatively slow adjustment of the external balance.

Germany's focus on the alleged fiscal crimes of countries now in crisis was an effort at self-exculpation: as the Eurozone's largest supplier of surplus capital, its private sector bore substantial responsibility for the excesses that led to the crisis. As Bagehot indicates, excess borrowing by fools would have been impossible without excess lending by fools: creditors and debtors are joined at the hip. A country that chooses to run current-account surpluses, indeed, one that has built its economy around generating improved competitiveness and increased external surpluses, has to finance the counterpart deficits and must, accordingly, bear responsibility for the wastage of funds. After all, the evidence of what was going on inside deficit countries was not hidden. What this might mean for future German policy will be considered further in Chapter Nine.

Some might respond that if the fiscal situation is not the root cause of the crisis in sovereign debt, why have the interest rates on the debt of some Eurozone sovereigns been so high (see Figures 6 and 7 above)? There are two answers to this question.

The first answer is that the fiscal position did become a big problem *after* the crisis, as Figure 14 shows. Fiscal indiscipline may not be the reason for crises, but crises certainly cause what will look like very serious fiscal indiscipline. That is one reason why it is important to avoid such crises.

The second and more directly apposite answer is that rates of interest on sovereign debt seem to be surprisingly high. Indeed, these very high rates have almost certainly been a consequence of defects in the

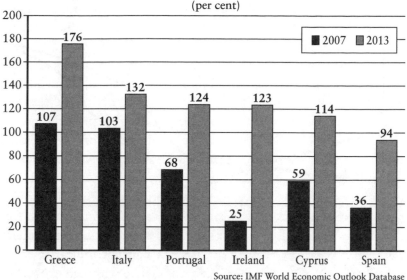

Figure 14. Ratio of Gross Public Debt to GDP
(per cent)

Source: IMF World Economic Outlook Database

Eurozone's structure and operation. Professor de Grauwe noted this in an important and influential paper published in 2011.[52] He showed that Spain and the UK had a similar profile for public debt, but the UK's long-term interest rates diverged far from Spain's, starting in the spring of 2010, reaching a maximum divergence of more than six percentage points in the summer of 2012, before falling after announcement of the OMT (see Figures 15 and 16).

How does one explain this apparent anomaly? There are three possible explanations. The first, advanced by Professor de Grauwe, is as follows:[53]

> Suppose that investors begin to fear a default by, say, Spain. They sell Spanish government bonds and this raises the interest rate. If this goes far enough, the Spanish government will experience a liquidity crisis ... The Spanish government cannot force the Bank of Spain to buy government debt and although the ECB could provide all the liquidity in the world, the Spanish government does not control that institution.[54] This can be self-fulfilling since, if investors think that the Spanish

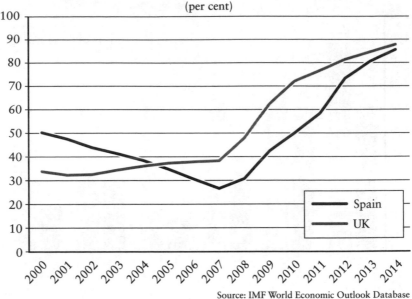

Figure 15. Ratio of Gross Public Debt to GDP
(per cent)

Source: IMF World Economic Outlook Database

government might reach this end point, they'll sell Spanish bonds in a way that turns their fears into a reality.

It doesn't work like this for countries capable of issuing debt in their own currency. To see this, re-run the Spanish example for the UK. If investors began to fear that the UK government might default on its debt, they would sell their UK government bonds and this would drive up the interest rate.

After selling these bonds, these investors would have pounds that most probably they would want to get rid of by selling them in the foreign-exchange market. The price of the pound would drop until somebody else would be willing to buy these pounds. The effect of this mechanism is that the pounds would remain bottled up in the UK money market, to be invested in UK assets.

Put differently, the UK money stock would remain unchanged. Part of that stock of money would probably be re-invested in UK government securities. But even if that were not the case so that the UK government cannot find the funds to roll over its debt at reasonable interest rates, it would certainly force the Bank of England to buy up

Figure 16. Spread Between UK and Spanish 10-year Bond Yields
(percentage points)

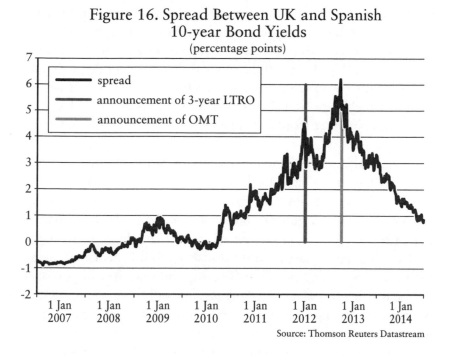

Source: Thomson Reuters Datastream

the government securities. Thus the UK government is ensured that the liquidity is around to fund its debt. This means that investors cannot precipitate a liquidity crisis in the UK that could force the UK government into default. There is a superior force of last resort, the Bank of England.

This is a compelling explanation of why interest rates on Spanish bonds were so much higher than on UK bonds: it is the result of not having a central bank of one's own. This can lead to multiple equilibria. Once a country's debt markets are stuck in a bad equilibrium, only a powerful force, such as determined intervention by the central bank, can move it to a good one. I find this argument persuasive.

Yet there are two other likely explanations. One is that there is a risk of break-up in the Eurozone. Thus, in the case of Spain, the possibility existed of a catastrophic redenomination of debt into a new currency. While there is also a risk of a meltdown of the pound, perhaps as a result of the hyperinflation that many (quite wrongly) find imminent, this is, in truth, a remote possibility. The second explanation is that if the Eurozone were not to break up, Spain would be stuck in a low-growth trap caused by a permanently overvalued real exchange rate. For this reason, investors had more confidence that the UK authorities would ultimately get its fiscal position under control than they had in the ability of the Spanish authorities to achieve the same thing. In other words, Spain is damned if it leaves and damned if it stays.

Interestingly, the turnaround for yields on Spanish debt came when the ECB announced its OMT programme. The same was true of other troubled countries (see Figures 6, 7 and 16). This strongly supports de Grauwe's argument. But it also supports the view that the risk of break-up mentioned explicitly by Mr Draghi in justifying the OMT programme matters. But Spanish yields still remained higher than UK ones throughout 2013. This suggests that the loss of monetary autonomy continues to matter, notwithstanding the OMT programme. Having a more proactive Eurozone central bank is not as good as having one's own central bank.

What is the conclusion? The existence of the single currency enormously increases the chances of devastating fiscal crises. That is an inevitable consequence of 'one-interest-rate-fits-all'. Before the crisis, the monetary policy that made sense for the Eurozone as a whole turned out to be too tight for some countries, notably including Germany, and too loose for others, notably including Greece, Ireland and Spain. The result was a massive divergence in credit growth, wages, prices and external balances that ended up in a crisis.

Participants have to be aware of these dangers and reduce the risks. This will only happen if people realize the underlying problem was not fiscal profligacy, but irresponsible lending (partly induced by the unavoidable defects of a single monetary policy), followed by 'sudden stops'. Slashing fiscal deficits in countries under pressure is a recipe for a depression. It is impossible to get fiscal deficits under control when the private sector is unable to borrow, without huge turnarounds in the external balance. Such turnarounds have indeed happened. But the path to this outcome has gone via depressions: forced austerity, failure to reduce fiscal deficits as planned, unwinding of the Eurozone's financial integration, persistent doubts over the solvency of banks, huge divergences in the cost of credit, and yet further economic decline.

THE ECONOMIC CONSEQUENCES OF THE CRISIS

The sudden stop in capital flows created huge crises in countries that had previously borrowed massively abroad. One might say that the victims were devastated by the very things that prompted the creation of the single currency: the single monetary policy and the desire to integrate financial markets and eliminate exchange-rate risk. But the flows reversed at the first sign of trouble, as one would expect of capital flows to emerging countries. Then the non-financial private sector, the financial sector and the governments of erstwhile capital recipients all fell into deep trouble.

The ECB eased the adjustment. But it also permitted the Eurozone economy as a whole to stagnate, thereby making the post-crisis adjustment far more difficult. The crisis has demonstrated that a currency union that is not a banking union and lacks some way of managing liquidity problems in public-debt markets ceases, in a crisis, to be a true monetary union. It was every national economy for itself, though with strong spillovers among the weak and from the weak to the strong. While everybody was affected, the institutions needed to manage such spillovers were lacking.

Meanwhile, the overriding pressures were towards fiscal retrenchment. All the vulnerable countries were forced to cut structural fiscal deficits rapidly after 2009. Indeed, vulnerable countries such as Cyprus, Greece, Ireland, Italy, Portugal and Spain had little choice, since they could no longer fund themselves. But the combination of private and public retrenchment generated deep recessions (see Figure 17). These made it more difficult for those countries to achieve the reductions in fiscal deficits demanded by the assistance programmes for Cyprus, Greece, Ireland and Portugal, and by the European Commission for Italy and Spain.[55]

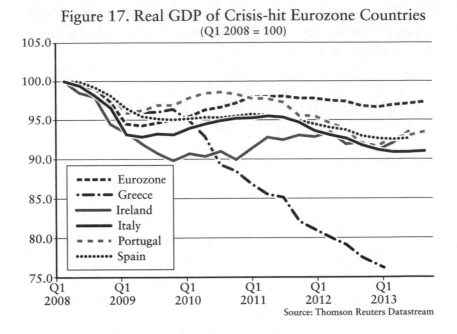

Figure 17. Real GDP of Crisis-hit Eurozone Countries
(Q1 2008 = 100)

Source: Thomson Reuters Datastream

The most important social consequence of the weak economies has been massively elevated unemployment (see Figure 18). In Spain and Greece, unemployment rates were recorded at 27 per cent in May and April 2013, respectively. The fundamental question is how long such depression conditions will last before society rebels. Will societies stick together long enough to implement the policies expected of them? In the end, after all, political accountability is national, not European. The distance between the locus of democratic politics and that of effective decision-making is wide: this is what the political philosopher Larry Siedentop, formerly of Oxford University, calls the 'democratic deficit'.[56]

The likelihood that politicians who reject the policies demanded by the outside world, and particularly by Germany, will be elected at some point is great. It nearly happened in Greece in 2012. With a need for multi-year economic adjustment ahead, the stresses are likely to grow. Above all, it has to be dangerous for its future that the project of European integration is now identified not with prosperity and stability, but with mass unemployment and economic crises.

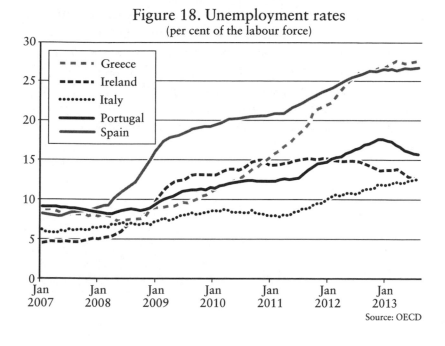

Figure 18. Unemployment rates
(per cent of the labour force)

Source: OECD

CONCLUSION

The crisis of the Eurozone changed what would, in any case, have been an enormous shock into a far more serious global crisis. The Eurozone, it turned out, was disastrously ill-equipped to cope with the sudden stops in private-capital flows that its creation had encouraged. Given that break-up seems unthinkable, the question is whether there exist plausible reforms that would make it work better. The discussion will turn to that question in Chapter Nine below.

Meanwhile, one of the most important global consequences of the crisis has been that the difficulties of Greece and the rest of the vulnerable countries were taken to be representative of the threats confronting high-income countries outside the Eurozone. This, in turn, justified the premature swing towards austerity across the high-income countries in 2010 that has surely slowed the recovery. But, as de Grauwe has argued, countries like the US and the UK were never threatened by a collapse in support for their government bonds.

Being sovereign monetary areas, their position was entirely different. Meanwhile, inside the Eurozone, Germany and other creditor countries benefited, via exceptionally low interest rates on their long-term bonds, from the difficulties of their partners. They showed no gratitude. That windfall gain did not increase their willingness to help their partners in difficulty. The opposition to any policy likely to stimulate demand in the Eurozone remains resolute. The result is a slow and painful recovery.

3

Brave New World

We're in the midst of an international currency war, a general weakening of currency. This threatens us because it takes away our competitiveness.

Guido Mantega, Brazilian finance minister, 2010[1]

Something remarkable happened during the successive waves of financial crises discussed in Chapters One and Two. Or, remarkably, something did not happen. The emerging and developing economies did not fall into serious crisis.[2] On the contrary, they survived largely unscathed. Indeed, it has turned out that the recovery of the high-income countries is possibly more dangerous to the emerging countries than the crises they suffered.

The post-crisis success of emerging economies demonstrated that they had become significantly more resilient in the years prior to the crisis. Yet it certainly does not mean they have 'decoupled' from what happens in high-income countries. The latter remain too important, as markets, as sources of finance, and as employers of temporary and permanent immigrants for that to have happened. The great recession that followed the worst of the financial crisis, in late 2008 and early 2009, hit many emerging and developing countries hard. Those who were least hit – China, above all – had to make bold policy decisions to offset the impact of the shock upon their economies. Those decisions also created troubling longer-term challenges.

The result, none the less, was an acceleration of the already rapid shift in the balance of the world economy from the high-income countries to the emerging countries, particularly China. This, in turn, partly reflected the increased resilience of emerging and developing countries. As important, however, was the fact that China had emerged as a new centre of the world economy. Yet China's economy is sure to slow from its trend growth rate of 10 per cent a year between 1980 and 2012.[3] If it slows modestly, the impact on economies dependent upon its demand, notably for commodities, should not be significant: after all, 7 per cent growth in 2013 would mean the same absolute increase as 10 per cent as recently as 2009.[4] If, as some fear, China's growth were to slow far more sharply, the impact on the world economy would be more serious.[5]

CRISIS AND RECOVERY IN EMERGING ECONOMIES

In the five years up to and including 2008, the average annual growth of emerging economies was an amazing 7.6 per cent. Asian developing and emerging economies led the way, with average growth of 9.5 per cent, pulled along by China and, to a lesser extent, India. The Commonwealth of Independent States (CIS) – the bulk of the former Soviet Union – also grew quickly, at an average rate of 7.6 per cent, pulled along by Russia's oil boom, itself largely driven by rising world commodity prices (see Figure 27). Behind them came sub-Saharan Africa, also pulled along by the commodity boom, with growth averaging 6.5 per cent. The Middle East and North Africa benefited from the oil boom, too, averaging growth of 6.3 per cent. Central and Eastern Europe also enjoyed a boom, averaging growth of 5.6 per cent in the five years up to and including 2008, though this boom blew up in 2008. Latin America and the Caribbean grew at an average rate of 5.3 per cent. Meanwhile, the advanced economies grew at an average rate of 2.4 per cent. The world economy as a whole grew at an average rate of 4.6 per cent.[6]

In 2009 the world economy shrank for the first time since the Second World War. But this decline was by no means universal. The gross domestic products of only four regions declined: the high-income economies, Central and Eastern Europe, and the Commonwealth of Independent States (CIS). Growth slowed sharply in sub-Saharan

Africa, the Middle East and North Africa, though it remained positive. Most important, the slowdown in emerging and developing Asia (the last including the emerging and developing countries of East, South East and South Asia, which contain slightly over half of the world's population) and in the two Asian giants, China and (to a lesser extent) India, was barely noticeable (see Figure 19).

Then came the remarkable recovery of emerging economies in 2010. Thereafter, most emerging regions grew reasonably well, the exceptions being Central and Eastern Europe and the CIS (see Figure 20).

The divergence in economic growth rates over the course of the crisis also meant rapid shifts in the relative size of economies. Between 2007 and 2012, economies of the high-income countries expanded by a grand total of 3 per cent. Over the same period, the economies of emerging and developing countries grew by 31 per cent and those of

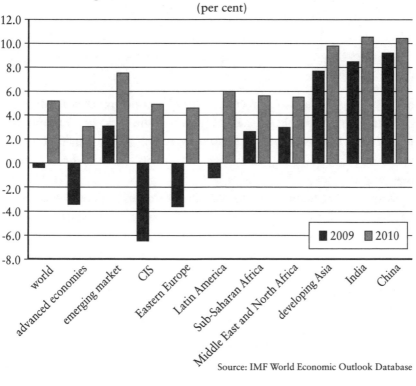

Figure 19. Growth in the Great Recession
(per cent)

Source: IMF World Economic Outlook Database

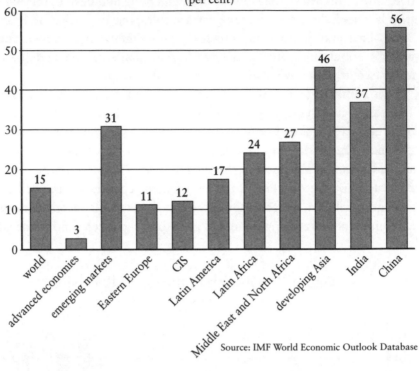

Figure 20. Increase in GDP 2007–2012
(per cent)

Source: IMF World Economic Outlook Database

developing Asia by 46 per cent. China's economy expanded by an even more remarkable 56 per cent and India's by 37 per cent (see Figure 20). The second-fastest growing region of the world economy was sub-Saharan Africa, at 27 per cent.[7] This then has been a brave new world.

Despite a big financial crisis, which hit the high-income economies hard and rendered them virtually stagnant over a period of five years, the emerging economies not only survived, after a swift recession (or, in some cases, just a slowdown) in 2009, but even thrived. This suggests something important had changed: not only were most emerging and developing economies quite resilient to the financial shock, but they returned to rapid growth relatively swiftly. This is quite different from the experience in the 1990s when the epicentre of big financial crises was often in emerging countries.

What explains these successes and are they likely to endure? These are the questions to be addressed in the rest of this chapter. What the answers tell us about the future of the global economy is a question to be addressed in the third part of the book and its Conclusion.

THE RESILIENCE OF EMERGING ECONOMIES[8]

During 2003–07, growth in emerging markets and developing economies accelerated, even though growth in advanced economies was weak. Then, as underlined by the International Monetary Fund, during 2009, the year that immediately followed the worst of the global financial crisis, 'more than half of emerging market and developing economies experienced negative growth . . . But they quickly bounced back, and during 2010–11 many of them grew at or above pre-crisis rates. As a result, they now account for virtually all of global economic growth.'[9]

This performance came after what had already been a substantial improvement. Between 1970 and 1989, the median annual growth of emerging economies was only 1.5 per cent; between 1990 and 2007, it reached 3.4 per cent.[10] Between 1970 and 1989, the median growth rate of low-income countries had been a calamitous minus 0.1 per cent; in the subsequent period, it reached 1.5 per cent – low, but still a huge improvement.[11] The variability of growth also fell substantially between the two periods.[12]

An optimistic view is that the ability of many emerging and developing countries to cope with the biggest financial crisis since the 1930s reflects improvements in policies and changes in economies, particularly diversification of the composition and direction of trade, of the sources of inflows of capital and of their entire economies. A pessimistic view is that recent growth has been supported by capital inflows, strong credit growth, booming commodity markets and, in the crucial case of China, an unsustainable growth of poor-quality investment. All this, pessimists note, is becoming far more challenging.

Optimists have evidence on their side.[13] Something has indeed changed for the better. Emerging and developing economies have been spending more time in expansion, while their downturns have become shallower and shorter. Their monetary policies have improved. Stronger fiscal positions have also facilitated the use of counter-cyclical fiscal policies. Where countries have fixed their exchange rates, they have built up substantial foreign-currency reserves as an insurance against shocks. Not surprisingly, the statistical analysis of the IMF shows that countries with superior policies and better underlying positions – in terms of monetary policies, public debt, fiscal deficits and foreign-currency reserves – also enjoyed longer expansions and stronger recoveries. The reduction in the frequency of shocks explains about two-fifths of the improved performance of emerging and developing economies. But 'Greater policy space [that is, the ability to use monetary and fiscal policy relatively freely because of strong initial conditions] and better policy frameworks account for the remaining three-fifths of the improvement in their performance.'[14]

In many respects, emerging and developing countries appear almost to have changed places with the high-income countries in the 2000s. The latter have suffered huge financial crises, big recessions, and correspondingly large rises in fiscal deficits and debt. This is the sort of picture we used to see in emerging and developing countries: one crisis came on the heels of another, notably the Latin American debt crisis of the 1980s, the 'Tequila crisis' in Mexico and then other Latin American countries in the mid-1990s, the Asian financial crisis of 1997–98, and the crises in Russia (1998), Brazil (1998–99) and Argentina (2000–01). But emerging countries suffered far fewer banking crises in the 2000s than in the 1980s and 1990s, largely because few had experienced big credit booms in the earlier 2000s. That left them in a good position to expand domestic credit in response to the crises of 2008 and 2009. Thereupon, after the immediate collapse in external demand was over, they mostly tightened credit again.

Better policies have, it appears, brought substantial rewards. Yet it is also vital to put these improvements in context. Not all emerging and developing countries have done well. Moreover, in many cases, the improvement may prove (or has already proved) unsustainable: India's performance deteriorated sharply after 2010, and Brazil started to stagnate. What makes it more likely that the improvement will prove unsustainable, in many cases, is that the greater resilience of the emerging and developing countries is, at least in part, a mirror image of the loss of resilience of the high-income countries. This might be called the 'law of the conservation of crises'. If one group of economies escapes the credit booms that are one of the chief precursors of crises, it is because another group has embraced them. Over the last four decades, the world economy does not seem to have functioned without huge financial excesses somewhere.

MIRROR IMAGES IN ECONOMIC PERFORMANCE

Why might one envisage such a negative relationship? After all, the prosperity of others normally enhances one's own by providing improved opportunities for trade. If that were always true, no reason for concern would exist: the faster growth of the emerging and developing countries, far from being detrimental to high-income countries in any way, would be a benefit. Certainly, it is normally true that countries benefit from the prosperity of others, as Lawrence Edwards and Robert Lawrence argue in an excellent study of the beneficial economic impact of the rising wealth of emerging economies upon the US.[15]

This is true, with one crucial proviso: cross-border finance must be reasonably stable and efficient. Alas, this has not been – and is not – the case.[16] If so, as the high-income countries become stronger, once again, many emerging and developing countries will become weaker.

How might this happen? The question can be addressed by looking at the emerging and developing countries that performed poorly during the crisis. As is clear from Figure 19, the two regions that did worst economically during the crisis were the Commonwealth of Independent States and Central and Eastern Europe. The former is a special case, since its aggregate performance is dominated by that of Russia, a very large commodity exporter. The fate of the latter, however, is interesting. For the salient characteristic of the countries of Central and Eastern Europe was their pre-crisis reliance on capital inflows, as shown by their enormous current-account deficits, far larger, on average, than those of other regions of emerging and developing countries (see Figures 21 and 22).

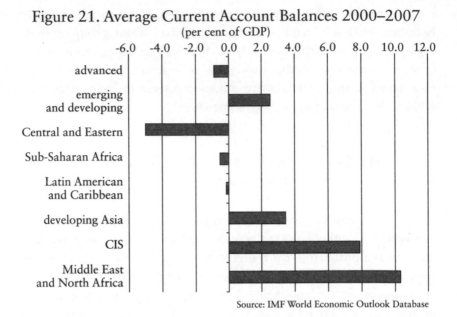

Figure 21. Average Current Account Balances 2000–2007
(per cent of GDP)

Source: IMF World Economic Outlook Database

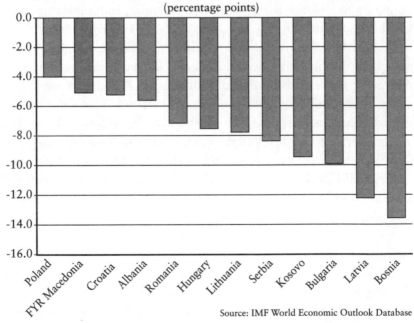

Figure 22. Average Current Account Balance 2000–2007
(percentage points)

Source: IMF World Economic Outlook Database

Like the countries of southern Europe discussed in Chapter 2, the countries of Central and Eastern Europe became vast importers of capital, at least relative to the size of their own economies, as Figure 23 shows. That did not end well.

During the crisis, the finance they depended upon dried up. This was another 'sudden stop', very much the same as those that afflicted Ireland and southern Europe at that time. For investors, flight to safety is almost always also a rush back home, except if the economy to which the capital previously flowed is the home of a reserve, or near-reserve, currency, and possesses triple-A or close to triple-A status as a sovereign borrower (such as the US). The countries of Central and Eastern Europe did not possess those attributes. So the money took flight, whereupon these countries were forced to retrench suddenly and brutally. The result was deep recessions, with few exceptions. (Poland did well during the recession year of 2009. But its current-account deficit was also relatively small in the period before the crisis.)

Figure 23. GDP Growth in Central and
Eastern Europe in 2009
(per cent)

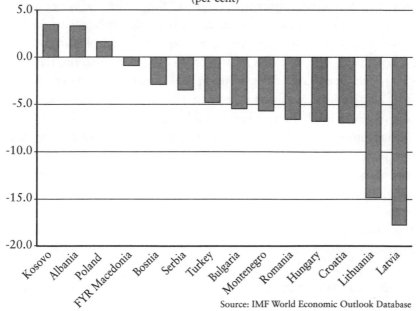

Source: IMF World Economic Outlook Database

We can confidently assert that most Central and Eastern European countries did not show strong resilience in 2009. (See also Figure 20, for post-crisis economic growth.) On the contrary, the recessions in this region were very deep. The explanation is that large current-account deficits are generally associated with asset-price bubbles, unsustainable domestic spending, strong surges in domestic credit, rising wages, construction booms, unsustainable increases in public spending and declining external competitiveness. If the boom is strong enough, the fiscal accounts may temporarily appear robust. But once the private-sector credit boom ends and spending collapses, the fiscal accounts will worsen, as happened to the crisis-hit Eurozone members (see Chapter Two). Large net capital importers lack resilience, therefore, because they are vulnerable to sudden stops in capital inflows.

This also helps explain why emerging and developing countries had become more resilient in the years before the crisis of 2007–08. As Figure 21 shows, emerging economies became capital exporters overall between 2000 and 2007, as did the most important emerging regions. The IMF's database shows that a sizeable number of small and very poor developing countries did run large current-account deficits between 2002 and 2007. This was to be expected, because these countries are recipients of large aid flows. But the larger emerging countries mostly ran surpluses or quite modest deficits: on average, current-account balances were close to zero or in surplus in the cases of Argentina, Brazil, China, India, Indonesia, Iran, Nigeria, Pakistan, Philippines and Russia. The economies of Central and Eastern Europe were somewhat exceptional among the more advanced emerging economies, though Turkey also ran a large external deficit.

So the improved resilience of emerging countries is, in part, explained by the development of their balance of payments. This development was not an accident: it is largely explained by the response of emerging and developing countries to the waves of financial crises they suffered in the 1980s and 1990s. This involved a deliberate policy of reducing vulnerability to external instability. This partly involved making domestic financial institutions better capitalized and better regulated, in response to earlier financial crises. Some important countries – notably, China and India – also retained exchange controls. But the most crucial and widespread policy was the decision to accumulate foreign-currency reserves on an enormous scale and so keep exchange rates down (see Figure 24). Surjit Bhalla, an Indian economist, argues in a recent thought-provoking book that this was excellent development policy: deliberate undervaluation of exchange rates promotes prosperity. By accident or design, many emerging and developing countries followed this policy in the 2000s, above all in East Asia and notably including China.[17]

In this way, many emerging economies turned themselves into net capital exporters. More precisely, they both recycled the inflow of foreign direct investment and ran substantial current-account surpluses. The most important of these economies were China and the oil exporters (including Russia). But if emerging economies became net exporters of capital, in aggregate, other economies had to become net importers of capital. The most important of these net importers were the US and countries on the western (Ireland and the UK), southern (Greece, Italy, Portugal and Spain) and eastern (more precisely, central and eastern) peripheries of Western Europe. All the large net importers of capital turned into epicentres of the crisis, though countries reliant

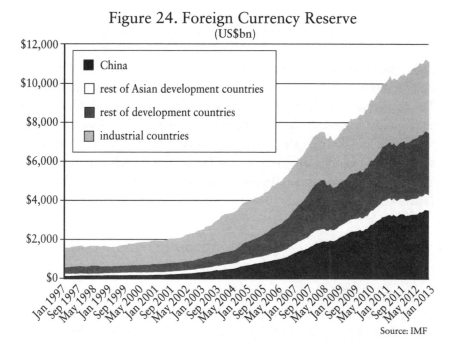

Figure 24. Foreign Currency Reserve
(US$bn)

Source: IMF

on them for markets (such as Germany and other European surplus countries) were also hit by their recessions indirectly. Once the crisis had occurred, the attraction of erstwhile capital importers to investors diminished or even disappeared altogether. The central banks of the troubled economies also slashed interest rates. The outcome was upward pressure on the exchange rates of emerging and developing countries.

To the Brazilian finance minister, Guido Mantega, this quite understandably looked in 2010 like a currency 'war'. In reality, it was a natural process of rebalancing after the crisis. Yet he was also correct on a crucial point. Emerging and developing countries did face a dilemma: should they accept higher exchange rates, reduced external competitiveness and large current-account deficits? Or should they resist that shift, intervening in currency markets, thereby risking a loss of monetary control, excessive credit growth, inflation and financial disorder? Against this background, the big question was whether the resilience lauded by the IMF was going to prove as evanescent as the 'great moderation', celebrated by Mr Bernanke (and others) before the crisis.

THE CHALLENGES AHEAD

Emerging economies did extremely well in the aftermath of the crisis. But they now confront at least four closely interrelated challenges. The first is the normalization of monetary policies of the high-income economies. The second is an economic slowdown that has structural roots. The third is the slowdown in China, the world's most powerful engine of economic growth. The last is the search for export-led growth by high-income economies, particularly in the Eurozone and Japan.

The Monetary Normalization of High-Income Economies

In May 2013, Ben Bernanke touched publicly on the mere possibility of 'tapering', or reducing the rate at which the Federal Reserve was expanding its purchases of US Treasury bonds, which were then $85bn a month.[18] This, note, was not an announcement of any reduction in the rate at which the Fed would purchase assets: that was not to come until December, when the Fed announced that it would reduce the rate at which it purchased assets by $10bn a month.[19] Also note that this was not an actual tightening. It was rather public speculation about a future reduction in the rate at which the Fed increased its holdings of assets. Nevertheless, the impact was an immediate rise in longer-term yields: between the beginning of May and the end of June, yields on ten-year Treasury bonds rose by just over eighty basis points, to 2.5 per cent. This triggered a 'taper tantrum', as markets reacted worldwide to the possibility of an end to the policy of ultra-easy money. This possibility had a particularly severe impact on emerging economies.

As Figure 25 shows, a sudden turnaround in financial flows to emerging economies followed. This triggered a substantial repricing of assets, notably bonds, equities and currencies. Significant – and, in the longer run, probably helpful – declines in exchange rates occurred between January and September 2013, notably for the Russian

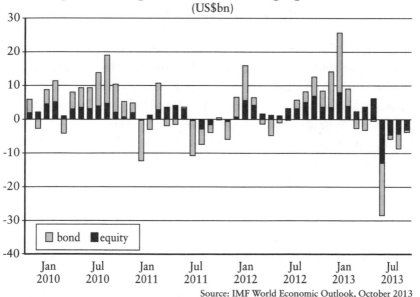

Figure 25. Capital Flows to Emerging Economies
(US$bn)

Source: IMF World Economic Outlook, October 2013

rouble, Indonesian rupiah, Indian rupee, Brazilian real, Turkish lira and South African rand.[20]

The impact caused by a non-event (after all, nothing happened for six months) is partly because it indicated the imminence of a turning point in monetary policy in the US. But also, and more significantly, it revealed vulnerabilities in emerging economies.

One set of factors explaining the vulnerabilities revealed by Bernanke's musing about tapering are financial developments. Domestically, many emerging economies experienced possibly unsustainable credit growth relative to GDP. Important examples were Brazil, China, India and Thailand. Ratios of private credit to GDP were particularly high in China, at around 120 per cent of GDP in 2012, according to the IMF. Any shock likely to slow credit growth, let alone large-scale losses and an actual reduction in credit outstanding, as happened in high-income economies after 2007, risked causing a sharp slowdown in growth in economies whose prior expansion was, to a significant extent, credit-driven.

In addition, argues Hyun Song Shin of Princeton University, among the world's foremost financial economists, the growth of demand for the private-sector bonds of emerging economies has created new external vulnerability.[21] External finance of emerging economies has changed in two ways since the crisis, he argues: non-banks have become bigger borrowers, relative to banks; and debt securities have largely replaced loans. Much borrowing is also done abroad. An indication is the widening gap between borrowing by place of residence and by nationality: Chinese companies, for example, issue foreign-currency bonds in Hong Kong, not the mainland. Brazilian and Indian companies have also floated bonds abroad.

The purchasers of these bonds have been searching for yield in the world of ultra-easy monetary policy by making riskier loans. The sellers, for their part, have taken advantage of the lower cost of bonds denominated in foreign currency. In the process, they have assumed a currency mismatch: foreign-currency debt against domestic-currency assets. These borrowers are speculating on their domestic currencies. Students of the Asian financial crisis of 1997–98 will find this disturbingly familiar.

Once funding conditions turn, such trades may become lethal. As the

Fed proceeds with tightening, the dollar might rise further, prices of dollar bonds are likely to fall and dollar funding might reverse, all of which was seen in the summer of 2013 (see Figure 25). As their bonds lose value, borrowers would be forced to post more domestic currency as collateral. That would squeeze cash flows and trigger a downturn in corporate spending. A fall in the exchange rate would exacerbate the squeeze upon them. Highly indebted non-financial corporations might go bankrupt, endangering domestic creditors, including banks.

Such a pattern of currency and risk mismatches partly explains the volatility in the summer of 2013. That stress is likely to return. Thus, even asset managers of high-income economies may prove to be a source of cyclical instability if they, too, behave pro-cyclically, just as banks have always done. The story underlines a point that emerged in previous crises in emerging economies: national balance sheets matter. Currency mismatches have repeatedly proved devastating to emerging economies, whether they have occurred in the government sector, the banking sector or the non-financial corporate sector.

What, finally, are the policy implications, beyond the fact that the combination of the most expansionary monetary policies in history with the private sector's reach for yield was sure to create fragility? One is that controls on capital inflows count for little if companies are allowed to borrow offshore. Another is that currency adjustments, albeit vital for managing our volatile world, as the IMF argues, will expose currency mismatches. Above all, managing a return to normal monetary conditions in high-income countries, without further global instability, will be tricky.

The Structural Slowdown of Emerging Economies

The impact of the discussion of tapering on emerging economies seems also to be related to something even bigger than financial vulnerabilities: the recognition of deteriorating growth performance. In the *World Economic Outlook* for October 2013, the IMF noted that 'projections for 2016 real GDP levels for Brazil, China and India have been successively reduced by some 8 to 14 per cent over the past two years. Together the downward revisions for these three economies account for about three-quarters of the overall reduction in projections for medium-term output for the emerging market and developing economies as a group.'[22]

According to the IMF's *World Economic Outlook* for October 2013, Brazil's growth fell to 0.9 per cent in 2012 and a forecast of 2.5 per cent for 2013, down from an already modest 2.7 per cent in 2011. China's growth fell to 7.7 per cent in 2012 and a forecast of 7.6 per cent for 2013, down from 9.3 per cent in 2011. India's growth was a mere 3.2 per cent in 2012 and a forecast of 3.8 per cent for 2013, down from 6.3 per cent in 2011 and 10.5 per cent in 2010. Russia's growth was 3.4 per cent in 2012 and a forecast of 1.5 per cent in 2013, down from 4.3 per cent in 2011. South Africa's growth was 2.5 per cent in 2012 and a forecast of 2 per cent for 2013, down from 3.5 per cent in 2011 and 10.5 per cent in 2010. In all, the slow-down has been severe, with China the only economy still growing quickly.[23]

Now turn to the broader picture. In 2011 emerging economies grew by 6.2 per cent. In 2012 and the forecast for 2013, this was down to 4.9 and 4.5 per cent, respectively. In developing Asia, growth rates were 6.4 per cent and forecast at 6.3 per cent, respectively, for 2012 and 2013, down from 7.8 per cent in 2011. In Latin America and the Caribbean, growth rates were 2.9 per cent and forecast at 2.7 per cent, respectively, for 2012 and 2013, down from 4.6 per cent in 2011. In Central and Eastern Europe, growth rates were 1.4 per cent and forecast at 2.3 per cent, respectively, for 2012 and 2013, down from 5.4 per cent in 2011. In the Commonwealth of Independent States, growth rates were 3.4 per cent and forecast at 2.1 per cent, respectively, for 2012 and 2013, down from 4.8 per cent in 2011. In sub-Saharan Africa, the slowing was modest: growth rates were 4.9 per cent and forecast at 5 per cent, respectively, for 2012 and 2013, down from 5.5 per cent in 2011.

In all, according to the IMF, 80 per cent of emerging economies have been slowing since 2011.[24] Analysis by the IMF suggests that the slowdowns are both cyclical and structural: cyclical, because the post-2009 recovery was unsustainably fast in many emerging economies; and structural, because the sources of previous rapid growth have frequently been exhausted. Past tailwinds – the commodity boom, high growth of trade and easy financing conditions – have become headwinds. But there are also deeper structural issues in many countries, which interact unfavourably with the more adverse external conditions: poor quality of labour forces; ageing of the populations, slowing growth of productivity; and rising external imbalances. Sustaining growth means continued reform. In its absence, sources of rapid growth weaken. That is probably a sizeable part of what we are seeing.[25]

Managing China's Inevitable Slowdown

The challenge for emerging economies is not just managing the global rebalancing. It is also that of adapting to what might become a big slowdown in the Chinese economy. One of the reasons many emerging economies did so well after the crisis is that China itself did so well (see Figure 20). It is not only the world's second-largest economy but significantly bigger than Brazil, India and Russia together. It is also the world's biggest source of demand for commodities. Its continued rapid growth helped both itself and the rest of the world through the crisis.

Particularly important was the fact that, after 2007, China's growth was driven by domestic, not external, demand. During the period from 2000 to 2007, in contrast, net exports had been an important source of demand for China: these rose from 2.1 per cent of GDP in 2001 to the extraordinarily high share of 8.8 per cent of GDP in 2007. At that point, China's trade and current-account surpluses were far and away the biggest in the world.

The crisis put an end to net exports as a driver of demand for the Chinese economy, as the Chinese authorities realized at once. So what took its place? The solution they adopted was a massive credit-fuelled investment surge, which brought the share of gross investment in GDP close to 50 per cent. Meanwhile, between 2007 and 2012 the share of private consumption remained around 35 per cent of GDP – an extremely low ratio by the standards of all other economies. Fortunately, the surge in investment fully offset the negative impact upon China's economy of declining net exports, particularly in 2009. Thereafter, the contribution of investment fell, as did economic growth itself (see Figure 26).

This extraordinary role of investment as a source of demand in

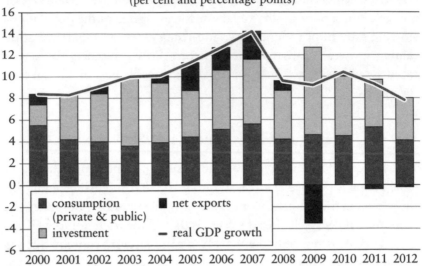

Figure 26. Demand Contributions to Chinese GDP Growth
(per cent and percentage points)

Source: Haver Analytics

China is unsustainable, for two reasons. The first is a long-run one: ultimately, the goal of production is consumption. Investment is merely an intermediate form of production. It makes no sense, in the long run, for investment to grow faster than consumption. If it does, it is likely that investment is excessive, excess capacity is extreme, and economic returns on investment are falling. The second is a shorter-run reason: the level of investment itself depends on the rate of economic growth: the higher the growth rate of an economy, the higher the share of investment in GDP is likely to be. As the Chinese growth rate slows, as everybody (including the government) expects – now that the country no longer enjoys the benefits of huge amounts of surplus labour and has become a middle-income country – the need for investment is likely to fall sharply. But that is also going to take away a crucial prop to demand.

The financial stresses discussed above are likely to accelerate the slowdown in China. The rapid growth of credit in the economy in recent years was driven by expectations of profits from continued ultra-fast growth. If growth disappoints and asset prices fall, much of this credit may prove unserviceable. While the Chinese government is certainly able to manage any conceivable losses, the experience will

Figure 27. Real Commodity Prices
(deflated by unit value of exports of manufactures from advanced countries;
December 1982 = 100)

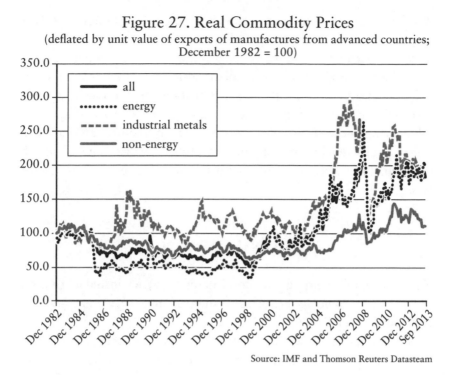

Source: IMF and Thomson Reuters Datasteam

make it far more cautious about credit expansion in future. In short, the chances of a sharper than expected slowdown in the Chinese economy in the short to medium term, followed by a significantly slower trend in growth, are quite significant.

If so, this would affect not just China, but the world economy. A particularly important possibility is weakness in real commodity prices after almost a decade of elevated levels (see Figure 27). If so, that would certainly have a sizeable impact on commodity exporters, many of which are emerging and developing countries.

GLOBAL REBALANCING

The emerging economies confront one final challenge: global rebalancing after the crises. They were able to take advantage of strong demand growth in high-income economies before then. Afterwards, they had room, for a while, to promote their own domestic demand.

But the weakness of demand in the high-income economies is likely to be permanent, not temporary. Indeed, under Germany's tutelage, the Eurozone is forcing itself into export-led growth. The emerging economies have to generate domestic demand-led growth, while financing resulting current-account deficits in a sustainable manner. The world economy, as currently constituted, may be unable to manage such rebalancing successfully. This would probably require, among other things, a substantial reform of global institutions, which is most unlikely to occur. The discussion will return to this point in the Conclusion below.

CONCLUSION

The success of emerging and developing countries in navigating the crisis is remarkable, by historical standards. But these countries now confront big challenges.

One derives from the fact that their post-crisis resilience was a mirror image of what made many high-income countries fragile: strong external payments positions. The fate of many countries in Central and Eastern Europe, which ran huge current-account deficits before the crisis, suggests that robust external positions were indeed an important reason for the resilience of many emerging economies. But between 2007 and 2012, 97 emerging and developing countries, out of a total of 151 for which IMF data were available, experienced a shift in their current-account balances towards smaller surpluses or larger deficits.[26] Many emerging and developing countries are going to find themselves increasingly vulnerable once again.

Another huge challenge is managing the return to something closer to normality in monetary policy and interest rates in the high-income economies. Making this more difficult will be what is happening to China. More than three decades of 10 per cent annual growth has come to an end. Managing such a slowdown smoothly is extremely difficult, particularly in an economy that is so dependent on an ultra-high investment rate for its demand. Financial excesses increase the danger of a sudden collapse in investment, growth and solvency. Yet China is not the only big emerging economy to confront such big challenges: Brazil, India and Russia have also been performing far worse.

I will return in Part III to the challenges of sustaining growth in emerging economies, as high-income countries rebalance. But first, I turn in Part II to the biggest question of all: why did this series of huge crises happen at all? Was it, as many apparently believe, just the result of a failure of the financial system, or was there, as I will argue below, something much deeper at work, namely huge shifts in the world economy?

PART TWO

The Shifts

Prologue

Why did the world's leading economies fall into such a mess?

The answer, in part, is that the people in charge did not believe that they could fall into it. By 'people in charge', I do not just mean the policymakers. One has to include those running financial institutions and those influencing how they ran. But these mistakes did not come out of the blue. They were, no doubt, themselves influenced by the incentives decision-makers faced: incentives to hope for the best and ignore the possibility of the worst – incentives for what I call 'rational carelessness'. That carelessness worked at many levels, from the policymakers via the regulators and on to those running financial institutions, those working in these institutions, those influencing how they were run, particularly outside investors, and, not least, economists. People did not understand the risks, partly because they really did not understand them and partly because they did not want to understand them.

The story is, however, not just about the failings of the financial system, important though these are. There was also the emergence of significant macroeconomic imbalances, revealed in huge net flows of savings across frontiers. Some argue that this was just the product of a credit boom caused by mistaken monetary policy. This is to confuse a symptom with a cause. The underlying cause was the emergence of a global savings glut (or, which comes to the same thing, investment dearth). The response of policymakers in a number of high-income countries was to tolerate – even encourage – an unsustainable credit boom, which then led to the interlinked global and Eurozone crises. The existence of the Eurozone exacerbated the financial and economic crisis, but did not cause it: it merely increased confidence before the crisis and removed certain adjustment mechanisms after it.

When the financial crisis then broke, the global savings glut became far worse, as investment fell and former borrowers were forced to save: this is shown by the simple fact that the high-income world hit the 'zero rate lower bound' in short-term interest rates and real interest rates became close to zero or even negative. Moreover, that happened even though the public sector became a massive dis-saver (by which is meant those who invest more than their annual flow of savings). If it had not, the high-income countries would surely have moved into a depression. The cause of this second and more severe manifestation of the savings glut was the unsustainable balance sheets bequeathed by the way policymakers had responded to the first manifestation, namely, allowing or even encouraging a credit boom. Making this worse were structural excess savings in the corporate sectors of important countries.

All this means that escaping from the crisis back to financial health may be more difficult than many suppose. This crisis was the product not just of easily fixable failings in the financial sector discussed in Chapter Four. It was also the product of failings of the global economic system to which the discussion will turn in Chapter Five. Moreover, both are among the consequences of fundamental shifts in the world economy. The links between these shifts and financial and economic shocks are central to our story.

It is possible to identify three huge shifts. The first is liberalization – the reliance on market forces across much of the world economy, including, notably, in finance. The second is technological change, in particular the information and communications technology revolution, which turbocharged the integration of economies, again, quite particularly, financial markets. The third is ageing, which transformed the balance between savings and investment in a number of high-income economies.

These underlying forces – the great shifts of our time – permitted or created significant further changes. Among the most important have been: the emergence of a globalized world economy; soaring inequality in most economies;[1] the entry of gigantic emerging economies, China, above all, into the world economy; the evolution of a liberalized and innovative global financial system (to be discussed in Chapter

Four); and a huge rise in net capital flows across frontiers (to be discussed in Chapter Five).

In brief, we have a world that is in the midst of historic shifts towards a more market-oriented, financially driven and globalized world economy. This new world is generating large increases in inequality within most countries, and notably so within the US. It is a world that has seen huge shifts in the relative size of economies and in the direction and scale of capital flows. It is a world that has seen downward shocks to the rate of inflation. It is also, it turns out, a world that is hugely crisis prone. How that has worked out is the topic of Chapters Four and Five.

4

How Finance Became Fragile

[A]t this point, the troubles in the subprime sector seem unlikely to seriously spill over to the broader economy or the financial system.

Ben Bernanke, 5 June 2007[1]

When the music stops, in terms of liquidity, things will be complicated. But as long as the music is playing, you've got to get up and dance. We're still dancing.

Charles 'Chuck' Prince, Former Chairman and
Chief Executive of Citigroup, 9 July 2007, Financial Times[2]

You never know who's swimming naked until the tide goes out.

Warren Buffett[3]

Simply stated, the bright new financial system – for all its talented participants, for all its rich rewards – has failed the test of the market place.

Paul Volcker, 2008[4]

What is most fascinating about the now notorious remarks by Chuck Prince, the man who led Citigroup into the disaster, is that he understood what might happen and yet felt he could do nothing to prevent it. Such was the pressure he was under, from both shareholders and the analysts to whom they listened, that he dared not try to prevent one of the world's biggest, most complex and most highly interconnected financial groups from going ever closer to the waterfall he could see ahead. By the time the boat went over the edge, a month later, it was too late. The government ended up having to rescue the boat, while he had to walk the plank, albeit with the consolation of a pay-off reported at $38m.[5]

Yet, in understanding the risks, Mr Prince seems to have been well ahead of Ben Bernanke, the world's most important regulator and central banker. The former appreciated the dangers of doing what he was under pressure to do. Yet, even two months before the crisis broke upon a largely unsuspecting world, the chairman of the Federal Reserve had next to no idea what was about to hit him, his institution and the global economy. To be blunt, he was almost clueless. The same was true of other important central banks, such as the European Central Bank and the Bank of England. True, warnings were given of financial excess. But none of these central banks understood the magnitude of the dangers or, if they did, they did not warn of them with adequate force. The central banks, particularly the Federal Reserve, responded well when disaster hit, as pointed out in Chapters One and Two. But they did not anticipate the nature or scale of the looming problems. This was certainly true of Mr Bernanke. It was arguably even truer of his predecessor, Alan Greenspan, Fed chairman from 1987 to 2006.

So what caused such a huge crisis and why was the danger missed? There are two closely linked answers: shifts within the financial system and shifts in the wider social and economic environment. This chapter discusses the former. The next chapter discusses the latter.

WHY FINANCIAL CRISES ARE ENDEMIC

In what Gary Gorton of Yale University calls the 'Quiet Period', between 1934 and 2007, during which the US experienced financial shocks but no systemic financial crises, policymakers and economists came to believe that such calamities were of purely historic interest or only befell benighted countries.[6] In the first part of this Quiet Period, finance was repressed. That certainly prevented crises. In the second part, from the 1970s onwards, finance was increasingly freed. It was during this latter period that confidence in the financial system's stability and the size of the system grew excessively. This insouciance about what was happening was widespread. In its *Global Financial Stability Report* of April 2006, the IMF stated that 'There is growing recognition that the dispersion of credit risk by banks to a broader and more diverse set of investors, rather than warehousing such risk on their balance sheets, has helped make the banking and overall financial system more resilient.'[7] This spectacularly mistaken view was a symptom of the dangers, not a sound analysis of the lack of them. Strangely, just before the publication of this report, in the summer of 2005, Raghuram Rajan, the IMF's economic counsellor (chief economist), wrote a now celebrated, but then heavily criticized, paper asking 'Has Financial Development Made the World Riskier?'[8] His prescient answer was that it had, because 'technological change, market liberalization, and institutional change', while creating opportunities, also bring additional risks, particularly in the presence of perverse incentives.[9] Professor Rajan was attacked at the Jackson Hole conference organized by the Kansas City Federal Reserve, where he presented this paper. His colleagues at the IMF ignored him. He has now become the governor of the Reserve Bank of India, where he has the opportunity to put his ideas into practical effect.

As Alistair Milne of the Cass Business School at City University London remarks, 'Financial markets are inherently unstable, veering from excessive optimism to excessive pessimism.'[10] So why are markets unstable and why does that instability make crises endemic (and epidemic) features of free-market finance? The answer comes from the links between debt, money and credit.[11]

The advantage of debt, as against equity, is that lenders do not have to monitor what borrowers are doing, which is inherently costly. Most lenders do not have the resources to do so. But, once lenders learn that important classes of borrowers are close to, or in, default, they are likely to become nervous. If enough lenders become nervous at the same time, interest rates will jump and the market value of tradeable loans will collapse. Lenders will then provide funds on ever-shorter maturities. Such maturity mismatches – situations in which liabilities have shorter terms than the assets they fund – make finance inherently unstable.

If lenders want to free themselves still further from the cost of monitoring borrowers, they can instead provide their funds to institutions (banks) that will borrow and relend their money, while promising to redeem it at short notice and at the same nominal value as the original deposits. Such debt is money.

Money is a means of payment. Above all, money guarantees one can pay one's way, *whatever happens*. That is why people hold money, despite the costs of doing so, relative to high-yielding assets or desirable goods and services. Money needs to be safe. Indeed, people keep their money in banks because this is normally safer and more convenient than if it is under a mattress. Moreover, people do not just deposit the money they have in banks. As Mr Milne also reminds us, 'banks create money by lending'.[12] Indeed, nearly all the money in a moderately sophisticated modern economy is a by-product of bank lending – the creation of credit – by these private businesses. Banks, in turn, are profit-seeking, risk-taking financial intermediaries. Inevitably, these institutions are least safe during a crisis, which is precisely when everybody is most concerned about their safety. From time to time, worried people will flee to assets deemed safer and more liquid than bank money, such as gold in a world of commodity money or cash and short-term government liabilities in a world of *fiat* (government-created, from the Latin for 'let it be made') money. As Professor Gorton explains, 'financial crises are en masse demands by holders of bank debt for cash – panics'.[13] Without a lender of last resort, a bank-based financial system will then implode.

Since the banking system provides most of the economy's money and credit, it is too vital to fail *in toto*. Since no society will accept the dissolution of the banking system, ways have been found to keep the system functioning in panics. In the nineteenth century, the Bank of England emerged as a lender of last resort, a process described and justified in Walter Bagehot's classic *Lombard Street*.[14] The US also found ways to deal with panics, despite lacking a central bank for most of the time between its founding and 1913, when the Federal Reserve was created.[15] The most important such mechanisms were concerted stays of payment – a decision to allow banks to halt payment to depositors.

The challenge for policymakers has always been to contain panic and the irresponsibility that breeds it, without stopping banks from taking risks. The state makes banks safer; bankers respond by making banks riskier. As Piergiorgio Alessandri and Andrew Haldane of the Bank of England note, 'The three longest standing state insurance devices for the banking system are liquidity insurance, deposit insurance and capital insurance.'[16]

Of these, liquidity insurance is the oldest: it is the central bank's role as lender of last resort, which consists of ensuring that solvent banks have access to the money they need to meet depositors' demands. Deposit insurance consists of a guarantee of deposits up to a pre-specified limit, even if the bank itself fails. Capital insurance consists of the state's willingness to inject capital into a bank, in order to prevent a disorderly bankruptcy. All three of these devices were employed in the most recent crisis. But the other side of insurance is regulation. Society tries to contain the consequences of the insurance it feels obliged to provide. But the institutions its agents seek to regulate work hard to evade restraints on their ability to exploit the opportunities they enjoy.[17] One way in which policymakers try to respond is to distinguish between a generalized panic (when they will intervene) and the failure of a particular institution (when they will not): that is, between general and idiosyncratic risk. But such a distinction is difficult to draw in practice – indeed, it emerges only *after* the consequences of failure become clear.

Financial systems also generate credit booms and busts: this is the chief reason for the instability of market economies. The late and, until recently, disregarded Hyman Minsky, with whom this book began, described the broad features of such booms and busts.[18] 'A fundamental characteristic of our economy,' wrote Minsky, 'is that the financial system swings between robustness and fragility and these swings are an integral part of the process that generates business cycles.'[19]

Minsky identified five stages in a bubble: 'displacement' – a trigger event, such as a new technology or falling interest rates; 'boom' – when asset prices start rising; 'euphoria' – when investors' caution is thrown to the wind; 'profit-taking' – when intelligent investors start taking profits; and 'panic' – a period of collapsing asset prices and mass bankruptcy.[20] Displacement is an event that raises optimism, such as an innovation, access to new economic resources, or maybe a decline in the cost of funds. As the cycle unfolds, credit expands relative to the economy. This allows more people to borrow, normally against collateral and often against property collateral. The borrowing is used to buy assets and spend on investment and consumption. The former raises asset prices. The latter stimulates the economy. Both effects encourage people to borrow and spend even more. Borrowing and spending create more borrowing and spending. As the happy days continue, this time is indeed thought to be different, partly because such times always are in some plausible respects. The pressure on prudent managers of financial institutions to participate is intense. The greater the competition, the greater the pressure to join Mr Prince's 'dance'. 'Participate now and maybe perish later' or 'perish now' seems to be the choice. People working for financial institutions are both the most expert and the most deeply invested in the solidity of the boom.

Trees do not reach the sky. Ultimately, the bubble will expand no longer. When new buyers can no longer borrow, prices stop rising. From ceasing to rise to starting to fall takes but a moment: nobody wants to hold assets that nobody wants to buy. This is the 'Minsky moment', a term coined by Paul McCulley, formerly of the Pacific Investment Management Company (PIMCO). Once the supply of 'greater fools' has dried up, those who have borrowed in the expectation of further price rises will be forced to sell, the institutions who have financed them will to try to get their money back, and those who have lent to such institutions will also want their money back. That triggers the panic, the systemic crisis and the recession. The financial sector and the economy crash. The Minsky cycle is complete.

Fraud is an inherent element of the fragility of finance. Finance involves transactions in complex instruments whose characteristics will often not be known until long afterwards. This makes it ripe for fraud. In Minsky's good times, when people are prone to believing just about anything, the level of fraud rises, but it mostly remains invisible. In bad times, when people want their money back, the fraud is revealed. The late John Kenneth Galbraith caught the process in his celebrated concept of the 'bezzle', introduced in his book on the 1929 stock-market crash:

> In good times people are relaxed, trusting, and money is plentiful. But
> even though money is plentiful, there are always many people who

need more. Under these circumstances the rate of embezzlement grows, the rate of discovery falls off, and the bezzle increases rapidly. In depression all this is reversed. Money is watched with a narrow, suspicious eye. The man who handles it is assumed to be dishonest until he proves himself otherwise. Audits are penetrating and meticulous. Commercial morality is enormously improved. The bezzle shrinks.[21]

Yet while fraud accompanies booms, it does *not* cause them. And while the discovery of fraud accompanies crashes, to the rage of the body politic, it does *not* cause them either. Fraud should be seen as an exacerbating consequence of the fragility of a system based on trust and so liable to excesses of both trust and mistrust. In such a system, the unscrupulous always find a place and, again, in a boom the regulators are most likely to allow them to do so. The most recent boom and bust were no exception.

In their book, *All the Devils are Here*, Bethany McLean and Joe Nocera remark of Ameriquest, one of the most notorious subprime lenders, that 'fraud was an everyday occurrence. "You'd look over and there would be a guy altering W-2s (Internal Revenue Service wage and tax statements)," says [Mark] Bomchill (a loan officer).'[22] Yet that is *not* the heart of the story. Vastly more important than the outright fraud that always accompanies credit booms is what was legal: 'NINJA' ('no income, no job, no assets') loans;[23] the right to repackage such loans into complex products, many of which were granted a triple-A rating by the rating agencies; the ability to hold such assets off balance sheet; the right to sell such complex products across the world; and the ability to operate with a leverage of fifty to one.

Crises, then, are rooted in the interaction between the financial system and human nature. The system is always fragile. From time to time, it becomes extremely fragile. That is what happened this time.

THE SHIFT TOWARDS FRAGILITY[24]

What is exceptional about the recent crises in the US and the UK – the countries in which the world's two premier financial centres, New York and London, are located – is that the preceding booms were so lengthy and the previous large busts occurred before living memory. In the US, the last truly systemic crisis was in the early 1930s. In the UK, it was arguably as long ago as 1866. Greed is hardly a good explanation for the scale of the crisis, since it is a perennial. But the fact that the last big crises in the US and the UK occurred so long before helps explain why the crisis became so huge. Unfamiliarity bred complacency. But so did the way the financial system evolved, in five key aspects: liberalization; globalization; innovation; leverage; and incentives.

LIBERALIZATION

The most important single reason for the end of what Gorton calls the 'quiet period' was simply financial liberalization, itself an element in the general move towards free markets discussed briefly in the Preface. This movement was one of the dominant – arguably, the dominant – social, economic, political and philosophical shift of the past four decades. Though challenged by the post-2007 crisis, it has not reversed.

Politically, this shift is associated with the names of Ronald Reagan and Margaret Thatcher, president of the US and prime minister of the UK in the 1980s, though our progeny might associate it more closely with the name of Deng Xiaoping, the paramount leader of China after 1978 and progenitor of the programme of 'reform and opening up' that brought such a profound transformation to China and the world. Historically, this shift is also associated with the collapse of the Soviet Union and the Soviet empire in Central and Eastern Europe and with it the left-wing revolutionary tradition born out of the French Revolution two centuries before. In the history of economic ideas, the shift is associated with a decline of belief in Keynesianism – and so of the influence of Keynes – and the rise of belief in monetarism and the free market – and so of the influence of the Nobel laureates Milton Friedman and Friedrich Hayek. At a yet more fundamental level, the shift reflects the rise of individualism and belief in the autonomous and self-reliant person over the collectivism and social solidarity born of the emergence of the industrial working class in the nineteenth and early twentieth centuries, two world wars and the Great Depression.

Once the general shift towards trust in markets over governments occurred, the rise of the liberal financial market was inevitable. Indeed, the latter closely accompanied the former. If governments are not to allocate resources, markets must do so. The logic is impeccable. Moreover, the passage of time and the experience of a long period of financial stability had robbed the Western world of the terror of financial instability born in the 1930s. At the same time, economics provided theories justifying the proposition that free markets would allocate resources optimally. We saw the rise, for example, of the efficient market hypothesis associated with Chicago University's Nobel laureate Eugene Fama and of belief in shareholder value maximization associated with Harvard University's Michael Jensen. Beyond these intellectual arguments in favour of financial liberalization there were also practical arguments against regulation. Over time, it was found increasingly difficult to make the regulations that existed stick, as financial actors increasingly found ways around them. The general move towards more open and market-driven economies that had already proceeded a long way in the 1950s and 1960s greatly increased this difficulty. By the 1980s and 1990s, a veritable bonfire of regulations was under way, along with a general culture of laissez-faire. The assumption increasingly was that markets knew best, while regulators knew next to nothing. This cultural context, more than specific regulatory practices, was the most important influence upon the financial sector. And so, increasingly, the activities of the financial sector became dominant, its rewards became exceptional. and its most successful practitioners became heroes.

GLOBALIZATION

A second and closely related transformation was globalization, itself a natural concomitant of liberalization. The globalization of finance, in turn, was a natural concomitant of the globalization of the economy. Big financial crises are almost always international, usually because a number of countries are affected by similar conditions.

That was very much true in the case of the post-2007 crises. But there are often also microeconomic reasons for the cross-border spread of fragility. That was also true in this case, for three principal reasons.

First, funding went global. This was particularly true of wholesale funding. The Turner Review of 2009 describes what happened in the UK as follows:

> The import of capital into the UK, funding the rapid growth of credit, in part took the form of foreign purchases of UK credit securities, in particular retail mortgage-backed securities (RMBS). Before 2000, unlike in the US, securitised credit had played a small role in the UK mortgage market but by 2007, 18% of UK mortgage credit was funded through securitization ... But the UK also saw the rapid growth of on-balance sheet mortgage lending, with UK banks expanding their loan books more rapidly than deposit bases, placing increasing reliance on wholesale funding. At the aggregate level, this implied a significant increase in overseas bank financing of the UK current-account deficit.
>
> A crucial feature of the UK system in the run-up to the crisis, was therefore the rapid growth of a number of specific banks – Northern Rock, Bradford & Bingley, Alliance and Leicester and HBOS – which were increasingly reliant on the permanent availability of a large-scale interbank funding and/or on their continuous ability to securitise and sell down rapidly accumulating credit assets, particularly in the mortgage market.[25]

Second, banking went global. This was true for many institutions and countries, but it was dramatically true of the UK. The balance sheet of the UK banking system grew from about 50 per cent of GDP for the century prior to 1970, to a little over 200 per cent in the late 1980s and over 500 per cent of GDP immediately before the crisis of 2007.[26] This partly reflected the increased debt within the UK economy, particularly household mortgage debt. But between the late 1990s and 2008, the consolidated foreign claims of UK headquartered banks also rose from less than $500bn to $4tn, or about 150 per cent of GDP.[27] Part of this was because of increased trading activity and part of it was because of mergers, particularly the 2007 takeover of the Dutch banking group ABN AMRO by the Royal Bank of Scotland. Ben Broadbent, a member of the UK's monetary policy committee, remarked in 2012 that 'the major UK-owned banks have lost around 15 times on non-UK mortgages what they have in the domestic market. Overall, around three-quarters of aggregate losses have been on their non-UK balance sheets.'[28] This is a consequence of going global.

It is also a consequence of a third phenomenon: holdings of the newly created assets also went global. Thus, not only banks but other investors found themselves holding toxic assets created by the 'originate and distribute' model of finance that increasingly replaced the traditional 'lend and hold' model in the US in the run-up to the crisis: thus institutions made loans, to be packaged into composite securities and sold on to outside investors, instead of holding those loans on their own books as they used to do. As we have seen, the argument for this wide distribution of assets had been that they would end up being held by those best able to understand the risks. In practice, however, many of them ended up being held by those least able to understand the risks (see Chapter Two above). This is asymmetric information at work. This was partly, no doubt, because better-informed sellers emphasized the upside of complex products, but did not go out of their way to make clear their downside. It is partly because the combination of greed with ignorance is a perennial feature of customers in financial markets. The good side of the wide distribution of the risks was that the total loss-bearing capacity of the investors who held doubtful assets was greater. The bad side, when it came, was that the panic affected far more institutions and countries than it would otherwise have done. Moreover, as the Nobel laureate George Akerloff of the University of California at Berkeley argued in a classic paper, once buyers realize sellers know much more than they do about the products they are selling, the market may disappear altogether.[29] That is exactly what happened to complex structured products.

Innovation

The third reason for the emergence of such a high degree of financial fragility was a series of intellectual and organizational innovations. Innovation usually increases fragility, because unfamiliarity is itself confusing. Innovations transformed the way the financial system operated: it became an around-the-clock and around-the-globe bazaar, selling ever more complex products. Making these innovations possible was the revolution in information and communications technology.

The most important innovation was, arguably, in the allegedly mathematically rigorous pricing of derivatives – financial assets that 'derive' their value from the prices of underlying assets, such as stocks or bonds, indices, or interest rates.[30] But, it should be noted, Nassim Nicholas Taleb, famous for the 'Black Swan' (an unforecastable event), views the theories underlying the pricing of derivatives as intellectually fraudulent.[31] But, aided by rising computing power, this almost universally accepted intellectual innovation led to an explosion in the invention and trading of ever more sophisticated products, including the infamous collateralized debt obligations (CDOs), synthetic collateralized debt obligations and CDOs squared, which triggered the global financial crisis of 2007–08. (These instruments are explained further below.) According to the Bank for International Settlements, between June 1998 and June 2008 the notional value of outstanding over-the-counter derivatives exploded from $72tn to $673tn (whereupon it stagnated), the latter being just under eleven times global gross product. The market value of such derivatives is, by necessity, far less than their notional face value, because a derivative is not a direct, but a conditional, claim on an underlying asset.[32] There is nothing inherently fraudulent or inappropriate about the relationship between notional and market values. But even the market value of derivatives rose from $2.6tn to $35.3tn in December 2008, itself more than half global output.[33] This had become a very large market.

Along with new products came organizational innovations. Much (though not all) of this is captured in the phrase 'shadow banking'. Its inventor, Paul McCulley, defined it as 'the whole alphabet soup of levered up non-bank investment conduits, vehicles, and structures'.[34] This new system was revolutionary. It created a parallel financial system that performed the functions of conventional banking. But few people realized that it was vulnerable to the risks of conventional banking, and it lacked both a lender of last resort and a competent regulator. Worse, conventional banks were also implicated in central aspects of shadow banking, the creation of – and trading in – complex securities and borrowing in short-term, collateralized debt markets, which replaced conventional bank deposits for many big lenders.

As is true of most revolutionary systems, the implications of shadow banking were widely misunderstood. It created new forms of non-deposit near-money – notably, money-market funds, predominantly held by households, which financed supposedly safe short-term securities, and repos (repurchase agreements), a form of secured lending by corporate treasurers to investment banks and the investment-banking operations of universal banks (banks that provide both retail and investment-banking services).[35] It allowed companies increasingly to issue commercial paper instead of relying on conventional bank loans. It converted conventional loans into tradeable asset-backed securities and CDOs (versions of asset-backed securities in which the repayments were 'tranched' or divided, with the highly rated paper receiving the first payments and the lower-rated paper receiving the later payments, if any). It created instruments that insured such assets, known as credit-default swaps, often deemed an adequate substitute for the capital required by regulators, even though they did not in any way increase the capital in the system. It led to the dissolution of the boundary between retail banking and wholesale markets. It created intense and non-transparent networks of financial relationships among institutions, both vertically and horizontally, in place of the vertically integrated silos characteristic of more traditional banking. It introduced far more competition into the financial sector. Not least, it facilitated enormous growth in credit and debt, in the US and elsewhere (see Figure 5).[36]

A particularly important component of the growth in debt occurred within the financial system: while debt was once held within vertical institutions, such as retail banks or mortgage lenders, it was now held through a chain of market relations among independent players. This was a measure of perhaps the most striking feature of the new financial system: its complexity. The gross debt of the US financial system (much of this consisting of loans among financial institutions) grew from 20 per cent of GDP in 1979 to 120 per cent in 2008. In the UK, the gross debt of the financial system reached two and a half times GDP in 2007.[37]

According to the official report of the US Financial Crisis Inquiry Commission, 'over the past 30-plus years, we permitted the growth of a shadow banking system – opaque and laden with short-term debt – that rivaled the size of the traditional banking system'.[38] This novel set of arrangements was of negligible size in 1980, but the total assets of shadow banking reached close to $13tn in 2007, about 90 per cent of US GDP. The shadow-banking system became bigger than the traditional system, in the early 2000s, and remained so until after 2008, even though the traditional system also grew substantially.[39]

The most important aspect of the new market-based system is that it was vulnerable to panic for exactly the same reasons as the traditional banking system: maturity and risk mismatches, but here magnified by the opacity and interconnectedness of the system. Unlike in traditional banking systems, with which policymakers were familiar, no effective insurance of the enormous quantity of liquid liabilities in the new system existed in a deep crisis. Indeed, in one of the best-informed analyses of the crisis, Perry Mehrling of Columbia University argues that 'it is not just the shadow banks but, more important, the larger capital-market based credit system that failed, and it is that failure that we must understand if we are to put the system back together again, and on more solid foundations this time. This financial crisis is not merely a subprime mortgage crisis or even a shadow-banking crisis; it is a crisis of the entire market-based credit system that we have constructed since 1970.'[40]

From the point of view of vulnerability to runs, a vital feature was that a new form of credit-backed money emerged. A working paper from the International Monetary Fund in 2012 summarized what happened:

> in recent decades, with the advent of securitization and electronic means of trading and settlement, it became possible to expand greatly the scope of assets that could be transformed directly, through their use as collateral, into liquid or money-like assets. The expansion in the scope of the assets that could be securitized was in part facilitated by the growth of the shadow financial system, which was largely unregulated, and the ability to borrow from non-deposit sources.[41]

In the event, central banks were driven to intervene. Yet, at its core, the failure was quite traditional: the excesses of a combination of financial innovation with mismanaged risk-taking generated a panic that devastated liquidity. As recounted in Part I, the markets froze.

Leverage

A fourth dimension of increased fragility, emphasized in a marvellous book, *The Bankers' New Clothes*, by Anat Admati of Stanford University and Martin Hellwig of the Max Planck Institute for Research on Collective Goods, was unprecedented leverage or gearing (by which is meant ways of funding investments that multiply the returns to investors on the upside and the losses to investors on the downside).[42] Leverage increased on three dimensions: leverage of non-financial borrowers, such as house buyers, who borrowed more relative to the value of houses; leverage embedded in new instruments, particularly derivatives; and leverage inside the financial sector itself, which became extraordinarily high in many institutions. Leverage generates profits on the way up, but also huge losses on the way down. That well-known fact is why panic hits when the possibility of such losses becomes immediate.

Many borrowers leveraged themselves dramatically during the 2000s. This was true in the US and the UK, but also in Iceland, Ireland, Spain, and parts of Central and Eastern Europe. It was true of households and companies, particularly investors in property, property developers and those engaged in leveraged buy-outs. With more debt relative to equity, and overvalued asset prices, the outcome was extreme vulnerability to crisis.

In addition, the market-based financial system embedded an enormous amount of leverage inside financial instruments. Collateralized debt obligations (CDOs) are an excellent example, with leverage inherent in the process of tranching cash inflows. Synthetic CDOs, which are created by pooling and tranching credit-default swaps on asset-backed securities and other bonds, involve much the same process. Think of the simplest possible CDO, one in which the underlying interest payments and mortgage repayments are divided into just two securities: the lower risk of these two securities would be entitled to receive the first 50 per cent of all the payments and repayments; the higher risk of these securities would get the rest. Even if half the underlying borrowings ended up in default, the lower-risk security would remain serviced, but the higher-risk security would be wiped out. Thus, relative to investing in a single security in which losses would be shared equally, holders of the riskier of the two new securities made a highly leveraged bet: their proportional losses would be twice as high as those on the underlying mortgages. Of course, they would demand a higher return on such a higher-risk security: leverage generates higher expected returns and higher risks. In general, investors seem to have been unaware that the leverage embedded in lower-rated collateralized obligations was far greater than in comparably rated corporate bonds.[43]

The new financial system generated leverage in other ways. A particularly important one was inside the financial system, via reliance on risk-weighted capital. Real capital could – and did – fall prior to the crisis as measured risk-weighted capital rose, because the perceived riskiness of the portfolio declined. Since the underlying models of risk were conceptually and empirically flawed (conceptually, because the presumed distribution of outcomes was wrong, and empirically, because the data were for vastly too limited a period), this had perverse results.[44] In 2011 the UK government's Independent Commission on Banking showed that the ratio of risk-weighted assets to un-weighted assets for the four largest UK banks (among the largest banks in the world) fell from close to 55 per cent to close to 35 per cent between 2004 and 2008: in other words, bankers (and, apparently, complacent regulators) deemed their assets progressively safer, just as they were, in fact, becoming riskier.[45] That underestimation of risk was in turn directly due to the lengthy prior period of economic and financial stability – the great moderation, in fact.

Perhaps the most elegant demonstration of the scale of the error in the models came from David Viniar, risk-management officer of Goldman Sachs before and during the crisis. He remarked, in August 2007 – shortly after large losses on Goldman-managed funds, but also long before the worst of the crisis – that 'we were seeing things that were 25-standard deviation moves, several days in a row'.[46] Goldman was not alone in seeing this. The response was to de-risk the institution as swiftly as possible. When repeated across the financial industry, it exacerbated the shocks Goldman and others observed and to which they responded. This is an excellent example of the idea of 'reflexivity' promulgated by George Soros, the well-known investor.[47]

The risk-management models were wrong. These assume a certain distribution of possible outcomes. A measure of the dispersion of possible outcomes is the 'standard deviation'. In one of the most frequently assumed distributions of outcomes – the so-called normal distribution – moves up to three standard deviations away from the mean (in either direction) would cover 99.8 per cent of all possible outcomes.[48] How likely then is a 25-standard deviation outcome, not once, but several days in a row? A paper from Nottingham University notes: 'If we observe a profit or loss once a day, then a mere 8-sigma (i.e. eight standard deviations of the distribution) event should occur less than once in the entire history of the universe.'[49] What, then, are the chances of experiencing a 25-sigma event two days in a row? It is as likely as winning the UK's national lottery forty-two times in a row. The supposed 'bad luck' of Goldman Sachs and its peers, which is what it would have to have been if their models were correct, makes Job appear a man blessed by good fortune. The alternative – and correct – explanation was that the models Goldman Sachs used to evaluate the riskiness of its strategies were totally wrong. These financial emperors were naked. They were clothed not in a silken weave of sophisticated mathematics and solid evidence, but in moonbeams.

Trust in such mistaken models of risk fuelled the embrace of high leverage within the financial sector.[50] It was thought that a well-managed institution would not need much capital since it could assess its risks precisely. This proved to be a delusion, partly because of the incentives for managers, traders and even shareholders to take risks and no less because of their lack of understanding of the risks. Lulled into complacent sleep, the UK banks and regulators allowed their median leverage ratio (the ratio of their total assets to fully loss-bearing equity) to more than double, from around twenty to one to nearly fifty to one in the years immediately before the crisis.[51] In April 2007, just before the financial crisis, the Bank of England's *Financial Stability Report* noted: 'The major UK banks remain highly profitable, with a median return on equity of 22% in 2006. Published capital ratios are well above regulatory minima.'[52] But those regulatory minima were themselves based on the highly unreliable risk-weighting of assets. Complacently, the opening words of the same report were that 'The UK financial system remains highly resilient.'[53] Because regulators were, like the firms themselves, trusting inaccurate measures of risk, they were also looking at misleading measures of leverage. This is an important respect in which stability destabilized, as Minsky argued. Regulators have still not fully rectified their mistaken reliance on risk-weighting, as will be noted in Chapter Seven below.

Subsequent work at the Bank of England has shown that the increased leverage was also the principal source of the increased returns on bank equity reported in the period before the crisis. This work concluded: 'Much of the "productivity miracle" of high return on equity in banking appears to have been the result not of productivity gains on the underlying asset pool, but rather a simple leveraging up of the underlying equity in the business.'[54] It's a simple, but dangerous, way to try to become rich: it involves no innovation, other than more borrowing – that is, more risk-taking.

Incentives

Behind many of the changes was a shift in incentives towards greater risk-taking. The most important changes were the shift from partnerships to public companies on Wall Street in the 1980s and 1990s, the embrace of stock options, and the payment of bonuses, frequently linked to a single year's performance, with little or no claw-back in the light of subsequent events. Accounting rules that allowed the recognition of profits on signing the deal, rather than over its life, also shifted incentives towards the short term. With each firm under pressure to perform, their employees increasingly mobile and the end of partnerships, management found it difficult to avoid entering the race for ever more generous rewards.[55] As Mary Schapiro, chairman of the Securities and Exchange Commission, told the US Financial Crisis Inquiry Commission, published in 2011, 'Many major financial institutions created asymmetric compensation packages that paid employees enormous sums for short-term success, even if these same decisions result in significant long-term losses or failure for investors and taxpayers.'[56]

These changes in incentives for employees, including management, came on top of those inherent in limited-liability companies, particularly those with very high leverage, in which shareholders take the upside, while the downside losses are capped. In an important paper, Lucien Bebchuk and Holger Spamann of Harvard University argue that aligning the interests of employees with those of shareholders is dangerous for this reason. Thus, 'while such measures could eliminate risk-taking that is excessive even from shareholders' point of view, they cannot be expected to prevent risk-taking that serves shareholders but is socially excessive'.[57] The problem became extreme in banking, because taxpayers took a large portion of the equity risk via the (as it turned out, correct) expectation that they would bail out creditors. In other words, the taxpayer is the shareholder of last resort, relieving creditors of the need to examine the quantity of equity in the business and so encouraging more one-sided risk-taking.

Conclusion

Crises are an inherent element of the market-based financial system, as we know it. They follow periods of rising fragility, created by the rise of apparently hugely profitable risk-taking generated within the system. So it was this time. Success bred excess and excess bred collapse.

HOW POLICYMAKERS FAILED

Where were the policymakers? Questions can be raised about policy in three hugely important areas: regulation, monetary policy and crisis intervention.

Regulation

Regulators made errors of omission and commission. Sins of omission are the result of excessively permissive regulation and supervision: they occur when regulators choose to ignore either gross malfeasance or excessive risk-taking. Sins of commission arise when regulators and lawmakers encourage financial institutions to take risks for social or political reasons. In the run-up to the crisis, both forms of mistake were made. Moreover, it is partly because both such mistakes are always made that making the regulatory regime work is so hard.

In explaining the origin of those sins of omission, Adair Turner, chairman of the UK Financial Services Authority, noted, in his eponymous review in 2009, that:

> At the core of [assumptions guiding pre-crisis regulation] has been the theory of efficient and rational markets. Five propositions with implications for the regulatory approach have followed:
>
> (i) Market prices are good indicators of rationally evaluated economic value.
> (ii) The development of securitised credit, since [it is] based on the creation of new and more liquid markets, has improved both allocative efficiency and financial stability.
> (iii) The risk characteristics of financial markets can be inferred from mathematical analysis, delivering robust quantitative measures of trading risk.
> (iv) Market discipline can be used as an effective tool in constraining harmful risk taking.
> (v) Financial innovation can be assumed to be beneficial, since market competition would winnow out any innovations which did not deliver value added.
>
> Each of these assumptions is now subject to extensive challenge on both theoretical and empirical grounds, with potential implications for the appropriate design of regulation and for the role of regulatory authorities.[58]

Behind all this was the assumption that self-interest would, via Adam Smith's invisible hand, ensure a stable, dynamic and efficient financial system. This is the view that Alan Greenspan, probably the most influential spokesman for that point of view, recanted, when he told a congressional committee in October 2008 that he had found a 'flaw' in his thinking on markets.[59] He then accepted that the pursuit of self-interest, however beneficial in the economy as a whole, does not necessarily lead to financial stability, because shareholders of financial institutions are either unaware of the risks their institutions are running or are prepared to let management make big gambles. By then, that was perfectly obvious.

The application of these naive ideas proved extraordinarily dangerous. Treating the financial system in the same way as, say, retailing does not make sense. No other industry has the capacity to create such widespread economic and social damage and, for this very reason, no other industry benefits from such large implicit subsidies.

Andrew Haldane of the Bank of England has elucidated the costs. He has argued that the present value of lost output caused by the recent financial crises may be 'anywhere between one and five times annual GDP. As Nobel-prize winning physicist Richard Feynman observed, to call these numbers "astronomical" would be to do astronomy a disservice: there are only hundreds of billions of stars in the galaxy. "Economical" might be a better description.'[60] Furthermore, adds Mr Haldane, the state provides a huge implicit subsidy to the financial sector, by insuring it against failure: 'For UK banks, the average annual subsidy for the top five banks over these years [2007–09] was over £50 billion – roughly equal to UK banks' annual profits prior to the crisis. At the height of the crisis, the subsidy was larger still. For the sample of global banks, the average annual subsidy for the top five banks was just less than $60 billion per year. These are not small sums.'[61]

This time may not be different. But finance *is* different. It was extraordinarily foolish to forget this. Yet, as the Federal Reserve's General Counsel, Scott Alvarez, told the Financial Crisis Inquiry Commission, the 'mind-set was that there should be no regulation; the market should take care of policing, unless there already is an identified problem . . . We were in the reactive mode because that's what the mind-set was of the '90s and the early 2000s.' Moreover, added the Commission's report, 'The strong housing market also reassured people. Alvarez noted the long history of low mortgage default rates and the desire to help people who traditionally had few dealings with banks become homeowners.'[62]

Similarly, in his review of the UK experience, Adair Turner argued that:

> the FSA's regulatory and supervisory approach, before the current crisis, was based on a sometimes implicit but at times quite overt philosophy which believed that:
>
> - Markets are in general self-correcting, with market discipline a more effective tool than regulation or supervisory oversight through which to ensure that firms' strategies are sound and risks contained.
> - The primary responsibility for managing risks lies with the senior management and boards of the individual firms, who are better placed to assess business model risk than bank regulators, and who can be relied on to make appropriate decisions about the balance between risk and return, provided appropriate systems, procedures and skilled people are in place.
> - Customer protection is best ensured not by product regulation or direct intervention in markets, but by ensuring that wholesale markets are as unfettered and transparent as possible, and that the way in which firms conduct business (e.g. the definition and execution of sales processes) is appropriate.[63]

Thus, as the shadow banking system evolved, the regular banking system joined it. These were not two distinct financial systems, but one, with two aspects: traditional retail banking and a more dynamic component built around structured finance and wholesale finance. Traditional retail banks participated fully in the latter, via conduits and special-purpose vehicles and, more fundamentally, via the integration of investment and commercial banking, the former historically focused on trading in securities and the latter focused on lending. Changes in the law happened along the way in the US, including the repeal of the Glass-Steagall Act in 1999, which had previously separated investment from commercial banking. The arguments for repeal were that the law had become either irrelevant or inefficient: irrelevant to the extent that it increasingly failed to prevent the entry of commercial banks into investment banking, and inefficient to the extent that it still posed an obstacle to the entry of commercial banks into such activities.

Yet sins of omission were not the only mistakes. There were also sins of commission. Two might have been particularly significant. The first was the zero risk-weighting of sovereign debt under the so-called 'Basel I', which turned out to be so problematic inside the Eurozone.[64] The assumption – convenient for governments, but very dangerous in certain circumstances – was that governments would not default. It is true that governments are unlikely to default in their own currencies, though even that is not absolutely certain. But governments frequently default in other countries' currencies – or, more precisely, currencies they are unable to create at will. This now includes all Eurozone members, with results discussed in Chapter Two above.

The second sin of commission was the strong encouragement of lending for home purchase, notably in the US. A particular complaint concerns the role of the government-sponsored enterprises (GSEs), Fannie Mae and Freddie Mac. Peter Wallison of the American Enterprise Institute, in his dissent to the majority report of the *Financial Crisis Inquiry Commission*, even argues that:

> the *sine qua non* of the financial crisis was U.S. government housing policy, which led to the creation of 27 million subprime and other risky loans – half of all mortgages in the United States – which were ready to default as soon as the massive 1997–2007 housing bubble began to deflate. If the U.S. government had not chosen this policy path – fostering the growth of a bubble of unprecedented size and an equally unprecedented number of weak and high-risk residential mortgages – the great financial crisis of 2008 would never have occurred.[65]

It is certainly possible to accept that enthusiastic government promotion of home ownership and, in particular, the GSEs, played some role. But the view that this was the principal cause is entirely unconvincing, for four reasons.[66]

First, Keith Hennessey, Douglas Holtz-Eakin and Bill Thomas, also Republican nominees to the Financial Crisis Inquiry Commission, note, in their own dissenting comment:

> The report largely ignores the credit bubble beyond housing. Credit spreads declined not just for housing, but also for other asset classes like commercial real estate. This tells us to look to the credit bubble as

THE SHIFTS AND THE SHOCKS

an essential cause of the U.S. housing bubble. It also tells us that problems with U.S. housing policy or markets do not by themselves explain
the U.S. housing bubble.

There were housing bubbles in the United Kingdom, Spain, Australia,
France and Ireland, some more pronounced than in the United States.
Some nations with housing bubbles relied little on American-style
mortgage securitization. A good explanation of the U.S. housing bubble should also take into account its parallels in other nations. This
leads us to explanations broader than just U.S. housing policy, regulation, or supervision.[67]

Evidently, this argument applies with just as much force to the argument of their fellow Republican nominee, Mr Wallison, who argues as
if this were solely a US crisis and solely a subprime mortgage crisis.

Second, the view that the GSEs played a central role in encouraging
the private sector to enter into the subprime housing mania is false.
Nobody forced sophisticated private financial institutions to enter
into the transactions that made up the 'originate, securitise, rate and
distribute model'. Mr Wallison also relied on the research of a colleague at the American Enterprise Institute to argue that Fannie and
Freddie made a great many subprime loans and other high-risk mortgages. But it turns out that these 'other high-risk mortgages' were
vastly safer than private subprime lending, because they did not in
fact share the same characteristics. Indeed, the expansive definition of
'high-risk mortgages', on which Mr Wallison relies, is extremely idiosyncratic: the number of such mortgages in this expanded definition
is over five times bigger than that used in a 2010 report by the US
Government Accounting Office. Above all, the loans supported by the
GSEs that Wallison's AEI colleague labels 'high-risk' did not in fact
have anything close to the failure rates of the subprime mortgages
promoted by private lenders.[68] Indeed, even Mr Wallison's fellow
Republican commissioners did not buy his argument that Fannie and
Freddie created the subprime crisis. As Bethany McLean and Joe
Nocera make quite clear, Fannie Mae and Freddie Mac were, in fact,
latecomers to the subprime party – followers, not leaders.[69]

Third, some argue that the villain of the piece was the US Community Reinvestment Act, designed to prevent 'redlining' – blanket bans

on lending in particular areas – by US banks. On this, the US Financial Crisis Inquiry Commission remarked that 'only 6 per cent of high-cost loans – a proxy for subprime loans – had any connection to the law. Loans made by CRA-regulated lenders in the neighborhoods in which they were required to lend were half as likely to default as similar loans made in the same neighborhoods by independent mortgage originators not subject to the law.'[70]

Finally, accept for a moment that Mr Wallison is right. (He is not.) Then the biggest financial crisis for eighty years, one that caused a worldwide recession and a prolonged slump, was all due to the desire of the US government to raise home ownership. If true, the financial system is indeed hopelessly fragile and unstable. But the entire point of Mr Wallison's argument is that it would not be were it not for the government's role in housing policy. His position is self-refuting: the fact that an alleged error in US housing policy can bring down the Western world's financial system demonstrates the hopeless fragility of the latter. It does not vindicate it. It condemns it.

My conclusion then is that the role of regulation was principally one of omission: policymakers assumed the system was far more stable, responsible, indeed honest, than it was. Moreover, it was because this assumption was so widely shared that so many countries were affected.

Monetary Policy

The second aspect of policy closely related to financial fragility is monetary policy. Much of the discussion of this issue will be left to Chapter Five, which looks at the economic origins of the crisis. Yet one thing is clear: policymakers thought stable inflation would deliver economic stability. They were wrong. Central banks did deliver stable inflation, but what ensued was still the biggest financial and economic crisis for eighty years, followed by a long-lasting economic malaise. The 'great moderation' proved to be a snare and a delusion.

Mark Gertler of New York University described the dominant pre-crisis recommendations of central bankers and orthodox macro-economists in his comments on the critical paper submitted by Claudio Borio and William White of the Bank for International Settlements at a 2003 symposium organized by the Federal Reserve Bank of Kansas City:

> Use prudential policy to prevent undesired financial risk exposure from building up. Then use active monetary policy to mitigate any harmful effects of a downturn ... [A] flexible inflation targeting framework (in conjunction with a cogent prudential policy) accomplishes exactly this goal. It induces a central bank to take the appropriate policy actions in response to financial market volatility and does so in a way that properly takes into account the real informational constraints the central bank faces. In particular, the central bank does not have to get into the business of figuring out fundamental market valuations. Nor does it have to figure out how the market will respond to policy actions or its perceptions of proper market valuations. Since, in my view, the Federal Reserve in recent years has acted as an implicit inflation targeter and done so in a way that has clearly mitigated any harmful effects from market volatility, it seems that recent events have only served to support our position.[71]

This point of view does not hold up so well a decade later. Maybe it would have worked if the right prudential policy had been used, though it is quite hard to believe that such a policy would have made the difference. In any case, a successful inflation-targeting monetary policy proved entirely compatible with a huge financial crisis and consequent economic instability. Indeed, the complacency it induced in the form of the idea of the great moderation played a big role in causing the crisis.

Crisis Intervention

The final question concerns how the policymakers responded to the crisis when it hit. In the panic, they were caught between two opposing pressures: the first was the view that those who made mistakes should be allowed to fail, to minimize 'moral hazard' (the risk that insurance makes the insured take greater risks); the second was the need to respond to a panic.

The concern about moral hazard is greatly exaggerated. Nobody argues there should be no fire service because the knowledge that it exists encourages people to take the risk of smoking in bed. We have fire brigades mainly because of the spillover impact on innocent people: if someone's house burns down, we may end up with the Great Fire of London, as happened in 1666. Likewise, the economic costs of systemic financial crises are mostly borne by people who had nothing to do with the decisions that led to it. Allowing a systemic financial collapse is no more the right way of dealing with a financial crisis than letting London burn down would be the right response to a domestic fire.

The right way of dealing with the risk of fire is precisely what we do: have a fire brigade, fire regulations and household fire insurance, secure in the knowledge that people still have a strong incentive to avoid a fire on their premises. In the same way, the right response to the risk of a systemic financial crisis is to prevent a collapse, impose financial regulations and offer deposit insurance, secure in the know-ledge that important decision-makers would still suffer significant losses. Thus, policymakers were right to halt the systemic financial collapse of 2008, because of the immense damage it would have done if allowed to proceed unchecked; they were right to seek to tighten financial regulations subsequently, to prevent dangers from building up to extreme levels again; and they are right to impose rules that ensure shareholders, decision-makers and unprotected and uninsured creditors would bear losses in future. What this means will be dis-cussed further in Chapter Seven below.

In retrospect, policymakers paid too much attention to moral haz-ard at the beginning and too little attention to stopping the financial blaze. In a systemic crisis, the danger of an overshoot in valuations of assets that generates mass insolvency of intermediaries is so great that, as Bagehot argued, policymakers must intervene. Indeed, Bage-hot offered a classic description of the role of a central bank in *Lombard Street*:

> A panic, in a word, is a species of neuralgia, and according to the rules of science you must not starve it. The holders of the cash reserve must be ready not only to keep it for their own liabilities, but to advance it most freely for the liabilities of others. They must lend to merchants, to minor bankers, to 'this man and that man', whenever the security is

good. In wild periods of alarm, one failure makes many, and the best way to prevent the derivative failures is to arrest the primary failure which causes them. The way in which the panic of 1825 was stopped by advancing money has been described in so broad and graphic a way that the passage has become classical. 'We lent it,' said Mr Harman, on behalf of the Bank of England, 'by every possible means and in modes we had never adopted before; we took in stock on security, we purchased Exchequer bills, we made advances on Exchequer bills, we not only discounted outright, but we made advances on the deposit of bills of exchange to an immense amount, in short, by every possible means consistent with the safety of the Bank, and we were not on some occasions over-nice. Seeing the dreadful state in which the public were, we rendered every assistance in our power.' After a day or two of this treatment, the entire panic subsided, and the 'City' was quite calm.[72]

Critics of the policy response in 2008 would argue that the failure to understand the consequence of a panic led to a far greater disaster than necessary, particularly in the autumn of 2008, after the failure of Lehman. Anatole Kaletsky argued in his thought-provoking book, *Capitalism 4.0*:

> Lehman precipitated 'a complete collapse of confidence' among the depositors and creditors of every major financial institution – in effect a run on every bank around the world ... The corollary is that the world economy would probably not have suffered a serious recession had the Lehman bankruptcy not been allowed to trigger the world's greatest financial panic.
>
> This panic could have been avoided in two ways: by saving Lehman or by putting in place immediately after its failure comprehensive and unconditional guarantees for other financial institutions, which governments all over the world introduced anyway, but a crucial month too late.[73]

The view that there was a panic that could – and should – have been prevented is consistent with what we know about financial crises in general and this crisis in particular. It is also consistent with evidence on the pricing of assets that were at the heart of the crisis. As Figure 28 shows, a substantial recovery of the AAA-rated tranches has occurred since the huge collapse in the price of subprime asset-backed securities. The panic, which saw values of these tranches fall to 60 per cent of par in early 2009, was overdone, as is usual. At the same time, the panic was due to something real, as the pricing of lower tranches shows. This also is usual. But it *was* a panic and that, as Bagehot had argued, had to be halted. It was halted, in the end, but only after it had caused huge damage. Many argued, both at the time and afterwards, that the panic should have been allowed to take its course, anything else being a 'bailout'. That is an understandable, but grossly mistaken, judgement, since allowing the panic to take its course would have caused a deep depression and so vast damage to innocent bystanders. It would have been to repeat the mistakes of the early 1930s: once in history is enough.

The real difficulty was not over the principle of intervening to halt a panic, but over deciding when to do so. It was only the consequences of Lehman's failure that created the political conditions in which subsequent action against the panic became possible. Saving Lehman would have been difficult because the case for doing so still rested on

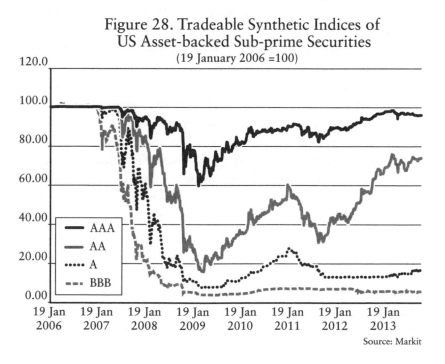

Figure 28. Tradeable Synthetic Indices of
US Asset-backed Sub-prime Securities
(19 January 2006 =100)

Source: Markit

a hypothetical – what would have happened if it had been allowed to fail. Not saving Lehman turned the hypothetical into a reality. That then made it far easier to act. So even if it might in theory have been far better to save Lehman, it was the failure to do so that made the crisis sufficiently bad to warrant the necessary actions. In that case, what happened was more a tragedy than a blunder. Tragedies are, alas, often inescapable in the realms of the hypothetical.

CONCLUSION

How then should we try to understand the origins of the panic that built up in 2007 and overwhelmed the financial markets in 2008? What does this disaster teach us?

First, the financial system is inherently fragile. It is prone to error and, of course, to fraud. But fraud is a natural concomitant of the processes that lead to crises. The financial system is also vulnerable to panics that exaggerate the underlying reasons for a crisis. This fragility is integral to the system and generated by it, in periods of boom and bust.

Second, the view that stabilizing inflation was a sufficient condition for economic stability has been proved grotesquely wrong. The truth is the opposite. A time of macroeconomic stability is precisely when the financial system is likely to become more fragile, because that is when people feel safe in taking on more risk.

Third, again, the view that market forces would make the financial system stable has also proved egregiously wrong. Market forces generate euphoria and panics, as was understood by Bagehot and his forebears, notably Henry Thornton, author of the classic *An Inquiry into the Nature and Effects of the Paper Credit of Great Britain* (1802).[74] This is largely because the assets upon which private households and businesses depend for their day-to-day lives are also overwhelmingly the liabilities of profit-seeking, risk-taking private businesses. When the creditworthiness of these businesses comes into question, as it did in 2008, panic is likely to ensue among uninsured short-term creditors: there will, in brief, be runs on the market. What then makes these panics systemic is the interconnection among institutions and their vulnerability to similar risks.

Fourth, the ignorance and arrogance of academics and policymakers, and the shortsightedness and grossly misdirected incentives of managers and traders, made the Western financial system increasingly fragile in the decades leading up to the crisis. The crisis became so severe largely because so many people thought it impossible.

Fifth, policymakers failed to act sufficiently decisively until the crisis reached its worst in the second half of September and October 2008. Until then they acted as if they did not understand the dangers. But they may have had little choice: it is difficult to get support for decisive action before it becomes evident to ordinary people that something has to be done. Remember that even after the crisis reached its climax, it took two attempts to get the Troubled Asset Relief Program (TARP), which gave the US government the funds it needed to rescue the financial system, through the House of Representatives.

Sixth, possibly most disturbing was (and is) the ability of the financial industry to use its money and lobbying clout to obtain the lax regulations it wanted (and wants). This has not ended. On the contrary, the push-back against post-crisis regulation demonstrates that it is very much with us. This is one of the reasons why crises will recur. Regulation will be eroded, both overtly and covertly, under the remorseless pressure and unfailing imagination of a huge, well-organized and highly motivated industry. This is not about fraud narrowly defined. It is more about the corruption of a political process in which organized interests outweigh the public interest.

Finally, regulators will never keep up with all this. They lack the resources, the motivation and, in the last resort, the knowledge to do so. The only solution is to create a financial system whose failure the world economy would survive relatively unscathed. How to do so will be a theme of Part III of the book and its concluding chapter.

Yet it is not enough merely to learn from past mistakes and then assume economies will swiftly go back to the old normal. They have to go to a 'new normal'.[75] Even without the crisis, pre-crisis trends in the global economy were unsustainable in certain important respects. This being so, the world cannot embrace its old future. It has to go forward to a different one. The crisis did not cause that necessity, but revealed it. In this sense, we cannot simply state that the post-crisis malaise is the consequence of the crisis. It would be better to say that it also represents the consequence of the end of the unsustainable processes that caused the crisis. In the next chapter, the discussion will turn to these deeper macroeconomic roots and consequences of the financial crises.

5

How the World Economy Shifted

To think that two and two are four
And neither five nor three
The heart of man has long been sore
And long 'tis like to be.

A. E. Housman[1]

The crisis takes a much longer time coming than you think,
and then it happens much faster than you would have thought.

Rudiger Dornbusch[2]

The financial system of the high-income economies shifted from stability to extreme fragility over the decades before the crisis. Nobody now disagrees about this. The question is why. The answer suggested by Chapter Four is that the instability developed within the financial system itself: the profit-seeking behaviour of people motivated to take certain sorts of risks made the system as a whole enormously more fragile. It is not clear whether they were aware of the risks they were creating. It is plausible that many were not. But that makes no difference. Even if they understood the risks they were taking, they hoped to be able to ride the waves – and some indeed did. Whether the bosses were aware or not, it was hard for any individual institution to stop dancing, as Chuck Prince, former head of Citigroup, suggested.[3] If Prince had tried to stop Citigroup from doing so, he would probably have been sacked in favour of someone who would not. This, then, was the failure of a *system*, not of individuals.

This chapter puts the point in a far wider context. It argues that the failure does not lie only or even mainly within the financial system or with financial regulators. The crisis had wider economic causes – and consequences. This matters because it would have been far more difficult to prevent the crisis than many now suppose. It matters perhaps even more because it means that the world economy cannot go back to the *status quo ante* – to where it was before. That will be the topic of Part III and the Conclusion.

That is not to suggest that a more robust financial system would not have helped: it would have helped a great deal. It would surely have avoided the extreme disruptions of 2008–09. Yet the path the world economy was on before the crisis could not continue.[4] As the late Herbert Stein, former chairman of the Council of Economic Advisers to Richard Nixon, famously remarked – what cannot go on must stop.[5] The challenge is to understand what was unsustainable and then work out how to respond. The purpose of this chapter is to answer the first part of this question. The purpose of the rest of the book is to answer the second.

Nobody doubts the crisis has had macroeconomic consequences, the difference being only over what they are and how long-lasting they will prove to be. But the view that the crisis had macroeconomic roots is controversial. Michael Dooley of the University of California at Santa Cruz and Peter Garber of Deutsche Bank, two of the authors of the influential 'Bretton Woods II' hypothesis (which explained and justified the fixed exchange-rate regimes adopted by many developing countries, notably China, as a sensible way of achieving rapid export-led industrial growth), reject the notion out of hand.[6] They argue that the blame lies 'with ineffective supervision and regulation of financial markets in the U.S. and other industrial countries driven by ill-conceived policy choices'.[7]

This chapter will argue, in opposition to this view, that understanding the underlying economics of the crisis is crucial. It notes, however, that those who agree on this advance two distinct views on what those macroeconomic roots were: savings glut and credit glut. These alternatives partly reflect different perspectives on how the economy works, differences that the crisis has brought out into the open. I will argue that the views are not as contradictory as many suppose. Indeed they share common roots in a series of profound and interconnected transformations of the world economy since around 1980.

THE SHIFT INTO THE GLOBAL SAVINGS SURFEIT

Ben Bernanke, when still a mere governor of the Federal Reserve, laid out the savings-glut hypothesis in a speech he gave in 2005. In this he stated that 'Over the past decade a combination of diverse forces has created a significant increase in the global supply of saving – a global savings glut – which helps to explain both the increase in the U.S. current-account deficit and the relatively low level of long-term real interest rates in the world today.'[8] Michael Pettis of Peking University has written an excellent book that elaborates this hypothesis: 'For almost any serious student of financial and economic history, what has happened in the past few years as the world adjusts to deep imbalances is neither unprecedented nor should even have been unexpected. The global crisis is a financial crisis driven primarily by global trade and capital imbalances, and it has unfolded in almost a text-book fashion.'[9]

In his speech, Mr Bernanke laid out three contributions to this savings glut. The first was the ageing of the high-income countries. But, he noted, that was a long-run condition, which had not changed in the recent past. The second was the then recent rise in oil prices, due to a combination of strong growth in demand, notably from China and other fast-growing emerging economies, and stagnant supply, partly because close to two precious decades of low prices had undermined the incentive to invest in exploration and the development of new capacity. These higher prices greatly increased the surplus savings of oil exporters, at least in the medium term. The third and most important reason for the emerging savings glut was the reaction of emerging countries to the financial crises of the 1990s. In particular, they engineered surplus savings, as we saw in Chapter Three, to reduce their vulnerability to what they had learned to view (rightly) as destabilizing private-capital inflows, above all, debt-creating flows.

As a matter of definition, observed savings must equal observed investment. So how does one identify a savings glut? Indeed, why should one call it a savings glut, rather than an 'investment dearth'? The answer to the second question is that one cannot. It is a matter of interpretation of the evidence. Often, it is more sensible to talk of an investment dearth than a savings glut. The answer to the first question is that one cannot identify the savings glut or the investment dearth directly. It can be observed instead in some combination of the reward for savings – that is, the interest rate – and the level of economic activity – that is, the degree of excess capacity. In brief, if people desire to save (that is, not spend) more than people desire to invest, the economy will adjust in a combination of two ways: via interest rates or via output and incomes. What is desired will not necessarily occur: the way the economy adjusts, to bring desired savings and investment together, will determine the actual outcome. In general, the economy will adjust via prices (the interest rate) if the price can adjust. But in a slump, with interest rates as low as they can go, it will adjust via levels of income and output.

Under the first of these alternatives, the interest adjustment, the supply of savings meets demand from would-be users in the market for 'loanable funds'. When the supply of savings rises, the rate of return falls and vice versa. If the demand from users of funds rises, the rate of return rises and, again, vice versa. The return on savings is the interest rate. Since we are talking here about savings and investment in real terms (that is, without considering inflation), the relevant rate of interest is the real rate (the rate after inflation).

Keynes introduced the second alternative to economic theory – adjustment via the level of output and incomes in a slump when short-term interest rates are zero and long-term rates are as low as they can go, because of 'liquidity preference' – the point at which people prefer to hold cash to bonds because the yield on the latter is too low to make holding them attractive (particularly since there is then a strong likelihood of falling bond prices, when the economy recovers).[10] The immediate impact of higher desired savings, he noted, is then to lower demand and so lower output and incomes. A part of this reduction in incomes will fall on desired consumption and a part will fall on desired savings: so both will shrink. Output and incomes will then go on falling until desired savings again match intended investment. Unhappily, as the economy weakens, desired investment might fall further. In that case the economy could just go on shrinking. A greater desire to save could then well be highly unwelcome, since it may result in a prolonged and deep recession. This is the paradox of thrift.

The standard ways to address the danger of a recession are for the central bank to cut interest rates, and for the government to spend more or cut taxes. A difficulty arises for the first of these solutions, if short-term interest rates are close to zero, as they are at the time of writing (see Figure 29). Note that Japan's central bank has been offering near-zero interest rates since 1995. The other three central banks – the Federal Reserve, the European Central Bank and the Bank of England – have been offering ultra-low interest rates since late 2008 or early 2009. Japan's monetary stimulus did not bring a strong recovery to its debt-laden economy. Much the same has been true of the more recent monetary stimuli offered by the other three central banks in response to the waves of financial crises since 2007.[11] The

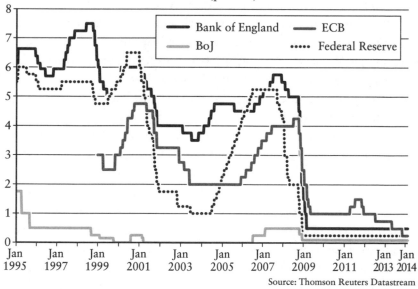

Figure 29. Central Bank Short-term Policy Rates
(per cent)

Source: Thomson Reuters Datastream

alternative policy option is fiscal stimulus. That, as we will see in Chapter Eight, makes good sense if interest rates are close to zero and yet are inducing no strong recovery in demand.

In brief, Mr Bernanke's global savings glut would be visible in a combination of two phenomena: weak economies and/or low interest rates. Today, this combination is precisely what we see in the high-income countries: ultra-low interest rates and recessionary conditions, with high unemployment. A global savings glut is also a condition of chronic excess supply. In a provocative recent book, Daniel Alpert, an investment banker, properly calls the present 'the age of oversupply'.[12]

The ultra-low short-term interest rates are offered by the central banks. Longer-term interest rates on safe bonds are set in the market, in the light of expectations of the short-term rates set by central banks. Expectations of inflation and of the real interest rates needed to achieve economic stability govern these expectations of future short rates. By economic stability I mean a level (and growth) of economic activity consistent with a stable rate of underlying inflation. This (by now standard) definition of stability harks back to the notion of a 'natural rate' of unemployment advanced by Milton Friedman and Edmund (Ned) Phelps in the 1960s, this being the rate of unemployment consistent with stable inflation. As we now also know, economic stability, thus defined, is consistent with substantial financial instability. That is one of the dilemmas addressed by this book.[13] Thus, the simplest indicator of a savings glut in non-recessionary times is not the level of savings or investment. It is the level of interest rates or, more precisely, the level of the real interest rate on what are thought to be the safest assets.[14]

Several important governments, notably including the US and the UK, have been selling index-linked bonds for quite a time (see Figure 30). The yields on these securities provide the most direct measure of real interest rates. In theory, the real interest rate on the liabilities of highly rated governments should be the same in an integrated global capital market. (The only qualification is that a country might have a lower real rate of interest than another if its currency is expected to appreciate in real terms, and vice versa.) Figure 30 shows that since January 2003 the yield on US Treasury index-linked securities (TIPS)

Figure 30. Yields on Index-linked Ten-year Bonds
(per cent)

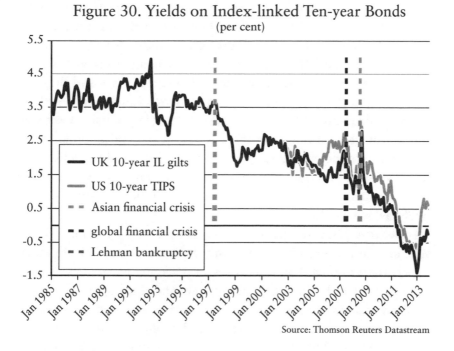

Source: Thomson Reuters Datastream

and UK index-linked gilts have tracked each other closely. This encourages us to accept that the longer-running UK data should offer a reasonable indication of the global real rate of interest without solvency risk.

The data in this Figure fall into three periods: up to July 1997, from July 1997 to August 2007, and from August 2007 until early 2014. In addition, there is a spike centred on October 2008. Thus, up to July 1997, the average yield on UK index-linked gilts was 3.8 per cent. Between July and August 1997, the average yield was 2.1 per cent. After August 2007, the average yield on UK index-linked gilts was 0.4 per cent and on US TIPS 0.9 per cent. During the October 2008 spike, yields briefly reached 2.5 per cent on UK index-linked gilts and 2.8 per cent on TIPS. Subsequently, yields even became negative. Remarkably, real interest rates remained extraordinarily low into early 2014, when recovery seemed well entrenched.

Conventional bonds, for which, naturally, much more complete data exist, show similar movements. Thus, between June 1997 and January 1999, the yield on US conventional ten-year treasuries

declined by 2 percentage points, on German bonds declined by
2.1 percentage points, and on UK bonds declined by 2.8 percentage
points. (The announcement of Bank of England independence in the
middle of 1997 probably explains part of the relatively large UK fall.)
Then, again, between the beginning of September 2008 and the middle of 2012, the yields on the same conventional bonds fell by
2.2 percentage points in the US, 2.6 percentage points in Germany
and 2.8 percentage points in the UK. Thus, the conventional bond
yields fall into the same three periods as the index-linked yields, provided we start in the mid-1990s. Before that, inflation was a bigger
concern and affected conventional bond yields more than index-linked
yields, as one would expect.

So what explains the periods noted above? July 1997 marked the
beginning of the Asian financial crisis, the last and most significant of
a succession of large financial crises in emerging economies. August
2007 marked the beginning of the global financial crisis, which reached
its worst point in October 2008. The picture on real interest rates then
suggests that the Asian crisis nearly halved the equilibrium real interest
rate on safe securities. The yield on UK index-linked securities never
recovered to where it had been pre-July 1997. Then, after August
2007, the yield collapsed again, to close to zero, with a lengthy period
of negative real rates. Finally, during the worst of the crisis, a panic
rush into the most liquid government securities occurred, which generated a short-lived, panic-driven spike in index-linked rates.

It is hard to think of any explanation for these massive shifts in real
rates, other than declines in the equilibrium price of savings in three
successive states of the world economy: buoyant demand for savings,
while emerging economies were willing to be large net importers of
capital up to the late 1990s; weak demand for savings, while emerging economies – those with the best investment opportunities – became
large net exporters of capital in the early 2000s; and collapsed demand
for savings, when high-income economies went into a 'contained
depression' after 2007.[15]

A fall in the global rate of interest will normally lower the real yield on
other long-lived assets and so raise their prices. This is the inevitable
result of arbitrage in the market: as investors shift from lower-yielding
government bonds to higher-yielding alternatives, they drive up the

prices and so lower the yields of the assets they buy. The longest-lived real asset is property. Not surprisingly, therefore, the impact of the fall in real interest rates was to raise the real price of property. That is exactly what happened in three important countries, all of which then experienced house-price booms: the US, the UK and Spain (see Figure 31). Again, not surprisingly, the rise in real house prices began in 1997, or shortly thereafter, as the real interest rate collapsed.

The fall in real interest rates that coincided with the Asian crisis was what Minsky called a 'displacement' event (see Chapter Four above), the trigger for a runaway rise in asset prices and credit. It began a rise in house prices that put in motion exceptionally large credit booms and associated overshoot of the relevant asset prices. The risk of such an overshoot derives from a very simple fact: a decline in real interest rates, which foretells a *fall* in long-run real returns in the economy, will initially *raise* the prices of long-term assets. This confuses people. They start to see the rising prices of assets as a long-term upward trend, instead of what it really is – a one-off adjustment. Furthermore, the rise in prices and subsequent overshoot can only occur in countries

Figure 31. Real House Prices and Real Index-linked Yields

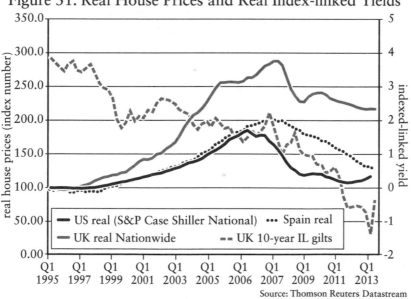

Source: Thomson Reuters Datastream

that allow, or encourage, an expansion in mortgage-related lending, because few people possess the cash to buy properties outright: they need access to elastic credit markets.

Again, because of the nature of property assets, which are traded in small parcels in relatively illiquid markets, the adjustment in prices is relatively slow, compared, say, to the prices of equities. In countries with a relatively elastic supply of building land, such as the US and Spain, rising house prices will then lead to expanding supply and, sooner or later, this will lower prices, once again. In the long term, therefore, the effect of the fall in interest rates is to increase the supply of new housing, not its price. That is indeed what happened in the US and Spain, though it took a decade to get there. So, if the real rate of interest rate falls, the prices of favourably located pieces of land should rise permanently. But the prices of houses on average should not do so. The experience in a country such as the UK, with restricted planning controls on land for house building, should be different. House prices rose more durably there, or so at least it appeared in 2014, because housing has been made artificially scarce. Some argue that the failure to expand housing supply is not because of artificial planning constraints, but because land is absolutely scarce in England. This is a myth. In fact, only 10.6 per cent of England is urban (and that includes urban parks and gardens, which themselves make up 79 per cent of the urban area).[16] It would be easy to expand supply if that were desired.

In the short run, then, a lower real interest rate raises asset prices; in the medium run, it generates credit booms and increased construction; and, in the long run, it leads to house-price collapses and financial stress. In a world of perfectly equilibrating markets with full foresight, none of these excesses would happen. This is *not* our world. In the actual world, as Minsky foretold, they do.[17]

THE SHIFT INTO THE GLOBAL IMBALANCES

At the global level, then, a savings glut would show itself as a fall in the real interest rate. It has done just that. But a global savings glut is unlikely to be evenly distributed across economies. On the contrary, some countries are likely to have big savings surpluses, while other do not, as Bernanke noted. Such country-specific savings surpluses show up in current-account surpluses – surpluses of exports of goods and services over imports of goods and services. Indeed, realized savings surpluses can only show themselves in current-account surpluses, which are identical (but of opposite sign) to a country's net exports of capital. What is striking in this case is that huge increases in global current-account surpluses and deficits did indeed occur in the decade after the Asian crisis, peaking shortly before the global financial crisis (see Figure 32).

Growth of the Global Imbalances

Between 1996, just before the Asian financial crisis, and 2006, these imbalances increased roughly five times relative to world output. Three categories of large net capital exporters emerged: China and

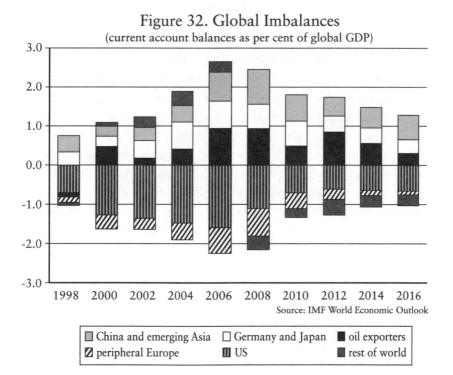

Figure 32. Global Imbalances
(current account balances as per cent of global GDP)

Source: IMF World Economic Outlook

| ▦ China and emerging Asia | ☐ Germany and Japan | ■ oil exporters |
| ▨ peripheral Europe | ▥ US | ■ rest of world |

emerging Asia; ageing high-income, export-oriented economies (Germany and Japan); and the oil exporters (the Gulf countries, Russia, Norway and so forth). There also emerged just two groups of large net capital importers – the US and 'peripheral Europe' – Western, Southern and Eastern Europe. It is no coincidence that the global financial crisis that began in 2007 hit these capital-importing economies hardest. Note the scale of what happened: in 1996 the cumulative current-account surpluses of all countries with surpluses added up to $298bn, of which the top ten countries contributed $228bn. By 2006, the total had risen to $1,527bn, of which the top ten contributed $1,037bn. In 1996 the largest surplus country was Japan, with just $66bn, followed by Italy with $39bn and the Netherlands with $22bn. In 2006 the largest surplus country was China, with $232bn, followed by Germany with $182bn and Japan with $171bn. Current-account balances and so net capital flows (the mirror image of the current-account balances) were transformed.[18]

As Peter Temin of the Massachusetts Institute of Technology and David Vines of Oxford University note in an enlightening book on the macroeconomic origins and consequences of the crisis, the ideal way to think about why this happened is in terms of an economy's internal and external macroeconomic balances.[19] By internal balance, we mean that the economy operates at close to full employment – in modern parlance, at a zero 'output gap', or the position at which underlying inflation is expected to be stable. By external balance, we mean that the economy has a sustainable external position – net trade or net capital flows (these just being two sides of the accounts, since net inflows of capital finance current-account deficits): a sustainable deficit is one that can be financed on affordable terms indefinitely. If the required net inflow of foreign financing is too large, financing will become increasingly expensive and may stop altogether, possibly suddenly. That is what happened to Greece in 2010, as was noted in Chapter Two above. A 'sudden stop' is the consequence of a collective decision by investors that deficits are indeed unsustainable: a stop has the characteristics of a bank run, since the decision by individual investors to withdraw funding is triggered by the perception that others are doing so. 'Sustainability' is, therefore, ultimately a subjective, not an objective, phenomenon. As

Hamlet tells us, 'There is nothing either good or bad, but thinking makes it so.'

Unfortunately and crucially, external sustainability is asymmetrical. It is possible for a country to run a large current-account surplus and so accumulate net claims on the rest of the world virtually without limit. It is usually impossible for a country to accumulate net liabilities in the same way. Sooner or later, its people run out of credit. Indeed, a central element of the Eurozone crisis, as argued in Chapter Two above, was the discovery that this is true even inside a currency union, contrary to the widespread (and foolish) belief that a currency union abolished the need for concern about the balance of payments. But it has not been true for the US (at least not so far). As issuer of the world's main reserve currency, it enjoys exceptionally elastic credit.

To summarize, after the Asian crisis, global macroeconomic balance increasingly coincided with severe divergences between income and spending within significant economies. The same was true inside the Eurozone. But this form of macroeconomic balancing turned out to be fragile, leading ultimately to a global financial crisis.

Drivers of the Global Imbalances

To understand how the global imbalances emerged, let us start with what drove the countries that shifted into surplus. Immediately after the Asian financial crisis of 1997–98, investment fell by about 10 per cent of gross domestic product in the crisis-hit countries – Indonesia, Malaysia, the Philippines, South Korea and Thailand.[20] This was an 'investment dearth'. Elsewhere, however, the phenomenon was more of a savings glut, particularly in Germany and the oil-exporting countries. In Germany, investment was weak, while profits and household savings were high. In the oil-exporting countries, the income from higher prices, which mostly accrued to the government, was almost automatically saved.

China's was a mixed picture: the rise in investment in the 2000s was remarkable, but that in savings even more so.[21] Justin Lin, the Chinese economist who became chief economist of the World Bank, argues that the structure of China's economy explains the extraordinarily high national savings rate, which far exceeded 50 per cent of GDP in 2008. Government and corporate savings account for some 60 per cent of these savings, with households making up the rest. Corporations, in particular, accounted for some 40 per cent of gross national savings. This is because of an array of policies and structural features of the economy that shift income from households to corporations. Professor Lin emphasizes, among these, the virtually non-existent taxation of profits, low royalties on natural resources, the use of the monopolistic state-owned financial sector as a way of taxing savers via low interest rates on deposits, and the monopoly power of financial and telecommunications industries. Yet, as Professor Pettis argues, currency intervention also increases corporate profitability, by keeping the real exchange rate undervalued.[22]

A crucial element in the story was massive intervention in currency markets by governments, mainly of emerging countries. It is possible to distinguish four reasons for this.

The first, particularly relevant to the oil exporters, was accumulation of supposedly high-quality foreign assets, often government bonds. In this case, a government is switching an asset in the ground – oil – for an asset abroad.

The second was pursuit of export-led economic growth – the most successful of all development strategies.[23] The outcome of the Asian financial crisis was to increase the incentive to pursue this strategy, particularly by the Asians themselves.

The third was supporting a high-investment, high-profit, high-savings development strategy. According to Pettis, this strategy, pioneered by Japan, is characterized by: systematically undervalued currencies; relatively low wage growth and so low wage shares in national income; and financial repression 'in which the state allocates credit and the central bank forces interest rates to below their natural or equilibrium rate'.[24] Asian countries needed export surpluses to export the surplus output and surplus savings that were the direct consequence of these strategies. This was particularly true of China, in the 2000s.

The last reason was increasing insurance against financial crises, partly by accumulating foreign-currency reserves and partly by reducing dependence on net inflows of fickle foreign finance. Many emerging countries had learned, painfully, that large net imports of financial capital were likely to drive property bubbles and irresponsible lending, at great cost to their people. They had also learned that in such a crisis they would receive inadequate help from the outside world and, worse, be subject to humiliating demands. Many then decided to 'smoke' in global financial markets, but not 'inhale'. A better alternative was to recycle the capital inflow out again as foreign-currency reserves.[25] The Chinese authorities, aware of past humiliations, surely felt this particularly keenly. Under no circumstances would they allow their country to become the plaything of international bureaucrats or US officials. The failure of the Western financial system to transfer resources into emerging countries in a responsible and sensible way in the 1970s, 1980s and 1990s led to blowback: once upon a time, the financial institutions of high-income countries exported crises; more recently, they have imported them.

Emerging economies are not the only ones to have pursued savings- and export-surplus growth strategies. Germany and Japan have done the same thing for much of the period since the Second World War. Professor Rajan describes the results as follows: 'So long as large countries like Germany and Japan are structurally inclined – indeed required – to export, global supply washes around the world looking for countries that have the weakest policies or the least discipline, tempting them to spend until they simply cannot afford it and succumb to crisis.'[26] Why these countries have ended up with structural savings surpluses and a concomitant tendency towards running substantial current-account surpluses is unclear. It may be that they put greater weight on production than on consumption. It may be that they see a need to reduce risks by becoming net creditors, as has also been true of China. It may be that they see success in export markets as a triumph in a form of peaceful economic warfare. It may be that the export-driven growth after the Second World War shaped their subsequent economic structures. In the German case, it may be because of a resolute rejection of demand management and so a need to rely on changes in net exports as a way to balance demand and supply (as explained in Chapter Two). In fact, the outcome has probably been shaped by all these things. It is no doubt also because of the ageing of societies. But that is not a sufficient explanation. Note that many ageing societies do not run large current-account surpluses (consider Italy, for example) and that Germany ran sizeable current-account surpluses before ageing had really set in (prior to German unification).

In the case of Japan, a floating exchange rate makes this policy more difficult to sustain than for Germany (as we will see later in this chapter), at least since the latter became part of the Eurozone. That is why Japan has periodically felt obliged to keep the yen down by accumulating foreign-currency reserves.[27] The aggressive monetary policies of Abenomics, introduced under Prime Minister Shinzo Abe, may also be an attempt to restore lost growth by improving external competitiveness: between November 2012 (that is, just before he became prime minister for the second time) and July 2013, the JP Morgan broad trade-weighted real exchange rate of the yen fell by 17 per cent.

We can only understand the challenges for US policymakers after 1997, particularly for the Federal Reserve, in the light of what was happening elsewhere. Their job, mandated in law, was (and is) to stabilize inflation and keep unemployment low in the US. We may define this combination as internal balance. Between 1997 and 2000, the stock-market bubble did a good job of sustaining demand without any need for heroic monetary policy (see Figure 29). But the bubble then burst. The Fed found itself confronting a much weaker economy. It slashed interest rates. Then came another shock – the terrorist attack of 11 September 2001. The recovery was weak. Worry grew that the US might fall into Japan's deflationary malaise. Mr Bernanke defined this concern, too, in an influential speech delivered in November 2002, entitled, tellingly, 'Deflation: Making Sure "It" Doesn't Happen Here'.[28]

The Federal Reserve's intervention rate was reduced to 1 per cent. The aim was to achieve internal balance and, for a time, the policy did just that. But then the policy blew up in the central-bank's face. It did so because the monetary policy worked by generating what turned into unsustainable rises in four areas: house prices; debt, particularly household debt; the financial deficit (the excess of spending over income) of the household sector; and financial-sector leverage.

Now consider the US external balance. In 2001 and 2002 the US current-account deficit (the balance of trade on goods and non-factor services) reached 3.7 per cent and 4.2 per cent of GDP, respectively, even though the economy was still in recession. This was far higher than it had been in 1997, at just 1.6 per cent of GDP. By 2006, this had reached 5.8 per cent of GDP, with the US deficit alone offsetting 60 per cent of the cumulative surpluses of the regions shown in Figure 32. The US had been a net source of demand for the world economy ever since the Asian crisis. But the combination of a recession in the early 2000s with a huge current-account deficit suggests (particularly in a rich country, which one would have expected to be a net exporter of capital, not an importer) that the real exchange rate – the price of non-tradeables (goods and services that cannot be easily sold internationally) relative to tradeables (goods and services that can be easily sold internationally) – was significantly overvalued. In other words, the incentive to produce tradeables was too weak, relative to the incentive to produce non-tradeables. That is what an overvaluation of the real exchange rate means. A big real depreciation would have helped stimulate the economy, via a rise in exports and a reduction in imports. That would have reduced the need to adopt such aggressive monetary policies. The Federal Reserve would presumably then have adopted a tighter monetary policy, which would have at least reduced the housing and credit bubbles. Given the fiscal policy of the administration of George W. Bush – unfunded tax cuts, unfunded health benefits and unfunded wars – the Fed's concern might even have been overheating, not the reverse.

Unfortunately, the US has little direct influence on the value of the US dollar, because of the currency's role as a reserve asset. Outsiders complain that this role of the US dollar is an 'exorbitant privilege' – a phrase first used by then French finance minister, Valéry Giscard d'Estaing, in the 1960s. Professor Pettis complains that it is, on the contrary, an exorbitant burden, because it deprives the US of control over its exchange rate and so forces it to 'import unemployment' from its trading partners, at their whim.[29]

It is easy to see the restricted downward flexibility of the dollar: as a result of their interventions, governments elsewhere, overwhelmingly in emerging countries, accumulated roughly $9.5tn in foreign-currency reserves between the beginning of 2000 and early 2013. Meanwhile, the cumulative current-account deficit of the US was $7.1tn between 2000 and 2012. Moreover, in the first quarter of 2013, 62 per cent of the world's foreign-currency reserves whose composition is published by the IMF were held in US dollars. If the same ratio held for all foreign-currency reserves, holdings by foreign governments of assets denominated in US dollars would have been around $6.9tn in early 2013. That would have made those holdings nearly as big as the accumulated US current-account deficit between 2000 and 2012.[30] In brief, governments were intervening massively to keep their currencies down against the US dollar and so financing the US deficit.

Because the dollar was too strong, US output of tradeable goods and services was relatively unprofitable and such output grew weakly. The Federal Reserve offset this drag on output and employment (and so inflation) by pursuing a more aggressive monetary policy. As domestic demand for both non-tradeables and tradeables expanded, a huge excess demand for tradeables emerged. The expansion of production abroad, notably in China, satisfied this excess demand, so generating huge trade and current-account deficits. Meanwhile demand and supply for non-tradeables returned to balance, producing the full employment the Federal Reserve was seeking. In this way, internal balance – full employment – was achieved, albeit temporarily, at the price of a huge external imbalance – excess demand for tradeables and so trade and current-account deficits.

The global market for the US dollar is rigged. It is one in which governments are prepared to buy massively, to prevent prices from reaching natural market clearing levels. We do not know how much lower the dollar would have been if there had been no such intervention, but surely it would have been substantially weaker and US monetary policy would have consequently needed to be less expansionary. As Pettis puts it, 'Excessive use of the US dollar internationally actually forces up either American debt or American unemployment.'[31]

Inevitably, the Fed chose debt over unemployment. Indeed, it is mandated to do so, because its task is to sustain the highest level of employment consistent with price stability (or, more precisely, stable and low inflation). Since the US has no exchange-rate policy and has been able to borrow freely in its own currency, and since, in addition, countries that target exchange rates usually do so against the dollar, the Federal Reserve has emerged automatically as the world's macro-economic balancer and the US economy as the one within which global balancing takes place. The Federal Reserve effectively is the world's central bank, because it issues the closest thing it has to a world currency. This is a role it has played, for better or worse, since the First World War.[32]

Meanwhile, the countries intervening in foreign-exchange markets and exporting savings had to stabilize their own economies. Among other things, this meant ensuring that the consequences of export surpluses, including the monetary results of the currency interventions, were offset or sterilized, to avoid chronic excess demand. Thus, when a foreign central bank buys dollars at a pre-determined exchange rate, it creates domestic currency, which it hands over in return for the holdings of foreign currency. This newly created domestic-base money is deposited in domestic banks, which then hold a claim on the central bank and a liability to their domestic customer. The central bank will then normally seek to contain the presumed effects on its overall domestic money supply of this expansion in the monetary base. It can do so by selling non-monetary debt instruments into the market, so withdrawing the monetary base (this being 'sterilization'), or by raising the reserve requirements of commercial banks (this being a way of offsetting the monetary effects of expansion of the monetary base).

With the US blocked from achieving external balance by policies adopted elsewhere in the late 1990s and first decade of the 2000s, its monetary policy was trying to fill a leaky bucket, because a substantial part of its domestic demand was exported abroad. In 2006, a year in which the economy was operating with a modestly positive output gap (that is, slightly over full capacity), aggregate domestic demand exceeded gross domestic product by nearly 6 per cent (that is, by the amount of the current-account deficit). This is because the difference between aggregate domestic demand and output is the current-account deficit, by definition: it is a consequence of national-income accounting. The logic is clear: if residents of a country spend more than they produce, the additional output they demand must be supplied from abroad: that is, imports must then exceed exports sufficient to offset the shortfall in output relative to demand. Thus, to turn this point around, if domestic output is to be sufficient to generate full utilization of capacity, aggregate demand must exceed domestic output by the size of the current-account deficit, at full employment. That was the challenge the Federal Reserve had to meet.

What made the challenge far more difficult is that the sector of the domestic economy best equipped to spend more than its income or, more precisely, invest more than its savings, is the corporate sector. It did just that at the peak of the stock-market bubble in the late 1990s: indeed its financial deficit, thus defined, reached 4 per cent of GDP. But from 2000 to the crisis of 2008, the business sector was in rough balance, despite the easy monetary policy (see Figure 33).[33] This is largely because gross business investment peaked at 13.6 per cent of GDP in the second quarter of 2000, as the stock-market bubble burst. It then fell to 10.1 per cent of GDP in the second quarter of 2003, before rising modestly to 11.8 per cent in the second quarter of 2007, as the economy recovered, just before the global financial crisis. It then collapsed, in response to the crisis and subsequent deep recession, reaching a nadir of 7.5 per cent of GDP in the third quarter of 2009. Since profitability remained consistently strong, the business sector ended up running a financial surplus after 2000, except briefly between late 2006 and late 2008. This was a big part of the savings glut. This left households and the government to run the deficits. In 2006 both were running financial deficits of around 3 per cent of GDP. President Bush bore substantial direct responsibility for turning the fiscal surpluses achieved by Bill Clinton into deficits – that is what his tax cuts and unfunded wars did; Mr Greenspan bore substantial indirect responsibility for stimulating household financial deficits – that is how his monetary policy worked.

Persuading the household sector to spend consistently more than its income is quite hard. The US household sector has almost always been a net provider of savings to the rest of the economy: that is, it has saved more than it invested in residential housing or durables. Now it had to play the opposite role. The way to achieve this rare outcome of a large household financial deficit was via a rise in house prices, which lowered household savings, and a residential construction boom, which raised household investment. Neither would have been possible without exceptionally easy credit.

Figure 33. US Financial Balances since 2000
(per cent of global)

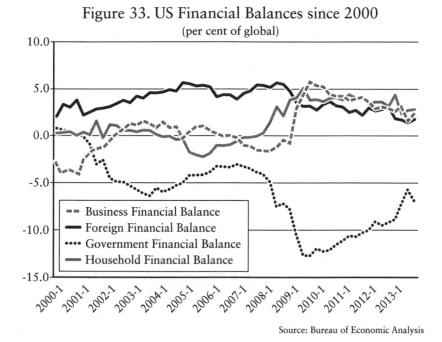

Source: Bureau of Economic Analysis

What makes this shift of the US household sector into such a large financial deficit even more remarkable was the massive increase in inequality among households. Other things being equal, one would have expected this to raise the overall savings rate of households, not lower it, because the rich tend to save more of their incomes.[34] As Raghuram Rajan notes, 'Of every dollar of real income growth that was generated between 1976 and 2007, 58 cents went to the top 1 per cent of households.'[35] The Congressional Budget Office reports that:

The share of income [after taxes] received by the top 1 percent grew from about 8 percent in 1979 to over 17 percent in 2007. The share received by other households in the highest income quintile was fairly flat over the same period, edging up from 35 percent to 36 percent. In contrast, the share of after-tax income received by the 60 percent of the population in the three middle-income quintiles fell by 7 percentage points between 1979 and 2007, from 50 percent to 43 percent of total after-tax household income, and the share of after-tax income accruing to the lowest-income quintile decreased from 7 percent to 5 percent.[36]

It is astonishing that such a huge increase in inequality did not lead to a higher household savings rate, rather than a lower one. The only plausible explanation is the ready availability of credit. This brings us to the underlying forces creating the global savings surplus and the emerging imbalances.

SAVINGS AND CREDIT

The savings-glut hypothesis is not the only explanation offered for the crisis. As Claudio Borio of the Bank for International Settlements argues, the rise in gross leverage and gross cross-border flows vastly exceeded net flows from surplus to deficit countries.[37] When the crisis hit, it was the size of gross balance sheets that determined how badly an individual country was hit. Borio notes, in addition, that the expansion in gross leverage (see, for example, Figure 5 for the US) was overwhelmingly inside high-income countries. Moreover, gross-capital flows across frontiers (the sum of inflows and outflows of direct, portfolio and other investments) vastly exceeded the net flows shown in Figure 32, rising from about 10 per cent of world GDP in 2002, to over 30 per cent of world GDP in 2007. Virtually all of these gross flows were among the high-income countries, because that is where all the main global financial centres are located. Thereupon, not surprisingly, the flows collapsed.[38]

The link between the (net) flows of financing, which are the mirror image of current-account deficits, and the rise in the gross flows and indeed in overall leverage, is that adoption of a monetary policy aimed at achieving internal balance, despite huge external imbalances, necessitated great excesses: large rises in house prices, excessive construction, huge increases in debt, and a massive increase in the size, profitability and leverage of the financial sector. Indeed, as Adair Turner has noted, the main activity of today's financial system is facilitating the purchase of *existing* assets, not the creation of new ones or even the direct funding of consumption.[39] But it is only the latter forms of lending and spending that directly determine actual demand in the economy. So a huge ratio of gross to net lending and a correspondingly huge increase in gross debt is inherent in what the financial system actually does. It has to generate a massive amount of leverage in the economy, directed at the purchase of ever more expensive existing assets, before it produces the internal balance the policymakers are seeking. Moreover, as noted in Chapter Four, within the brave new global financial system, these excesses were exported across the world: the export of toxic securitized assets and of unstable wholesale financing are two examples.

The irony is that policies aimed at achieving internal balance ultimately generated yet greater internal imbalances. That is the lesson for today, when the effort made by central banks to generate internal balance is even bigger and made against even greater economic headwinds. Indeed, in retrospect it would probably have been better if the needed additional demand had been generated via even larger fiscal deficits in the US and other external deficit countries rather than via the huge private deficits generated by aggressive monetary policy.

There are two aspects to the way in which these policies resulted in even bigger disequilibria than those to which monetary policymakers initially responded in the early 2000s. The first concerns the scale of the leverage created by the credit boom. The second concerns the finer structure of balance sheets.

The first of these is straightforward. Interest rates were set to achieve internal balance in the US, given external imbalances, themselves largely determined by economic structures and policies adopted elsewhere. Since the external imbalances were large – indeed, in some ways, extraordinarily so – the policymakers needed to launch credit expansions sufficient to sustain spending in the household sector. As shown by the increase in gross debt, those credit expansions were huge, for the reasons discussed by Turner. A huge stock of gross debt means that some Americans owe a great deal to other Americans. When the asset prices that back such debt collapse and the economy shrinks, a chain of bankruptcies threatens the economy, including large parts of the financial sector. Such a 'balance-sheet recession' is the biggest danger consequent upon a huge credit boom.[40]

The second aspect concerns the structure of balance sheets. Overall demand for high-grade assets – particularly investment-grade bonds – exceeded the supply in the years preceding the crisis, driving prices up and yields down. This was partly because of those huge current-account surpluses, foreign-currency interventions and consequent demands for safe assets. Many investors – particularly those concerned with providing incomes in retirement, such as pension funds – needed higher returns than government bonds provided, while stocks looked less attractive after the collapse of the market in 2000. The market's response was to mass-produce higher-yielding, pseudo-high-grade assets. In an inversion of Joseph Schumpeter's idea of 'creative destruction', Jagdish Bhagwati of Columbia University called this 'destructive creation'.[41] It was the new structured finance that provided investors with what they thought they wanted. As Lloyd Blankfein, chairman of Goldman Sachs, pointed out in 2009: 'In January 2008, there were 12 triple A-rated companies in the world. At the same time, there were 64,000 structured finance instruments . . . rated triple A.'[42] In short, what the market demanded the innovative financial sector duly supplied. Never can there have been a better example of the need to be careful about what one wishes for.

The best analysis of how the nature of demand for financial assets generated risk within the financial system is by Anton Brender and Florence Pisani of Paris Dauphine.[43] In essence, they argue, foreign governments accumulated assets on which they took the foreign-currency risk. But, so far as they could, they took no other risks. They were looking for riskless assets. In essence, the financial system had to convert foreign lending that would not take credit risk into financing of risky domestic assets. In doing so the system itself accumulated a great deal of risk. But it did so by creating instruments so opaque that they were perfectly designed to conceal that risk – from the point of view of almost every player.

Those who were worried about the consequences of these credit booms were correct. Something both big and bad happened to balance sheets: debt exploded relative to incomes; assets became increasingly leveraged; and the financial sector grew hugely. In the process, the financial sector itself became more unbalanced, with more leverage, more reliance on short-term wholesale funding, and more complexity, irresponsibility and dishonesty. It is easy to argue that all this was the immediate consequence of excessively easy monetary and regulatory policies. The question is why such policies were adopted. The answer is that they were the way to sustain demand in an economy suffering from demand-deficiency syndrome. It is what central banks were told to do. And they did it.

CREDIT BUBBLES AND MONETARY POLICY

The argument here then is that the global savings glut and associated imbalances drove the policies of the monetary and, to a lesser degree, financial sector that created the credit glut. Many object that the causality was the other way round, from irresponsibly loose monetary policy to financial fragility. Among the people who have argued for this position, albeit in different ways, have been Andrew Smithers of London-based Smithers & Co. and his co-author, Stephen Wright of Cambridge University, Claudio Borio of the Bank for International Settlements in Basel and his erstwhile colleague William White, former chief economist of the BIS, and Richard Duncan, a well-known market economist.[44] These analysts were prescient about the looming disaster. Also highly critical, in post-crisis writing, has been John Taylor of Stanford University, inventor of the eponymous 'Taylor Rule', which states that central banks should determine interest rates in response to divergences of actual inflation from target inflation and of actual GDP from full-capacity (or potential) GDP.[45] Claudio Borio has argued more recently that the crisis is the consequence of excessive expansion in credit due to mistaken monetary policies.[46] Justin Lin argues, on similar lines, that US monetary irresponsibility explains what has happened.[47]

The arguments can be put into two groups. The first contains arguments that no savings glut existed and that the global imbalances were solely the consequence of mistaken monetary policies in the high-income countries, above all the US. The second contains arguments that monetary policy was too loose, whether or not there was such a savings glut: Mr Bernanke may have had the right analysis, but the Fed's was the wrong response, made worse by the failure to regulate the financial system.

On the question of whether a savings glut existed (indeed still exists), the answer has to be that it did: it can be seen in post-1997 real interest rates and in huge and growing net exports of savings from a range of surplus countries. Even Lin, who is especially critical of US policy and particularly concerned to defend Chinese policy, does not deny this. Not only does he discuss the roots of China's extraordinarily high savings, but his idea of 'a massive global infrastructure initiative' is a way of absorbing what he clearly recognizes as global excess savings.[48]

Mr Duncan does argue that no savings glut has ever existed. He insists, instead, that 'most of the money those countries [East Asian surplus countries] invest in the United States is not derived from savings. The money those countries invest is newly created fiat (state-created) money. When the PBOC [People's Bank of China] created $460bn worth of yuan in 2007 to manipulate its currency by buying dollars, that $460bn worth of yuan was not "saved", it was created from thin air as part of government policy designed to hold down the value of its currency so as to perpetuate China's low-wage trade advantage.'[49]

This is wrong. If a Chinese business sells exports for dollars, it has earned an income. Instead of selling its dollars to other private individuals, the firm sells them to the PBOC at the price set by the PBOC in return for newly created money. The Chinese firm may either hold or spend the yuan it receives. Throughout, its transactions enter into the normal cycle of income and spending. Yes, it is true that the Chinese money supply has risen. But a rise in the money supply is not an increase in income. It is a rise in the stock of a particular asset, which may affect income. Through its sterilization policies the PBOC does, in fact, seek to contain those effects. Mr Duncan confuses money with income.

An opposite argument is that monetary policy needed to be considerably tighter, whatever the global context. Professor Taylor, for example, argues that a tighter monetary policy between late 2001 and early 2005 would have prevented the boom and bust in housing starts.[50] But this proposition raises at least three important questions.

A first question is how far such a tighter monetary policy would have weakened the economy and so undermined the ability of the central bank to meet its explicit or implicit inflation target. In particular, Professor Taylor and others who argue on similar lines fail to recognize how far the external environment compromised the ability of the Federal Reserve to achieve its mandate. One can find an optimistic response to this line of argument. If the Federal Reserve had not pursued a policy likely to expand US demand in the way it did, the emerging countries would still have faced the challenge they did in 2008, but a few years sooner: either expand domestic demand or accept a sharp slowdown. They might then have pursued more expansionary fiscal and monetary policies than they did, instead of relying on the US as spender of last resort. If that had happened, they would not have accumulated so many reserves and they would have ended up with far weaker macroeconomic fundamentals than those on which they now pride themselves (see Chapter Three). China, in particular, might have faced problems with excess domestic credit far sooner. Would such a world have been a better alternative? Possibly so, but that is true largely in the light of hindsight. The sheer scale of the crisis to come was unknown in the early 2000s.

A second question is how much tighter monetary policy would have had to be, given the rate of house-price inflation from the late 1990s to the middle of the first decade of the 2000s. If house prices are rising at, say, 10 per cent a year, one needs a very high interest rate indeed to persuade people not to seek to buy. Indeed, the Bank of England had substantially higher interest rates than the US (see Figure 29). It is hard to believe US rates could have been higher than UK ones. Professor Taylor certainly does not suggest that was appropriate. Yet the UK experienced even faster rises in house prices than the US. This suggests that a plausibly tighter monetary policy might not have made as much difference to asset-price inflation as many hope, given the environment of low long-term real interest rates. Of course, a monetary policy tight enough to cause a big recession might have done the trick on house-price inflation. But there was no chance that central banks would have got away with such a policy in the absence of general inflationary pressure. It would have violated their explicit mandates. Anybody who argues for such a policy is, in essence, arguing for a different monetary regime.

The final question is how far it is possible to live with a financial system capable of imploding in response to what was no more than a modest policy mistake, given the obvious reasons for loose monetary policy after the implosion of the stock-market bubble in 2000 and the terrorist attacks on the US of 11 September 2001. That is perhaps the biggest question of all, to which I will turn in Part III.

For all these reasons, the argument that what was needed was a tighter monetary policy does not get us far. The question is how much tighter and with what consequences. In essence, critics of monetary policy in the early 2000s and again today are suggesting that fine-tuning the economy via monetary policy risks dangerous unintended consequence.[51] This is correct. But, in a savings-glut world, not using monetary policy also has risks and costs.

THE EUROZONE FINANCIAL CRISIS

In the above discussion, I have focused on the US as much the biggest and most important economy directly affected by the global financial crisis. The UK was affected so heavily in large part because London and the UK banking system were deeply enmeshed in the US-centric financial system. Particularly important was the role of wholesale markets as sources of finance for the soaring mortgage lending of UK financial institutions, and the role of a number of the big UK banks in global finance. But the Eurozone is a distinct story. There, too, many institutions and markets were heavily involved in the activities that led to the global financial crisis, not least as active participants in US financial markets and as buyers of toxic US securitized assets. But the Eurozone was also in a crisis of its own making, one that can be best viewed as a by-product of external imbalances in the context of fixed exchange rates – in this case, indeed, the ultimate fixed exchange-rate regime, namely, a currency union. The Eurozone has turned out to be a dreadful monetary marriage. While some are still trying to join, quite a few must be regretting their entry. But nobody can see a way to an easy divorce.

As I have noted in Chapter Two, the conventional wisdom inside the European Union is that the blame lies with irresponsible borrowers, mostly public, but also private, and so with the governments of the directly affected countries – Greece, Ireland, Italy, Portugal and Spain. This view is wrong. As the quote from A. E. Housman reminds

us, 'two and two are four', however much we might like it to be otherwise. And so it must also be the case that one country's exports are
other countries' imports, one country's current-account surpluses are
other countries' current-account deficits, and one country's capital
exports are other countries' capital imports. This being so, the logic of
external and internal balances can, again, be applied in the Eurozone.
Once we do that, it becomes obvious that the biggest challenge has
been created not by excess demand on the periphery, but chronically
deficient demand at the core. The problem, in brief, is Germany and –
to a far lesser degree, because they are so much smaller – other creditor
countries inside the Eurozone. Why this is so is the theme of this section. What to do about it is the theme of the Conclusion.

The Eurozone is a large multinational economy – the second biggest economy in the world, after the US. In 2012, for example,
Eurozone GDP, at market prices, was a little short of 80 per cent of
that of the US. The Eurozone also has a floating fiat currency that no
other important country targets (unlike the US dollar). It is reasonable therefore to assume that the external balance is market
determined. Moreover, as it happens, since the creation of the Eurozone the external current-account surplus has been a small share of
GDP: internal imbalances have been far more significant than external
ones, at least until after the crisis (see Figure 34). Two are particularly
striking, because they are mirror images of each other: the massive
swing of Germany into a current-account surplus and Greece, Ireland,
Italy, Portugal and Spain (GIIPS) into a matching deficit from the
beginning of the 2000s. Was this an accident? Hardly.

What happened? In essence, three things that, in many ways, parallel what happened on the global level, but with one vital difference. At
the global level, the debtor – the US – is more powerful than the creditors; in the Eurozone, the creditor – Germany – is more powerful
than the debtors. American creditors cannot force adjustment via
deflation on the US, however much they would like to do so. Germany can, however, force deflationary adjustment on Eurozone
debtors, so long as they remain inside the Eurozone. The reason for
this difference is simple: Germany (more or less) controls the relevant
central bank; China does not.

The first of the three things that happened was a massive shift

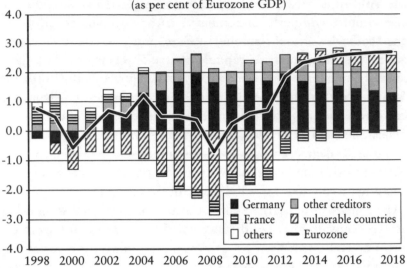

Figure 34. Eurozone Imbalances on Current Account
(as per cent of Eurozone GDP)

Source: IMF World Economic Outlook Database

by Germany towards external imbalance, in the form of a current-account surplus. Figure 35 makes the point in a simple way. During the 1990s, after reunification, Germany ran what were, by its standards, uncomfortably high fiscal deficits. By the end of the decade, the desire to tighten government finances had become strong as the post-unification infrastructure spending in the old East Germany came to an end. Moreover, for much of this decade, Germany even ran a (decidedly modest) current-account deficit (net inflow of foreign capital), which it also found uncomfortable. The fiscal deficit and the current-account deficit were linked, of course: they were both the result of the costs of unification.

So how was the country to eliminate its fiscal deficit and restore its traditional and 'virtuous' current-account surplus? The answer can be viewed in two ways that are two sides of one coin. The first side lies in the economy's macroeconomic balances: run a large private-sector financial surplus (excess of private savings over investment) matched by a current-account surplus, to absorb the excess private savings. German policymakers did not do so deliberately: it just happened. The other side of the coin, which they did think about, was improved competitiveness: keep the rise in wages down to a negligible level, thereby ensuring that real wages grew more slowly than productivity. This would, over time, make Germany's traditionally strong manufacturing export sector even more competitive. It would also raise the share of profits and so corporate savings in GDP. The reforms of the labour market introduced under the government of Gerhard Schröder in the early 2000s, known as the Hartz reforms, after Peter Hartz, chairman of the Commission that recommended them in 2002, certainly helped achieve these aims.

Professor Pettis describes the policies adopted as follows: 'The high German savings rate ... had very little to do with whether Germans were ethnically or culturally programmed to save – contrary to the prevailing cultural stereotype. It was largely the consequence of policies aimed at generating rapid employment growth by restraining German consumption in order to subsidise German manufacturing – usually at the expense of manufacturers elsewhere in Europe and the world.'[52] These were 'beggar-my-neighbour' policies and they achieved just that: they beggared Germany's neighbours.

Now turn to the second thing that happened: financial integration.

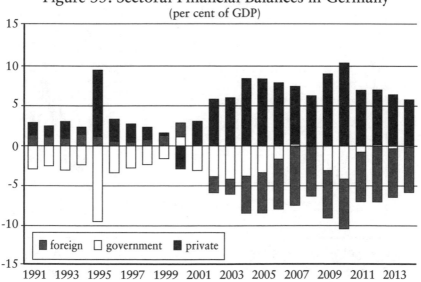

Figure 35. Sectoral Financial Balances in Germany
(per cent of GDP)

Source: IMF World Economic Outlook Database

In the mid-1990s spreads between yields on Italian and Spanish government bonds and those on German bunds were around five or six percentage points (see Figure 36). These spreads disappeared quite soon after the launch of the euro – until the crisis hit. (See Figures 6 and 7 for what happened from the middle of the last decade.) Effectively, investors ceased to apply any notion of country risk. People enjoyed the borrowing opportunities of a lifetime. With the exception of Greece, those who took advantage of these opportunities were overwhelmingly in the private sector.

The third and last thing to happen was that the European Central Bank pursued a monetary policy designed to stabilize the rate of inflation in the Eurozone as a whole. That, after all, was its mandate. With demand in Germany weak, the only way to achieve this was by expanding demand elsewhere. That then occurred in countries where the exceptionally low interest rates granted by euro entry would drive a huge credit boom. Of these countries, much the most important turned out to be Spain.

The burgeoning surplus of production over demand in 'creditor

Figure 36. Spread on Government 10-year Bond Yields over Bunds
(percentage points)

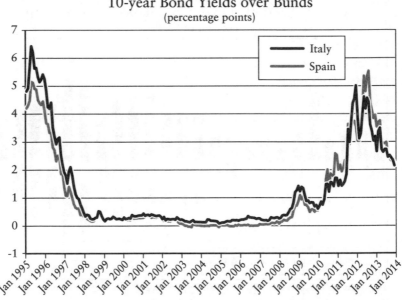

Source: Thomson Reuters Datastream

Eurozone' was perfectly matched by the burgeoning surplus of demand over production in 'debtor Eurozone'. The burgeoning surplus of output of tradeable goods, relative to domestic demand, in creditor Eurozone was matched by a burgeoning deficiency in output, relative to demand, in debtor Eurozone. The surplus of savings over investment in creditor Eurozone was matched by the surplus of investment over savings in debtor Eurozone. And, last but not least, the boom in investment in debtor Eurozone took the form of investment in non-tradeable goods and services, notably property-related investments, because the most competitive suppliers of tradeable goods in the domestic market were those in creditor Eurozone. Symptoms of these divergences included the crucial divergence in inflation and relative unit labour costs discussed in Chapter Two. The balance sheets of borrowers, including financial institutions, located in debtor Eurozone became ever more stretched, as those in creditor Eurozone apparently became ever more solid. But this is, in part, an illusion. Thus, the question raised of the global system is just as relevant within the Eurozone: where did the risks lie in the event of a reversal in willingness to lend?

How could debtor countries have better responded to the policies of the creditor Eurozone and the ECB? They had four options: accept the imbalances described above, through either higher investment or lower savings, and just hope for the best (the policy they actually adopted); accept the imbalances, but seek to offset the greatest danger by thwarting any significant increase in leverage within their own financial system (which the Spanish central bank sought to do through 'dynamic provisioning' inside the banking system); tighten fiscal policy sufficiently to reverse the market's effort to generate a huge current-account deficit (tried to a limited extent by Ireland and Spain); or, finally, impose controls on imports of capital or of goods and services (precluded by the rules of membership of the EU, not just of the Eurozone).

The idea that debtor Europe had some simple way of avoiding the disaster is a fantasy. With the Eurozone in internal and external balance and creditor Eurozone seeking internal balance via ever-larger external imbalances in the form of current-account surpluses, debtor Eurozone could only attain internal balance with ever-larger external imbalances in the form of current-account deficits. Debtor Eurozone had to choose between unemployment and debt. In practice, it chose the debt first and got unemployment afterwards, when the crisis washed away the debt path.

To regard the behaviour of the creditor countries as axiomatically prudent and that of the debtor countries as axiomatically profligate is asinine. After all, the borrowing would have been impossible without the lending. It is stupid to finance profligacy and then complain about the consequences of one's own choices. Yes, the Greeks should have paid their taxes and run their government more responsibly. But the fact that they behaved in this way was really no secret. *Caveat creditor* – let the lender beware – is a good motto. The result of the imprudence of both lenders and borrowers is a rolling crisis, characterized by prolonged recessions and resentments in debtor Eurozone and exasperation in creditor Eurozone. The result that we also see is a profound set of political and policy challenges.

UNDERLYING DRIVERS OF THE GLOBAL SHIFTS

The emergence of the global savings surfeit and associated global and Eurozone imbalances were huge events for the global economy. So, too, was the failure of investment in the high-income capital-importing countries, particularly the US, to employ productively the surplus funds imported from the outside world. Instead, the resources were wasted in building unneeded and unaffordable houses or in fiscal deficits caused by unfunded wars, unfunded entitlement spending and unfunded tax cuts. The capital imported by the US, in particular, was wasted on a colossal scale.

What were the deeper forces behind these huge shifts in global patterns of saving, investment and capital flows? The answer is to be found in three transformations.

The first was the shift towards economic liberalization – the embrace of the market as the organizing principle in economic life, already discussed in Chapter Four. Back in the 1970s, the high-income economies mostly still had extensive regulations on product markets and even employed direct controls on wages and prices, either permanently or temporarily. Marginal tax rates on high incomes were above 70 per cent in both the US and the UK.[53] While the high-income countries had substantially liberalized trade in goods in the 1950s, 1960s and 1970s, trade in services was still highly restricted and most countries retained foreign-exchange controls. In developing economies, controls over markets were far more extensive. Many economies also had high levels of public ownership of industry. In India, the economy was constrained by what had come to be known as the 'licence raj'. In the socialist economies of China, the Soviet Union and the Soviet empire in Central and Eastern Europe, comprehensive economic planning and public ownership remained in effect. The developing countries and socialist bloc also imposed comprehensive barriers, including high tariffs, on cross-border flows of goods, services, foreign direct investment, other capital flows and people, in both directions.

Ideas and associated events transformed this world of closed and highly regulated economies into the globalized and liberalized economy of the early 2000s. Arguably the most important change was the embrace of 'reform and opening up' by China after 1978, under the leadership of Deng Xiaoping. The election of Margaret Thatcher as British prime minister in 1979 and of Ronald Reagan as American president in 1980 began a revolution in the high-income countries, including privatization of what previously had been publicly owned companies. The European Union's Single European Act – triggered partly by the desire to inject economic vigour and partly by the desire to relaunch the project of European integration – was agreed in 1986 and started a move towards a single market. The Maastricht Treaty ratified in 1993 put the EU on the path towards the abolition of exchange controls and the currency union, which was launched in 1999. In 1989 the Soviet empire in Central and Eastern Europe collapsed. In 1991 the Soviet Union abandoned communism and disintegrated. In the same year, India began a process of extensive external and domestic liberalization. The Uruguay Round of multilateral trade negotiations was then completed in 1994. The World Trade Organization replaced the General Agreement on Tariffs and Trade in January 1995. Subsequently, China joined the WTO in 2001. This was a resurgence of global capitalism.

The second source of the underlying transformation was technologi-cal. Changes in transportation technologies during this era were not dramatic, though developments and improvements in container ships and high-volume air freight were significant. Improvements in informa-tion and communications technology, notably the personal computer, the internet, mobile telephony and the mobile internet were of far greater significance. These revolutionary developments permitted the organiza-tion of production and distribution across the world on a more systematic and timely basis than ever before. That in turn provided the opportunity for the accelerated development of export-oriented manufacturing, not-ably from China, and export-oriented information technology services, notably from India.

The third (and less important) source of transformation has been age-ing, notably in Germany and Japan. As populations aged and the proportion of young people in the population rapidly declined, the need to invest in new infrastructure and capital equipment shrank. Mean-while, corporate and household savings generally tended to remain strong. The result has been chronically weak demand. This weakness in domestic private demand was then offset either by prolonged fiscal defi-cits (as in Japan) or by large current-account surpluses (as in Germany, the Netherlands and other northern European countries).

These three underlying drivers – liberalization, technology and ageing – proceeded to shift the world economy into a new shape, one that created huge gross and net capital flows across borders, growing inequality within countries, radical shifts in the location of investment and the rise of liberalized credit. These shifts led high-income econo-mies into 'secular stagnation' – a world of structurally deficient aggregate demand, identified by Lawrence Summers, the former US treasury secretary, following the Keynesian Alvin Hansen, who invented this term in the 1930s.[54] These forces in turn help explain the low real rates of interest before 2007 and the still lower real rates after the crisis, which was caused in large part by the policy responses to pre-crisis recessionary forces.

Let us start with trade. Without the explosive rise in global com-merce and particularly the growth of exports and production in emerging countries, especially China, the scale of the imbalances shown in Figure 32 could not have emerged. This rapid growth in trade, driven in turn by liberalization and technological change, was also associated with a rapid shift in production from high-income economies to cheaper low-cost producers. China emerged over a remarkably short time as the world's largest manufacturing country and largest exporter of goods. This was the first time since the Industrial Revolution that a still relatively poor developing economy played such a huge role in world production and trade. That was made possible by the ease with which know-how could be transferred across frontiers. That in turn followed in part from the rise of integrated global companies, which were themselves the product of liberalization and improved information and communications technology.

Consider also the rise of state capitalism. The emergence of economies open to trade and financial flows allowed net and, as we shall soon see, gross capital flows to reach levels, relative to global and national economies, not seen since before the First World War. Yet, somewhat paradoxically, many of the new cross-border investors were governments. The emerging economies of East Asia, again particularly China, and the oil-exporting economies as well, directly controlled their countries' integration into the global financial system and managed their capital outflows. This showed up in the huge increase in foreign-currency reserves shown in Figure 24. It showed up, as well, in the rise of vast sovereign wealth funds, which, for lack of other high-quality, liquid and apparently safe opportunities, also put most of their assets in the markets of high-income countries.[55] While economies became more open, states played an enormous role in determining the scale of net capital flows and their corollary, the balance of trade. Of those states, China was the most important.

There was also the shift into structurally low inflation. Globalization seems to have been one of the most important explanations for this development. Kenneth Rogoff of Harvard University, for example, argued in 2003 'that the most important and most universal factor supporting world-wide disinflation has been the mutually reinforcing mix of deregulation and globalization, and the consequent significant reduction in monopoly pricing power'.[56] An aspect of this was the fall in the dollar prices of many manufactured commodities and labour-intensive services (such as call centres). This, in turn, was partly due to the entry of low-cost producers into the world economy on prices and partly due to the rapid decline in the prices of anything incorporating information and communications technology. Moore's law – the exponential fall in the cost of computing power first noticed by Gordon Moore of Intel in 1965 – continued to operate.[57] In itself, the fall in prices should not affect overall inflation in the medium run. It may, however, generate a short-term gain that allows central banks to hit their inflation target more easily. Taken together, these changes in market conditions not only permitted, but encouraged, inflation-targeting central banks to pursue aggressive monetary policies without having to worry much about inflation. Those policies then supported asset prices and associated credit growth.

A further crucial change has been the rise in inequality, driven by both rising inequality among working people and rising shares of profits in national income.[58] The changes have, as discussed above, been large. Yet, while there have been clear rises in inequality in the high-income economies, notably inside the US, this has probably not been true for the distribution of income across the globe as a whole. This is because the economies of some big poor countries (China and India, above all) grew faster than high-income countries, offsetting the general rise in inequality within almost all countries. Indeed, it appears from work at the World Bank that the clear losers from the economic developments of the last three decades have been the lower and middle classes of the high-income countries, whose incomes fall between the 75th and 95th percentiles from the bottom of the global income distribution.[59]

The forces driving the rise in inequality are complex. Technology helped create 'winner-takes-all markets' in which the most successful and productive participants could reap the lion's share of the gains. This became notably true in the high-tech sector and in finance, which emerged as the most dynamic industries in high-income economies. Technology also increased the relative demand for skilled workers and lowered the demand for less-skilled ones. Globalization directly affected the supply of relatively high-waged, but only modestly skilled jobs, particularly in manufacturing. Globalization also greatly strengthened the forces weakening trades unions. Reductions in taxation increased the incentive of managers to raise their pay: the relationship between the incomes of managers and ordinary workers was transformed.

The rise in the role of the financial sector also seems a potent driver of inequality: this sector has obtained a substantial proportion of corporate profits in high-income countries and it has probably had a role, along with trade and technological change, in the shift in labour incomes as well.[60] The Nobel laureate Joseph Stiglitz stresses the way in which the primacy of market norms has permitted a shift in the balance of power between the owners of capital, managers and financiers on the one hand, and ordinary workers on the other. One important aspect of this is rent-extraction by well-connected elites – that is, the ability to earn incomes over and above their economic contributions, by virtue of their powerful position within the economic system.[61]

An important proposition here is that the liberalization of credit interacted with rising inequality. Indeed, a chapter in Raghuram Rajan's book on the crisis was titled 'Let Them Eat Credit'.[62] Thus, as real incomes stagnated for a large proportion of the population, liberalized credit provided a way to sustain rising consumption. Soaring house prices also made households apparently able to afford more credit than before. This then led to rapid rises in household debt in many countries, notably the US and the UK, which then became highly problematic once asset prices started falling and economies started weakening.

Finally, technology seems to be having another important effect: the prices of investment goods are falling rapidly relative to goods and services in general. This is particularly true for investment in information and communications technology. This means that for any given level of nominal spending the real value is rising relatively rapidly. Thus, between its nadir in the third quarter of 2009 and the fourth quarter of 2014, the share of private investment in US nominal GDP rose by just 3.9 percentage points (from 12.4 to 16.3 per cent). But over the same period the share of private investment in real GDP rose by 6.3 percentage points, from 18.3 per cent to 24.6 per cent. Thus, both the level, relative to GDP, and the buoyancy of investment in real terms have been much higher than in nominal terms. This fact must also have strongly reinforced the tendency towards a financial surplus in the corporate sector.

This, then, has been a world transformed. The new world economy allowed the emergence of huge shifts in the balance between investment and saving across economies. These, in turn, reflected shifts in comparative advantage, in the global location of production, in the distribution of income, and in the functioning of the financial system. Behind these lay even deeper forces: the shift to liberalized market economies, technological transformation and ageing. The economy thus generated has, alas, proved to be highly unstable.

CONCLUSION

The global and Eurozone crises were not only financial crises. They were also crises with far deeper roots. It is essential to make the financial system less fragile. It would then be both better able to cope with shocks and also less likely to cause them. But that is only a necessary, not a sufficient, condition for a less unstable economy. The trends of the pre-crisis era were unsustainable, particularly the accumulations of household debt in a number of high-income countries. These were related to persistent global imbalances. And these, in turn, were driven by failures of monetary and financial systems in our newly globalized and market-driven world economy. So what are the solutions? That is the subject of Part III of this book.

PART THREE

The Solutions

Prologue

The crisis put all our thinking about economics, finance, the performance of economies and the future of the Eurozone into question. The following four chapters provide preliminary answers. They show how far orthodox thinking failed and consider in what ways it has to change.

First and foremost, this is a crisis of economics and particularly of conventional macroeconomics. The discussion of the shocks and then the underlying shifts in Parts I and II demonstrates quite clearly that the waves of huge crises which hit the high-income economies was *not* a result of events outside the economic system, such as an unexpected war or a vast natural disaster. On the contrary, they were the result of developments within the system. Those developments included the expansion of the financial sector, the growth of private debt, and the leveraging-up of much of the property assets of a number of important countries. Behind these developments in finance were the emergence of huge external imbalances, massive foreign-exchange intervention and the euphoria generated by the creation of the Eurozone. Yet, while some of this can be laid at the door of policymakers, much of it was the responsibility of the financial system itself and the operation of the vaunted free-market economy. So the starting point has to be with the failures of economics. That accordingly is the subject of Chapter Six, which is about the failure of economic orthodoxy and the search for a satisfactory replacement.

Second, this has been a crisis of the financial system. Naturally and inevitably, big efforts have been made to tighten up regulation and improve the resilience of the system. These efforts are not insignificant. But, in essence, they are conservative: an attempt to preserve the essence of a system that we already know is extremely fragile, and which is sure to implode once again in our current world of global financial integration, fast trading and huge flows of funds across borders. So the question is whether one can do simple things that would make the system more or less on its present lines more robust, and if not what the alternatives might be. That is the subject of Chapter Seven.

Third, this leads the discussion to the big macroeconomic challenges. How should we manage a world of savings glut – or, which comes to the same thing, excess supply? Is there a real chance of secular stagnation and, if so, what might be done about it? These are in fact plausible worries. In particular, our big problem is the addiction to ever-rising debt, and the most worrying debt is not the public debt with which policymakers are obsessed but private debt, whose collapse, as we have seen, creates huge public-sector debt problems. It is extremely disturbing, however, that the policies being pursued in the big high-income economies amount to an attempt to get the credit machine going again. So this raises a question. Is it possible to balance our economies without such a huge reliance on ever-rising leverage? The answer is: yes. This can be done in two complementary ways. One is to close external imbalances. The other is to use the government's ability to create non-debt money. The latter is regarded as unthinkable. But it may in fact be the least dangerous way of running our economy. These then are the issues addressed in Chapter Eight.

Finally, there is the question of the future of the Eurozone. It has become a bad marriage, but one from which it is immensely costly to escape. The question is whether it will be turned into a good marriage – one that all members would join again. At present, this seems highly unlikely. Instead, it will continue to fail to achieve full economic adjustment or provide the basic insurance needed to cope with untoward events as well. Moreover, there is a real danger of falling into a deflationary trap, because of the fundamental asymmetries in the adjustment processes and the failure of the European Central Bank to do its job. This being so, one cannot conclude that the crisis is over. On the contrary, it is perfectly possible to imagine that it would recur. This, then, is the topic of Chapter Nine.

6

Orthodoxy Overthrown

The message London's success sends out to the whole British economy is that we will succeed if like London we think globally. Move forward if we are not closed but open to competition and to new ideas. Progress if we invest in and nurture the skills of the future, advance with light touch regulation, a competitive tax environment and flexibility. Grow even stronger if this is founded on a strong domestic market built on the foundation of stability.

And whether it be in advanced high value-added manufacturing, our creative industries, pharmaceuticals, digital electronics, in fast-growing education exports, I believe, just as you have done in financial services, we can demonstrate that just as in the 19th century industrialization was made for Britain, in the twenty-first century globalization is made for Britain too.

Gordon Brown, Mansion House Speech, 21 June 2006[1]

Why did nobody notice it?

Question of Her Majesty Queen Elizabeth II at the London School of Economics, 4 November 2008[2]

[T]hose of us who have looked to the self-interest of lending institutions to protect shareholder's equity (myself especially) are in a state of shocked disbelief. Such counterparty surveillance is a central pillar of our financial markets' state of

balance. If it fails, as occurred this year, market stability is
undermined.

Alan Greenspan, Testimony before the House of
Representatives Committee on Oversight and Government
Reform, 23 October 2008[3]

Credit means that a certain confidence is given, and a certain
trust reposed. Is that trust justified? and is that confidence wise?
These are the cardinal questions. To put it more simply – credit is
a set of promises to pay; will those promises be kept? Especially
in banking, where the 'liabilities', or promises to pay, are so large,
and the time at which to pay them, if exacted, is so short, an
instant capacity to meet engagements is the cardinal excellence.

Walter Bagehot, Lombard Street[4]

On 4 November 2008, at the height of the financial crisis, Queen Elizabeth II visited the London School of Economics, one of the world's leading centres of academic economics, to open a new building. While she was there, she asked a group of dignitaries a simple question: 'Why did nobody notice it'?

In response to the Queen's question, the British Academy convened a forum on 17 June 2009. Shortly after these deliberations, a reply was sent to her Majesty.[5] In brief, it argued that the big failures lay in not recognizing how large the risks were to the system as a whole, how bad risk management was, and how big the mess bequeathed by the crisis would turn out to be. The institutional and political failure was the inclination of both politicians and regulators not to look the gift-horse of pre-crisis prosperity in the mouth.

This is hardly an adequate answer. It is easy to accept that the timing of a crisis is unknowable. An economic system is too complex for a precise prediction of the timing of a crisis: indeed, such a prediction, if widely agreed, must be self-defeating. But it is not enough to blame institutional failure, because the institutions that failed were those many economists had lauded, particularly those central to modern finance. This then was not an institutional failure, but an intellectual one. The remark at the head of this chapter by Alan Greenspan, chairman of the

Federal Reserve from 1987 to 2006, underlines this point. Rational pursuit of self-interest is the core ideology of the free-market economy. But, at the height of the crisis, Greenspan stated the loss of his faith that self-interest would deliver financial stability. It is as if the Pope declared he no longer believed in the Resurrection of Jesus Christ.

Here is another indication of intellectual failure. On 8 April 2011, at the conference of the Institute for New Economic Thinking (INET) in Bretton Woods, New Hampshire, I interviewed Larry Summers, winner in 1993 of the John Bates Clark medal for American economists under the age of forty, former US treasury secretary, and recently departed director of President Obama's National Economic Council.[6] I asked what economics, if any, he had found relevant to the task of putting the US and world economies together again, after the crisis. He responded: 'There are things economists didn't know. There are things economists were wrong about. And there were things where some economists were right . . . There is a lot in Bagehot that is about the crisis we just went through, there's more in Minsky and perhaps more still in Kindleberger . . . I think economics knows a fair amount. I think economics has forgotten a fair amount that's relevant. And it has been distracted by an enormous amount.'[7] Later in the interview, when asked what he found useful as a policymaker in deciding on the response to the crisis, Mr Summers referred to Keynes.

What did these four thinkers named by Summers have in common? They were all dead and their work was so far outside the contemporary academic mainstream that they had become Orwellian 'unpersons'. True, central bankers were aware of the great Victorian economic journalist, Walter Bagehot. But his work was gathering dust on a shelf marked 'irrelevant to contemporary concerns'.[8] Many of today's leading macroeconomic theorists, notably including Chicago's Nobel laureate Robert Lucas, probably the most influential of all, regard the work of John Maynard Keynes as embarrassing and that of the post-Keynesian Hyman Minsky with something bordering on contempt.[9] Charles Kindleberger of the Massachusetts Institute of Technology was an economic historian and, as a result, far below the salt where princes of academic economics sat.

The economics that dominated academe and has shaped thinking for several decades proved useless in predicting, tackling or even imagining the biggest financial debacle in the world's most advanced economies for eighty years. During the crisis, moreover, the people in authority ran as fast as they could back to Bagehot and even Keynes – indeed, Bagehot and Keynes on steroids. Yet the fact that a meltdown of the world's most advanced financial systems had occurred for a second time is significant. One great depression might be a fluke. A second such crisis begins to look like a pattern. True, policymakers learned lessons from the great economists who had themselves learned from the 1930s. They stopped another depression. But it was still a huge recession from whose effects the affected economies had not emerged six years later.

So what went wrong intellectually and what can be done about it?

THE FAILURE OF OFFICIAL ECONOMICS

In a lecture given at the South African Reserve Bank on 2 November 2012, Adair (Lord) Turner, outgoing chairman of the UK's Financial Services Authority, addressed exactly this question: what had economics got wrong? His answer was:

> The financial crisis of 2007 to 2008 was caused by excessive credit creation, excessive leverage, and too much maturity transformation. The fact that these excesses caused such havoc, and that private incentives and market disciplines failed to check their development, reflects three facts which are fundamental to understanding financial system dynamics and risks.
>
> (i) First, debt contracts create specific financial and economic stability risks; and those risks intensify as the proportion of all contracts which take a debt and in particular a short-term debt form increase.
>
> (ii) Second, that the existence of banks as we know them today ... exacerbates these risks because banks can create credit and private money, and unless controlled, will tend to create sub-optimally large or sub-optimally unstable quantities of both credit and private money.

(iii) Third, that bank or shadow-bank lending secured against real assets which can change in value, can be even more volatile and pro-cyclical, resulting in credit and asset price cycles which end in crashes and subsequent recessions.[10]

The most sophisticated modern economics ignored these dangers because they had been removed by assumption. The workhorse macroeconomic analytical tool used by central banks was a 'dynamic stochastic general equilibrium model' in which finance barely appeared: the underlying models were of movements towards equilibrium in the demand and supply for real goods and services in the economy, not ones in which financial forces had independent effects, on the lines suggested by Minsky.[11] Meanwhile, modern theories of finance focused on how markets would or should price assets, without paying attention to the impact of big shifts in asset prices on the economy as a whole.[12] The dominant assumption of the macroeconomic models was rational expectations and that of financial theory was market efficiency. As Felix Martin notes, in his book on money, 'By ignoring the essential link between the financial securities traded on the capital markets and the monetary system operated by the sovereign and the banks, academic finance built a theory of finance without the macroeconomy just as neoclassical macroeconomics had build a theory of the macroeconomy without finance.'[13] In effect, the compartmentalization of money and macroeconomics from finance and market efficiency removed an understanding of the interconnections among these aspects of the economy.

This brings us back to Lord Turner's analysis. In the words of staff at the Bank of England, 'In the modern economy, most money takes the form of bank deposits. But how those bank deposits are created is often misunderstood: the principal way is through loans made by commercial banks. Whenever a bank makes a loan, it simultaneously creates a matching deposit in the borrower's bank account, thereby creating new money.'[14] Thus, in making an advance to a would-be borrower a bank simultaneously creates a debt owed to it by the borrower and a deposit in favour of the borrower. Thereafter, the deposit may be transferred to somebody else, as payment or as a gift: it has become money. In this way banks create almost all of the money in the economy. Of course, individual banks need to hold on to deposits. Otherwise, they would have to shrink their balance sheets. But the deposits they lose would go to other banks (unless customers actually flee into cash). So the system as a whole would not lose deposits and it is the system as a whole that matters to the economy.

True, the distinction between banks and non-bank financial intermediaries must not be exaggerated. Most such institutions generate maturity mismatches and high leverage inside the economy.[15] But banks have two advantages over other intermediaries: the central bank will always provide the reserves that solvent banks need to ensure the 'moneyness' of their liabilities, namely, their ability to be redeemed or used in payment, at par with central-bank (that is, government) money;[16] equally, since the 1930s an increasing number of governments have guaranteed the value of at least a proportion of deposits explicitly, regardless of the solvency of the banks, and are implicitly believed to be behind even more of the deposits – quite possibly all of them. Banks, particularly big banks, should be viewed as more a part of the state than of the private sector. These valuable privileges allow banks to expand their lending in good times with next to no constraint. It is easy, after all, for banks to hold on to the deposits they need to fund their expanded lending, precisely because of the public confidence generated by the support provided to banks by the government and central bank. Banks are explicitly part of the government's monetary system. Of course, once the Federal Reserve offered equivalent support to money-market funds in September 2008, the latter came to have much the same characteristics as banks.

What then stops the bank-led financial system from expanding credit and money without limit? The obvious answer would be that it would stop when participants ran out of profitable opportunities. But this is not a convincing answer if the activities of the hyperactive intermediaries in aggregate *create* the perceived opportunities: credit growth breeds asset-price bubbles that in turn breed credit growth. This is, at core, a disequilibrating process. That is why microeconomic financial theory is next to useless in explaining it. It is a macroeconomic process, moreover, not a microeconomic one: it shapes the entire economy.

There could then be two further answers to the question: what stops credit expansion? One is that a crisis stops it. That is all too unpleasantly true: in the end the elastic credit system snaps back into a credit crisis: that is the 'Minsky moment', when panic sets in. A more pleasant answer is that the central bank stops credit expansion by raising interest rates. The implicit answer of the pre-crisis official orthodoxy was that central banks would stop the excess credit expansion in time, or at least not too late, by responding to rising inflation in the prices of goods and services. But that signal would fail if rising asset prices and expanding credit were not closely related to inflation. That is precisely what happened in the 2000s.

Thus, the period before the crisis saw strong external demand for assets denominated in the currencies of the economies in which credit and money were growing rapidly, and a lack of inflationary pressure in the world as a whole, largely because of a huge expansion of capacity and employment in the production of tradeable goods. Even a huge credit expansion generated no overt inflationary pressure. But asset prices – house prices, above all – rose substantially.

The reason orthodox economics failed to pick up the risks was, in short, that it ruled out what most mattered. Modern financial economies do not equilibrate smoothly. They are dynamic systems characterized by uncertainty and 'animal spirits', in which the most powerful destabilizing force is the ability of the private financial sector to generate credit and money and so to produce euphoric boom and panic-stricken bust.

So what now? Let us start with what the official sector and the economists who advise it tell us they have learned. Then let us look at fundamental critiques.

THE OFFICIAL RESPONSE TO ITS ERRORS

In the fourth of a series of lectures on 'The Federal Reserve and the Financial Crisis', delivered in Washington DC in March 2012, Chairman Bernanke addressed 'The Aftermath of the Crisis'.[17] Mr Bernanke was not only the chairman of the Federal Reserve, the world's most important central bank and the epicentre of policymaking throughout the crisis, but is also a distinguished academic economist. He should be viewed as an authoritative source for the opinions of most officials and informed academics.[18] In this lecture he did two important things. The first was to defend the interventions of the Federal Reserve and other important central banks after the crisis. The second was to lay out the agenda for post-crisis policymaking. This is what he said:

> [W]e began by noting the two principal tools of central banks, serving as lender of last resort, to prevent or mitigate financial crises, and using monetary policy to enhance economic stability. In the Great Depression, as I described, those tools were not used appropriately. But, in this episode . . . and I should say that . . . other major central banks have followed . . . very similar policies to those of the Fed . . . these tools have been used actively. And in my belief, in any case, we avoided – by doing that, we avoided – much worse outcomes in terms of both the financial crisis, and the depth and severity of the resulting recession.
>
> A new regulatory framework will be helpful. But again, it's not going to solve the problem. The only solution in the end is for us regulators and our successors to continue to monitor the entire financial system and to try to identify problems and . . . respond to them using the tools that we have.[19]

Mr Bernanke then made three fundamental points about the role of central banks, in the light of the crisis.

First, the interventions during the crisis, though huge in scale, were 'very much in keeping with the historic role of central banks, which is to provide lender-of-last-resort facilities in order to calm a panic. And what was different about this crisis was that the institutional structure was different. It wasn't banks and depositors. It was broker-dealers and repo markets. It was money-market funds and commercial paper but the basic idea of providing short-term liquidity in order to stem a panic was very much what Bagehot envisioned when he wrote *Lombard Street* in 1873.' This is broadly correct, so far as central-bank operations are concerned, though the interventions of finance ministries went well beyond standard lender-of-last resort operations, since they involved buttressing the solvency of failed institutions.

Second, these interventions saved the economy from another 'Great Depression', by preventing a cascading collapse into bankruptcy not just of the financial sector, but of large parts of the US and world economies. We do not know the counterfactual and never will, which makes it easy for opponents of these interventions to argue they were unnecessary. But it is hard to believe that an unmanaged implosion of much of the Western world's financial system, at a time of overextended balance sheets in much of the private sector, would not have created a global depression at least rivalling that of the 1930s. No sane policymaker could have taken that risk and, fortunately, after the post-Lehman shock, they did not do so. We were forcibly reminded of the dependence of the financial system on the unique capacity of the state to create the money that people want when they trust nothing else.

Third, the way oversight of the stability of the financial system as a whole will work is for 'the regulators and our successors to continue to monitor the entire financial system and to try to identify problems'. This is in addition to a host of more detailed changes – to be discussed in Chapter Seven – aimed at making institutions and markets less fragile. The financial sector, argues Mr Bernanke, will need the permanent, persistent and penetrating oversight of a paternal state. The core of the market economy – its brain, so to speak – cannot be trusted to operate without adult supervision. This is not a small matter.

Mr Bernanke emphasized, then, that 'maintaining financial stability is just as an important a responsibility as monetary and economic stability. And indeed, this is ... very much a return to where the Fed came from in the beginning. Remember the reason that [the] Fed was created was to try to reduce the incidents of financial panics, so financial stability was the original goal of [the] creation of the Fed. So now we sort of come full circle.' But he did not forget the other goal: monetary stability. On this he argued that:

> ... markets have been confident that the Fed will keep inflation low, inflation expectations have stayed low. And except for some swings up and down related to oil prices, overall, inflation has been quite low and stable.
>
> At the same time, while we've kept inflation low, we've also made sure that inflation hasn't gone negative ... Those of you familiar with the Japanese situation understand that's been a big problem for their

economy now for quite a few years. We certainly wanted to avoid deflation. I talked about deflation also in the context of the Great Depression. So, monetary ease also guarded against the risks of deflation by making sure that the economy didn't get too weak.[20]

In sum, Mr Bernanke offers the following conception of the three roles of the central bank in the economy: inflation targeting (in other words, macroeconomic stabilization); financial oversight; and unlimited crisis intervention. All important central banks now accept these tasks, though the Federal Reserve, with its dual mandate, would also state that its aim is to achieve the highest employment possible, consistent with achieving the inflation target.

How then might one summarize post-crisis central-bank orthodoxy or, as I will call it, the 'new orthodoxy'? It comes in three parts. First, central banks still believe in seeking to stabilize inflation, a lesson the high-income economies learned in the inflationary era of the 1970s.[21] Second, they seek a second set of instruments, to achieve stability in the financial system as a whole. These instruments fall under the title of 'macroprudential policy'.[22] Third, central bankers are strengthened in their role as lenders of last resort, but want to avoid rescuing insolvent institutions. So they need ways of resolving (reorganizing the financial structure or even closing) institutions, ways that won't trigger financial Armageddon. Financial institutions should, accordingly, not be allowed to become too big, too complex or too interconnected to fail.

This approach is, however, open to powerful objections. Three are particularly important.

First, this new orthodoxy gives enormous discretionary power to bureaucrats in managing the financial system in particular, which is the heart of the supposedly market economy.

Second, the new orthodox doctrine does not resolve the confused relationship between the state and the private sector as suppliers of money. On the contrary, it reinforces that confusion.

Third, the doctrine assumes that monetary policy can be targeted at price stability, while macroprudential policy is targeted at financial stability. More important, it is assumed that they will not get in each other's way, with monetary policy sometimes undermining financial stability by encouraging excessive credit creation, and macropruden-tial policy undermining monetary policy by halting credit creation.

Not surprisingly, given the poor performance in the run-up to the crisis and the doubts about the workability of the new doctrines, many object to the emerging official post-crisis ideology. These objec-tions have their roots in the work of important economists from the past: Knut Wicksell; Ludwig von Mises and Friedrich Hayek; Henry Simon; John Maynard Keynes and Milton Friedman; and Abba Lerner. This is a very old set of debates. But they are as relevant today as ever before.

ALTERNATIVES TO THE NEW ORTHODOXY

The power of the financial system to create credit and money is enor-mous, for both good and ill. The mixed public-private arrangement of today is certainly not the only way this system could work. The choice of alternatives is far from a purely technical matter. It has, inevitably, deep political implications.

So what are the alternative visions of financial, monetary and fiscal systems?

Knut Wicksell on the Market and Natural Rates of Interest

The big lesson of recent experience is that private-credit provision can be highly destabilizing even when inflation is under control. The new central-banking orthodoxy described above is, of course, an attempt to stuff the genie of financial-sector-driven instability back into the bottle.

The view that the credit system is destabilizing is one shared by post-Keynesians, such as Minsky, and Austrian economists, such as von Mises.[23] The man from whose ideas these very different strands descend is the great Swedish economist, Knut Wicksell (1851–1926), whose classic work, *Interest and Prices*, was published in 1898. In this, he started from the observation that banks were able to create credit-backed money, as explained in the quotation from the Bank of England above.[24] Given the existence of such credit-backed money, Wicksell argued, two interest rates operate in the economy: the 'natural' rate and the 'money' rate. The former cannot be observed directly: it is the real return on new capital, as seen by profit-seeking entrepreneurs. The latter can be observed directly: it is the lending rate of the banking system.

In Wicksell's theory, when the money rate is below the natural rate, banks expand credit to meet rising demand from business. What is driving businesses to borrow is their belief that the return on investment (the natural rate) is above the cost of borrowing from banks (the money rate). The demand for new lending then expands credit and money (in ways already discussed above) and so drives the real economy and ultimately inflation upwards. When the money rate is above the natural rate this process goes into reverse: credit and money contract. There is then a risk of deflation. Since credit expansion and contraction are cumulative processes, with today's credit expansion or contraction influenced by yesterday's expansion or contraction, via their effects on activity and prices, changes in credit and money have powerful real effects on the economy.

Wicksell influenced both Austrian economists and Keynes, but in different directions. A contemporary descendant is the influential neo-Keynesian, Michael Woodford, of Princeton University, whose work provides support to management of expectations via inflation targeting, in line with contemporary orthodoxy.[25] Woodford focuses on Wicksell's concern with achieving stable inflation. Other descendants include William (Bill) White, former economic adviser and head of the monetary and economic department of the Bank for International Settlements, and Claudio Borio, Deputy Head of the Monetary and Economic Department and Director of Research and Statistics at the BIS (already mentioned in Chapter Five).[26] These economists focus more on Wicksell's insights into credit, insisting that deviations between natural and market interest rates may emerge in destabilizing credit expansions and contractions rather than in measured inflation or deflation, other than in the very long run.[27]

The problem, these economists emphasize, is that central banks have allowed the credit system to become excessively elastic. This is, they argue, why the incidence of financial crises has increased. The current orthodoxy, they note, is that macroprudential regulation will control such elasticity. But they question whether regulation can curb the impact of a monetary policy pushing in the opposite direction. Their conclusion is that monetary policy must 'lean against the wind' of credit expansion.[28] Bill White argues similarly that policy is now on a treadmill, with a succession of ever more desperate monetary policies designed to remedy the malign longer-term impacts of the last set of such policies. He is concerned that the result of the policies adopted in response to the post-2007 crisis will be even worse. All this occurs, argue such Wicksellians, because the money rate of interest has been kept below the natural rate for far too long.[29]

The latter group of neo-Wicksellians argue, correctly, that inflation targeting, far from stabilizing the economy, may destabilize the financial system and so the economy, in the medium term. Yet, while this diagnosis is persuasive, the policy recommendations are not.

First, it is impossible to hit two targets – price stability and financial stability – with one instrument. Second, the natural rate of interest is unknown: attempts to use the rate of economic growth as a proxy for the natural rate, as White does, are unpersuasive. That relationship would only hold in a long-run equilibrium. But the dominant feature of our economy is that it has not been in such an equilibrium: a world of fast growth and very low real rates of interest is a disequilibrium world. This is because of the once-in-a-century impact of the rise of China and the other emerging economies on the world stage, what I have called the 'shifts' in Chapter Five.[30] Third, the extent of the needed 'leaning against the wind' is unknown and unknowable – the links between monetary policy and asset prices are not subject to precise control, according to current knowledge. Fourth, it is unclear how a legal mandate upon the central bank to achieve both monetary and financial stability via monetary policy could be made operational. Finally, seeking to stabilize finance might destabilize inflation and inflation expectations, thereby making the real economy more unstable, not less so.

The neo-Wicksellians have indeed identified a problem, but not put forward a workable solution. The conclusion I draw is that in an environment of rapid credit growth, monetary policy should be tighter than strict inflation targeting would suggest. But monetary policy cannot achieve two targets at once: other instruments will indeed be needed to make the financial system less destabilizing, as the new orthodoxy would suggest.

The Austrians on Bank Credit and Malinvestment[31]

Wicksell greatly influenced the Austrian economists, Ludwig von Mises (1881–1973) and Friedrich Hayek (1899–1992), both of whom played an important role in academic debates on money and finance in the 1920s and 1930s. They lost these debates in academic and policy circles partly for methodological reasons – their rejection of the growing role of mathematics in economics – but far more for political ones – the opposition to any policy response to the greatest crisis that had ever befallen capitalist economies, other than letting it burn itself out. Paradoxically, their defeat in academe liberated Austrian economics. It has become politically influential, principally in the US, where Austrian economics has become a favourite economic ideology of libertarians and so of parts of the modern Republican Party: former Congressman Ron Paul is a devotee. The reason for this appeal is that, unlike the Chicago School, in which the late Milton Friedman was the dominant post-war figure, the Austrian economists see no case for a government role in managing the market economy, including even the money supply. Many contemporary 'Austrians' favour a return to the gold standard. Naturally, they are opposed to every element of the new (or old) orthodoxy on monetary and financial policy. They are purist adherents of laissez-faire. This is why 'they have condemned the Federal Reserve's policies during the great recession'.[32] Instead, they see depressions as healing events.

Von Mises followed Wicksell in his attention to the natural and money rates of interest. But he added a great deal of detail to the role of banks in a credit expansion. As the Spanish Austrian, Jesús Huerta de Soto, explains, 'According to Mises, the amplification of any inflationary process, via credit expansion will sooner or later spontaneously and inexorably reverse and provoke a crisis or economic recession in which the investment errors committed will be revealed and massive unemployment will emerge along with the need to liquidate and reallocate all the resources wrongly invested. To eliminate recurrent economic cycles Mises proposes the establishment of a banking system with a 100 per cent reserve requirement for demand deposits.'[33] Ironically, a great apostle of the free market wished to suppress the free market in the provision of money. In this way, he recommended, the ability of banking institutions to create credit and money would be ended, by legal fiat, though the reserve backing would come from gold.

Hayek argued that divergences between natural and money rates of interest would lead to distortions in the structure of production. Thus, if a positive gap opened up between the natural and money rates of interest, possibly because of the efforts of the central bank to expand credit, expected profits would rise, since the real returns on new investments (the natural rate) would be above the rate at which business could borrow (the money rate). This would encourage a credit expansion (that is, false savings), via greater leverage in the banking system, and a move towards more capital-intensive (in Austrian terminology more 'roundabout') methods of production: the lower the cost of capital (in this case, proxied by the money rate) the more capital-intensive will become the most profitable techniques of production. Such forced adoption of capital-intensive techniques is 'malinvestment'. The bigger the divergence between the two rates of interest, the bigger the boom and the bigger the bust.[34] In particular, Hayek blamed the Great Depression on the expansionary credit policies of the Federal Reserve during the 1920s.[35] In the words of Mr Huerta de Soto, 'Hayek views the Keynesian remedy for the Great Depression as nothing more than a temporary solution with adverse consequences. Indeed any artificial rise in aggregate demand will severely distort the productive structure and can only generate unstable employment.'[36] In later years, Hayek devoted his attention to the idea of privately issued money, rather than the 100 per cent reserve-backed money of von Mises.

In the debates of the 1930s, the Austrians lost the public argument on business-cycle theory to the Keynesians and, subsequently, the monetarists. They ceased to have much influence on ideas about macroeconomic policy for a long time. Both economics and politics explain this failure. The economic explanation was the scale of the slump. It was impossible to argue that no more was involved than the reversal of the malinvestment during the 1920s. Indeed, this theory is puzzling, particularly given that it comes from such passionate believers in laissez-faire. Why should business people be so misled by mistaken monetary policy? If business can be so wrong about this, what else might it be wrong about? Moreover, why should the reversal of malinvestment lead to a depression? It should lead, instead, to the scrapping of some capital, along with a boom in more profitable investments.

A far more plausible view is that the scale of the downturn in the Great Depression was due to a steep decline in demand, largely due to the banking and monetary collapses. This decline in demand also generated massive involuntary unemployment. The Austrian School's support for the 'liquidation' recommended by US Treasury Secretary Andrew Mellon and its opposition to any remedial intervention by government was (rightly) judged indefensible in the place where it counted: the electoral process.[37] In the US, Franklin Delano Roosevelt became president. In Germany, Adolf Hitler became chancellor. What these two vastly different leaders shared was their rejection of laissez-faire. By the end of the 1930s, a defeated Hayek abandoned his efforts at business-cycle theory, moving more to political philosophy and the economics of information, in both of which he made influential contributions.

Today's adherents of the Austrian school, such as former Congressman Paul, tend to argue in favour of a return to nineteenth-century political economy: the gold standard (with its direct link between the supply of money and the supply of gold); abolition of the central bank; ending of financial – and other forms – of regulation; elimination of social safety nets; and so forth. If people with this set of views had been in charge in 2007 and 2008, the results would probably have matched those of the 1930s. That would have discredited them for another two generations. In the US, however, a frightened Republican administration was shortly followed by an activist Democratic one. This allowed Austrian economists and other libertarians to blame the disappointing aftermath of the crisis on those who sought to cure it. Indeed, in the US, it has become conventional wisdom that the Obama administration's stimulus programme failed when it was just insufficiently large, partly because of fierce Republican opposition and partly because of what turned out to be false optimism among economists working for the administration.[38] Given this mistaken view on what had just happened, Austrian liquidationism may be tried in the next great crisis, with predictably dire results. Yet it is hard to believe that the nineteenth-century gold standard could be successfully reintroduced into a modern democracy.[39]

This is not the only reason why the approach of the Austrian School has to be rejected. They are right to argue that the conditions leading to a crash are important. But their recommendation that the right response to the crisis itself is to do nothing does not follow from their (correct) view that significant mistakes caused it. Doctors do not refuse to treat someone who owes his heart attack to overeating, recommending that he just go on a diet instead. First, they treat him, and then when he is better he can go on a diet.

Nevertheless, the Austrian School's critique of the official orthodoxy has value, even if their theory and policy ideas do not. First, the credit system is, as they remind us, destabilizing. Second, stable inflation does not guarantee economic stability. Third, booms will create malinvestment and excess debt, which will then have to be dealt with in one way or another. It is not surprising, therefore, that construction, finance and debt itself all shrank after the boom ended. Finally, the idea that regulators will be able to fine-tune monetary policy on the basis of economic forecasts, and safeguard the stability of the financial system on the basis of their analysis of systemic risk, is rather optimistic. Indeed, we must assume at least a degree of failure.

Henry Simons and the Chicago Plan

Mises concluded that the ability of private institutions to create debt-backed money out of thin air, as a by-product of their lending (as discussed above), needed to be brought under control, via 100 per cent reserve banking – that is, a system in which deposits are backed by central-bank reserves, one to one. The Chicago School – another group of free-market economists – came to the same conclusion in the 1930s, for the same reason: they concluded that the bank-based monetary system (which we still have today) was itself unstable and so destabilized the economy. The economists involved were hugely distinguished and respected: Frank Knight (1885–1972), who pioneered the crucial distinction between calculable risk and uncertainty; Henry Simons (1899–1946), author of the most complete version of the Chicago monetary plan; Irving Fisher (1867–1947), the most famous pre-Second World War American economist; and, after the war, Milton Friedman (1912–2006).[40] Again, as with the Austrians, these free-market economists concluded that the ability to create credit-backed money had to be ended if the market economy was to be protected from ruinous crises.

The thrust of the plan, which was first proposed in 1933 at the trough of the Great Depression, was to give government the exclusive right to create money, thereby taking it altogether away from private businesses (that is, banks). All versions of the plan required 100 per cent reserve backing of deposits. In other words, households and businesses would keep their holdings of deposits in banks, which would, in turn, hold accounts at the central bank or, possibly, hold government debt. Deposits would, therefore, fund the government. The economic argument is that only in this way would there be no banking crises: banks could not fail. The philosophical argument is that a monetary system is both a social contrivance and a public good. Society should gain the reward from what society has created. The plan then proposed that the money supply, now under full government control, would expand in accordance with a rule – probably a target rate of growth based on expected growth of the economy, expected changes in demand for money and an inflation target.

If reserves backed deposits 100 per cent, what would finance lending to the economy? This is the crucial question for all such schemes. The original Chicago Plan proposed replacing traditional banks with investment trusts that issue equity and sell their own interest-paying securities. But, as we have learned from the emergence of the money-market funds and the repo markets, which played a central role in the shadow-banking system, such debt can once again become an attractive replacement for money, with lethal consequences for stability. Two alternatives were proposed, both of which aimed at eliminating this risk. Under one, recommended by Simons, all private property would take the form of currency, government bonds, corporate stock or real assets. Thus, the investment trusts would take the form of equity or property mutual funds. Under the other alternative, banks would borrow from the government, not the private sector, to fund their riskier assets.

The essential aim of the plan is to give the government a monetary monopoly: private institutions would not issue money-like liabilities except when backed by government money. What would be the advantages? Fisher claimed four. First, preventing banks from creating and then destroying credit and money in self-reinforcing cycles would eliminate the biggest source of instability in the economy. Second, 100 per cent reserve banking would eliminate the possibility of bank runs: banks would be completely safe. Third, if the government financed itself by issuing money at zero interest, rather than borrowing at interest, debt interest and net government debt would fall dramatically. Indeed, in almost all countries, government would become a net creditor. Finally, since money creation would no longer need private debt, the level of such debt could fall dramatically. Indeed, in the transition, the government could use the excess of the total supply of money over its own debts to fund a dramatic decline in private debt, through buy-backs. I would add to these benefits that the extinction of conventional bank-created money would almost certainly shrink the financial sector, reduce the aggregate incomes earned by bankers and so improve the distribution of income.

The fiscal implications alone would be dramatic. According to an important International Monetary Fund working paper on the Chicago Plan by Jaromir Benes and Michael Kumhof, total bank deposits in the US are around 180 per cent of GDP.[41] Assume the demand for money merely grows in line with nominal gross domestic product, at about 5 per cent a year. If it failed to do so, interest rates would rise and the economy might be pushed into deflation. So each year the money supply would need to grow by 9 per cent of GDP if it were to remain at 180 per cent of GDP. This would fund about 40 per cent of the Federal government in normal years, allowing a dramatic reduction in taxes. Republicans should love that! To this should be added savings on government-debt interest (on the assumption that these would not be interest-earning deposits) and the earnings on any money lent to the private sector.

Also dramatic would be the implications for the operation of monetary policy. The central bank would have direct control over the money supply. It could be told to follow a strict rule, as the Chicago School proposed, which would include a precise inflation target. The central bank could set any interest rate it liked, including negative rates, up to the point that people preferred to hold cash instead of deposits. The stabilization of the economy would become a relatively simple challenge because the main obstacle to it would have been eliminated.

Not surprisingly, the opposition of the banking industry forced abandonment of the Chicago Plan in the 1930s. Those who enjoy such an extraordinary privilege – in this case to create state-backed money at will – would not willingly give it up. But the idea of what is called narrow banking – an important part of the Chicago Plan – returns, quite understandably, in every generation. Minsky, though a post-Keynesian, also endorsed 100 per cent reserve banking in 1994.[42] The plan for Limited Purpose Banking, proposed by Laurence Kotlikoff of Boston University in his book *Jimmy Stewart is Dead*, has close similarities to the Chicago Plan.[43] On the political left, James Robertson, a British environmentalist, has gone further in his proposal that the central bank should create all money directly and hand it over to the government to spend as it sees fit. But, from a monetary point of view, that is the same as 100 per cent reserve banking.[44] More recently, Andrew Jackson and Ben Dyson have endorsed a similar approach for Positive Money, a UK campaigning organization.[45] The crucial point is that these proposals for replacing private debt-created money with government-created money are perfectly feasible and would bring substantial benefits: far less private debt and far less private indebtedness.

The self-interest of private bankers would again be a significant factor in opposing such ideas. But there are also intellectual objections. Walter Bagehot opens *Lombard Street* by arguing that:

> . . . much more cash exists out of banks in France and Germany, and in all non-banking countries, than could be found in England or Scotland, where banking is developed. But that cash is not, so to speak, 'money-market money': it is not attainable . . . But the English money is 'borrowable' money. Our people are bolder in dealing with their money than any continental nation, and even if they were not bolder, the mere fact that their money is deposited in a bank makes it far more obtainable. A million in the hands of a single banker is a great power;

he can at once lend it where he will, and borrowers can come to him, because they know or believe that he has it.

Bagehot attributes British economic dynamism to the public's willingness to trust their money to risk-taking private banks. Yet we do not know that economic progress depends on the instability of a credit-creating banking system. Certainly, the authors of the Chicago Plan and others in their intellectual tradition pose a profound challenge to the contemporary new orthodoxy that some combination of inflation targeting with skilful macroprudential regulation will allow the world economy to ride the financial tiger in reasonable safety. Unfortunately, while something as radical as the Chicago Plan may be a necessary condition for stability, it is unlikely to be a sufficient one: the market economy could still be unstable. Moreover, the gains for dynamism generated by a risk-taking private system might outweigh the risks to stability.

The rational strategy is to make more changes now than the new orthodoxy suggests (which will be discussed in Chapter Seven and the Conclusion) *and* plan to move to still more radical ideas if huge crises recur. But it would be too disruptive and risky to make a massive shift in the nature of our economies towards the Chicago Plan without first trying more limited reforms, albeit radical ones by the standards of the new orthodoxy. It would also be rational to encourage some (possibly smaller) countries to experiment with still more radical plans for eliminating banking as we know it. Indeed, so great has been the failure of the financial system that the idea of a monoculture of banking and financial systems, governed by the same global rules, seems inordinately foolish. We simply do not know enough to settle on just one system. Experiment is essential. The Chicago Plan or variants upon it is *definitely* an experiment worth making.

Keynes versus Friedman on Fiscal versus Monetary Policy

The economic debates of the 1930s bequeathed an agreement between John Maynard Keynes (1883–1946) and his successors, on the one hand, and the monetarists on the other hand, over one decisive matter: that aggregate demand matters. The economy does not automatically operate at full employment. Potential output does not automatically become actual output in a complex monetary economy. In these respects, Keynesians and monetarists are very much on one side, since they are both concerned about aggregate demand, and the Austrian economists are on the other, since they reject this concern altogether. A divide did emerge, however, between Keynesians and monetarists on which tools to use and how. That divide still exists today. Indeed, the debate over the relative importance of fiscal and monetary policies in the post-crisis period was among the most important debates of all.

This is not true in normal times, when interest rates are significantly positive. In these circumstances, most (though not all) of the descendants of Keynes would agree with Milton Friedman and his successors that monetary policy can deliver the desired stability of demand. Important disagreements remain, however. First, Friedman's view emphasized not the price of money (the interest rate), but its quantity. He was a quantity theorist in the tradition of Irving Fisher: he argued that what mattered was not the price of money, the rate of interest, but its quantity, the stock of money. Friedman believed that the rate of interest does not tell one whether monetary policy is loose or not. Only the rate of growth of the money supply does that. His underlying assumption was that, despite radical changes in monetary institutions towards a credit-based – and away from a commodity-based – monetary system, it is possible and desirable both to define what money is and control its growth more or less precisely. Furthermore, argue quantity theorists, if one achieved a steady rate of growth of the money supply, the growth of nominal demand would also be stable: there is, in other words, a direct relationship between the money supply and nominal spending in the economy. Second, Friedman argued that the best approach would be to follow a rule for growth of the money supply, rather than rely on the discretion of central bankers. If one did that, any short-term disruptions to the real economy generated by vagaries in the supply of money would be ironed out, leaving the underlying real economy to function as smoothly as it could.

Monetarism's great successes were in the 1960s and 1970s when naive Keynesianism blew up because it underplayed

inflationary expectations and believed too confidently in macroeconomic fine-tuning. The assumed trade-off between unemployment and
inflation broke down, whereupon Keynesian fine-tuning of the real
economy, via active fiscal and monetary policies, became largely discredited and was subsequently abandoned. Of course, it was logically
possible to have a Keynesian view of the role of fiscal policy in demand
management, while accepting the crucial role of expectations. Nor was
it essential for Keynesians to believe in macroeconomic fine-tuning.
Given our ignorance, they could have believed in coarse-tuning,
instead – namely, the use of fiscal policy to guide the economy only
in extreme circumstances. Similarly, it would have been perfectly possible to believe money is of great importance, but not pay much
attention to expectations, while believing in a degree of fine-tuning.
But, as a matter of historical fact, the Keynesians of the 1960s mostly
downplayed inflation expectations and largely believed in fine-tuning.
This opened up a vulnerable intellectual wing to the monetarist
counter-attack, which combined the role of expectations, the centrality
of money, and the difficulties inherent in discretionary macroeconomic
fine-tuning.

When monetarism was tried in the 1980s and 1990s, it failed, since
neither defining nor controlling the money supply proved at all easy.
This then led to the pre-crisis orthodoxy of inflation targeting by the
central banks, which relied on interest rates not quantitative control
over money. At the back of policymakers' minds was the notion of the
'natural rate of unemployment' proposed by Milton Friedman and
Edmund Phelps, or, as it would be called today, the non-accelerating
inflation rate of unemployment (NAIRU) or, alternatively, a zero output gap. This, then, was a kind of synthesis between Keynesianism
and monetarism: natural-rate Keynesianism, implemented via active,
indeed fine-tuning, monetary policy.

This orthodoxy also broke down, first in Japan in the 1990s, then
in the West after 2007, because of what both Keynes and Friedman
both ignored: the tendency of the credit system to run riot, as Wicksellians, Austrian School economists and 'Minskyans' emphasize.
After the crisis, much of the world found itself with close to zero nominal short rates. At that point, the debates revived. Both monetarists
and most adherents of the contemporary orthodoxy argued that

monetary policy could still work effectively, either by expanding the quantity of money or lowering the yield on other securities, particularly long-term bonds. One policy, it was thought, would achieve both those outcomes: quantitative easing, by which was meant the expansion of the monetary base. By using newly created central-bank money to buy bonds, the central bank could, it was believed, both expand the money supply and lower yields.

Figure 37 shows what happened to US M2, the broadest measure of money the Federal Reserve publishes, after 1980.[46] M2 consists of currency held by the public, plus deposit liabilities of financial institutions principally belonging to households. Figure 37 also shows the 'monetary base'. This consists of currency, again, and the deposits of banks at Federal Reserve banks (that is, the central bank). The monetary base is the government-created money in the system: it is a liability of government. The rest of the money supply is the liability of banks. The monetary base is sometimes called 'outside money' and the bank-created money supply 'inside money'. Until the recent crisis, virtually all M2 was inside money – a by-product of the rapidly expanding lending activities of private financial intermediaries. The monetary base barely grew. In the early years of the crisis, however, lending to the private sector by financial intermediaries shrank. By expanding the monetary base, principally through quantitative easing, the Federal Reserve compensated for the cessation of bank lending to the private sector, thereby keeping M2 growing. This is exactly what Milton Friedman would have recommended. From the monetarist point of view, it was the obvious thing to do. Since monetarists are generally viewed as being on the 'right wing' economically, it was amusing to watch the scorn with which many on the political right wing treated these actions by the central bank in the US.

Keynesians argue that when short-term rates are close to zero, monetary policy is no longer very effective. Certainly, apparently reasonable monetary growth, measured by M2, did not generate a vigorous recovery, though it almost certainly stopped a far deeper recession. The difficulty, as we saw in Chapter Five, is that the economy suffers from a savings glut – desired savings exceed desired investment, despite the extremely low interest rates. In the well-known expression: money is pushing on a string.[47] Moreover, though the short-term rate may be

Figure 37. Backing for US M2
(US$bn)

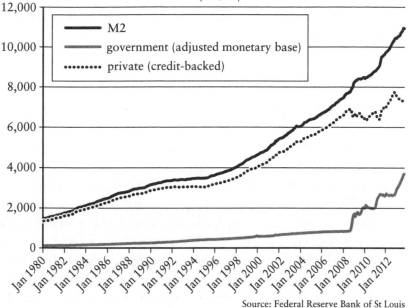

Source: Federal Reserve Bank of St Louis

near to or at zero, it is impossible to bring the long-term rate that low, because of 'liquidity preference': at negligible long-term rates, the downside for holders is large (since investors would lose a fortune if yields returned to normal) and the upside negligible. So people will not hold the long-term bonds if the yield falls below a certain level. If the central bank wanted their yields to go still lower, it would have to buy almost all of these bonds outright: in effect, it would find itself financing the government directly. A better solution, argue Keynesians, is to lower desired savings directly, while keeping rates of interest at zero. To do that, the government has to spend more itself or implement tax cuts that will encourage the public to spend more. This is the simplest and most direct way to revive the economy. Furthermore, such a fiscal policy will have no effect on short-term interest rates and will raise long-term interest rates in countries with their own central banks only if it encourages confidence in a recovery. The risks of default are more or less zero in this case.

This debate between Keynesians and monetarists on the best

macroeconomic policy response to a crisis is very much live, both within academe and more publicly. It will be a big part of the discussion in Chapter Eight, where it will inform our analysis of the new orthodoxy in action.

Minsky's Instability Hypothesis

Hyman Minsky (1919–1996), fascinatingly, a post-Keynesian product of the Chicago School, developed one of the most comprehensive critiques of pre-crisis and, by implication, the post-crisis new orthodoxy too.[48] As we saw in the Preface, Introduction and Chapter Four, his crucial points were three: first, he believed that instability is an inherent feature of a dynamic capitalist economy, not just of the financial system; second, he doubted whether any regulatory rules could contain this instability durably; and, finally, he believed that the combination of 'Big Government' with the 'Big Bank' (the central bank) was the only way to contain the consequences of severe instability.

While disagreeing, rightly, with the notion that inflation targeting could deliver stability, Minsky would have appreciated the need, stressed by Mr Bernanke, for regulatory watchfulness and with the efforts of the Federal Reserve to rescue the economy from the crisis. He would have emphasized that the economy is now in a depression mode and will take a great deal of government-led effort to escape from a more severe crisis. All these are very important lessons, to be considered further in Chapter Eight.

Lerner, Chartalism and Modern Monetary Theory

A final school of thought, which is called 'chartalism' (from the idea that money is just a token, for which the Latin word is *charta*), argues that the conceptual failure of the contemporary monetary and fiscal orthodoxy is not that it gives too much room for central-bank or government discretion, but that it gives far too little: thus, it goes beyond Keynes and most Keynesians.[49] The essential idea is that the purpose of monetary and fiscal policy is to ensure full employment. In an economy based on freely floating fiat (government-created or government-backed) money, the government suffers from no fiscal constraint: it can always create money that residents have to accept. The constraints are only macroeconomic, particularly excessive inflation.

Adam Smith made reference to the idea of state-created paper money, noting that the governments of the British colonies in North America 'find it for their interest to supply the people with such a quantity of paper money as is fully sufficient and generally more than sufficient for transacting their domestic business'.[50] But the theory emerged in full form in 1895, the heyday of the gold standard, with the publication of Georg Friedrich Knapp's analysis of the role of the state in creating money.[51] Taxation makes money valuable, he argued, since private citizens need it to pay those taxes. This, in turn, makes paper money acceptable in the economy at large. It is simply the most readily transferable of all possible credits, since the government is the most powerful and most permanent of all possible debtors and all money is just transferable credit: its value derives from the willingness of people to trust in it.

This idea influenced Keynes and was taken up in 'functional finance' proposed by the influential post-Keynesian, Abba Lerner (1903–1982).[52] Since the government can issue currency at will, the level of taxation and the extent of borrowing are tools to influence the economy. They have nothing to do with any need to finance the government, since it can fund itself by creating money. Thus all forms of balanced-budget household economics applied to the government are nonsense unless it has ceased to be able to create money (as has happened inside the Eurozone). In Lerner's words, 'Government should adjust its rates of expenditure and taxation such that total spending is neither more nor less than that which is sufficient to purchase the full employment level of output at current prices. If this means there is a deficit, greater borrowing, "printing money", etc., then these things in themselves are neither good nor bad, they are simply the means to the desired ends of full employment and price stability.'[53] So long as these policies do not generate excess demand, there is no reason to fear their inflationary effects. This does not mean no constraint on monetary policy exists, but those constraints come from inflation and the associated risks of sharp declines in the value of the currency against other currencies.

Today's proponents of this set of ideas call it 'modern monetary theory'.[54] An essential point is that the private sector can be a net accumulator of financial assets if and only if the government runs a deficit or the economy as a whole runs a current-account surplus (that is, foreigners run a financial deficit). If the government runs a financial surplus in good times, as orthodox Keynesians propose, the private sector will, in the absence of a current-account surplus, run a financial deficit. The latter deficit will need to be financed by the creation of bank credit, which may ultimately prove destabilizing.

A crucial and unquestionably correct point in modern monetary theory is this: *banks do not lend out their reserves at the central bank*.[55] Banks create loans on their own, as already explained above. They do not need reserves to do so and, indeed, in most periods, their holdings of reserves are negligible. Only the central bank (by open-market operations), government (by spending and taxation) or private individuals (by reducing or increasing their holdings of cash) can change the aggregate level of bank reserves. Nor is the amount of money that banks create related in any direct way to reserves in the contemporary monetary system, as central banks have discovered: reserves increased dramatically after the crisis, but lending did not. The amount of money that banks create is dependent only on how much they think they can profitably lend at the interest rates set by the central bank.

Because the risk perceptions of banks vary dramatically, depending on the economic climate (for which they themselves are, in aggregate, in large part responsible), their willingness to create loans will also vary dramatically, from feast – a time of credit boom – to famine – a time of credit bust. If a bank needs reserves to meet settlement or cash obligations, today's central banks will freely supply them at the rate of interest it has determined. Thus, this rate of interest will then determine the rates at which banks lend. If the central bank engages in quantitative easing (that is, it creates money with which to buy assets from the public), it will increase aggregate banking reserves automatically. The central bank pays members of the public in return for the bonds it buys from them. Members of the public then deposit this money in their accounts at commercial banks, which then have increased liabilities to the public and a matching increase in deposits at the central bank. Those matching deposits are, of course, bank reserves.

Moreover, to repeat, banks themselves can do nothing to lower the aggregate levels of bank reserves, since the only use of reserves is to settle accounts with other banks. Other businesses and households do not hold accounts at the central bank. So one bank's loss of reserves (deposits) at the central bank is always another bank's gain. It does not affect the total quantity of reserves outstanding. Of course, the government and central bank can change the quantity of reserves by buying and selling assets in the market. Similarly, the public can change the quantity of reserves by asking for cash, instead of bank deposits. The banks, in turn, get the cash from the central bank, in return for their reserves or by borrowing from the central bank, which creates the reserves. In brief, one should envisage the relationship between banks and the central bank as being identical to the one between the public and the banks. The central bank is the banks' bank.

Modern monetary theory poses another fundamental challenge to the official orthodoxy. It argues that in an economy based on fiat money, the job of the central bank and government, together, is only to stabilize the economy. Moreover, these entities can always create the needed demand by spending the money they create. Of course, there is a constraint: too much demand relative to supply will indeed generate inflation. But this will not happen just because of quantitative easing, unless its effect is to increase the overall supply of (broad) money faster than the public is willing to hold it. That has certainly not happened during this crisis, which is why the hyperinflation some feared has turned out to be an illusory danger. Deflation is a far greater risk.

The reason not to give the government the power to use its ability to create money as a tool of stabilization, in this direct way, is not that it is technically difficult. It is rather that many view it (with reason) as politically dangerous, because it puts too much discretionary power in the hands of politicians whose estimate of full-capacity output might be dangerously optimistic. The answer to that concern is institutional: give the power to decide how much money to create to the central bank, but ask the central bank to do this directly via the creation of outside money, not indirectly via the expansion of inside money. Interestingly, the MMT view of monetary policy and the

Chicago Plan are essentially the same, the difference being mainly the institutional setting within which the state creates money, rather than private banks.

CONCLUSION

The people who have developed the critical perspectives outlined above differ on political values and so on whether the aim should be less state and more private or less private and more state intervention. They differ on whether policy should be guided by rules or discretion. They differ on whether the state should have an active role in managing the economy. They differ on whether money and credit are the sole source of instability in the economy. But, on one point, they agree: the balance between the role of the state as ultimate supplier of money, and that of the private sector as actual creator of almost all of the credit and money we use, is highly destabilizing. We have made a pact with the devil. It is not a new bargain. On the contrary, it goes back many centuries. But we have recently been reminded that the dangers are huge. Moreover, the liberalization of finance seems to lead to crises almost automatically. Surely this strongly suggests a need for a new kind of system.

Let us now turn to the twin challenges the authorities are attempting to address: getting out of the present malaise; and restoring a stable and dynamic world economy. What, precisely, are they trying to do? Does it have a chance of working? What else might be needed? These are the questions to which we turn.

7

Fixing Finance

[W]e ... committed to reach agreement expeditiously on stronger capital and liquidity standards as the core of our reform agenda and in that regard fully support the work of the Basel Committee on Banking Supervision and call on them to propose internationally agreed rules to improve both the quantity and quality of bank capital and to discourage excessive leverage and risk taking ... It is critical that our banking regulators develop capital and liquidity rules of sufficient rigor to allow our financial firms to withstand future downturns in the global financial system.

Communiqué of finance ministers and central-bank governors of the G-20, 5 June 2010[1]

Capital comes at a cost – both to banks and to the economy at large in the form of forgone lending as institutions shrink to meet extreme capital-to-asset ratios ... It's no surprise that loan levels in the US and Europe have suffered over the past five years and will continue to do so with regulators' demands for even higher levels of required capital.

To tell banks they need more capital and then complain that some borrowers are not getting funding is a political statement, not an economic one. The incentives are obvious. When regulators set rules, they should not be surprised that banks naturally adjust to the incentives they created. Yet too often

banks get blamed for making rational decisions based on the
rules that have been set by their regulators.
Frank Keating, President and Chief Executive, American
Bankers' Association, 22 August 2013[2]

The breakdown of the financial system was so spectacular that the principal legislatures, policymakers and regulators have indulged in an orgy of law- and rule-making. A plethora of labels – 'Basel III', 'Dodd-Frank', 'Volcker rule', 'Vickers' and 'Liikanen' – have become familiar to readers of the business press. Yet what is behind all this? Will these reforms succeed? Will they cost too much? Is there something better we could do? In addressing these questions, the focus of the discussion will be on the attempt to rescue a system that, in its essence, will remain much like the one that went into the crisis. The aim is to tame the tiger of banking and finance, not turn it into another animal. Then, in the next chapter, the discussion will turn to the macroeconomic context – monetary reform, both domestic and global, and the rebalancing of the world economy.

CLOSING STABLE DOORS

Among the most important consequences of the crisis was the decision to convene a G-20 summit of the leading high-income and emerging countries in Washington in November 2008 and thereafter make this informal gathering the focus of global economic decision-making. This marked a shift from bodies dominated by a limited number of high-income countries, most recently the finance ministers and central-bank governors of the G-7 (US, Japan, Germany, France, UK, Italy and Canada) and the heads of government of the G-8 (the G-7, plus Russia). It recognized fundamental shifts in global power. In consequence, it was the G-20 that set the post-crisis reform agenda. The 'Declaration on Strengthening the Financial System' of 2 April 2009 outlined commitments to:[3]

Establish the Financial Stability Board, to oversee global financial stability.

Widen the scope of regulation to cover 'all systemically important financial institutions, markets, and instruments', with particular attention being paid to 'large and complex financial institutions'. Oversight of hedge funds was also to be included.

Strengthen prudential regulation, including by imposing more and better-quality capital, ensuring firms build up bigger capital buffers in good times, and supplementing risk-based capital requirements with 'a simple, transparent, non-risk based measure which is internationally comparable, properly takes into account of off-balance sheet exposures, and can help contain the build-up leverage in the banking system'.

Ensure that 'compensation structures would be "consistent with firms" long-term goals and prudent risk-taking'.

Improve standards for valuation of financial instruments.

Make oversight of credit-rating agencies more effective.

This indicates the immediate regulatory response to the crisis. This, in turn, reflected a consensus that almost everything had gone wrong: inadequate oversight; insufficient capital; regulatory arbitrage; irresponsible behaviour; misleading accounts; and misleading credit ratings. Subsequently, the authorities added yet more objectives: structural change (altering the way banks are allowed to organize themselves internally), stress tests (assessments of the ability of banks to survive extreme conditions), resolution regimes (new legal mechanisms for reorganizing the finances of failing financial institutions), changes to market structure (shifting trading from over-the-counter markets towards exchanges and clearing houses); and reforms of regulatory structures. They were trying to close all the stable doors at once.

So what has happened with this complex agenda?

Basel III

A first area of focus was reaching agreement on a new Basel III accord (after the failures of Basel I and II demonstrated by the crisis) governing bank capital, risk-management – including management of market risk – macroprudential regulation and liquidity risk.[4] Basel I, which imposed a minimum set of capital requirements for banks, had been agreed by the Basel Committee on Banking Supervision in 1988. Ironically, one of its main aims was to weaken the feared competition from undercapitalized Japanese banks, which then promptly failed in the financial crisis of the 1990s. The essence of Basel I was risk-weighting of assets, with assets allocated to five risk classes. Ironically and dangerously, these weights treated government debt as riskless and put triple-A-rated mortgage-backed securities into the next least risky category. International banks were required to fund themselves with capital equal to 8 per cent of their risk-weighted assets. But that meant far lower ratios of equity capital to assets if the risk weights of many of the assets that individual institutions held were themselves low.[5] Basel II, initially published in 2004, was an extension of Basel I. It paid far more attention to market and operational risks, for example, than had Basel I, and also encouraged banks to use their own value-at-risk models.[6] In the event, the crisis occurred before Basel II had been fully implemented. Basel III is now replacing Basel II, though it is very much the progeny of the two earlier accords. It still relies on risk-weighting, for example, even though that approach failed in the run-up to the crisis, as noted in Chapter Four above.

On capital requirements, regulators agreed to raise common equity, plus retained earnings, to 4.5 per cent (up from 2 per cent in Basel II) and 'Tier 1' capital (including preference shares and perpetual subordinated debt) to 6 per cent of 'risk-weighted assets'. They agreed to add a further 2 per cent in 'Tier 2' capital (subordinated debt with a maturity of more than five years) and a mandatory minimum 2.5 per cent 'capital conservation buffer', to give room before a firm fell to the regulatory floor. They also decided to add up to a further 2.5 per cent of risk-weighted assets in a 'countercyclical buffer' and a further 1–2.5 per cent extension of this countercyclical buffer for global systemically important banks (G-SIBs). Together, this could bring capital, broadly defined, to 15.5 per cent of risk-weighted assets for the G-SIBs, in good times. The hard minimum of broadly defined capital would be 8 per cent of risk-weighted assets.[7]

In addition, Basel III substantially tightened oversight of the risk-weighting procedures adopted by financial institutions. This was partly because the latter had proved hopelessly over-optimistic prior to the crisis and partly because different institutions applied radically different weights to the same assets. Because risk-weighting is vulnerable to gaming by financial firms, policymakers also agreed to impose a leverage ratio without risk-weighting. But the ratio under discussion among regulators in Basel has been a mere 3 per cent.

Basel III promotes macroprudential regulation, by introducing strong stress tests, estimating probabilities of losses over long time-horizons and calling on regulators to pay attention to the building up of systemic risks. It also made a number of significant changes to liquidity requirements. Finally, it demanded important changes in the structure and conduct of financial markets: better-integrated management of market and counterparty risk; stronger capital requirements for counterparty credit exposures; and movement of trading in over-the-counter derivatives towards centralized clearing houses.

Some jurisdictions have gone – or are considering going – beyond these globally agreed minima. The US plans to impose a 5 per cent simple leverage ratio on bank holding companies with more than $700 billion in consolidated total assets. Insured depositary institutions that are subsidiaries of these holding companies must maintain a supplementary leverage ratio of at least 6 per cent to be considered 'well capitalized'.[8] The eight US bank holding companies (Citigroup, JP Morgan, Bank of America, Bank of New York Mellon, Goldman Sachs, Morgan Stanley, State Street and Wells Fargo) included in the globally agreed list of G-SIBS are affected by these US rules, which are due to come into effect in 2018.[9] Switzerland has told UBS and Credit Suisse – its two global systemically important banks – to raise their capital to 19 per cent of risk-weighted assets – of which 9 per cent can be in contingent convertible bonds ('CoCos'), designed to convert into equity once a pre-set trigger is breached. The UK's Independent Commission on Banking recommended that the UK's systemically significant banks be required to have a minimum loss-absorbing capacity of between 17 and 20 per cent of risk-weighted assets, including 'bail-inable bonds'.

Resolution

A second area of focus has been 'resolution', particularly resolution of systemically significant banks.[10] Resolution allows the authorities to reorganize the finances of troubled institutions by imposing losses on shareholders and creditors in an orderly way. Individual firms would, at the same time, need to develop their own resolution plans – so-called 'living wills'. The aim of this effort is to eliminate the widely advertised threat of 'too big to fail'.

One of the arguments for ring-fencing subsidiaries with separate capital and 'bail-inable' debt (debt issued under the clear understanding that it could – and probably would – be converted into equity if the issuing institution was deemed to need additional capital) is that it would make it much easier to 'resolve' banks that get into trouble. Consider, for example, a retail bank with independently capitalized subsidiaries and the bail-inable debt required by the host regulators. The Spanish bank, Santander, or the UK bank, HSBC, might be examples of such federal institutions. Suppose a subsidiary got into serious trouble. Suppose, too, that the parent institution was unable (or unwilling) to rescue it. Then the host regulator of the subsidiary could seize the subsidiary and resolve it, by converting an appropriate proportion of the bail-inable debt into equity. Indeed, with appropriate triggers this could even happen without regulatory involvement. This is very much the process envisaged by the UK's Independent Commission on Banking.

Now turn to the more difficult example of a global investment bank such as Goldman Sachs or Morgan Stanley or the investment-banking subsidiaries of universal banks. Such banks have integrated global balance sheets and so cannot be resolved by host-country regulators without causing global chaos. Far and away the best way to solve such problems is via orderly resolution of the bank holding company by the home-country regulator. The Federal Deposit Insurance Corporation and the Bank of England are cooperating in developing such a 'single-point-of-entry (SPOE)' approach. The aim is to concentrate the losses on shareholders and long-term unsecured debt holders of the parent holding company. To achieve this, the holding company would need to carry an appropriate amount of debt, distinct from the debt of its subsidiaries. The SPOE approach should reduce incentives for creditors and customers of operating subsidiaries to 'run' and for host-country regulators to engage in ring-fencing or other measures disruptive to an orderly resolution of a failing global firm.[11]

Employee Incentives

A third important area has been employee incentives. The aim is to better align the interests of employees with those of stakeholders, including the public at large. In 2010 the Committee of European Banking Supervisors finalized rules requiring 40–60 per cent of the variable pay of bank executives to be deferred for three to five years and at least 50 per cent of variable pay to be in shares.[12] The Federal Deposit Insurance Corporation has introduced broadly similar requirements for American bankers.[13] In 2013 the European Union imposed a maximum one-to-one ratio of bonus to salary.[14] This rule is inevitably controversial. Some suggest it will drive banking outside the EU and raise base pay, thereby making pay more inflexible and creating unnecessary job losses in downturns, and reducing rewards for exceptional performance. But others counter that it will reduce incentives for one-sided risk-taking, thereby turning banks into the sober utilities they should become.

Some have proposed going far beyond mere changes in compensation regime. In the UK, the Parliamentary Commission on Banking Standards has recommended that 'a criminal offence . . . be established applying to Senior Persons carrying out their professional responsibilities in a reckless manner, which may carry a prison sentence; following a conviction the remuneration received by an individual during the period of reckless behaviour should be recoverable through separate civil proceedings.'[15] This draconian approach reflects a widely shared belief that the managers of banking institutions have taken little responsibility for the consequences of their decisions.

Structural Reform

A fourth area of focus has been structural reform, on which much has happened. The US introduced the Volcker rule, named after its promoter, Paul Volcker, redoubtable chairman of the Federal Reserve between 1979 and 1987: 'The Rule generally prohibits a banking entity from engaging in proprietary trading or acquiring an ownership interest in, sponsoring, or having certain relationships with a hedge fund or private equity fund.'[16] The comprehensible aims of this rule are to reduce conflicts within firms between their own and their clients' interests and to ensure that any form of implicit or explicit public subsidy is not employed in trading for their own account. The difficulty is that it is hard to distinguish proprietary trading from the essential service of market-making. The Rule was agreed in December 2013 and is due to go into effect only in April 2014. It is accordingly too early to tell whether it can be made effective and, if so, can also make a difference. The UK's Independent Commission on Banking (of which I was a member) concluded that the Rule was not well targeted and would not work well.

In the UK, the incoming coalition government established the Independent Commission on Banking in June 2010 under the chairmanship of Sir John Vickers of Oxford University, former director general of the Office of Fair Trading. In September 2011 the Commission recommended that retail banking be ring-fenced from investment banking in a separately capitalized subsidiary.[17] In the Commission's proposed arrangement, household and small-business deposits would be held within the retail bank, trading activity would be inside the investment bank, and large corporate deposits could be on either side of this ring fence. The aims of these proposals were to help insulate domestic retail banking from external financial shocks, facilitate resolution of a banking group in difficulty, and make it more credible that the government would not back trading activities. At the same time, the Commission rejected the idea of a full split, rather than a ring fence, arguing that the diversity of businesses within a large group and the diversification of their assets might improve stability in a crisis. The UK government subsequently brought in legislation in line with the Commission's proposals, with the strong support of the Parliamentary Commission on Banking Standards. The Banking Reform Act based on these proposals was passed into law in late 2013.

The ICB's recommendations were a response to the worrying fact that before the crisis the assets of the UK's banking sector amounted to five times the country's GDP, largely because of the huge scale of its globally active banks. Indeed, the total assets of the UK banking sector in 2009 were not significantly smaller than those of the US banking sector. In the size of its banks relative to the economy, the UK was like Switzerland and the Netherlands. One of the aims of the ring fence was to protect domestically oriented banking from whatever might happen in the globally oriented activities.[18]

Reacting to the publication of the report of the Vickers Commission, the internal market commissioner of the European Commission, Michel Barnier, established a high-level commission under the chairmanship of Erki Liikanen, governor of the Bank of Finland, to examine the possibility of a similar structural reform of banking in the EU.[19] The Commission published its report in October 2012. Its central structural recommendation was that:

> ... [p]roprietary trading and other high risk trading activities should be assigned to a separate legal entity if the activities to be separated amount to a significant share of a bank's business and are above a certain threshold. This would ensure that trading activities beyond the threshold are carried out on a stand-alone basis and separately from the deposit bank ... The long-standing universal banking model in Europe would, however, remain untouched, since the separated activities can be carried out in the same banking group. Hence, banks' ability to provide a wide range of financial services to their customers would be maintained.[20]

Thus the Liikanen Commission's structural recommendation was almost a mirror image of that of the UK's Vickers Commission: the former recommended ring-fencing trading from the rest of the business; the latter recommended ring-fencing retail banking from the rest of the business instead. This would leave standard investment-banking activities – mergers and acquisitions, initial public offerings and corporate finance – outside both ring fences. Moreover, the Liikanen Commission's proposed ring fence was generously defined. Necessary, not sufficient, conditions for considering a separation into a separate entity were that the tradeable assets of a bank be 15–25 per cent of total assets or that those assets amounted to at least €100bn.[21] As of the time of writing in early 2014, it is unclear what if anything will come of these proposals. The attachment of important European countries, particularly France and Germany, to the universal banking model is powerful. Moreover, how these proposed reforms, if enacted, would fit with the UK's structural reforms, which will be largely in line with the recommendations of the Vickers Commission, remains unclear.

Reform of Regulatory Institutions

A fifth and final important area has been institutional reform. In the US, the passage of the Dodd-Frank Act in 2010 established the Financial Stability Oversight Council charged with overseeing the overall stability of the financial system. In the UK, the government rearranged the entire regulatory furniture, abolishing the Financial Services Authority created in 1997 by Chancellor Gordon Brown, on whom they wished to cast blame for the crisis, and putting all prudential regulatory authority inside the Bank of England. As part of this upheaval, the government established a new Financial Policy Committee inside the Bank, also charged with overseeing the overall stability of the financial system. Finally, the Eurozone crisis has also triggered a fundamental shift in regulatory responsibility, with oversight moving to the European Systemic Risk Board within the European Central Bank. In all these cases, the power of the central banks is set to increase, though this is least clear in the US, where responsibility for systemic oversight was not given to the Federal Reserve. But, given its institutional and intellectual strengths, the Fed seems likely to dominate the Financial Stability Oversight Council.

A LABOUR OF SISYPHUS

In brief, the authorities have responded to the crisis with a bout of frenetic reform. Unfortunately, the new regulatory regime is astonishingly complex and demanding. In a brilliant paper, Andrew Haldane and Vasileios Madouros of the Bank of England note the increasing demands of regulation on many dimensions. Among the most striking is the sheer volume of rule-making:

> Contrast the legislative responses in the US to the two largest financial crises of the past century – the Great Depression and the Great Recession. The single most important legislative response to the Great Depression was the Glass-Steagall Act of 1933. Indeed, this may have been the single most influential piece of financial legislation of the 20th century. Yet it ran to a mere 37 pages.

The legislative response to this time's crisis, culminating in the Dodd-Frank Act of 2010, could not have been more different. On its own, the Act runs to 848 pages – more than 20 Glass-Steagalls. That is just the starting point. For implementation, Dodd-Frank requires an additional almost 400 pieces of detailed rule-making by a variety of US regulatory agencies.

As of July this year, two years after the enactment of Dodd-Frank, a third of the required rules had been finalised. Those completed have added a further 8,843 pages to the rulebook. At this rate, once completed, Dodd-Frank could comprise 30,000 pages of rulemaking. That is roughly a thousand times larger than its closest legislative cousin, Glass-Steagall. Dodd-Frank makes Glass-Steagall look like throat-clearing.

The situation in Europe, while different in detail, is similar in substance. Since the crisis, more than a dozen European regulatory directives or regulations have been initiated, or reviewed, covering capital requirements, crisis management, deposit guarantees, short-selling, market abuse, investment funds, alternative investments, venture capital, OTC derivatives, markets in financial instruments, insurance, auditing and credit ratings.

These are at various stages of completion. So far, they cover over 2000 pages. That total is set to increase dramatically as primary legislation is translated into detailed rule-writing. For example, were that rule-making to occur on a US scale, Europe's regulatory blanket would cover over 60,000 pages. It would make Dodd-Frank look like a warm-up Act.[22]

Cynics will be reminded of the remark in Giuseppe Tomasi di Lampedusa's *Il Gattopardo*: 'If we want everything to stay the same, everything must change.' They will conclude that this manic rule-making is designed to disguise the fact that the thrust of it all has been to preserve the system that existed prior to the crisis: it will still be global; it will continue to rely on the interaction of vast financial institutions with free-wheeling capital markets; it will continue to be highly leveraged; and it will continue to rely for profitability on successfully managing huge maturity and risk mismatches. But the new structure of regulatory oversight and rules displays something equally important: the breakdown of trust between authorities and finance.

That was hardly surprising, given the huge costs of the crisis. Nevertheless, the authorities want largely to preserve a system they also mistrust. That is why the regulatory outcome has been so complex and insanely prescriptive, though that has also been affected by the complexity of modern finance itself and by lobbying.

The question remains: will this complex regulatory effort deliver a financial system that is both robust and dynamic? In essence, after all, we need a financial system that will cope with inevitable shocks while not generating huge shocks of its own. Will these reforms provide it? In a word, no. The sheer complexity of the regulatory structure makes it virtually inconceivable that it will work. Nobody in charge of a bank is going to know and understand all the rules it is supposed to obey. Indeed, nobody is, be they in the regulatory bodies or the regulated institutions. Operating in such a regulatory quagmire makes it certain that institutions will end up operating contrary to the rules without meaning to do so. It will also create pervasive uncertainty. It is highly undesirable.

To illustrate the problems beyond these crucial points about complexity and uncertainty, this chapter will look at two central issues: capital and macroprudential regulation. But it will first look at ideas for more radical reform.

THE CASE FOR RADICAL REFORM[23]

There is a simple and telling reason why, notwithstanding all the regulatory reforms, the system is bound to fail again and again: it is designed to do so. The reason for this, elucidated in Chapters Four and Six, is that the fragility is built in. The financial system makes promises that, in certain states of the world, it cannot hope to keep. The reason for this is that institutions finance long-term, risky and often illiquid assets with short-term, safe and highly liquid liabilities. The people who provide the funds regard their deposits and other loans as a very close substitute for – if not exactly the same thing as – money. But the assets held by the institutions to which they have lent are not in the least like money: they are subject to significant solvency and liquidity risks. At a time of trouble, providers of funds will panic:

it always makes sense to try to be among the first to leave a burning theatre or even a theatre that might be burning. In withdrawing their funds, providers will trigger what they fear. The assets held by the institutions will be dumped at fire-sale prices, turning illiquidity into insolvency. Figure 28 shows, for example, that AAA-rated sub-prime asset-backed securities had lost two-fifths of their initial value by February 2009, devastating the net worth of any leveraged business that held a large quantity of these supposedly safe assets.

This is the world's Faustian bargain. Some (such as members of the Austrian School and the authors of the Chicago Plan, discussed in Chapter Six) argue for a drastic solution: abolish it. Make term-transforming finance, in general, and conventional banking, in particular, illegal. Replace it with 100 per cent reserve banks, which cannot fail, using the huge additional demand for reserves at the central bank to back the deposits of the public at commercial banks as a way to finance the government.

Charles Goodhart of the London School of Economics, doyen of British analysts of finance, responds to such suggestions as follows:

> A problem with proposals of this kind is that they run counter to the revealed preferences of savers for financial products that are both liquid and safe, and of borrowers for loans that do not have to be repaid until some known future distant date. It is one of the main functions of financial institutions to intermediate between the desires of savers and borrowers, i.e. to create financial mismatch. *To make such a function illegal seems draconian* [my emphasis].[24]

We permit many things that are far less than perfectly safe. Consider motorcars or aeroplanes. These are regulated, but not banned, because their benefits exceed their costs. That, as I noted in Chapter Six, is what that shrewd and practical observer, Walter Bagehot, believed about banking and the money markets. Yet we can identify two exceptional features of finance, as distinct from other examples of risky products and activities: first, it has huge negative 'externalities' – that is the irresponsibility of some can create a generalized panic and crisis; and, second, the economic and social costs of financial crises are enormous. In the UK, for example, the financial crisis has delivered the fourth worst fiscal shock in the last two hundred years, after the

Napoleonic Wars, the First World War and the Second World War. Relative to the pre-crisis trend, it seems quite likely to cost something quite close to six times annual GDP; it might be much worse. In Ireland, the crisis has imposed a rise in net public debt of close to 100 per cent of GDP. Professor Goodhart is right in saying there is a strong preference for a financial system that mismatches maturity, not to mention riskiness. But one must ask: at what price?

The upheaval involved in moving towards anything similar to the Chicago Plan or Kotlikoff's updated version might be large.[25] The same is true of plans to replace conventional banking with government-created money.[26] It is understandable that few want to take the risk of embarking on such a contentious and complex reform. Bankers managed to see off the Chicago Plan even in the depth of the 1930s. Nowadays, their task would be far easier, because the slump has thankfully been milder.

A halfway house to a shift to the Chicago Plan does exist, however. It would consist of insisting that demand deposits or maybe just insured deposits would be backed by safe and highly liquid assets: central-bank reserves or short-term government securities. This is narrow banking. Such narrow banks could be separate institutions or parts of bigger ones. The problem with narrow banking, to which both the Chicago Plan and Limited Purpose Banking might be an answer, is that the fragility would migrate elsewhere in the system, as happened with shadow banking. The Federal Reserve had no plans for intervening in money-market funds or wholesale markets, though the latter is where many of the most significant mismatches had migrated. Thus if narrow banking were really to work, it would be necessary either to ensure that the fragility did not emerge somewhere else (previously unrecognized) in the financial system, as the more radical proposals for reform suggest, perhaps by insisting that all other finance took the form of equity contracts, or to make it credible that the central bank and government would never intervene to help the rest of the financial system if it fell into trouble. But such a promise is, as economists inelegantly say, 'time inconsistent'. If someone had asked the Federal Reserve whether it would ever bail out AIG, the shadow provider of shadow capital to the shadow-banking system, its answer would surely have been: no. But that was before September 2008, and then suddenly it was another world.

It would be fascinating to see the Chicago Plan or Kotlikoff's Limited Purpose Banking tried. Even an experiment with narrow banking would be informative. But the difficulties involved in making such a transition would be huge. So let's first consider less radical ways of buttressing a system that would still be much like our own. For that, we must begin with equity, the only unquestionably loss-absorbing form of finance.

A CAPITAL SOLUTION[27]

A bank can fund its assets with two sources of funds: equity and debt. Depositors often believe that the money they have put into their bank belongs to them. In fact, it is just part of their bank's debts. Of course, they are a politically important part of a bank's debts. This is why deposit insurance has become universal. It is unthinkable that banks would be allowed to default on small deposits in a universal-suffrage democracy. Indeed, when Iceland's banks got into such severe difficulty in 2008, the government imposed default on their foreign creditors, since the combined balance sheets of the banks, at eleven times GDP, were far too big for it to guarantee, but it protected domestic depositors.[28] Elsewhere, in the worst of the crisis, blanket government guarantees turned not just the insured deposits, but almost all bank debt, effectively into public debt. In some cases, the creditworthiness of the state was put at risk in order to guarantee the debt of banks. Ireland is an extreme example of this unconscionable development: the debt taken on by the Irish state merely to fund the bailout of the creditors of its banks was around a third of GDP.

The Business Model of Banking

A cynic would say that the business model of banks consists of creating enormous quantities of explicit and implicit public debt – in the UK case, not far short of five times GDP – as a by-product of their other activities. That is why one might view bankers as merely exceptionally highly paid civil servants. But creating implicit public debt is not the whole of the business model. The other – and closely connected – part is minimizing reliance on shareholders' equity as a source of funding. It is then easy to set a high target for the return on equity, unadjusted for risk. Before the crisis, that target used to be 15 per cent or even more. Achieving that target was then used as a benchmark for paying out generous bonuses to employees.

In a non-financial business, promising to raise the return on equity by increasing the ratio of debt to equity – that is, by increasing the leverage – is not seen as a wealth-enhancing strategy. It is a zero-sum speculative strategy. Indeed, one of the fundamental theorems in finance – known, as the Modigliani-Miller theorem (after its discoverers, Franco Modigliani and Merton Miller, both winners of the Nobel Prize in economics) – is that the way a business is financed does not influence how valuable it is, apart from any tax benefits from leverage.[29] Finance merely determines how risk is distributed among those who fund the business. Indeed, since bankruptcy is normally destructive and high leverage makes bankruptcy more likely, well-established businesses generally avoid it. If British Petroleum (BP) had been as leveraged as a bank, the disaster in the Gulf of Mexico in 2010 would have bankrupted it.

Higher leverage makes debt riskier and so its cost higher. The expected return on equity rises, but this is compensation for the rising volatility of the returns. The investors who buy shares in businesses with risky funding models are those who like the combination of higher return with higher risk. When banks tell the world that their shareholders want the high expected returns they promise, they are probably right. But the shareholders are self-selected. People who would like an expected return of, say, 8 per cent with low volatility would not now buy bank shares. When banks told shareholders they intended to earn 15 per cent returns on equity, they were telling them they intended to run a risky business. They were also, as we know, telling the truth.

There is, however, one reason why high leverage might be attractive to shareholders, even in the absence of government guarantees: debt overhangs. In their important book on the perils of high bank leverage, professors Anat Admati of Stanford University and Martin Hellwig of the Max Planck Institute for Research on Collective Goods use the example of Kate, a woman who has borrowed $270,000 to buy a house for $300,000. Suppose she inherits $50,000 and uses that money to pay off part of her loan. She then owes $220,000. Now, the creditor is fully protected against loss if the house loses $80,000 in value instead of the protection of $30,000 the creditor obtained from Kate's initial equity. But what does Kate gain from putting an extra $50,000 into the house? She gains nothing, unless her rate of interest is lowered. If she cannot obtain a reduction in the rate of interest she pays, Kate has no incentive to repay any of the loan, because the benefit goes to her creditor, not to her. If she can find an investment with a higher post-tax return than the cost of her mortgage, she should put her money in that instead. If the value of her house rises, Kate will even have an interest in adding a second mortgage, to limit her potential losses.[30]

Now consider an extreme – but, alas, plausible – scenario for both house buyers and banks. Suppose Kate's house fell in value to $150,000. Her equity in the house would then fall from plus $30,000 to minus $120,000. If she were to put her inheritance of $50,000 into repaying the mortgage, she would still owe $70,000 more than the house was worth. On the assumption that this is a non-recourse loan (one where the creditor has no claim against her assets or income, beyond whatever the house is worth), the only entity that would benefit from her putting in the extra $50,000 is the creditor, whose loss would be reduced by that amount. Kate would gain nothing. It would make more sense for Kate to put her $50,000 in a risky investment. If it came off, the money would be hers. If it did not, she would be no worse off than if she sank the money into her house, since this would only benefit her creditor: it does not matter to her, after all, whether her creditor loses $120,000 or $70,000. Her loss is still limited to the initial $30,000 she invested. So Kate would chose 'gambling for resurrection'. It is what one would expect anybody with negative equity to do.

This is also relevant to banks. These are businesses with next to no equity in good times whose shareholders enjoy the benefits of limited liability: in other words, loans to banks (or any other company) are non-recourse. If the bank were to fall into negative equity – extremely likely to happen, in fact, given how leveraged they are – the downside would no longer matter to shareholders, since the losses fall on creditors or the government. So it would make sense to gamble on 'resurrection' or 'go for broke'. They can do this quite easily by taking on riskier loans and adopting riskier trading strategies.

Yet banks also enjoy explicit and implicit guarantees from the state (as is true of some house buyers). This means that not only shareholders, as we have seen, but even creditors fail to benefit if the shareholders decide to put more equity into the business. The only people who benefit from there being more equity in banks are taxpayers and other outsiders. Thus, those engaged in the wider economy would be less likely to suffer the results of a contagious panic and a huge recession if banks were better capitalized. In this situation, what is the optimal amount of equity for shareholders to put in? The answer is: as little as they can get away with. In the run-up to the crisis, that turned out to be amazingly little – just before the crisis, the median leverage ratio (ratio of debt to equity) in UK banks – that is, the value in the *middle* of the distribution, not at the extremes – was 50:1.[31] In other words, the median equity (equity of the bank in the middle of the distribution) was roughly 2 per cent of assets. And this means that the value of those assets needed to fall about 2 per cent before the business was bankrupt.

So the business model of contemporary banking is this: employ as much implicitly or explicitly guaranteed debt as possible; employ as little equity as one can; invest in high-risk assets; promise a high return on equity, unadjusted for risk; link bonuses to the achievement of this return target in the short term; ensure that as little as possible of those rewards are clawed back in the event of catastrophe; and become rich. This is a wonderful business model for bankers. But how is it for the rest of the world? The evidence suggests executives fared spectacularly well. But even shareholders have fared poorly. For everybody else, it was a disaster.[32]

The solution seems clear: force banks to fund themselves with equity to a far greater extent than they do today. A fragile business based on extreme maturity and risk mismatches (long-term and risky assets funded by short-term liabilities and notionally safe liabilities), needs the capacity to bear large losses, particularly if failure is likely to cause a global economic meltdown. Much higher equity would protect creditors, remove debt overhangs and eliminate the shareholders' incentive to go for broke. It would also make government promises not to save creditors more credible, since the failure of one institution would be less likely to bring down many others.

The Case for Higher Capital

So how much capital would do? A great deal more than the 3 per cent ratio being discussed in Basel is the answer. How can anybody seriously imagine that it is sensible to allow such important businesses and ones whose failure would cause such damage to operate with such a tiny equity cushion? A mere 3 per cent decline in the value of its assets would bankrupt the business. Well before it reached that point, the bank would be unable to raise funds on market terms and so would cease to be a going concern. If one wants to understand why such tiny equity slivers will not do, just look at the reported profits of

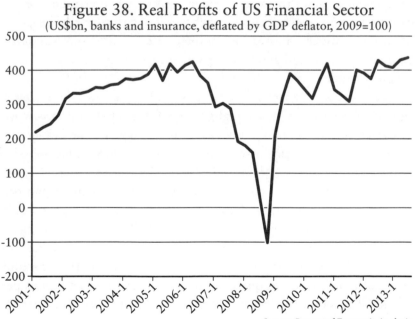

Figure 38. Real Profits of US Financial Sector
(US$bn, banks and insurance, deflated by GDP deflator, 2009=100)

Source: Bureau of Economic Analysis

the US financial sector during the 2007–08 crisis. The banking system has to be able to bear huge losses, because it is so cyclical. Remember, too, that without government intervention, the losses would have been vastly bigger as financial institutions went down like ninepins (see Figure 38).

An important paper co-authored by David Miles, a member of the Bank of England's monetary policy committee, recommended that bank capital be at least 20 per cent of risk-weighted assets.[33] Their fascinating analysis is based on the actual volatility of GDP for many countries over the past two hundred years and on the assumption that changes in the value of the risk-weighted assets of banks would be proportional to changes in GDP. It also assesses the present value of the economic costs of a financial crisis that would follow a large negative shock to the economy. This turns out to be at least 140 per cent of GDP. The conclusion of their cost-benefit analysis is that leverage should be a half to a third of what is now proposed, which would imply a ratio of common equity to bank assets of about 10 per cent. But the required equity could well be even higher. That depends on the chances of even bigger shocks and the benefits of a banking system able to survive them. The paper even argues that under certain not implausible assumptions the right level of capital might be 45 per cent of risk-weighted assets (more than 20 per cent common equity). In their book, Admati and Hellwig suggest a ratio of up to 30 per cent common equity.

There can be no exact science in this. Nobody knows, for example, how big the losses of banks might be in a future crisis. But it is worth stressing that fairly small underlying losses triggered the devastating recent series of financial crises in high-income countries. Future crises could easily be bigger. Nobody knows either whether higher equity would mean a (or even any) significant loss of economic opportunities, though lobbyists for banks suggest that much higher equity ratios would mean the end of our economy. This is wildly exaggerated. After all, banks are for the most part not funding new business activities, but rather the purchase of existing assets. The economic value of that is open to question. Moreover, the market would presumably generate alternative ways of financing good investment opportunities if highly leveraged bank lending were reduced. Finally, the degree of safety that is to be chosen is a matter of values. How much risk a society is willing to take is something it has to decide for itself. In making that decision it also has to decide how much banking risk it can bear, which will depend on the size of the banking sector relative to the economy and the solidity of the government's financial position.

In all one might regard a leverage ratio of 10:1 as a reasonable maximum and so an (unweighted) common equity ratio of 10 per cent as a minimum. Moreover, it is also vital not to rely much on risk-weighting. Andrew Haldane and Vasileios Madouros conclude from an analysis of failure among one hundred of the world's biggest and most complex banks in 2006, that 'simple-weighted measures [of capital] appear to have greater pre-crisis predictive power than risk-weighted alternatives'.[34] 'Keep it simple, stupid' is as good a rule in regulation as it is in life. There is yet another reason for emphasizing equal weighting of all risks, rather than complex risk-weighting: the latter gives a strong competitive advantage to mega-banks able to manipulate complex models. It would be best then to rely first on a straightforward leverage ratio, but add to it for the big banks whose failure would cause the biggest damage. Risk-weighted assets can play a secondary role. That way one would have a 'belt-and-braces' approach: a strong leverage ratio, plus a risk-weighted capital ratio as a back-up.

There is no doubt that substantially greater capital (measured at market value, not on an accounting basis) would bring greater stability to the banking system. There is also no doubt that financial crises are spectacularly costly. Furthermore, there is no doubt that banks do not internalize those costs. Moreover, would a bank now happily lend to borrowers with just 3 per cent equity in their business or home? Hardly. So why should governments permit institutions as important as banks to operate with such small equity cushions? The case for higher capital requirements seems overwhelming. It also has the great merit of being relatively simple, particularly if the capital that regulators rely upon most is common equity, with no risk-weighting of assets, measured at market value.

Objections to Higher Equity Capital

The demand for substantially higher equity capital is controversial. That is hardly surprising, since it would kill the lucrative business model of banking on the state. So what are the objections? Here are seven.

First, it is objected that higher equity capital 'would be expensive for banks, because the money sits on banks' balance sheets and essentially can't be invested to bring in more profits'.[35] This is a surprisingly common blunder. Such comments show a confusion between liquid assets (such as government debt), which banks do indeed hold, with equity, which is just a way of funding the balance sheet, its advantage being that it is unambiguously loss-bearing. In other words, this reveals a fundamental confusion between the two sides of banks' balance sheets: their assets, which are what banks own, and liabilities, which are how banks fund themselves. Equity is a liability: it is a way of funding a bank, not an asset (investment) owned by a bank. Equity in banks is an asset of shareholders.

Second, it is objected, as I have just noted, that higher capital would be too costly to the banks. This objection is at least intellectually coherent, albeit wrong. The general answer is that it would cost nothing, except to the extent that it reduced the benefits to the bank of the tax deductibility of interest (which would not be a cost to society) or reduced the benefits to the bank of state guarantees of bank debt (which would be a gain to society). Otherwise, the effect of lower leverage in raising the cost of funds should be offset by a lower expected return on equity (because the volatility of returns would fall) and a lower cost of debt (because bank liabilities would be safer). In his co-authored paper, Professor Miles concludes from an empirical examination that a halving in the leverage of British banking from 30:1 to 15:1 (assets over Tier 1 capital – common equity, retained earnings and preferred stock) would raise the weighted average cost of all capital by a mere eighteen basis points (0.18 per cent).[36] Of course, this would still leave leverage too high. But a move to 10:1 or far lower would not impose prohibitive costs. Of course, it would lower the return on equity. But such a reduction would be highly desirable: it would reflect a decision to make banks safer. Higher capital would only be bad for bankers, who could no longer make themselves rich by promising high risk-unadjusted returns on equity with a straight face.

Third, it is objected that demanding higher bank capital would damage the economy. As Frank Keating of the American Bankers' Association argues in the opening quotation of this chapter, 'Capital comes at a cost – both to banks and to the economy at large in the form of forgone lending as institutions shrink to meet extreme capital-to-asset ratios.'

Bankers frequently argue that, if their overall lending were restricted, business must suffer. But the loans on the balance sheets of banks are overwhelmingly not to business, but rather to households and other financial companies.[37] In the case of the UK, for example, as of August 2013, 34 per cent of outstanding lending from banks was to other financial businesses, 43 per cent was to individuals, secured on dwellings, 4 per cent was to other loans to individuals, 10 per cent was to real estate and construction, and the remaining 9 per cent was to all other beneficiaries, including to non-financial businesses (other than real estate and construction).

Banks could reallocate their funds towards funding business if they wanted to do so (or found it sufficiently profitable to do so). This would also be desirable. Loans to other financial institutions are an indicator of the complex network of connections among banks, which exacerbated the panic in 2008–09. Most loans to households and a large portion of the loans to business simply leverage up the property assets of the country, thereby creating significant fragility for at least questionable economic gains. The benefits of further rises in lending for home purchase in particular are therefore social rather than economic: such lending widens home ownership, albeit at the price of imposing heavy mortgage burdens on young households. Moreover, recent work, notably at the Bank for International Settlements, indicates that increasing the financial development of the economy beyond a certain point lowers productivity growth, rather than raises it.[38] Many of the high-income countries seem to be beyond that point.

Alan Greenspan has made much the same argument in a more sophisticated form: 'Any excess bank equity capital also would constitute a buffer that is not otherwise available to finance productivity-enhancing capital investment.'[39] In other words, equity, being scarce, should not be wasted on making banks safer.

This is a puzzling argument. Remember that equity is not an idle buffer: it is merely another liability of banks, just like their debt and so a safer and less crisis-prone way to fund lending. Furthermore, if more equity went to funding banks, then the leverage in other (today far less leveraged) businesses would rise, as equity shifted towards banking. That would make the economy as a whole less vulnerable to waves of financial sector bankruptcy, but without affecting its overall wealth. After all, as Mr Greenspan himself notes, 'Consolidated, the net capital stock of a nation must equal the sum of the equity of households, businesses of governments, adjusted for the national's net international investment position.' A nation's debt nets out to zero if one ignores claims on – and liabilities to – foreigners. Shifting equity from one sector would not change the total net equity (wealth) of a society. Net equity claims of the public held via banks would increase and net equity claims held via direct investment would shrink. That is all.

In February 2014, 5 per cent of the value of the US stock market and 12 per cent of the value of the UK equity market consisted of shares in banks. Assume that the total equity of banks had to rise threefold and that other companies reduced their equity by borrowing, with the total value of the stock market remaining the same. Then, on the same date, the market capitalization of US banks would be 19 per cent of the US stock market and 55 per cent of the UK stock market. The former looks conceivable. The latter does not. But UK banks are global entities. The likelihood is that many of the shares would end up being held by foreigners. Indeed, the companies in the UK stock market hold so many foreign assets that looking at this as a national market is highly misleading.

None the less, it is unlikely that the world's shareholders would want so much of their wealth (net claims on the economy) to be channelled through (and managed by) a small number of very big banks. The likelihood then is that if equity requirements were raised, the balance sheets of the banks would be forced to shrink and risk-taking would move outside the banking sector. In and of itself, this would be hugely desirable, though it would involve a significant transitional problem, and new institutional forms might need to be created for the finance of entities that could not borrow directly in the bond markets. Among other things, the revival of markets in securitized debt would be necessary. But, crucially, the risk-taking capacity of the society would *not* fall, because its total equity would not fall.

During the (possibly lengthy) transition, it would be possible to raise the equity of banks other than by letting them shrink their balance sheets. The obvious way to achieve this would be to prevent them from paying dividends or buying back their shares until equity has reached the level needed to fund desired balance sheets at lower leverage. Yet it is of course possible – even likely – that today's huge stock of bank assets could not generate the returns on equity desired by shareholders at lower leverage. This would be because a previous subsidy (free implicit insurance provided by governments), which encouraged excessive leverage in the economy, is being withdrawn. The government might wish to use some of that now withdrawn subsidy to pay for de-leveraging directly, by promoting the write-down of excessive debt.

A more subtle argument that Mr Greenspan might be making is that if banks were to be still allowed to create leverage on the present scale, the total quantity of economic activity would be greater than it otherwise would be. This would be true, however, if and only if the economy had redundant resources that could be mobilized in this way alone. But it would be possible to achieve the same effect by exploiting the ability of the central bank (or the government) to create money directly and spend it within the economy or transfer it to citizens or residents to spend in the economy. Mobilizing redundant resources does not depend on allowing the banking sector to become massively (and dangerously) leveraged.

In addition, if the problem with lower leverage is that bank loans would become more expensive to borrowers, the central bank can lower interest rates, at least when it is not up against the zero bound. Even in the latter situation, the government could lower the cost of bank loans by targeted subsidies rather than by permitting excessive leverage.

Also remember that crises due to excessive leverage impose enormous costs. For this reason, a study prepared for the Basel Committee on Banking Supervision concluded that the net economic impact of significantly higher capital standards was strongly positive, because they could lower the incidence of crises significantly.[40]

Fourth, it is objected that illiquidity is a more important danger to banks than lack of capital. The response is well laid out by professors Admati and Hellwig: 'If ... institutions are highly indebted, it does not take much of a shock for solvency concerns to arise. Such concerns can lead creditors to withdraw their money as soon as they can, causing liquidity problems for banks.'[41] Moreover, acting as lender of last resort becomes far easier for the central bank if it has no doubt about the solvency of the institution it is temporarily funding. Professor Goodhart makes the suggestion that a bank's capital requirements might be lowered as its liquidity position strengthens or raised as it weakens. Thus the closer it came to becoming a narrow bank, the lower its capital requirements would be.[42]

Fifth, it is objected that shrinking the balance sheets of banks must lead to a calamitous shrinkage of the money supply. This can be answered, in part, by ensuring that balance sheets do not shrink, by insisting on target *levels* of equity, rather than ratios. But there are at least two other considerations. One is that it is hard to believe that the borderline between money and non-money is well defined in today's economy. This is why reliance on the quantity of money in monetary policy turned out to be so disappointing. The other consideration is that the central bank can create money by other means if it wishes to do so. One possibility would be to continue to purchase assets from the non-bank private sector, thereby raising the latter's holdings of cash and increasing the reserves of banks. In order to prevent this from leading to the shrinkage of bank holdings of other assets, the regulator would need to specify that the holding of central-bank reserves does not count against a bank's capital. This obviously makes sense, since default by the issuer of a fiat currency is inconceivable.

Sixth, it is objected that the combination of bail-inable debt (debt that is contractually available for conversion into equity if required) with effective resolution regimes is an adequate substitute for higher capital requirements, while allowing banks to continue to benefit from the tax deductibility of interest.

There are at least two general problems with this. The first is that the lower the equity and the more plausible bail-in becomes, the more the bail-inable debt would have the characteristics of equity, in which case it would not be a cheaper alternative for banks, apart from tax deductibility. Second, the combination of resolution with bail-in of certain classes of debt generates the risk of a funding cliff: as banks approach the trigger point, willingness to buy such securities might dry up completely. This is why governments saved the owners of hybrid securities – debt securities supposedly convertible into equity – in the crisis. They turned out to be useless as a way of creating equity for undercapitalized banks.[43] The triggering of conversion of hybrid debt turned out to be 'time inconsistent' – a promise the authorities did not dare to keep. Triggering conversion would be less of a problem if hybrids had very long maturities. But that would merely make them even more like equity. So why not just rely on equity?

The most intriguing proposal aimed at getting round such difficulties is that for Equity Recourse Notes (ERNs), proposed by Jeremy Bulow of Stanford University, Jacob Goldfield, formerly at Goldman Sachs, and Paul Klemperer of Oxford University.[44]

ERNs are a form of 'contingent capital' that would start life as debt but convert into equity payment if the issuer suffered large losses in market value. The market would trigger conversion, while the value at conversion would be tied to the share price on the date of issue. If, for example, an ERN were issued when a bank's share price was $80, the bank would be required to pay in shares on any subsequent date on which an interest or principal payment was due if its shares traded at less than 25 per cent of the price on the issue date (in this case $20). The issuer would have the right, but not the obligation, to pay in shares if the stock were trading at a higher price than this. Moreover, the shares would be valued at the trigger price. In the example above, if a payment of $100,000 were due to bondholders and shares were trading at or below $20, the bank would be required to pay out 5,000 common shares ($100,000 divided by $20). Finally, the conversion would take the form of payment when due. Whether any given payment is to be made in shares or cash is determined by the share price on the due date of the payment. In the example, if the share price were $18 on one payment date but climbed to $22 on a later payment date, the bank would have to make the first payment in shares but would have the option of making the second payment in cash.

It is evident that this form of debt would become equity automatically if it were needed. That makes it an attractive form of bail-inable debt. But is it superior to equity, apart from the fact that it should benefit from the unjustifiably favourable tax treatment of debt? The answer is: maybe so, but not obviously.

Proponents argue that ERNs have a number of advantages over equity. Thus, although ERNs are always equity in the states of the world that matter for protecting taxpayers, they remain debt in other states, and many also argue that equity is intrinsically more costly than debt (rightly or, more plausibly, wrongly). Again, since ERNs represent an apparently less radical (though also more unfamiliar) alternative to more equity, it might be possible to require significantly more capital in this form than in the form of common equity. Proponents also argue that with higher equity, riskier activities might migrate to other parts of the financial system. They suggest as well that people might believe banks with high equity are so much safer that management and regulators would become laxer and more accident-prone.

Yet none of these arguments is decisive. The assertion is frequently made that equity is costly. But the reasons for this are never made entirely clear (if we leave aside fiscal and other subsidies). Furthermore, with higher leverage, the 'debt overhang' problem continues: shareholders would have less interest in running a bank prudently because much of the benefit of their doing so would accrue to creditors, including surely owners of ERNs. Again, if ERNs were seen as an onerous and costly regulatory requirement, as is inevitable, then the pressure for migration of risk to other parts of the industry would remain. To reiterate, if high equity ratios made management and regulators laxer, so would ERNs. Indeed they might be worse because owners of ERNs would have no managerial control over the bank before conversion into equity. There might also be enhanced instability as a bank's share price comes close to a trigger point. Moreover, the advantage of ERNs in halting a cash drain when a bank became distressed might be available to equity if the latter included a provision allowing a halt to pay-outs when share prices reached a trigger point.

In all, while ERNs are clearly an excellent form of bail-inable debt, it is not clear they are superior to additional equity. In general, the simple beats the complex if it does the same job. And equity is simpler than complex hybrids.

A seventh objection is that relying solely on leverage relative to total assets, rather than relative to risk-weighted assets, again risks arbitrage, with banks choosing riskier assets since they would not be penalized for doing so and might, in this way, hope to meet their return on equity targets. Peter Sands of Standard Chartered has made this argument.[45] But shareholders should only be interested in their risk-adjusted returns. If taking on more risk does not raise risk-adjusted returns, shareholders should flee. If it does raise risk-adjusted returns, it should have happened anyway. Moreover, with substantially higher equity, banks could take on more risk safely. Finally, the disaster came from what banks wrongly thought to be safe. Risk-weighting is extremely unreliable, because the samples from which the weights are derived are always too small or irrelevant.

A similar objection arises over regulatory arbitrage: with high levels of equity imposed on banks, risk would migrate elsewhere, as happened prior to the crisis of 2007–08. It would be extremely important, therefore, to ensure that the balance sheets of significant financial institutions are fully consolidated. It would be equally important to ensure oversight over the system as a whole, to check where risks might be emerging. That is part of macroprudential regulation, to which we turn in the next section.

Raising the capital requirements of banks would certainly not fix everything. But if it were combined with significantly higher capital requirements still for the biggest and most interconnected institutions, it would take us a very long way in the right direction, in a relatively simple manner. Indeed, the higher the capital requirement, the less important changes in structure become. Mr Haldane and Mr Madouros add the possibility of taxing interconnectedness, which would seem to make much sense.[46] But capital is key. A basic leverage ratio of 10:1, with conservation, countercylical and large-firm buffers on top, might lead to leverage ratios in good times of six to one. That would be a vastly safer system.[47]

The many changes now under way do not do the simple thing that would render the financial system less fragile: make it far better able to bear losses. Indeed, so long as the system allows leverage of 30:1, these businesses are designed to fail. The belief that failure of a business can be managed smoothly and without systemic effects, with hybrid capital instruments, resolution regimes and living wills, is naively optimistic.

BEING MACRO-PRUDENT

Making sure that individual financial institutions and particularly large global institutions fund themselves with more equity capital is the most important way to make them – and so the system as a whole – more resilient to the inevitable shocks. But there is another equally important challenge, that of ensuring the resilience of the system as a whole. That is the task of a newly discovered regulatory activity: 'macroprudential supervision' – the official label for the job of regulating the stability of the financial system as a whole. So can it work?

First, here is some background. The fundamental assumption of orthodox policy, prior to the crisis, was that the combination of inflation targeting with microprudential supervision would deliver stability. Should it, by any chance, fail to do so, it would be better to be 'clean' than 'lean': it would be both easier and more effective to clean up a financial mess after it had emerged than use monetary policy to try to prevent it.[48] This orthodoxy has taken a hammering. It is now generally agreed that it is hard to clean up after an asset-price bubble accompanied by (or indeed caused by) a credit boom. So this is where macroprudential policy comes in. The idea of macroprudential regulation is to look at how the activities of the financial system as a whole are destabilizing the economy and so increasing risks for all financial institutions. This raises five big questions: What is this regulation for? Why is it needed? How should it be done? Who should be in charge? Will it work?[49]

The Purpose of Macroprudential Policy

Macroprudential policy has two, mirror-image functions: to protect the financial system from the economy and the economy from the financial system. In its former guise, macroprudential policy recognizes that a monetary policy designed to achieve price stability can encourage destabilizing developments in the financial system. The aim, then, is to prevent or at least reduce the undesirable consequences of such a development. In this guise, then, macroprudential policy is concerned with financial stability. It works by, for example, raising equity requirements of lenders or borrowers in a boom. In its latter guise, macroprudential policy is aimed at protecting the economy from the excesses of the financial system, in both boom and bust. It works by actions that curb lending.

Macroprudential regulation borders on microprudential regulation at one end, and monetary policy at the other. In theory, targeting monetary policy at price stability and macroprudential policy at financial policy ought to work, at least in normal times. When interest rates are at the zero lower bound, however, the problem will be far bigger: with a badly damaged financial system, monetary policy works badly, if at all. So fixing the financial system – a task for macroprudential policy – becomes a necessary condition for effective monetary policy. Alternatively, another macroeconomic policy – probably fiscal policy – needs to be employed. Moreover, if monetary policy has historically worked by creating destabilizing financial bubbles, as argued in Chapter Five, the new macroprudential policy might weaken the effectiveness of monetary policy, possibly making the zero lower bound a more frequent event. In short, the assumption that targeting monetary policy at price stability and macroprudential policy at financial stability will be easy is optimistic.

The Need for Macroprudential Policy

The argument for macroprudential policy is that a financial system in which individual institutions look sound may be unstable, because of their exposure to (and generation of) common risks. Each institution may be diversified. But they will be vulnerable if all are diversified in the same way. Worse, being subjected to similar microprudential regulation makes it *more* likely that firms will end up being diversified in much the same way and exposed to many of the same risks.

So what are the common risks to which financial firms might be exposed? An obvious example is to the economic cycle or, worse still, the property cycle. A second set of shared risks will be the same funding markets. A third set of shared risks will be the same accounting rules, particularly mark-to-market accounting in a crisis. A fourth set of shared risks will be the same suppliers of insurance against shared risks. A fifth set of shared risks will be use of the same risk-management models. A sixth set of shared risks will be the rating agencies. A seventh set of shared risks will be the same regulatory standards implemented in the same way.

A system becomes risky if all its members are significantly exposed to the same risk. Riskiness of the system as a whole is quite different from the perceived riskiness of individual institutions. National banking families become risky when all their members are risky in the same way; they become safer when their members are risky in different ways. Yet there is something more to it even than that. It is not only that members of the financial system are exposed to common risks. It is also that they generate common risks, for one another and for the economy as a whole. Financial systems are not just absorbers of risks, but creators of risks. This, in essence, is why macroprudential policy is necessary.

The Implementation of Macroprudential Policy

Macroprudential policy needs to be as automatic and non-discretionary as possible. It is desirable, for example, to relate capital requirements of – or provisioning by – financial institutions to the rate of credit growth: the faster the latter, the higher the former. It will be crucial to ensure that not only institutions, but the mass of their borrowers, can take large losses without too much difficulty. Similarly, it will be important to impose constraints, in the form of charges or higher capital requirements, on extreme maturity transformation – that is the funding of ultra long-term and risky assets with short-term and safe liabilities. Much of this can, in principle, be done automatically. But there are some things that cannot be done in a mechanical way. One of the most obvious is watching over regulatory arbitrage: if risks are migrating out of the formal system, regulators will need to remain very alert. Unfortunately, this is not the only area where discretion will be necessary. Another is being aware of the systemic risks created by regulation, particularly the tendency to force regulated institutions to take the same risks in the same way and so become more homogeneous and thus more exposed to identical surprises. Mono-crop economies are vulnerable to a disaster to that one crop. Similarly mono-risk financial systems are also vulnerable to concentrated disasters.

The Responsibility for Macroprudential Policy

Given the close connection between macroprudential policy and monetary policy, the responsibility should rest with the central bank, in conjunction with the prudential regulators. It is not clear whether or not a separate group should be responsible for macroprudential policy. The argument in favour of a separate official body is that it should include expertise not relevant to monetary policy, such as that of the prudential regulator. The argument against is that monetary policy and macroprudential policy will interact closely and frequently will be alternative ways of achieving the same objective. It would be desirable for countries to experiment with the alternatives of separation and integration. In any case, monetary policymakers will have to be very aware of what the macroprudential regulators are trying to do, since it will have a profound effect on the course of monetary policy.

The Effectiveness of Macroprudential Policy

Finally, will it actually work? Nobody knows. The idea that it might is an example of what Friedrich Hayek would have called the 'fatal conceit' – the assumption of knowledge where it does not exist. On the other hand, the alternatives to trying all seem to be worse: having further huge crises or relying on the blunt instrument of monetary policy. But it also has to be recognized that the macroprudential regulators will be subject to political pressures, to conflicts with the direction of monetary policy, and to their own ignorance. It is a valiant but risky undertaking. That is why higher capital is so important. If crises will still happen, as Minsky argued, then the core of the financial system has to have the ability to survive, just as bridges need to survive hurricanes.

CONCLUSION

The reaction to the crisis has included a host of ambitious regulatory efforts. Many are important, but two seem to be vital: raising capital sharply and making macroprudential regulation work. The former has definitely not yet gone far enough. It is all too easy to imagine shocks that would, once again, decapitalize the financial system. The case for reducing the leverage ratio to no more than 10:1 is overwhelming. The present situation in which banks are stuck to the state like a Siamese twin must not endure. It creates huge problems of incentive and so increases vulnerability to crises in the long run. Furthermore, macroprudential regulation, though certainly greatly helped by higher capital standards, must also be made to work. The most important element will be automatic adjustment to capital and liquidity standards over the cycle.

At present, the financial system is designed to fail. Yet, strengthening it is only part of the answer. The other part is fixing the macroeconomic mess into which the world has fallen. That is the topic of Chapters Eight and Nine.

8

The Long Journey Ahead

There is a risk that synchronized fiscal adjustment across several major economies could adversely impact the recovery. There is also a risk that failure to implement consolidation where necessary would undermine confidence and hamper growth. Reflecting this balance, advanced economies have committed to fiscal plans that will at least halve deficits by 2013 and stabilize or reduce government debt-to-GDP ratios by 2016.

G-20 communiqué, Toronto, 27 June 2010[1]

There are some people who think we don't have to take all these tough decisions to deal with our debts. They say that our focus on deficit reduction is damaging growth. And what we need to do is to spend more and borrow more. It's as if they think there's some magic money tree. Well let me tell you a plain truth: there isn't.

David Cameron, UK prime minister, 7 March 2013[2]

How do high-income countries restore their economic vibrancy? Is this possible or does a 'new normal' dictate miserable performance? Is the current policy approach right and, if not, what would be better? Where do emerging economies fit in? These questions are to be addressed in this chapter, which examines the global picture, and then Chapter Ten, which will focus on the Eurozone.

This chapter's focus is on one topic: how to restore a sustainable macroeconomic balance in high-income economies and so in the world. This necessitates both moving out of the post-crisis slump and away from the extreme private-sector savings glut revealed by today's low real interest rates and chronic global imbalances. It also necessitates doing both of these things without a return to accumulation of excessive private debt. This combination is going to be hard to achieve. We seem, in brief, to confront a nasty choice between an inadequate recovery and an unsustainable one.

These are, of course, not the only economic challenges confronting high-income economies, let alone the rest of the world. Yet the immediate tasks of restoring stability to these economies and fixing the conditions that caused the instability are not only important in themselves: they are necessary conditions for dealing with those other challenges. The first part of the solution, discussed in Chapter Seven, is making the financial system more robust. The second, to be discussed in this chapter, is overcoming the macroeconomic challenges of deficient demand, excessive debt and global imbalances.

The best way of thinking about this – also relevant to the Eurozone crisis – is in terms of flows, stocks and reforms. The flow challenges are those of adjusting income and spending, and borrowing and lending, to deliver full employment and growth in line with potential. The stock challenge is that of dealing with the overhang of private and, in some cases, public debt. The reform challenge is that of creating better-balanced domestic and world economies, supported by functioning institutions that deliver stability and widely shared prosperity. At the end of these adjustments, balance sheets need to be sound, the financial system needs to be healthy, and spending needs to be consistent with high levels of economic activity and employment.

It all sounds so simple. Alas, it is not. Far more likely is an enduring slump in high-income countries, at least relative to pre-crisis expectations. That would impose huge costs – of investments unmade, of businesses not started, of skills atrophied and of hopes destroyed. Should that fate be avoided, another temporary credit-driven boom might emerge, followed by another and still bigger crash. Worst of all, in a world marked by domestic economic stresses and a global transition of power, a breakdown in cooperation might occur.

This has to be avoided. So how? To answer that question, the discussion will be divided as follows. First, it will show that this is indeed a large slump. Second, it will analyse the debate over austerity. Third, it will consider how to manage debt. Fourth, it will examine structural obstacles to growth. Finally, it will turn to complementary global adjustments and reforms.

THE SLUMP

Chapters One and Five have already looked at what has happened to the crisis-hit economies and, above all, the costs in terms of output and employment. Figures 39 and 40 give a longer-term picture for the crisis-hit economies on which this chapter will focus – the US and the UK – with the Eurozone to be discussed in Chapter Nine.

In the US, a fitted quarterly trend growth rate is shown for 1950 to the end of 2007, just before the crisis hit. The trend growth of the US economy was 3.4 per cent a year over this lengthy period. The UK's trend growth over the 1955–2007 period was 2.8 per cent. Moreover, deviations of actual growth from the fitted trends (also shown, on the

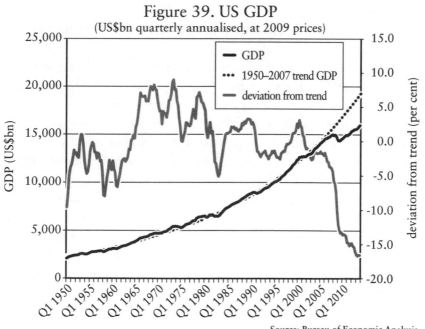

Figure 39. US GDP
(US$bn quarterly annualised, at 2009 prices)

Source: Bureau of Economic Analysis

259

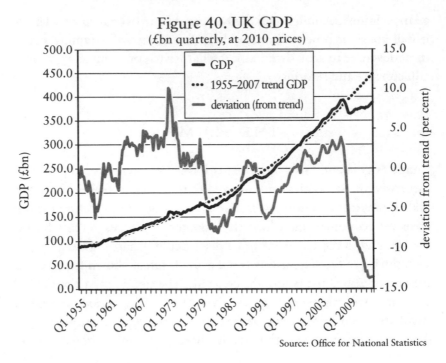

Figure 40. UK GDP
(£bn quarterly, at 2010 prices)

Source: Office for National Statistics

right-hand scale) were fairly modest in both directions, in both the US and the UK.

Then came the post-2007 'great recession'. By the last quarter of 2013, US GDP was 17 per cent below the historic trend. The UK's reduction was smaller, at 14 per cent, largely because it had been somewhat above trend levels before the crisis (see Figure 40). These are gigantic shortfalls. Assume, optimistically, that the US economy manages to grow at 3 per cent a year from now on. Assume that the relevant real rate of interest for discounting future GDP is also 3 per cent. Then the cumulative present value of the lost US GDP over the next century would be seventeen times the GDP of 2013.[3] If the discount rate were lower than the rate of growth, the amount of lost GDP would be still bigger. Such costs are greater than those of world wars. Indeed, both the US and the UK managed to regain or exceed the pre-Second World War trend level and rate of growth after that conflagration was over. Thus, the long-run economic costs of wars, in terms of subsequent levels of GDP, have been far smaller than those of big financial crises. The collapse of financial systems and the need to de-leverage impose enormous costs.

Current estimates of output gaps – the gap between actual output and estimates of potential or full-capacity output – are far smaller than the deviations from trend shown in the Figures. The reason for this is that estimates of potential output always follow actual output. In its November 2013 *Economic Outlook*, the Organisation for Economic Co-operation and Development (OECD), for example, estimated the US output gap at 3 per cent of potential output and the UK output gap at 2.5 per cent in 2013 – substantial, but far smaller than the output shortfalls relative to trend, in that year. For the pessimistic view that the potential level of output today has fallen far below the pre-crisis trend level of output (to be precise, about 14 per cent below trend in the case of the US and 11.5 per cent in the case of the UK), one might suggest three explanations. The first is that the pre-crisis trend exaggerated potential (or at least sustainable) output. The second is that the crisis destroyed potential output. The third is that the OECD and other forecasters that have reached similar conclusions are far too pessimistic.

The Pre-Crisis Trend was Exaggerated

It is easy to accept that the boom in credit and the measured output of the financial sector exaggerated both true output and potential output. One reason for this would be that it is easy for the extension of credit to be converted into incomes. If someone takes a flat fee out of a bad loan, it will appear as income in the national accounts. Yet there are arguments against the view that such spurious activity means that true, long-run potential output was vastly below actual output in 2007.

The first is that, as Figures 39 and 40 show, there was no rise in output above trend in the US in the 2000s – rather the opposite, in fact. Even in the case of the UK, output was only 4 per cent above the long-run trend in the second quarter of 2007. Second, there was no sign in wage or price inflation of a huge excess of actual over sustainable output during the pre-crisis period. Third, if the story were essentially sectoral, and so not about the economy as a whole, one would expect falls in employment to be concentrated in crisis-hit sectors. In the US, employment in construction did decline by 26 per cent between 2007 and 2012, while that in real estate fell by 11 per cent. But employment in finance and insurance fell by only 6 per cent, against a fall of 4 per cent in the economy as a whole. Employment fell by 7 per cent in wholesale and retail distribution, 11 per cent in media and related industries and, astonishingly, 14 per cent in manufacturing. In other words, the collapse in employment was across the board. This strongly supports the proposition that the output and employment declines were due to a collapse in aggregate demand.[4]

The Crisis Devastated Potential Output

The second explanation for the contrast between the huge shortfalls in output relative to long-term trends and relatively modest estimates of the current output gap is that the crisis has damaged potential output and its rate of growth. This is certainly correct. One can propose two explanations. The first is that the crisis damaged the financial system's ability to service the economy. The second is that the slump lowered both investment and employment. The long-term unemployed then become less employable. Note, however, that these costs were largely unnecessary. Stronger action to sustain demand could have reduced them substantially.

Forecasters are too Pessimistic

The third explanation is that forecasters are just too pessimistic. Yet one strong argument in favour of the forecasters' pessimistic position can be made: the stability of inflation. If there was a huge amount of slack, why has inflation not fallen further or even turned into outright deflation? There are two responses. The first, proposed by the International Monetary Fund, is that expectations are anchored by the inflation-targeting of central banks.[5] The second is that the principal determinant of inflation remains labour costs. But there is very strong resistance to nominal wage cuts, even in depressed economies.

The Case for Action

Consider two policy alternatives: strong stimulus on the one hand and austerity on the other. If one adopted the first strategy when a great deal of economic slack existed, the outcome would be a stronger recovery. If one were to adopt the stimulus strategy when there was no excess capacity in the economy, there would be inflation, current-account deficits, or both. Now turn to the second alternative: austerity. If there were economic slack, the economy would adapt to the policy by shrinking potential output towards its actual level, largely through shrunken investment. If there were no slack, the policy would deliver the predetermined outcome. In other words, austerity would become a self-fulfilling prophecy.

So, if one were wrong to be optimistic, the cost would be an inflation overshoot, followed by a policy correction. If one were wrong to be pessimistic, the cost would be a permanently smaller economy. The former error is less damaging than the latter. The right risk to take then is stimulus, because the costs of greater austerity would be higher. Moreover, the likelihood is that in fact there is a great deal of slack after such huge falls in output. That reinforces the case for taking the risk of expansionary policies.

HOW TO STIMULATE ECONOMIES[6]

Countries with flexible exchange rates, such as the US and the UK, can employ both fiscal and monetary policies, one of these options, or neither. So, let us start by accepting arguments for some form of stimulus, before looking briefly at the arguments for using neither.

The Limits of Monetary Policy

Is it sensible to rely on monetary policy alone? Here are four arguments against doing so.

First, one obviously needs to use the most effective policies available. The busts that follow prolonged credit booms are both very costly and very hard to remedy.[7] One reason for this is that with interest rates at or close to the zero bound, the effectiveness of monetary policy is constrained, though not zero. Prolonged periods of ultra-low interest rates, together with quantitative easing and 'forward guidance' – indications of low policy rates far into the future – have brought only a modest recovery. Thus, as of early 2014, neither the US nor the UK had achieved rates of growth higher than before the crisis. The recovery had, accordingly, not even begun to close the proportional gap between actual output and the pre-crisis trend.

Second, as Simon Wren-Lewis of Oxford University notes, the impact of unconventional monetary policy is quite hard to calibrate.[8] Nobody doubts that a monetary policy capable of generating adequate growth of nominal demand exists. But when both the right way to carry out the monetary policy and its impact are so uncertain, caution must be advised. As John Williams, president of the Federal Reserve Bank of San Francisco, points out: with multiple-policy instruments, the 'optimal strategy is to rely on the instrument associated with the least uncertainty and use alternative, more uncertain instruments only when the least uncertain instrument is employed to its fullest extent possible'.[9] When interest rates are close to zero, the least uncertain policy is quite likely to be fiscal policy.

Third, aggressive monetary policy creates risks of its own. It may keep zombie companies alive too long. It may distort price signals, so creating wasteful investment. Above all, it may encourage another round of irresponsible lending and spending. Indeed, this is the argument made by some critics of such policies, including William White, former chief economist of the Bank for International Settlements, and Raghuram Rajan, now governor of the Reserve Bank of India.[10]

Finally, an aggressive monetary policy by the US, producer of the world's reserve currency, might be particularly destabilizing, since it confronts other countries with a painful choice: import US monetary policy and risk domestic destabilization; or refuse to import US monetary policy and risk exchange-rate instability; or impose controls on capital inflows and so seek to separate the economy from global capital markets.

Some economists go further by arguing that the aggressive monetary policies, particularly unconventional policies, risk causing high inflation or even hyperinflation. Austrian economists have long believed this must be the case. Some monetarists believe it, too: Allan Meltzer of Carnegie Mellon University is an influential example.[11] The argument is that the expansion of the monetary base must lead to a multiple expansion of bank lending and so of the money supply, ending in high inflation.

This is nonsense. Consider the misnamed 'money multiplier' – the supposed relationship between the banks' holdings of reserves at the central bank and the money supply (see Figure 37). As Figure 41 shows, the ratio of US M2 (the broadest measure of the money supply now published by the Federal Reserve) to bank reserves doubled between 1994 and 2008, whereupon it collapsed when unconventional monetary policy began. By February 2014, the multiplier was only four. Bank reserves rose from $95bn in April 2008 to $2.7tn in February 2014. There was no multiplier effect on M2. Moreover, the central bank, not the banks, controls the quantity of reserves (with a little help from the public's desire for cash).[12] It can create and liquidate reserves, by buying and selling assets or by lending and withdrawing loans to and from the banks. Finally, the central bank can sterilize

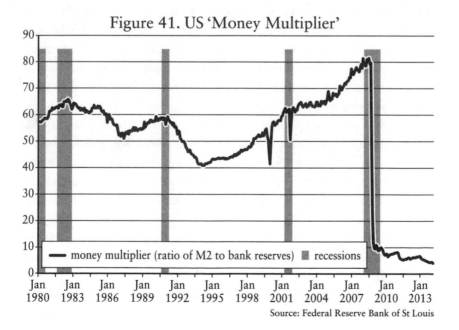

Figure 41. US 'Money Multiplier'

money multiplier (ratio of M2 to bank reserves) ■ recessions

Source: Federal Reserve Bank of St Louis

reserves by changing reserve requirements, and it can decide how onerous to make such requirements by determining the rate of interest it pays on reserves.

If interest rates were to remain at zero when a normal appetite for risk returns, credit and money would start to grow too fast, the economy would overheat, and everything would end up as critics fear. *But the conditions that caused interest rates to fall to zero are the very conditions that prevent such a credit explosion.* When the conditions change, policies must change. And, we must assume, they will.

Yet even if the hysteria about hyperinflation is wrong, the objections to an exclusive reliance on monetary policy create a *prima facie* case for using fiscal policy. So why has it been widely rejected?

The Case against Fiscal Austerity

The starting point for any discussion of the role of fiscal policy is over the size of fiscal 'multipliers' – the ratio of the change in national income to the change in government spending that drives it. A widely shared conclusion is that, at the zero rate bound, these multipliers are likely to be 0.5 or so at their lowest and, more likely, to be well over one.[13] The reasons why fiscal multipliers should be high in today's circumstances are as follows: economic agents are far more likely than normal to be unable to borrow freely and so spend now out of future income, which is what borrowing permits; cutting public spending is likely to make many would-be borrowers less creditworthy and so in a worse position to take advantage of the aggressive monetary policy; and many countries are tightening simultaneously. In 2012, J. Bradford de Long of the University of California, Berkeley, and Lawrence Summers, then back at Harvard University after his period in the White House, added two other points. The first was that if shortfalls in output damaged potential output – an idea known as 'hysteresis' – the case for expansionary fiscal policy would be stronger. Second, if real interest rates were low enough and multiplier and hysteresis effects strong enough, fiscal stimulus would even pay for itself. Deficits could be a free lunch.[14]

Yet, as we know (see Chapter One above), opposition to fiscal stimulus was strong. One justification for this was the classical view that the economy operates at full capacity at all times. If one believes that, the explanation for the sharp reduction in output during the 'great recession' might be that the workers of the world decided to take a vacation, while only pretending they were unemployed. In other words, the equilibrium output capacity collapsed, because people suddenly decided to withdraw their labour instead of being involuntarily unemployed. Yes, it does sound silly: that is because it is.[15]

Some economists argued for 'expansionary fiscal contraction': thus, the confidence benefits of a return to sustainable public finances, particularly if achieved by slashing spending, outweighs the depressing effect on demand. Alberto Alesina of Harvard University and Silvia Ardagna of Goldman Sachs wrote the most influential paper arguing this case.[16] Paul Krugman, the Nobel laureate economist and *New York Times* columnist, ridiculed it as belief in a 'confidence fairy'.[17] But the most influential criticisms came from the staff of the International Monetary Fund.[18] First, they noted, the cases in which policymakers made an attempt to tighten fiscal policy were not necessarily those in which cyclically adjusted fiscal balances – on which Mr Alesina and Ms Ardagna relied – were cut. Second, they insisted, 'large spending-based fiscal retrenchments are contractionary, as are fiscal consolidations occurring in economies with a high perceived sovereign default risk'. Third, they pointed out, 'the decline in private consumption and private investment is mitigated by a rise in net exports associated with a fall in the value of the domestic currency'. Thus, it was not austerity that was expansionary, as claimed, but beneficial changes elsewhere in the economy, largely driven by depreciation of the currency. Not surprisingly, they added, 'this offsetting channel is less potent in economies with pegged exchange rates.'[19]

Then, in 2013, Roberto Perotti of Bocconi University, an early supporter of the idea of expansionary contractions, pointed out that depreciation and fast export growth had been offsets to fiscal consolidation in four widely cited European exemplars of expansionary austerity: Denmark (1983–87), Finland (1992–96), Sweden (1993–97) and Ireland (1987–89).[20] The IMF's World Economic Outlook of October 2010 added another possible offsetting channel: a fall in interest rates. The US, the Eurozone, the UK, not to mention Japan, are far too big to achieve export-led growth in the near term.

Moreover, the US and the UK already enjoy rock-bottom interest rates. Only the crisis-hit Eurozone member countries can benefit from these.

In brief, the decision to withdraw fiscal support for the recovery, taken at the G-20 Summit of June 2010, delivered a longer and deeper slump than necessary (see Figures 42 below and 3 above). It has also meant relying on a more uncertain tool – that of unconventional monetary policy – and abandoning a less uncertain one – that of fiscal policy. According to Alan Taylor of the University of California, Davis, UK GDP was 3 per cent smaller in 2013 than it would have been if the austerity of 2011–13 had been postponed.[21]

It is interesting to ask why countries that did have a choice to slow fiscal austerity or even expand deficits temporarily did not do so. In the US, austerity was the result of a political stand-off between the two parties. But in the UK it was a deliberate policy.[22] An influential argument was that the UK had too much public debt, even though the ratio of debt to GDP has remained below its average of the past three centuries.

Research by Carmen Reinhart and Kenneth Rogoff, both at Harvard University and celebrated as authors of *This Time is Different*, a

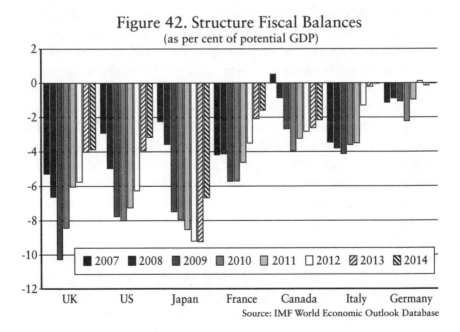

Figure 42. Structure Fiscal Balances
(as per cent of potential GDP)

Source: IMF World Economic Outlook Database

justly influential book on financial and fiscal crises, supported the idea that public debt was becoming dangerously high and so that an early shift towards fiscal austerity was both necessary and wise. Thus, in a paper published in 2010, they argued that growth was close to zero when the ratio of public debt to GDP exceeded 90 per cent.[23] Thomas Herndon, Michael Ash and Robert Pollin of the University of Massachusetts at Amherst have provided a widely noted critique.[24] They argue that the paper contained a coding error, data omissions and strange aggregation procedures. After correction, they argue, average annual growth in advanced countries with debt above 90 per cent of GDP was 2.2 per cent between 1945 and 2009. This contrasts with 4.2 per cent when debt was below 30 per cent, 3.1 per cent when debt stands between 30 per cent and 60 per cent, and 3.2 per cent when debt is between 60 per cent and 90 per cent.

So slower growth is indeed associated with higher public debt. *But an association is not a cause.* It is very hard to argue that high public debt caused the UK's slow post-crisis growth. After all, in the years immediately prior to the crisis, UK net public debt was close to its lowest ratio to GDP in the past three hundred years. Thus, the higher debt today than before the crisis is a *result* of slow post-crisis growth. This is not to rule out two-way causality. But the impulse has mostly gone from private financial excesses to crises, slow growth and high public debt, not the other way round. In assessing the consequences of high public debt for growth, one must therefore ask why debt rose in the first place. Again, the reasons why deficits are high and debt rising will affect the costs of austerity. After a financial crisis, an excess of desired private savings is likely to emerge, even with interest rates close to zero. In that situation, fiscal austerity will drive the economy into a recession, so limiting the government's ability to reduce its deficits and debt. So the issue is not only the direction of causality, but also the costs of trying to avoid high public debt in the aftermath of a financial crisis.

In its April 2013 *World Economic Outlook*, the IMF noted that fiscal support for recovery had been exceptionally weak during this recession, compared with previous ones.[25] Not surprisingly, therefore, the recovery has been feeble. True, countries in the Eurozone that could not borrow had to tighten, in the absence of support from their partners. Others with room for manoeuvre, such as the US and even the UK, could – and should – have taken a different course. Because they did not, recovery has been weaker and the long-run costs of the crisis almost certainly greater than was necessary.

This is a controversial view, particularly since the UK economy grew by 2.8 per cent from the fourth quarter of 2012 to the fourth quarter of 2013 and the US economy continued to grow once more from mid-2009 (see Figures 39 and 40). In the end a crisis-hit economy will expand. By and large modern market-led economies do not stop growing forever. So the question concerns a counterfactual: would alternative policies – in this case less contractionary fiscal policies – have led to faster recovery and a stronger economy in the long run? We can never know for certain the answer to this counterfactual. But three arguments suggest that less contractionary fiscal policies would have been helpful in securing a stronger and earlier recovery.

First, the recovery has been decidedly weak, as already pointed out above. In the case of the US, the economy has grown consistently more slowly than the long-term pre-crisis trend. As a result, the short-fall of output relative to that long-term trend has grown year after year. It is possible to argue that this was the best that could be managed. But it is not evident why that should be so, given the persistently low employment and weak investment. No doubt some loss was indeed inevitable, but one as big as this in terms of both levels and rates of growth of GDP needs meticulous justification, particularly for a country that had exceptionally low short-term and long-term interest rates. It could certainly have borrowed and spent more if it had wished to do so. Again, in the case of the UK, the economy was still smaller in early 2014 than six years earlier, despite the upsurge in growth in 2013. True, this dismal performance – the slowest recovery on record – was partly because of the contraction in the output of North Sea oil. Nevertheless, the recovery had been very slow in coming. Moreover, the rate of growth still had not surpassed its historic trend. Furthermore, in the UK, too, short- and long-term interest rates remained very low, even though the actual fiscal deficits greatly exceeded those planned by the incoming coalition government in 2010. It is hard, given these facts, to argue that policy in the US and the UK was the best that could be managed.

Second, the decision to allow a more supportive fiscal policy until these economies had recovered strongly would have brought forward spending, particularly investment, to a time when idle resources were available, notably in construction. Shifting spending from a time when it would have crowded out other activities to a time when it would not have done so is exactly what a government – the economy's largest and longest-lived borrower – should do. Moreover, as Bradford de Long and Lawrence Summers argued (see above), using resources that would otherwise lie idle is not just a free lunch in that income might be higher now, without lowering it in future. It might even make the economy better off in every subsequent year by keeping people employed instead of jobless and businesses functioning instead of bankrupt.

Third, by persisting with strongly supportive fiscal policies until the recovery was well entrenched, the pressure on monetary policy would have been reduced. This could have brought the benefit of not relying so much on a policy that amounts to manipulating asset prices and encouraging further borrowing. The risks of such an expansionary monetary policy, even if effective, are real. Furthermore, while not as unmanageable as some critics allege, exit from unconventional monetary policy, including massively expanded balance sheets and forward guidance, is sure to create bumps along the road. With a more expansionary fiscal policy, monetary policy could have been less extreme than it was.

For all these reasons, the decision to tighten fiscal policy after 2010 was almost certainly premature and unwise. It would have been better to rely more on fiscal policy and less on monetary policy. Of course, by 2014, this debate had largely become an historic one. The choice had been made.

Liquidationist Folly

The above discussion essentially assumed that battered economies needed policy support. The debate was over which policy should be employed – monetary, fiscal, or both. But some respectable organizations have argued that the right recipe is fiscal and monetary tightening. This has become the house perspective of the Bank for International

Settlements and the Organisation for Economic Co-operation and Development. These have called for monetary and fiscal tightening even though economic growth has been weak, unemployment high and inflation low.[26] It has been hard to work out why this has seemed the right policy when it is so easy for government to borrow and inflation has been so low. It is hard to believe they think that Greece, Ireland and Spain have been so successful that everybody should follow their example. Even if they did think that, they must also realize that the success of such crisis-hit economies depends on rapid improvement in their external balances. Such shifts are going to be far more difficult if big economies, particularly the US, pursue strongly contractionary economic policies. Fortunately for their own and other economies, American and British policymakers have not listened to such calls for across-the-board fiscal and monetary contraction, since that would have risked a far deeper slump. But, partly as a result of this pressure, the policies actually chosen have not delivered sufficiently fast healing. However, it could have been worse – and, next time, given the persistent strength of such sentiments, it could be.

HOW TO RESTRUCTURE DEBT

Since there is now more debt than can be easily managed, de-leveraging has been the order of the day. De-leveraging can be achieved by growing out of debt, via a combination of real growth and inflation, or by paying down and restructuring debt. De-leveraging involves one, or often all, of these processes. How well the strategy of 'growing out of debt' works depends on the relationship between rates of interest and growth. The lower the former and the higher the latter, the better. That is why 'financial repression' – a deliberate reduction in the costs of debt by lowering returns to creditors – is common in a de-leveraging episode.

Aggressive monetary policy lowers interest rates and supports nominal incomes. This is why the decision of central banks to move the short-term interest rate to near zero was right. It is also one of the reasons why higher inflation would help. An aggressive fiscal policy can also help de-leveraging. It does so by supporting nominal incomes, offsetting private-sector financial surpluses and even by directly sub-sidizing debt restructuring.

Many insist 'one cannot get out of debt by adding more debt'. That is wrong.[27] If one wants the private sector to pay down its debt, it will tend to run a large financial surplus: those who are over-indebted will spend less and so shift into financial surplus; but those who are not over-indebted will not suddenly wish to borrow more. (Figure 43 shows this for the UK.) In aggregate, then, the private sector is likely to move towards a surplus, which must be offset elsewhere in the economy, since, by definition, financial surpluses (differences between income and spending) add to zero across the economy as a whole once the foreign sector is included. The sector best suited to run the countervailing deficits in a crisis is the government. The response to the objection that it makes no sense for the public sector to go into debt in order to help the private sector de-leverage, is that the new debts will effectively be borne by different people. This then is a way of replacing bad debts with better ones.

A vital element, however, is orderly debt restructuring. The govern-ment can help with this by subsidizing or supporting debt-for-equity swaps, particularly in housing finance. Given the way many banks behaved before the crisis, their shareholders should also pay. Robert Kuttner, an American commentator, justly complains that 'The same financial elites who instrumentally rely on Chapter 11 [of the US bankruptcy code] to rearrange assets and shed debts warn of the shameful improvidence of families caught in a general downdraft of housing values.'[28]

Yet the US has been relatively successful in de-leveraging, with pri-vate debt back to levels last seen in the early 2000s, relative to GDP (see Figure 5). This is due to more growth, more restructuring and more repayment than in most other high-debt countries. The McKinsey Global Institute notes that a standard path for de-leveraging goes in two phases. In the first, the private sector reduces debt while the econ-omy is weak and the public sector runs large fiscal deficits. In the second, the public sector de-leverages too. This is what happened in Finland and Sweden in the 1990s. As of late 2011, the US was well on this path, with substantial reductions in private-sector leverage. But, noted the McKinsey Global Institute, 'deleveraging in the UK and Spain is proceeding more slowly. The ratio of UK debt to GDP has continued to rise and UK households have increased debt in absolute terms. In Spain, households have barely reduced debt ratios and corporations continue to carry the highest level of debt relative to GDP in our ten-country sample [namely, the ten biggest high-income economies]. It could take many more years to finish an orderly deleveraging in the UK and Spain.'[29]

In brief, what is needed to handle the debt overhang is a strategy for demand expansion, low interest rates, reconstruction of the financial system, and restructuring and reduction of non-financial debts. Of the big countries, the US has come closest to this combination, though the others have been slowly and painfully following behind.

Inevitably, creditors do not like the strategy of low interest rates and debt restructuring. Yet what they want – all borrowers to pay high interest rates in full and punctually – they cannot now have. If a boom has created more credit and debt than can be sustained, the stock of claims, the returns upon them, or both, must be reduced. The alternative is stagnation and, at worst, the nightmare of debt deflation explained by Irving Fisher in 1933.[30] Since that must be prevented, the alternative of debt restructuring is the inevitable and rational choice.

STRUCTURAL LIMITS AND SECULAR STAGNATION

The challenges discussed in this chapter hitherto are those of sustaining demand and restructuring debt – the flows and the stocks – during post-crisis recession. But many commentators argue this is beside the point. They insist that structural obstacles to sustained recovery are insuperable.[31] This is partly because of slowing, if not collapsing, trend growth and partly because of structural constraints on demand.

Slowing Growth

Underlying economic growth is indeed almost certain to slow in high-income countries. The principal reason is demographic: the ageing of societies. Over the next four decades, the proportion of the population that is of normal working age will fall considerably and the proportion of the population aged over sixty-five will rise substantially. In the US, for example, according to UN forecasts, the proportion aged twenty to sixty-four will fall from 60 per cent to 54 per cent between 2010 and 2050, whereas the proportion over sixty-five will rise from 13 per cent to 21 per cent. In a country that is ageing more rapidly than the US, such as Germany, the proportion of people aged twenty to sixty-four will fall from 61 per cent in 2010 to 50 per cent in 2050, whereas the proportion over sixty-five will jump from 20 per cent to 31 per cent. In Japan, the forecast is even more extreme, with the population aged twenty to sixty-four down to 47 per cent by 2050.[32] Even if we assume that retirement ages will rise substantially, as they should, the impact on potential growth is evident: not only will the labour force shrink absolutely in many countries, as the population falls, but the proportion of it that is young, flexible and innovative will decline further. Moreover, age-related public spending on health and pensions also seems bound to rise in most high-income economies over the next few decades unless there are extraordinary medical innovations or the rest of the population refuses to pay.[33]

With the labour force growing more slowly than previously, or even shrinking, growth is bound to slow, other things being equal. But the other component of economic growth – rising productivity – is even more important than demography in determining the rate of growth over the long run. It is also the principal determinant of incomes per head.

Nobody knows what will happen to productivity over the coming decades, but some well-informed people have put forward reasonable arguments that it must slow. Among these are Robert Gordon of Northwestern University and Tyler Cowen of George Mason University.[34] An important reason why the pace of innovation might be slowing is that many opportunities have already been exploited: the population of the high-income countries is already highly educated and highly urbanized; the economy has already exploited the most readily available natural resources; people have already enjoyed the fruit of many life- and economy-transforming innovations, such as running water and sanitation, inoculation, electricity, chemicals, pharmaceuticals, the internal combustion engine, civil aviation, telephony, the computer and the internet. While nobody knows what is still to come, it would have to be impressive indeed to match this record of past achievements. Yet, it should be stressed, this relatively pessimistic view is far from universally shared. Erik Brynjolfsson and Andrew McAfee of the Massachusetts Institute of Technology argue, instead, not only that the measured decline in productivity growth in recent years is a product of a failure to measure output correctly, but that an age of accelerating technological progress is ahead of us, as intelligent machines and 'big data' transform our economy and our lives.[35] At this stage, the only sensible thing to say is that we do not know what promise of a more productive future new technologies hold, though it seems likely that if it is as dynamic as some expect, it will also tend to generate even bigger increases in inequality of earnings and incomes between digital haves and have-nots.

If one takes these elements together, the growth rate of the high-income countries may be substantially slower in the future than it was even in the decades leading up to 2007, let alone the magnificently prosperous years from 1945 to 1975 – *les trentes glorieuses*, as the French call those three decades of economic boom. This will have many difficult consequences: the distributional struggle will be more intense and political stability less assured; the relative power of the high-income countries will shrink; the public finances will be more difficult to manage; and the beneficiaries of public spending – particularly the old – will find the resources at their disposal shrinking. Given all this, it becomes even more important to return to potential output as swiftly as possible and then pursue policies likely to stimulate economic growth. Such policies will need to be heterodox, with a strong focus on supporting scientific research and risk-taking innovation.[36] The high-income countries cannot afford years, even decades, of unnecessary stagnation, due to inadequate demand.

Weak Demand

The second part of the structural argument comes down to the proposition that there exist longer-term constraints on demand. If so, the pump-priming by governments and central banks will ultimately fail, since economies will return to their depressed state as soon as policy is reversed. This view fits with the analysis in Chapter Five of longer-term reasons why demand in the high-income countries had to be supported by aggressive monetary policy and an ultimately unsustainable credit boom, particularly after the Asian financial crisis and the collapse of the stock-market bubble of the late-1990s. The argument for secular stagnation made by Lawrence Summers is that demand has become structurally weaker over the past decade.[37] Daniel Alpert's *The Age of Oversupply* is about much the same thing.[38] The principal piece of evidence of secular stagnation is, as Mr Summers also notes, the combination of rapidly growing credit and high asset prices with weak economies, even before the crisis hit.

The first explanation for structurally deficient private-sector demand in the absence of credit bubbles is rising inequality. A number of authors, from different sides of the policy spectrum, have made a direct link between inequality, structurally deficient demand and credit booms.[39]

The Nobel laureate economist Joseph Stiglitz of Columbia University has argued, for example, 'Unemployment can be blamed on a deficiency in aggregate demand (the total demand for goods and services in the economy, from consumers, from firms, by government and by exporters); in some sense, the entire shortfall in aggregate demand – and hence in the U. S. economy – today can be blamed on the extremes of inequality.'[40] Similarly, James K. Galbraith of the University of Texas at Austin argues 'In rich countries such as the United States, we find that economic performance has become dominated since 1980 by the credit cycle; financial booms and busts drive the performance of employment and thus prosperity is associated with rising income inequality.'[41]

Finally, Raghuram Rajan, now governor of the Reserve Bank of India, argues:

> Recognizing the need to find new sources of growth, the United States towards the end of Jimmy Carter's term, and then under Ronald Reagan, deregulated industry and the financial sector, as did Margaret Thatcher's United Kingdom. Competition and innovation increased substantially in these countries. Greater competition, freer trade, and

the adoption of new technologies, increased the demand for, and incomes of, highly skilled, talented, and educated workers doing non-routine jobs like consulting. More routine, once well-paying, jobs done by the unskilled or the moderately educated were automated or outsourced. So income inequality emerged, not primarily because of policies favoring the rich, but because the liberalized economy favored those equipped to take advantage of it.

The short-sighted political response to the anxieties of those falling behind was to ease their access to credit. Faced with little regulatory and supervisory restraint, sometimes based on the faith that private incentives worked best in this best of all worlds, the financial system overdosed on risky loans to lower middle class borrowers, aided and abetted by very low policy interest rates.[42]

What is interesting is the similarity of the underlying analysis among analysts with quite different ideological perspectives: liberalization, particularly of finance, led to massive rises in inequality. This then generated structural deficiencies of demand (not to mention the disappointment of stagnant or declining real incomes for many people), which were papered over by a temporary credit boom. Once that collapsed, the government took the private borrowers' place as borrower and spender of last resort. But the only way to restore demand in the private sector has been via ultra-expansionary monetary policies, with the disturbing longer-term consequences discussed above. All this is a plausible internal complement to the analysis of external imbalances in Chapter Five (and see further below). It explains why it has been so hard to offset the depressive effects on demand of external imbalances.

Jeffrey Sachs, also at Columbia University, argues, in *Price of Civilization*, that the crisis is the result of a moral collapse in the American elites.[43] Rising inequality, ineffective and unpopular government, out-of-control finance and deteriorating external competitiveness are, in this view, symptomatic of a deeper social and ethical failure. Pumping up demand in the short run cannot deliver the longer-term prosperity the US needs. This is surely correct. However, one could view such a policy not as a solution but as, at best, a stepping stone to a renewed vision or, at worst, as a way of making the best of a bad job. Getting back to full employment through stimulus policies would not resolve the difficulties of the US, but it would reduce the immediate misery. One cannot let the best be the enemy of the good.

Andrew Smithers of London-based Smithers & Co. suggests yet another structural constraint. In *The Road to Recovery* he argues that the bonus culture distorts the behaviour of corporate management, particularly in English-speaking countries, in a destructive direction.[44] Above all, it focuses managerial attention on ways to raise reported earnings and share prices in the short run, since managers are unlikely to be in charge very long. Their goal is to cash out as successfully as possible and as quickly as possible. They can do this not only by using the earnings to buy shares in their own companies, but also by borrowing to fund yet more such buy-backs. In the process, they leverage up their businesses, making them more financially fragile, and reduce investment, weakening long-term prospects. This is particularly true in activities that demand patience and long-term investment, such as large-scale manufacturing. One result of this behaviour is of particular macroeconomic importance: it creates a structural financial surplus (excess of retained earnings over investment) in the corporate sector, notably so in the US and the UK.

In a healthy economy, the corporate sector would be a net importer of savings from the rest of the economy. After all, it is responsible for virtually all the investment, other than in human capital. If the corporate sector is profitable, but does not invest, policymakers have two headaches: the first is that their economy's growth will be harmed; the second is that the savings surplus of the corporate sector will need to be offset by spending elsewhere if a slump caused by a savings glut is to be avoided. Until the crisis, the offsetting spending was in the construction of homes and in household and government consumption. Then, after house prices fell and particularly after the financial crisis, the onus fell on the government deficit alone. The huge post-crisis fiscal deficit was not a surprise: it was a predictable – and predicted – event for those who understood the financial balances of the economy.

This brings us to a fourth structural concern, already discussed at length in Chapter Five: the external sector. If the corporate sector runs a financial surplus, the remaining sectors must run deficits. But what happens if the external sector also runs a structural surplus, as seems to be the case in both the US and the UK (see Figures 33 and 43). Even in a deep recession, both countries have continued to run current-account deficits, which means they remain net importers of savings from the rest of the world. This is happening for two interconnected reasons: foreigners are running savings surpluses (as explained in Chapter Five), which they are sending to the capital-importing countries; and, in the process, foreigners are also subsidizing their tradeable industries and taxing those of the capital-importing countries, via shifts in real exchange rates.[45]

In countries with structural current-account deficits domestic demand must exceed income in order to offset the export of a part of their demand to foreign producers of goods and services. If both foreigners and the corporate sector are running structural (or cyclically adjusted) financial surpluses – by which one means the surpluses that would emerge if output were as close as possible to what used to be

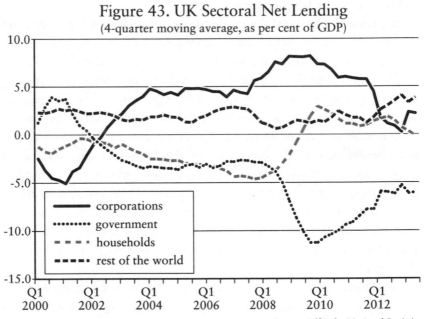

Figure 43. UK Sectoral Net Lending
(4-quarter moving average, as per cent of GDP)

Source: Office for National Statistics

called 'full employment' – other sectors have to run deficits. Prior to the crisis, this task of running deficits fell both to households and government in the US and the UK. Since the crisis it has fallen on the government alone.

So what would happen if the government tried to eliminate its fiscal deficit too? If this is to be combined with high levels of economic activity, the offsetting changes must be expansionary. If so, one or some combination of three things *must* happen: a swing towards financial deficits by households, almost certainly driven by another credit boom; a swing towards financial deficit in the corporate sector, driven by a surge in corporate investment; or a move towards structural surplus in the current account of the balance of payments, driven by a sustained improvement in competitiveness. Of these three possibilities, the first is undesirable. This leaves investment and net exports.

Those concerned with structural constraints are right: the needed sustained improvements in investment and net exports are unlikely to happen swiftly. One can envisage policy changes that would help. It would be possible, for example, to redistribute incomes among households so that the need for excessive expansions in credit, in order to intermediate between the haves and have-nots, would substantially diminish. But since a large proportion of this intermediation is also between the old and the young, it would still not disappear. It would be possible, in addition, to change the corporate tax code to give a stronger incentive for investment and a reduced incentive for borrowing. But whether that would make a big enough difference either is open to question. Similarly, it would be possible to imagine changes in real exchange rates that deliver the shift in competitiveness that is desired. But there is no way for a single country to deliver this, so long as it has an open capital account and a monetary policy oriented towards domestic price stability. This is particularly true for a country that issues a reserve currency: it effectively loses control over its exchange rate.

So this brings us to one of the biggest issues raised by the argument in this book, particularly in Chapter Five: global rebalancing.

GLOBAL REFORM

One way out of the apparent demand trap would be via global rebalancing. The evidence at present is that high-income countries are no longer able to absorb the savings that would be generated by their private sectors if their economies were running at something close to full capacity and were also not experiencing an unsustainable credit expansion.[46] This is why activity has been persistently weak and real interest rates low. Whether this is inevitable or the result of rising inequality and failures in corporate governance is unclear: probably a bit of all of these. The condition of excess private-sector savings still exists. So, if these excess savings are not to be absorbed in the fiscal deficit (to which we will return in the next section), the only alternatives are to eliminate them via a depression or export them. In brief, all the high-income countries would then become like Germany and the rest of the world economy would become large net importers of capital.

Let us think this through via some simple illustrative calculations. Assume that the private sectors of the high-income countries wish to run financial surpluses – excesses of savings over investment – in normal times (that is, when credit is not exploding and asset prices are reasonably stable) of around 4 per cent of GDP. Assume also that these countries wish to bring their public debt back down from the relatively high levels of recent years. On the assumption that real economic growth is going to be about 1–2 per cent a year (lower in Europe and Japan and higher in the US, largely for demographic reasons), and inflation is also going to be around 2 per cent, growth of nominal GDP would be 3–4 per cent. If the public debt ratio in high-income countries is to trend back towards, say, 50 per cent of GDP, the cyclically adjusted fiscal deficit needs to be 1.5–2 per cent of GDP. This implies an aggregate cyclically adjusted current-account surplus (capital-account deficit) for the high-income countries of 2–2.5 per cent of GDP.

That is where the Eurozone seems to be painfully going, under German tutelage, though it is, alas, achieving such a current-account surplus at depressed output, not at potential output (see Figure 34). But if the Eurozone adjustment planned by Germany – towards more restricted domestic demand – is to succeed, that is probably what has to happen. Japan has embarked on the path of 'Abenomics', with dramatically looser monetary policy and a substantial real depreciation. The latter is not an explicit objective of the policy: how could it be, since the overt adoption of a 'beggar-my-neighbour' policy is a 'no-no' for respectable high-income countries? But if one looks at the huge structural financial surpluses of Japan's corporate sector (in the neighbourhood of 10 per cent of GDP) and the desire to reduce the fiscal deficit, a large current-account surplus seems inevitable. The fall in the exchange rate may ultimately help achieve this. In the US and the UK, such shifts also seem necessary if fiscal deficits are to be reduced substantially, while avoiding further credit bubbles. Of course, credit bubbles are the more likely outcome. But we are discussing a hypothetical world.

The high-income countries, together, generate a little over 60 per cent of global GDP (at market prices) and are currently close to aggregate external balance. But this is partly because of the slump. The full employment current-account deficit of the high-income countries is probably now closer to, say, 2 per cent of aggregate GDP. So the needed swing in their aggregate current-account balance would be to 4–4.5 per cent of potential (or full employment) GDP, to allow the desired fiscal deficit of 1.5–2 per cent of GDP. Remember that an economy's financial balances must sum to zero. If the private-sector surplus were 4 per cent of GDP and the government's deficit were 1.5–2 per cent of GDP, the foreign balance (that is, draft on foreign savings) would be minus 2–2.5 per cent of GDP. This is equivalent to a current-account surplus of 2–2.5 per cent of GDP, since the countries in question would be exporting surplus savings, not importing them. Such an external surplus would be needed to allow the high-income countries to balance their economies' demand and supply at positive real interest rates and at something close to full employment, without needing to rely on unsustainable credit and asset bubbles.

A swing in the current-account balance of the high-income countries of 4–4.5 per cent of GDP to a structural surplus of 2–2.5 per cent of aggregate GDP implies a swing of 6–6.75 per cent in the current-account deficit of the rest of the world and an actual deficit of 3–3.75 per cent of GDP. If this were distributed evenly, it should be just about manageable, given that, taken as a whole, the rest of the world is where the best investment opportunities should now be. But such an even distribution is most unlikely. The chances are, instead, that a number of emerging economies would end up with very large current-account deficits and rapid accumulations of net external debt. But we know from both experience and research that the accumulation of large quantities of net debt, particularly if denominated in foreign currency, is a harbinger of a crisis.[47] Naturally and wisely, given painful experience, the emerging and developing countries would be most unwilling to embark on an experiment with large external deficits merely to make the lives of the high-income countries a bit easier.

Why, after all, should they take this risk? The answer to this rhetorical question might be that the availability of foreign savings should, in principle, allow emerging and developing countries to invest and consume more, raising the welfare of the population. But this only makes sense if the inflows are indeed properly used and, in addition, the potential recipients of net capital inflows are adequately insured against the risks, particularly of a sudden reversal of inflows. No sensible economist would today – after so much painful experience – advise these countries simply to open their capital accounts to the world and ignore the risks of excessive inflows: asset and credit bubbles, distortions of the productive structure, particularly falling incentives for the production of tradeable goods and services, and severe financial and economic crises.

Nothing suggests that a change in the global balance of payments big enough to turn the high-income countries into large net exporters of capital is at all likely. Surplus countries do not want to give up being surplus countries. As noted in Chapter Five, a number of important countries have become highly export-dependent and have been willing to intervene massively in foreign-currency markets to reinforce this orientation. Germany does not need to do so: it is nicely locked into the Eurozone with countries that are, by now, more or less permanently uncompetitive (a topic to which the discussion will turn in Chapter Nine). But countries in East Asia, in particular, have often intervened in foreign-currency markets to support their competitiveness. In theory, the 'mutual assessment process' (MAP), initiated by the G-20 at the Pittsburgh Summit in 2009, should be doing something about this.[48] Certainly, China, the most important of the currency interveners, has let its currency appreciate considerably in real terms. But this may be difficult to sustain now the economy is slowing sharply. Overall, there seems to be little chance that changes in policy will be large enough to reverse the current pattern of global imbalances (see Figure 32).

What needs to happen to make this desirable outcome – a large flow of net savings from rich countries to poor ones – even conceivable? We would need to look at a combination of policies.

First, encourage less risky flows of finance. The most productive and least risky forms of finance are foreign direct investment and, to a lesser degree, purchases of equity. The obstacles to such flows need to be identified and overcome, wherever possible by improving security of property in emerging economies. But it is also possible to consider far more imaginative forms of debt or quasi-debt finance, such as GDP-linked bonds or bonds whose terms are automatically altered in the event of pre-specified contingencies. Institutions like the World Bank and the regional banks should be putting a great deal of effort into creating and marketing such novel forms of finance. Much progress has also already occurred in the development of local-currency bond markets, replacing riskier foreign-currency finance. This must be taken still further, with more innovation. Finally, there need to be procedures for managing bankruptcy conditions, not just for the public sector, but also for the private sector in emerging and developing countries.

Second, increase insurance. The massive reserve accumulations by emerging and developing countries are, in part, self-insurance. This was a waste: their people had to work hard to earn the dollars that the Federal Reserve so easily prints. But the insurance is valuable, even if excessive. It helped reserve holders to survive the crisis of 2008–09 relatively unscathed. It is also possible that many emerging countries will conclude that their present reserves are quite big enough. An alternative to such huge reserves is a much bigger International Monetary Fund that offers far more unconditional finance. This means both more resources and more say for potential users. Alternatively, the emerging and developing countries could now go further in pooling their own resources.

Third, create a global money. The most radical suggestion is the creation of a global reserve asset. The idea was recently presented by a panel of experts commissioned by the UN Secretary General:

> [T]he idea of an international reserve currency issued by a supranational bank is not new. It was broached more than seventy-five years ago by John Maynard Keynes in his 1930 *Treatise on Money*, and refined in his Bretton Woods proposals for an International Clearing Union. There currently exist a number of alternative proposals for a new global reserve currency, for how the system might be administered, how the emissions of the new currency might be allocated, and how the transition to the new system might be managed. Considerable international discussion will be required for the international community to decide the precise arrangements. However, this is an idea whose time has come.[49]

Needless to say, the US will oppose this idea. Yet it is far from clear that the US benefits from being the supplier of the reserve currency. On the contrary, the evidence from the recent crisis is that the consequences for financial stability in the US are highly adverse. It seems likely that the Chinese government will have that view of a comparable role for the renminbi. It surely should do so. Maybe, the possibility of a transition to the kind of monetary regime Keynes envisaged may now emerge. It is at least clear that the world of floating fiat currencies, one of which is a reserve currency, is highly unstable. The experience already forced a drastic shift in the policies of emerging and developing countries after 1997, as this book has noted (see Chapter Five). Now the owner of the monetary and financial dog has been bitten too. The system needs to be changed. If it is not, there is a good chance of a real currency war, not a phony one, as countries struggle to gain a share of chronically inadequate global demand.

MONETARY FINANCING

Yet imagine that it proves hard to create the most desirable offsets to falling fiscal deficits, namely, surging investment and rising net exports from today's crisis-hit high-income countries. This does not mean that the effort to solve the problem of deficient demand evident since the

1990s must fail. But since the effort to create another credit boom, particularly one focused on excessive leverage of the household sector, would be risking even more trouble down the road, we need to consider more radical options.

Yet before pondering that possible outcome, let us return to another even more radical possibility that would bring together our discussion of structural determinants of the private-sector financial balances with the discussion of the Chicago Plan in Chapters Six and Seven and of the balance between fiscal and monetary stimulus earlier in this chapter. If the choice is between letting the creation of money be the by-product of irresponsible private lending, as was seen in the US and Europe in the 2000s, or the by-product of government spending, the latter would be a better choice. Indeed, that was the point made – rightly, properly and persuasively – by Adair Turner, former chairman of the UK's now defunct Financial Services Authority, in a seminal speech in early 2013.[50]

Lord Turner noted that Milton Friedman himself argued 'in an article in 1948 not only that government deficits should sometimes be financed with fiat money but that they should always be financed in that fashion with, he argued, no useful role for debt finance'.[51] Instead of granting the private sector the right to create almost all the money in the economy, as a by-product of often bad lending decisions, let the money be created by the state, instead, for its own use. Other economists have argued for such a policy in the event of crises, among them Keynes with his celebrated suggestion that people be paid to dig up bottles full of pound notes, and Ben Bernanke, when considering policy options confronting Japan in the early 2000s.[52]

This seems a solution to any long-term problem of structural-demand deficiency. Instead of relying on private-sector credit booms to generate a temporary return to full employment or accept a semi-permanent depression, let the government use its capacity to create money, already accepted when countries moved to floating exchange rates. This is not only what many in the Chicago School would have accepted. It is also the recommendation of those who believe in Modern Monetary Theory (see Chapter Six above).

Meanwhile, control over the quantity of money to be printed would be left with the central bank, which would create the amount of money it deemed non-inflationary. The government would be forced to borrow to cover deficits beyond those funded by the central bank. But the aim would be to make the monetary expansion decided by the central bank a semi-permanent part of the assets of the commercial banks. As a result the reserve requirements of banks would also need to be adjusted.

THE CASE FOR ACTION

The crisis was a huge moment. Much of the political and financial establishment pretends that everything will soon return to the old normal, with a few regulatory changes and bashing of innocent beneficiaries of public spending. This is not going to work. There are reasons to believe growth will be slower in future. That will make achieving better-balanced economies even harder than it might be. But the big problem is that policymakers have permitted the crisis to do much more damage than it needed to do in the short to medium term *and* have failed to ensure a path to a balanced economy in the longer term. They allowed stimulus, particularly fiscal stimulus, to diminish too soon. But, more important, they have failed to tackle longer-term constraints on achieving balanced domestic and world economies.

Once one thinks about these issues, it is evident that needed changes will be very hard to achieve. We have apparently become dependent on unsustainable credit booms. It is necessary to consider alternative ways of balancing demand with potential supply. Among such ways are radical domestic and global monetary reforms. Indeed, the world of floating fiat currencies and debt-backed money has been so unstable that radical reform must be on the agenda. It will not happen this time. But after the next crisis its time will surely have come. So prepare now. How to do so will be discussed in the Conclusion. But first let us look at another important story: the future of the Eurozone.

9

Mending a Bad Marriage

Ubi Solitudinem faciunt, pacem appellant (They make a desert and call it peace)

Tacitus

It is an error to think that fiscal austerity is a threat to growth and job creation. At present, a major problem is the lack of confidence on the part of households, firms, savers and investors who feel that fiscal policies are not sound and sustainable. In a number of economies, it is this lack of confidence that poses a threat to the consolidation of the recovery. Economies embarking on austerity policies that lend credibility to their fiscal policy strengthen confidence, growth and job creation.

Jean-Claude Trichet, Interview with
Libération, 8 July 2010[1]

The euro has been a disaster. No other word will do. A project intended to strengthen solidarity, bring prosperity and weaken German economic domination of Europe has achieved precisely the opposite: it has undermined solidarity, destroyed prosperity and reinforced German domination, at least for a while.

For all its cultural and economic achievements, Europe has a long history of catastrophic errors, which have usually been the result of blind arrogance and wishful thinking bordering on insanity. In the year this book is published, the world is mourning the centenary of perhaps the most significant of all of Europe's follies – the First World War, which led, not inevitably, but ultimately, to the Second. Then, over half a century of patience, under US protection, the Europeans brought forth upon their continent peace, prosperity and partnership, only to succumb to a new, far less calamitous, but even less necessary, piece of arrogance – the idea that an irrevocable currency union among sovereign states with diverse economies and very different cultures could work smoothly.

The crisis has made clear how foolish this view was. For all their mistakes in running the Eurozone, German policymakers and economists, to their credit, understood the risks. The only other large European country to do so was the UK. Thoughtful Germans, particularly those working at the Bundesbank, realized that in the modern world a currency is a product of a state and a polity. It must come after their creation, not before it. But other Europeans decided to put the cart before the horse by creating the monetary union before a proper union of states. The report of the Committee for the Study of Economic and Monetary Union, established in 1988 and chaired by Jacques Delors, president of the European Commission, contained no discussion of the political underpinnings of a currency union.[2] It was instead merely a technical guide to the path towards it. Caught in the throes of its internal unification, for which it sought its partners' support, and committed to the European ideal, Germans felt they could not reject this plan. The Maastricht Treaty establishing a path to the currency union was duly agreed in 1991 and, in the course of time, almost every member of the European Union sought to join. The rest is the history described in Chapters Two and Five.

The contrast with the emergence of the American monetary union is extreme. As professors Kevin O'Rourke of Oxford University and Alan Taylor of the University of California observe:

> The US began with a secure political union from which exit . . . is now unthinkable and this provided a stage on which economic and monetary union . . . could be slowly constructed. The US national constitution embodied key assumptions about the existence and permanence of the national debt (a key collective safe asset) [and] federal taxing power (ultimate central fiscal capacity), as well as the common currency and the commerce clause (truly free interstate trade). Onto this, after major crises, a banking union and an economically meaningful fiscal union

were later grafted. In comparison, neither the eurozone nor the European Union comprise a political union; exit is conceivable from both and openly discussed; there is no central fiscal authority in either, nor any common debt, and there seems to be no appetite on the part of creditor nations to go down that route. Recognising these limits means that what is desirable for the eurozone may not be feasible.[3]

Five member countries – Greece, Ireland, Italy, Portugal and Spain – fell into deep depressions, with extremely high rates of unemployment and soaring public debt (see Chapter Two, especially Figures 17 and 18). In Greece and Portugal, the youth unemployment rate has exceeded 55 per cent. Not just a decade is being lost, but sizeable parts of an entire generation. By early 2014, one could see signs of a feeble recovery, but unemployment is likely to remain very high until the end of the decade or even later. Cyprus even imposed capital controls in 2013, thereby establishing what everybody already knew: a euro is not a euro, unless it is a physical note or a coin. A euro in a bank account in Cyprus is not necessarily the same thing as a euro in a bank account in Germany: the latter can be used freely as a means of payment at all times and anywhere; the former cannot.

Trust in European institutions has fallen sharply. Extremist political forces are emerging in some countries; resentment among the peoples of Europe is emerging everywhere. The post-war domestic and European settlement is fraying. Meanwhile, a stream of 'austerian' platitudes and over-optimistic forecasts flows from those in charge. Europe is under the sway of the ideas of Heinrich Brüning, German chancellor between 1930 and 1932, whose disastrous policy of austerity prepared the way for Adolf Hitler.[4]

Proponents thought eliminating multiple currencies would also end balance-of-payments crises. But credit crises and long-running traumas of external adjustment emerged instead. Proponents thought providing a single currency would ensure the beneficial integration of cross-border finance. But national banking crises emerged instead. Proponents thought the act of creating a single currency would eliminate the fear of break-up. But the survival of national politics ensured this remained a live question instead. Proponents thought that creating a currency union would bring the peoples of the Eurozone closer together. Crises divided them into contemptuous creditors and resentful debtors instead. This has been a march of folly.

Think of the Eurozone as a polygamous monetary marriage entered into by people who should have known better, in haste and with insufficient forethought, without any mechanism for divorce – deliberately so, since the more unfeasible a divorce, the less credible it becomes. The groom came to the altar out of a sense of duty, not out of a strong belief in the monetary marriage. The brides did not understand what they were doing. Then came an irresponsible honeymoon when everybody seemed to be getting what they wanted. The brides were able to borrow freely at far lower rates of interest than ever before: predictably, they went shopping. The groom went back to hard work, building up a hugely competitive export sector and a vast external surplus matched by growing claims on the debtors. Then came the crisis. The groom complained that the brides had wasted his money. The brides complained that the groom was forcing them into penury. So the marriage went very bad, in part because it always was a bad idea, but also because the honeymoon had been so irresponsible. Then, when the crisis came, everybody made big mistakes.

Consider the possible outcomes: divorce; continuation of a bad marriage; or creation of a good marriage. Today, the members are dangling between the first two alternatives. The marriage is pretty bad, but divorce looks frighteningly painful. What is needed is to turn this into a good marriage. Action must again cover flows, stocks and reforms. First, everybody must return to a reasonable level of prosperity. Second, the Eurozone must deal with the overhang of stocks of bad debt inherited from the recent or, in some cases, more distant past. Third, it must put in place reforms that make its future more prosperous and secure. It seems really unlikely that all this is going to happen. If so, the likelihood is either divorce, though probably only after a lengthy period of a truly bad marriage, or, more likely, an almost intolerably bad marriage forever.

The discussion will begin with the legacy of the honeymoon. It will then look at what an enduring bad marriage might mean and next what a divorce might look like. Finally, it will examine how to achieve a good marriage – and whether that is even feasible.

HONEYMOON ILLUSIONS

The strangest feature of the Eurozone story is that it was almost as if three fairy godmothers had attended the wedding. The first said: you will all get exactly what you want. The second added: after ten years, you will then get your worst nightmares. The third concluded: yes, you will get your worst nightmares because you first got exactly what you wanted.

So, in those happy honeymoon years up to late 2008, countries that had previously suffered from weak public finances, high interest rates and vulnerable currencies enjoyed some happy combination of low interest rates, fast economic growth, rising real wages and growing current-account deficits. They did not all have all of these things: Italy and Portugal did not enjoy fast economic growth, for example. But, overall, this was a contented period. Meanwhile, Germany and to a lesser extent other northern countries, enjoyed rising competitiveness and net exports, partly because of access to the markets in the Eurozone, but also because the euro was much weaker than the Deutschmark would have been. Needless to say, the happiness of the borrowers and that of the lenders were two sides of one coin.

Then the honeymoon came to an end, this time in the midst of a global financial crisis. Suddenly market participants, policymakers and the people realized they had made huge mistakes: Greek public debt was *not* as good as German debt; current-account deficits of around 10 per cent of GDP and net external debts of close to 100 per cent of GDP (as in Greece, Portugal and Spain) were *not* sustainable even in a currency union; countries did *not* become rich by building houses potential purchasers did not want or could not afford; economies did *not* become enduringly competitive by expanding their construction, property and financial sectors; countries would *not* remain competitive if they let their labour costs rise faster than those of the Eurozone's anchor country, year after year after year; and it really did *not* make sense for countries whose industries were competing with those of China to allow their labour costs to rise faster than in countries, like Germany, whose industries were complementary to those of China. In sum, it had been worse than ten wasted years; it had been ten years of travel in the wrong direction.

That is why the crisis was so bad. The Eurozone was not constructed to cope with the mixture of economic, fiscal and financial crises that emerged after 2008. But the position would not be quite so bad if people had not believed in it so much in the first decade of its existence.

LIVING IN A BAD MARRIAGE

Economic processes are cumulative. Powerful forces can reinforce the success of some regions and the failures of others. Today, resources themselves do not matter that much. But network externalities matter a great deal. The factors that start driving economies in opposite directions may initially be accidental, but that will not matter in the long run. If a particular region has succeeded over time in bringing together people skilled in a particular set of activities, created the physical, social and cultural infrastructure that supports their work, built up the amenities they desire and has gained the taxable wealth to reinvest in ever more of this, it can gain extraordinarily durable advantages. Think of the contrast between northern and southern Italy, Boston and Mississippi, Bavaria and Brandenburg, Manhattan and Detroit, or London and any other British city.

The Marriage Trap

What has this to do with the bad Eurozone marriage? We know the vulnerable countries are suffering economic depressions and difficulties with debt likely to last many years. It would be extraordinary if their economies were to be back to their pre-crisis levels a decade after the crisis. It is also unlikely any of them would have unemployment below 10 per cent of the labour force before, say, 2018. Some may have unemployment over 20 per cent. It is still likely that at least one and possibly more than one of them are going to be forced to default on their public debt, with devastating consequences for confidence in the only governments these countries have.

This is all bad. But one must also appreciate the longer-run costs of such disasters. Any able and enterprising young person will contemplate emigrating and in the worst-hit countries many are already doing so. With depressed investment and an anxious younger generation, these countries may be eating their seed-corn. At worst, they could enter a downward spiral of slumps, fiscal difficulties, emigration of the enterprising, a yet more unbalanced demographic profile, and back to worse slumps. If so, what we would be witnessing is not just a temporary Eurozone crisis, however extended, but the emergence of something like the old Mezzogiorno, Italy's poor southern region, but across whole countries, not just regions.

Such a prognosis may seem alarmist. But it is conceivable. Figure 17 above shows the Irish and Portuguese economies expanding in 2013. But in neither case was GDP decisively above 2012 levels. Moreover, both economies were still about 7 per cent smaller in late 2013 than at their pre-crisis peaks. Neither Italy nor Spain showed much recovery in 2013, while Greece languished in a deep depression. Note, too, that the unemployment rate consistently rose after the crisis in Greece, Italy and Spain, and fell quite slowly, from high levels, in Ireland and Portugal (see Figure 18). These are true depressions.

Note, again, that the signs of improving competitiveness one can see in Figure 44, particularly in Ireland and Spain, is largely because of higher productivity. As professors O'Rourke and Taylor note, nominal wages are still sticky downwards, as they have been in most high-income countries since the First World War.[5] Among these countries, only Greece saw significant falls in nominal wages. To achieve that, the economy shrank by 25 per cent. Moreover, if higher productivity and declining nominal wages are the route to competitiveness, employment has to collapse, thereby raising productivity directly and putting downward pressure on wages indirectly. The mechanism of Eurozone adjustment is simply that of the old gold standard.

If we are to understand why adjustment is proving so hard, we need to look at what is happening in the Eurozone as a whole. The economy has, alas, been allowed to stagnate (see Figure 45). Moreover, Eurozone annual headline and core inflation (less food, energy, alcohol and tobacco) were both just 0.8 per cent in the year to January 2014. This is far below the European Central Bank's admittedly

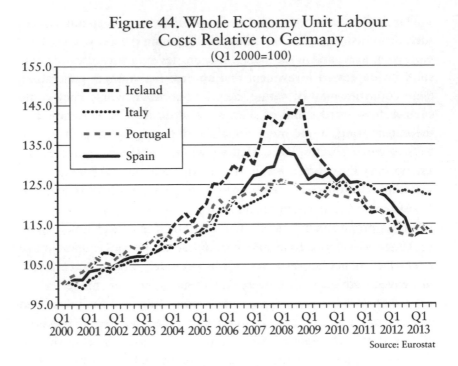

Figure 44. Whole Economy Unit Labour
Costs Relative to Germany
(Q1 2000=100)

Source: Eurostat

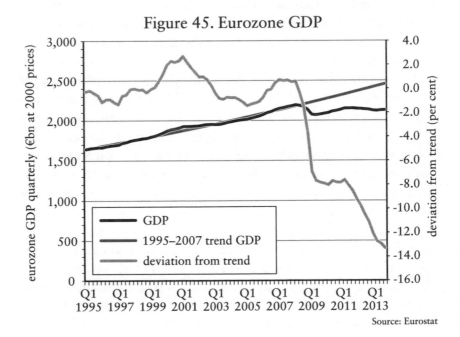

Figure 45. Eurozone GDP

Source: Eurostat

ambiguous inflation target, which is for 'rates of below, but close to, 2 per cent over the medium term'.[6] It would be far better for the ECB to raise inflation above its medium-term target of 2 per cent rather than let it fall below it. Such a rise in inflation and inflation expectations could lower real interest rates and so encourage spending and growth. If very low inflation is bad, deflation will be worse: it will raise real interest rates and the real burden of debt still further.[7] The ECB has failed to do its basic job by allowing inflation to become too low and the economy too weak. Worse, the Eurozone is now probably just one adverse shock away from a deflationary outcome.

Higher inflation would also make needed adjustments in competitiveness among economies quicker, given resistance to nominal wage declines. But the dispersion in inflation between creditor and debtor countries needed to accelerate the adjustment in competitiveness is not happening fast enough, because the average level of inflation is too low (see Figure 46). In the year to January 2014, core consumer price inflation was only 1.2 per cent in Germany, against 0.9 per cent

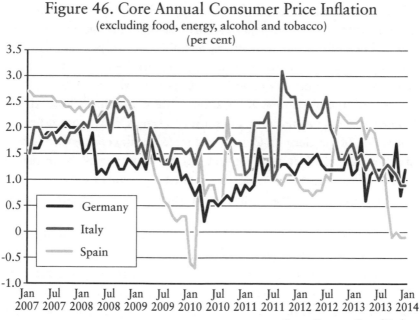

Figure 46. Core Annual Consumer Price Inflation
(excluding food, energy, alcohol and tobacco)
(per cent)

Source: European Central Bank

in Italy, though it was -0.1 per cent in Spain. Germany's core consumer price index rose by 6.7 per cent between January 2008 and January 2014, against 9.3 per cent in Italy and 5.3 per cent in Spain. Thus German core inflation is very low, forcing the countries seeking improvements in competitiveness towards deflation, which Greece had reached in the year to January 2014 and Ireland and Spain were close to, with the inevitable adverse results for the real levels of their euro-denominated debt.

Adjustment is occurring, but by shedding labour. If the productivity improvements prove sustainable in the long term, newly profitable businesses should expand production, using lower inputs of labour per unit of output. But it is going to take a long while for this to drive up employment in entire economies, particularly larger and less trade-dependent ones.

All this sets the stage for debt deflation: nominal GDP is depressed; and nominal interest rates on longer-term government bonds, though much lower than before the announcement of its Outright Monetary Transactions programme by the ECB in the summer of 2012, were still some two percentage points above German levels in early 2014 (see Figures 7 and 36). Baseline forecasts made by Zsolt Darvas in September 2013 for Bruegel, the Brussels-based think tank, suggest that Italy's ratio of public debt might fall from 130 per cent of GDP now to 110 per cent in 2028, while Spain's will rise further, to 110 per cent, by 2020, before falling to around 95 per cent by 2028.[8]

Both of these important countries are travelling along debt's knife-edge path, given their vulnerability to any spike in interest rates. The ruling of the German Constitutional Court in February 2014 that the Outright Monetary Transactions programme is inconsistent with the treaties establishing the monetary union, though not yet blocking it outright, might make it much harder to operate in practice.[9] Markets might yet be shocked by this realization. Thus, default or a restructuring of some kind is certainly conceivable, which can only itself increase the risks of a spike in interest rates.

Ultimately, debt manageability depends on the relationship between the growth of nominal GDP and the interest rate. The relationship between the two is delicately poised in the crisis-hit countries: they have low prospective growth of nominal GDP, at probably no more than 3 per cent, given these countries' necessarily ultra-low inflation, if they are to regain competitiveness in a low-inflation Eurozone; and they still had long-term interest rates on public debt at 4 per cent in early 2014. Any loss of confidence could cause this relationship to shift adversely both quickly and dramatically. As professors O'Rourke and Taylor remark, based on interwar experience, 'large public debts are difficult or impossible to stabilize when deflation is increasing the real value of the debt and slowing economic growth'.[10]

The Baltic Example[11]

At this stage, some bright spark, seeking to counsel the desperate, will point to tiny Latvia, deemed a great success of the 'internal devaluation' and 'austerity' strategy. But this is largely an illusion. What is possible for tiny open economies, without their own banking systems (and so no need to bail out the banks) and next to no government debt before the crisis, is impossible for others.

All three small Baltic states – Estonia (population 1.3 million), Latvia (population 2 million) and Lithuania (population 3 million) – enjoyed credit-driven booms prior to the financial crisis. In 2007, Latvia's current-account deficit was 22 per cent of GDP, Estonia's was 16 per cent and Lithuania's 14 per cent. The domestic counterparts of the capital inflows were huge private-sector financial deficits: 23 per cent of GDP in Latvia, 19 per cent in Estonia and 13 per cent in Lithuania. As usual, the booms flattered fiscal positions: Estonia's net public debt was minus 4 per cent of GDP in 2007, Latvia's 5 per cent and Lithuania's 11 per cent.

Then came the four horsemen of financial crises: 'sudden stops' in capital inflows, asset-price collapses, recessions and fiscal deficits. In response, the Baltics decided to stick to currency pegs and embrace austerity. A substantial rescue package was also negotiated for Latvia in late 2008, with support from the European Union, the International Monetary Fund, the Nordic countries and others. Yet some doubted whether the programme would work. Olivier Blanchard, the IMF's economic counsellor, stated in June 2013 that 'Many, including me, believed that keeping the peg was likely to be a recipe for disaster, for a long and painful adjustment at best, or more likely, the eventual abandonment of the peg when failure became obvious.'[12] He was wrong. According to the IMF, Latvia tightened its cyclically adjusted general government deficit by 5.3 per cent of potential GDP between 2008 and 2012, to achieve a small surplus of 0.8 per cent in the latter year. Over the same period, Lithuania tightened its cyclically adjusted deficit by 3.3 per cent of potential GDP. (The IMF does not provide these data for Estonia.) But Greece's tightening was 15 per cent of potential GDP between 2009 and 2012.

How well has the strategy worked? Defenders point to recent rapid growth. Latvia's economy grew by 20 per cent between its trough, in the third quarter of 2009, and the fourth quarter of 2013. But it shrank by 24 per cent between the fourth quarter of 2007 and its trough. In the fourth quarter of 2013, Latvian GDP was still 9 per cent below its pre-crisis peak. This is no better relative to the pre-crisis starting point than Ireland, Italy, Portugal and Spain. The other two Baltic states have done better, returning where they were in the first quarter of 2008 by the fourth quarter of 2013, though also after huge slumps.

These huge recessions do matter. For Latvia, the cumulative loss from 2008 to 2013 added up to 89 per cent of the country's pre-crisis annual output. On the same basis, the loss was 43 per cent for Lithuania and 39 per cent for Estonia. Unemployment has been falling, but it was still 12 per cent of the Latvian labour force in December 2013, despite heavy emigration.

In brief, Latvia, worst hit of the Baltic countries, suffered one of the biggest depressions in history. Moreover, it cannot be a model for far bigger economies, such as Greece, Ireland and Portugal, let alone Italy and Spain. The Baltic states have four huge advantages in pursuing a strategy of combining economic expansion with fiscal contraction.

First, according to Eurostat, Latvian labour costs per hour, in 2012, were a quarter of those of the Eurozone as whole, 30 per cent of those in Spain and 50 per cent of those of Portugal. Given the potential for further rapid rises in productivity and its integration into the Scandinavian economic system, Latvia did not need a big real depreciation to become competitive.

Second, these are very small open economies. The more open the economy the larger is the portion of output not dependent on recession-hit domestic spending. This makes external adjustment a more potent alternative to domestic stimulus than in larger economies. Between 2007 and 2012, Latvia's current-account deficit shrank by 21 per cent of GDP. The same absolute adjustment would amount to just 0.3 per cent of Italian GDP. External markets will hardly notice Latvia's adjustment. But they would certainly notice a comparably large Italian one. Again, Latvia's population shrank by 7.6 per cent and Lithuania's by 10.1 per cent between 2007 and 2012. That has to flatter the unemployment picture, which is still pretty dreadful. If Spain and Italy had lost the same proportion of their populations, there would have been 11 million economic refugees. Such a massive movement of people from collapsing economies can hardly be a politically or socially viable part of the contemporary European settlement.

Third, since foreign-owned banks play a central role in the Baltic economies, the banking system survived the economic downturn and fiscal stress. But, today, at least, Italy and Spain have a domestically owned banking system.

Finally, the Baltic states embraced their European destiny as an alternative to falling back into Russia's orbit and they have prospered as a result. Their peoples have reason to prefer painful adjustment to appearing to waver in this political commitment. Other crisis-hit countries also have reasons for the commitment to Europe, but to a lesser extent.

The Baltic states, and particularly crisis-hit Latvia, are not a model of expansion driven by fiscal contraction. The fiscal contraction itself was indeed contractionary. Subsequently, they were able to combine a colossal external adjustment, greatly facilitated by their small size, with restoration of growth, though joblessness has remained high and emigration has been huge.

Latvia is not a plausible model for others, particularly for far bigger countries. The idea that we should view every economy, let alone many economies taken together, as if they were small open economies that do not interact with one another, is an intellectual disease. It is why Eurozone policymakers are happy to ignore demand. It is also why the adjustment process has been so grim. One can argue that Latvia is a model for tiny countries. But it is crazy to think it is a model for Europe as a whole.

Turning the Eurozone into a Bigger Germany[13]

Germany thinks of itself as the model on which the new European economy should be built. But the German model – that of an open export-dependent economy – works only because other countries are its mirror image.

Germany has always used shifts in its external balance to stabilize the economy: a rising surplus when domestic demand is weak, and the reverse when demand is strong. Germany's economy may seem too big to rely on a mechanism characteristic of small and open economies. It has managed to do so, however, by relying upon its superb export-oriented manufacturing and ability to curb real wages. In the 2000s, this combination allowed the country to regenerate the current-account surplus lost during the post-unification boom of the 1990s. Between 2000 and 2007, Germany's current-account balance moved from a deficit of 1.7 per cent of GDP to a surplus of 7.5 per cent. This, in turn, helped bring modest economic growth, despite feeble domestic demand.

For this approach to work, a large export-oriented economy needs buoyant external markets. Within the Eurozone, domestic credit booms drove demand in several countries. As noted in Chapters Two and Five above, after the financial crisis, capital inflows halted and private spending collapsed, creating huge fiscal deficits. The mistaken consensus swiftly emerged that this was a fiscal crisis. In truth, except in the case of Greece, it was a financial crisis with fiscal consequences. But crisis-hit countries had to tighten their fiscal positions, despite their deep recessions. Unfortunately, the Eurozone's healthier countries also hewed tightly to the stability mantra. So they, too, tightened fiscal positions. The IMF has forecasted that the Eurozone's cyclically adjusted fiscal deficit will have shrunk by 3.2 per cent of potential GDP between 2009 and 2013, ending up at just 1.1 per cent of GDP. The European Central Bank also continues to show next to no interest in spurring demand and is allowing inflation to fall far below target.

Unsurprisingly, Eurozone demand is becalmed. That leaves external adjustment. According to the IMF, by 2018 every current Eurozone member, except Finland, will be running a current-account surplus.

The Eurozone as a whole is forecast to run a current-account surplus of 2.5 per cent of GDP. Such reliance on balancing the domestic economy via external demand – that is, using an external imbalance (a current-account surplus) to offset an internal imbalance (a shortfall of domestic demand relative to potential output) – is exactly what one would expect of a Germanic Eurozone. This has, after all, been the macroeconomic policy of Germany for most of the past half-century.

If one wants to understand how far the folly goes, one must study the European Commission's work on its 'macroeconomic imbalances procedures'.[14] Its features are revealing. Thus, it takes a current-account deficit of 4 per cent of GDP as a sign of imbalance. Yet, for surpluses, the criterion is 6 per cent. It can hardly be an accident that this happens to be Germany's surplus. Above all and amazingly, no account is taken of a country's size in assessing its contribution to imbalances. In this way, Germany's role is brushed out. Yet its surplus savings create huge difficulties when interest rates are close to zero. The omission of Germany makes the Commission's analysis of 'imbalances' indefensible. Imbalances are a *systemic* issue, not a country-specific one. What matters is the scale of the imbalances relative to the Eurozone economy. In this broader context, Germany's surpluses are crucial.

The implications of the attempt to force the Eurozone to mimic the path to adjustment taken by Germany in the 2000s are profound. For the Eurozone it makes prolonged stagnation, particularly in the crisis-hit countries, probable. Moreover, as it starts to work, the euro itself is likely to appreciate, so increasing risks of deflation, and undermining the austerity-driven increases in net exports of vulnerable countries. Not least, the shift of the Eurozone into surplus is a contractionary shock for the world economy.

The Eurozone is not a small and open economy, but the second-largest economy in the world. It is too big and the external competitiveness of its weaker countries are too frail to make big shifts in the external accounts a workable post-crisis strategy for economic adjustment and growth. The Eurozone cannot hope to build a solid recovery on this mechanism, as Germany did in the buoyant 2000s. Once this is understood, the internal political pressures for a change in approach will surely become overwhelming. Europe will not become a bigger Germany. It is foolish to believe it ever could.

The Political Challenge

The difficulty is not only that the economic outcomes have been so terrible, but that a complete separation has emerged between the national level of accountability and the Eurozone level of power. Democracy has been nullified, as politicians of foreign countries – more precisely of one foreign country – and their official lackeys dictate to sovereign nations not just temporarily, in a period of crisis, but indefinitely. This structure cannot hold and, if it can, it should not.

FEAR OF DIVORCE

If the bad marriage is miserable and in the long run probably unsustainable, only two alternatives remain: divorce or a good marriage. A good marriage is one in which the partners stay together not because they are frightened of the consequences of leaving, but because they would prefer remaining in it to any conceivable alternative. Indeed, faced with the initial choice, but knowing all they now know, they would still tie the knot. So what might a divorce look like? Here the first question is what would happen if just one country tried to leave, the second is what would happen if a comprehensive break-up occurred.

Managing Partial Exits

One can envisage two possibilities: a disorderly exit and an orderly exit.

A cessation of external official funding, perhaps because a country refused to abide by an agreed programme, might trigger a disorderly collapse. The government of the country in question would default. The European Central Bank would argue that the banks of the country in question no longer possessed acceptable collateral, which would prevent it from operating as a lender of last resort. Comprehensive bank runs would occur. The country would impose exchange controls, introduce a new currency, redenominate domestic contracts and default on external contracts denominated in euros. These defaults would be by both the public and the private sectors. Chaos might break out. Unpaid police officers and soldiers would be unlikely to keep order. Looting and rioting would occur. A coup or civil war would become conceivable. Any new currency would be sure to depreciate sharply. Inflation would soar. In the medium run, however, order would presumably be restored in some way, even at enormous cost.

In time, after a huge devaluation, the economy would probably thrive, as happened to the East Asian economies after their post-crisis devaluations in 1997 and 1998. The devaluation would help adjust the current account radically, generating a strong growth impulse over time. Of course, the government might make a mess of this opportunity. Indeed, after a crisis of this magnitude irresponsible populism is all too likely. The consequences would then look a bit like Argentina ten years after its default and devaluation.

An agreed and so orderly departure would end up in much the same place, but much sooner. Outsiders could support the banking system and pay beneficiaries of public spending during transition to a new currency. That should limit unrest as well as reducing the currency collapse and inflationary upsurge.

In either case, a big challenge would be to manage the contagion. An exit, particularly a disorderly one, would surely trigger bank runs and capital flight from other members. It could also cause collapses in the prices of financial and other assets. A flight to safety, to Germany or beyond the Eurozone, would occur.

A decisive response from the Eurozone would be required to halt the contagion. The ECB would need to act as a lender of last resort on an unlimited scale, replacing money taken out in bank runs. Interest rates on sovereign debt would need to be capped. Above all, the commitment to keep the rest of the Eurozone together would have to be reinforced. The Eurozone either is an irrevocable currency union or it is not. If countries in difficulty leave, it is just an exceptionally rigid fixed-currency system. So any departure would have a destabilizing effect: people would trust in the Eurozone's survival even less and the economic benefits of the single currency would dwindle.

The least destabilizing exit would be by a creditor country, notably Germany, as George Soros has argued.[15] But even this would be highly destabilizing. Exit could never be a surprise in a law-governed society.

In the run-up to an exit, there would be flight into German financial assets, which the German authorities would have to manage in conjunction with the European Central Bank, from which they intended to exit. Agreeing rules on conversion would create prolonged and profound uncertainty, which would spread to other creditor countries likely to follow Germany's lead – notably Austria and the Benelux countries. After introduction of the new currency or, more probably, reintroduction of the Deutschmark, German financial institutions would suffer losses on their holdings of euro-denominated assets. German manufacturing would be hit. The credibility of Germany's commitment to the European project – the core of its post-war political identity – would be shattered and its relations with important partners, notably France, put into limbo.

Comprehensive Break-Up

Suppose the Eurozone members agreed to break the whole structure up instead of watching the departure, be it orderly or disorderly, of just a few members. In principle, it would be possible to divide every euro and redenominate every euro contract in the component currencies, weighted as they were when they joined the euro. But this would mean telling the citizens of, say, Germany, that their euro accounts and euro claims suddenly contained a substantial proportion of French francs, Italian lire, Spanish pesetas and all the rest. This would be very unpopular. German citizens would surely feel cheated.

In fact, governments would want to redenominate domestic money and contracts in their restored national currencies. Individual countries' experiences would vary, depending upon their exposure to foreign trade and financial interlinkages. But inflation would soar in the devaluing debtor countries; in creditor nations, deflation would be likely to set in. Inflation should erode the debt mountains of peripheral nations, provided they were promptly redenominated in the new domestic currencies. The value of the foreign assets of core countries would fall, their new currencies would soar relative to erstwhile partners and their economies shrink. It would be painful for all.

The mechanisms at work would be both powerful and disorderly: runs; the imposition of (illegal) exchange controls; legal uncertainties;

asset-price collapses; unpredictable and unknowable shifts in balance sheets; freezing of the financial system; disruption of central banking; collapse in spending and trade; and enormous shifts in the exchange rates of new currencies. Further government bailouts of financial systems would surely be needed, at great cost. Big recessions would also worsen already damaged fiscal positions. Such a chaotic break-up would also trigger legions of lawsuits.

The sad truth is that an orderly break-up is a contradiction in terms. The very notion would create too much instability while being discussed and agreed among so many countries. Worse, it is the sort of thing that could only happen in a crisis. It would be born of crisis and generate bigger ones. The EU would be cast into legal and political limbo, with its most important treaties and proudest achievement in tatters. It is impossible to guess at the result of such a profound change in the European order.

Winners and Losers

There would be no winners from a comprehensive break-up. But it is a good guess that creditors would be even more damaged than debtors. Export-dependent Germany might find itself suffering much the same longer-term fate as Japan, if not even worse. As noted above, Germany's financial system would be damaged as the value of its external assets tumbled, while its manufacturing industry would surely shift much of its activity into neighbouring countries, just as Japan has shifted much of its production into its neighbours, particularly China. Germany would emerge as a wealthy, but stagnant, rentier economy and society, earning a living off its foreign assets and, still more, its know-how, rather than off its domestic production. And this ignores the consequences of isolation from its neighbours and partners – the very fate that its wisest leaders have sought to avoid since the end of the Second World War. Neither as economic nor, still less, as political partners, could Russia or China give Germany what a thriving EU gives – a secure and predictable place in the world, and the company and support of those who share its values. The achievement of a unified, peaceful and democratic Germany anchored in a prosperous EU is not to be cast aside lightly or indeed at all. All wise German leaders know this. And all the evidence we have is that the German people agree, as indicated by their consistent choice of pro-EU and pro-euro politicians.

Global Dangers

These perils are not of concern to the Eurozone alone. Taken as a whole, it is the world's second-largest economy, with the largest banking system. The risk that a bigger Eurozone upheaval would cause a global crisis is real. Moreover, beyond that, a stable Europe is among the greatest achievements of the post-Second World War order and surely the finest triumph of American statecraft. It cannot – and must not – be thrown away. However bad an idea the Eurozone might have been, break-up would be worse.

TOWARDS A GOOD MARRIAGE

So, if the marriage is bad and divorce terrifying, the challenge is to turn the bad marriage into a good, or at least a tolerable, one. In considering what would need to happen, one must start by recalling what critics knew in the early 1990s: this is not a natural economic union. The economic forces driving these economies apart are far greater than in other federal monetary unions, because of their economic diversity, while the institutional and political underpinnings of the union are far weaker, because of their political diversity. What needs to be done in the Eurozone is to discover a set of practices and develop a set of supporting institutions that do enough to manage the diversity among its economies, while not demanding too much of the diversity among its polities. Can this be done? We do not know. Can we define what needs to be done? Yes, we can.

The Limits of Eurozone Integration

If we compare the Eurozone with the most obvious economy in terms of scale, political values and level of development, we end up looking at the US. But, as one would expect, given not just its lengthy history as a united country, its common language, shared legal traditions and mobile population, the US economy is far more integrated than that of the Eurozone: US internal trade is bigger, relative to GDP; and US labour mobility is far greater.

Yet perhaps even more important is the fact that the US offers two insurance mechanisms for its states. It also offers a critical background condition. The background condition is that break-up is not an option. Fear of secession will not generate flight from a state's (government or private) liabilities. The Civil War resolved that question. Fortunately, nobody would go to war to keep the Eurozone together. Unfortunately, this also means that the risk of break-up cannot be eliminated. The first of the US insurance mechanisms is a federal tax and spending system, which ensures not only an important offset to economic shocks but also that individuals and businesses can survive even the bankruptcy of a local or state government relatively unscathed compared with what default means in the Eurozone. The second and possibly even more important insurance mechanism is support for the financial system from the US Treasury and Federal

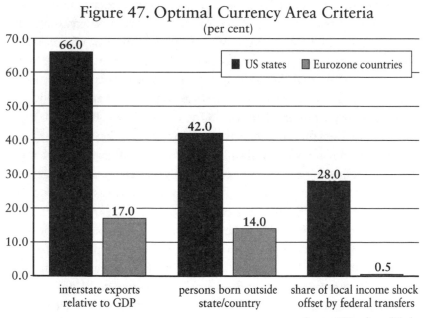

Figure 47. Optimal Currency Area Criteria
(per cent)

Source: O'Rourke and Taylor

Reserve. It is horrifying even to consider what would have happened in 2008 if responsibility for managing the collapse of the US financial system had fallen to the state governments of New York, South Carolina or California, all homes of huge financial institutions (see Figure 47).

Adjustment of Income and Spending

The immediate challenge confronting the Eurozone is adjustment. The vulnerable countries need to achieve internal and external balance once again: sustainable external accounts; sustainable fiscal positions; and full employment.

The reason why the process of adjustment has been so painful is only partly because the exchange rate has been removed as an instrument, but even more because it is so asymmetrical. Indeed, it is not clear that the vulnerable countries can live with creditor countries that run such huge persistent current-account surpluses (see Figure 34). If Germany and other surplus countries were to earn those surpluses in trade with economies outside the Eurozone, the result would probably be an appreciation of the euro. That would once again undermine the competitiveness of the vulnerable economies. In effect, the current-account surpluses of creditor countries are sucking demand out of vulnerable countries. It makes little sense to insist that the latter become more competitive if overall demand does not expand. This is a zero-sum game. Building the future of the Eurozone on such a game is folly.

This has important implications. One is that the ECB must do more to promote demand in the Eurozone. It should be willing to use unconventional policies. It should also target a higher rate of inflation, to facilitate needed adjustments in relative prices. Aggregate inflation of 3–4 per cent a year would not be a disaster. A nominal GDP target for the Eurozone would also make a great deal of sense.

Another implication is that the Eurozone's new imbalances procedure must bite. The most important contributor to the Eurozone's internal imbalances is Germany. It needs to find a way to reduce its current-account surplus. If it does not wish to use fiscal policy, let it try something else. It would also help if the Eurozone's internal capital flows did not take the form of debt, in general, and bank debt, in particular. Banks have played far too big a role in the Eurozone's finances. A move towards greater reliance on capital markets would help, though care would have to be taken to avoid the disaster of shadow banking in the US.

Financing Adjustment

Symmetrical adjustment is essential. But so is the financing of economies in difficulty. The well-understood reason for this is that private financing usually turns around faster than any economy can adapt, creating unnecessarily deep and socially costly collapses. Such financing is going to be even more important in the absence of a flexible exchange rate.

In the Eurozone, the role of financier of last resort falls to the ECB. Yes, the creation of the European Stability Mechanism, together with funding (and intellectual input) from the International Monetary Fund, provides a backstop. But what members of the Eurozone, particularly Italy and Spain, needed most during the worst of the market panic was insurance against illiquidity in their markets for government and bank funding. They lacked what the UK and the US possess: a supportive central bank. Indeed, as Paul de Grauwe, now at the London School of Economics, has argued cogently, the panic in financial markets, the threat to national banking systems, and the inability of governments to fund themselves were due to the failure of the ECB to ensure liquidity in debt markets, a responsibility the Federal Reserve met during the crisis.[16] The main reason weak banks ended up in a terrifying embrace with weak states – two drunks holding each other up – is that it was widely believed that the ECB would allow liquidity crises in the markets for government bonds to turn into sovereign defaults.

Governments do not offer collateral. So government debt markets are always lifted by their own bootstraps: the willingness to lend depends on the perceived willingness of others to do so, now and in future. Such markets are exposed to self-fulfilling runs and so need a credible buyer of last resort: that is the central bank. The UK has such a central bank. Eurozone members do not. In effect, they borrow in a quasi-foreign currency.

Note that if the ECB succeeded in stabilizing government bond markets, it would automatically stabilize banks as well, since fears of sovereign defaults drove worries over insolvency of banks. The capital needed to protect the European banking system from defaults by important sovereigns does not exist. It is ridiculous to suppose that sovereigns can provide insurance against their own default. Yet since there is no good reason for a well-managed Eurozone to suffer illiquidity-driven defaults, the answer is to stop them at source.

The ECB had the firepower to do this and finally it did it, via its OMT programme in the summer of 2012, with remarkable success, enormously easing the pressure on the two pivotal vulnerable countries: Italy and Spain (see Figure 7). It is a tragedy that it did not do this earlier. Yet even the OMT programme might fail if put to the test: the ECB's promise to offer unlimited, but conditional, support is inherently contradictory, as noted in Chapter Two. It is easy to imagine circumstances in which the ECB would feel unable to help, because elected politicians refused to meet the conditions imposed upon them. Unfortunately, the circumstances in which this conflict happened would be ones of extreme crisis. One must hope it never comes to this. But it could.

Financing must not be so generous that it prevents adjustment, but rather gives adjustment the time it needs. The stress on governments and credit markets in vulnerable states is quite large enough, despite the ECB's interventions, to ensure this, as shown by the massive shifts in current accounts, weak economies and high rates of unemployment. Worse than that is neither morally justifiable nor practically needed.

Debt Restructuring

Adjustment, financing and growth are the start of what is needed to put the Eurozone economy back on track. Together they would handle the 'flow' problems – those concerning flows of incomes and spending, including the balance of payments. But there is also a stock problem – the overhang of private and public debt from past mistakes. The lower the interest rates paid, the easier debt is to handle. Nevertheless, the vulnerable countries are all going to end up with very high public debt, which it will take a very long time to reduce to manageable levels. Moreover, we now know from experience that, if they are to use fiscal policy to cushion recessions in future, they need low debt burdens. More fundamentally, members of the Eurozone do need to have relatively low levels of public debt because they are semi-sovereign countries locked inside a currency union without access to their own central bank or a solid demand for their sovereign debt as a safe asset.

A credibly one-off debt restructuring might be necessary in a number of cases, notably Greece (see Figure 48). This would certainly create problems, notably for the banks: it might be necessary to restructure bank debt as well, as has happened in Iceland and Cyprus. But the long-established practice of protecting bank creditors at the expense of taxpayers must be ended in any case. It is unconscionable. An alternative to the nuclear option of debt restructuring would be agreement on lower interest rates and much longer maturities, supported by the creditor countries directly, via ECB involvement, or both. Since, as argued in Chapter Five, the creditor countries bear a full share in the responsibility for the mess, they should expect to bear

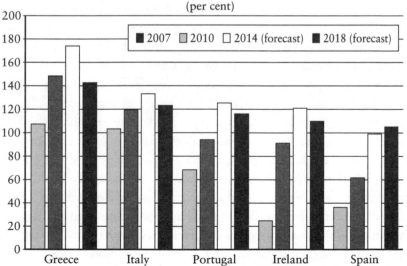

Figure 48. Gross Public Debt over GDP
(per cent)

Source: IMF World Economic Outlook Database

a full share in its resolution as well. There is another alternative: rapid economic recovery. But that will depend on the speed of adjustment.

Reforms

Let us assume that the Eurozone does manage the adjustment, financing and restructuring needed to put the economies on a sounder footing. What else is needed if it is to be a minimally viable currency union among otherwise sovereign countries? Here is what must happen and what must not.

First, the Eurozone must have a proper banking union. It is now clear that vulnerable countries are unable to provide the backstop for their banks that has, hitherto, seemed normal. This is why a banking union, similar to that already achieved by the US, is vital. It requires several elements: an effective resolution regime for all banks, however large, that will impose losses on bail-inable debt smoothly (see Chapter Seven for an explanation of this concept). Because of the difficulty of doing this, the case for much higher capital ratios, also presented in Chapter Seven, is particularly strong for the Eurozone: these semi-sovereign countries need banks that can stand on their own. Such a banking union will require strong central regulation and supervision and, in particular, strong macroprudential regulation, at least to try to prevent the sort of runaway credit booms that led to such disasters. The Eurozone has gone quite a long way to meeting these conditions in its agreement on banking union of March 2014.[17]

Yet if a banking union is to work, there must exist an adequate supply of unimpeachably safe assets, thereby breaking the doom loop between the sovereigns and their banks. Relying on the debt of just a few countries, principally Germany, is inadequate, particularly since Germany wishes to lower its public debt relative to the economy. For this reason, there has to be an adequate supply of eurobonds – bonds for which the Eurozone states are jointly and severally liable. As a collectivity, the Eurozone could certainly support eurobonds up to, say, 60 per cent of the GDP of each member state (and so of all of them together), leaving members on their own in financing debt above that level. A eurobond market on that scale would bring huge advantages: it would be the second-biggest bond market in the world and so very liquid; finance would, accordingly, be cheap; it would give banks a safe asset; and it would give the ECB ideal collateral and so the possibility of operating unconventional monetary policies, such as quantitative easing, quite easily. Turning a substantial portion of existing bonds into eurobonds would sharply reduce current anxieties. It would make restructuring the remaining debt much simpler, since it would not threaten the credibility of a substantial proportion of outstanding debt.

Second, with banks holding eurobonds, it would be far easier to restructure remaining public debt, making the 'no-bailout clause' credible. A no-bailout rule is far simpler than the undemocratic attempt to operate an economically arbitrary and hard-to-measure-and-interpret restriction on structural (or cyclically adjusted) fiscal deficits, as implemented in the Treaty on Stability, Coordination and Governance in the Economic and Monetary Union signed in March 2012.[18] This not only calls on governments to run budget deficits of less than 3 per cent of GDP, but also requires them to run structural (cyclically adjusted) fiscal deficits of less than 1 per cent of GDP if debt is under 60 per cent of GDP and 0.5 per cent if it is over 60 per cent. These rules are to be enforced through domestic legal procedures. But what sort of procedure can implement an inherently imprecise economic concept such as the structural fiscal deficit? Precisely because it makes more economic sense than just focusing on the existing fiscal deficit, it is also even less amenable to legal interpretation. Even more important, in a currency union, fiscal policy is the only national stabilizer left. It should not be lightly abandoned in favour of such arbitrary rules. The Eurozone needs to abandon this 'discipline union' approach, replacing it with a more effective no-bailout clause.

Third, the ECB needs to become a true modern central bank determined to underpin stability in the Eurozone economy. Demonstrably, it has failed to do this. The changes in fiscal and banking arrangements outlined above would be a big help. But it may ultimately be necessary to change the treaty to give it more freedom of manoeuvre in exceptional circumstances, including the ability to finance governments directly. That might become obvious if, as is possible, the OMT is tried at some point and turns out not to work.

Finally, the proposals outlined above evidently presuppose a form of fiscal union, not in the form of ongoing fiscal transfers, but in the form of collective backstops for the banking union as well as of eurobonds. Over time, it will probably be necessary to transfer a part of the fiscal responsibilities of member states to the centre. It will also be necessary to generate some capacity for fiscal stabilization policy at the centre.

WHY THE ROAD AHEAD IS HARD

A small Eurozone that contained Germany and its long-standing partners, together possibly with France, would have surely worked. But the broader and more dysfunctional Eurozone actually created has bequeathed huge and long-lasting depressions and resentments. It is dividing Europe rather than uniting it. It has, as critics warned, become a bad marriage. Yet divorce, as this chapter has argued, is a very tough option too. The economic and political consequences could prove devastating. Fear of these dire consequences might keep the parties together indefinitely. But locking parties together in a marriage that makes everybody miserable merely because divorce would be even worse would be a horrible outcome for Europe. A far better outcome would be to turn it into a good marriage instead.

The Eurozone has definitely not achieved that. Yes, the will to improvise during the crisis was remarkable. But what happened was 'just enough, almost too late'. The British would call it 'muddling through'. More fundamental changes will be needed to achieve a good marriage. The obstacles to success are three. First, with the best will in the world, making a currency union work well is bound to be difficult, particularly in view of the great differences in the economic structure of these countries, in their economic culture and in their politics. Second, the divergence in economic ideology remains substantial. Yes, Germany is powerful enough to impose its views for the moment. But that does not mean they are universally accepted. Nor does it mean they will be universally implemented. Germany may be the hegemon, but it is not all-powerful. Third, the peoples of the Eurozone do not like one another very much at the moment and, more important, they do not identify with one another very much either.

Since politics remain national, democratic legitimacy undermines cohesion. This is bad now. It could get even worse.

The obstacles to creating a good marriage are indeed high. But perfection is unnecessary, since economic arrangements are always imperfect. What is needed is rather a 'good enough' system. For the marriage to strengthen Europe rather than weaken it, the Eurozone must generate symmetrical adjustment, debt restructuring and further fundamental reform, including of its fiscal arrangements. The adjustment needed and the reforms required both go beyond what Germany is today prepared to contemplate. But Germany's insistence on retaining its huge external surplus, on keeping inflation so low, on national responsibility for bank debts and on ever-tighter fiscal discipline will not work. The Eurozone needs to become something different. The question is whether it can reach a more successful and balanced resolution of its failings before it is too late.

Conclusion: Fire Next Time[1]

But this long run is a misleading guide to current affairs. In the long run we are all dead. Economists set themselves too easy, too useless a task if in tempestuous seasons they can only tell us that when the storm is long past the ocean is flat again.
John Maynard Keynes, Tract on Monetary Reform, 1923[2]

Of all the many ways of organising banking, the worst is the one we have today.
Mervyn King, 'Banking from Bagehot to Basel, and Back Again', 2010[3]

Since 1980, the world has suffered six globally significant financial crises: the Latin American debt crisis of the early 1980s; the Japanese crisis of the 1990s; the Tequila crisis of 1994, whose epicentre was Mexico, but which also affected many parts of Latin America; the East Asian crisis of 1997–99; the global financial crisis of 2007–09; and the Eurozone financial crisis of 2010–13. This list leaves aside many national crises – the 2001 crisis in Argentina, for example – and significant regional crises, including the Scandinavian crisis of the early 1990s. Indeed, one authoritative source estimates there were 147 banking crises between 1970 and 2011.[4]

Driven by trade and foreign direct investment, economic globalization has produced impressive results, notably the successful integration of China and, to a smaller degree, India, into the world economy, together with large reductions in mass poverty in these and other emerging and developing countries. Nothing in this book contradicts these wonderful results. But financial crises are *not* among those wonderful results. On the contrary, they are a plague. Indeed, it is far from clear that the globalization of debt-creating flows, particularly those generated by banks, has brought much, if any, benefit to the world economy, as opposed to those who work in the financial industry.

Most frightening is that the crises seem to have become bigger and more globally devastating over time. The last two – the global and Eurozone financial crises – struck the core of the world economic system, affecting economies that generate not much less than half of global economic product (if we treat the Eurozone as a single whole). The emerging and developing countries managed the consequences relatively well. But that story is not over: it may well turn out that the ways in which these economies responded to the crisis – particularly, fiscal loosening and credit expansion – have brought substantial longer-term fragilities.

The high-income countries had the monetary and fiscal resources to prevent this crisis from becoming a complete economic meltdown. But they were also compelled to adopt extreme measures, notably, many years of close-to-zero short-term interest rates, huge expansions in the balance sheets of central banks, and fiscal deficits that had previously only been seen during world wars. Moreover, as shown in Chapters Two and Three above, their recessions were still deep and the recovery was weak. The full consequences of the measures taken cannot yet be known. Moreover, the events leading up to the crisis and the crisis itself have bequeathed a large overhang of private and public debt. It is unlikely that the high-income countries could cope with another such crisis within the next decade or two without large-scale defaults in the private or public sectors, either openly or via inflation. It might indeed be the fire next time.

This is a desperate situation. Keynes was right: hopes and fears for the long run must not be the enemies of decisive action in the short run. In the 1930s policymakers tried to do nothing or, worse, imposed austerity with dire economic and political consequences. As was argued in Chapters Eight and Nine, policymakers must deal with the problems they confront. But they must also do what they can to prevent them recurring. The ever-rising scale of the crises, combined with the ever-increasing desperation of the measures used to combat them, tells us that something is seriously amiss, as Mervyn King, then governor of the Bank of England, argued just after the height of the crisis. Somehow, the interaction between liberalization and globalization has destabilized the financial system. Why has this happened? What is the legacy? What is to be done? Why does it really matter? These are the questions addressed in this final chapter.

WHAT HAPPENED?

If we look at the debate on what happened, we find several explanations: a global savings glut and associated global imbalances; an expansionary monetary policy that ignored asset prices and credit; an unstable financial system; and naive, if not captured, regulation.

This list reminds us of the story of four blind men who are asked to tell an audience what is in front of them. One says it is a snake; another a sail; a third a pull rope; and the last, four trees. The answer is: an elephant. What we have here is just such an economic elephant. All of the explanations have validity. Above all, they fit together. Our story would go not in seven ages, but in seven stages. Here, then, is the story of shifts and shocks told in this book.

Unstable Credit

Our liberalized financial system is a credit-, debt- and leverage-creating machine. The banks are at the core of this activity, but not on their own. The creation of credit, debt or leverage is inherent in banks' on-book lending, but also, to varying extents, in the 'originate and distribute' model of securitized finance, in the strategies of private equity and hedge funds and, not least, in the markets for derivatives. Our public-private, credit-backed monetary system is explosive in good times and implosive in bad ones. During the explosions it creates excessive confidence, credit and leverage, not to mention excessive behaviour, legal, shady and downright illegal. During the implosions, it creates panic, collapsing credit, de-leveraging and hunts for scapegoats and villains. It was ever thus. Indeed, contrary to the views of many academic Panglossians, informed observers have long known this (see Chapter

Six). But it seems that, given contemporary information and communication technologies, modern financial innovations and globalization, the capacity of the system to generate complexity and fragility, surpasses anything seen historically, in its scope, scale and speed. Fortunately, the willingness and ability to respond has also increased. But it was quite a close-run thing in 2008 globally, and after 2009 in the Eurozone. Without the policy response, the outcome would have been worse than in the 1930s. It may also be impossible, financially or politically, to repeat this response in a similar situation, at least in the relatively near future.

The Reaction of Emerging Countries

Emerging countries learned the truth about financial markets from their painful experiences in the 1980s and 1990s. Many then decided to protect themselves against the vagaries of international finance by accumulating foreign-currency reserves and relying on export-driven rather than credit-driven economic growth. Let others create those debt mountains this time, they decided. And so those others – predominantly a few high-income countries, notably including the US, and the European emerging countries – did just that, big time. This shift by emerging economies looked shrewd. After all, the high-income countries had a substantial advantage in managing financial crises: their financial institutions were at the core of the global financial system; and they issued the world's principal reserve currencies. These countries could print their way out of the worst of a crisis – a luxury unavailable to almost any internationally open emerging economy. To be safe, an emerging economy needed an impregnable external position. When the crisis hit, China had built one, as a result of its massive accumulations of reserves, huge current-account surpluses and exchange controls. It used its position, to great effect, in 2008 and 2009, though the resulting credit boom created symptoms of financial fragility.

The Global Savings Glut

Thus, developing countries shifted into substantial aggregate current-account surpluses, led by the emerging colossus – China. Similar shifts into current-account surplus (by definition, a surplus of income over spending or savings over investment) occurred in high-income countries, notably Germany. The Japanese private sector has run an enormous savings surplus ever since the collapse of its bubble economy in 1990. As commodity prices soared in the 2000s, yet another group of savings-surplus economies emerged, namely, the commodity exporters, particularly the oil exporters, such as Saudi Arabia and other states of the Persian Gulf. In a number of high-income countries, not least the US, the non-financial corporate sector also ceased to need funds from outside. On the contrary, with rising profits and a weak desire to invest, the non-financial corporate sector became a net supplier of savings to the rest of the economy. Finally, there was a huge shift in the distribution of income inside many economies, notably including high-income countries, from wages to profits and, within wages, from those at the middle and bottom towards the top, partly due to globalization, partly due to technology, partly due to financial liberalization, and partly due to changes in social norms, particularly corporate governance.[5] The net result of all these changes was a marked rise in propensities to save relative to propensities to invest and so low long-term real interest rates in a world economy characterized by rapid economic growth (see Figure 30).[6] This, then, was the global 'savings glut' to which Mr Bernanke pointed, rightly, in the early 2000s. It might just as well be called a global 'investment dearth'. In the short run, ultra-low real interest rates will raise the prices of long-lived assets, particularly real estate. In the longer run, a savings glut will generate 'secular stagnation' – a situation in which the equilibrium long-term real interest rate is negative, as was the case after 2008 and might have been the case in the run-up to the crisis, as Lawrence Summers, former US treasury secretary, has argued.[7]

Global Imbalances

In the terminology used in Chapter Five, a host of countries achieved internal balance by pursuing external imbalance – or, more precisely, by exporting excess savings via current-account surpluses (which is the same thing, in a different language). If some countries export excess savings, others *must* import them. The only way to import excess savings is to run a current-account deficit. But, if this is not to depress output and so cause internal imbalances, domestic demand must rise. Now consider the options of central banks confronted with this internal imbalance caused, in large measure, by external imbalances. What can they do? The answer is: promote domestic spending, to offset the contractionary forces. This is what their mandate tells them to do: keep output near potential and so keep inflation on target. But, in the aftermath of the collapse of the equity bubble in 2000, this no longer worked via higher corporate investment. On the contrary, non-financial corporations were part of the problem of excess savings, not part of the solution. (In some cases the need to close pension-fund deficits also contributed to the financial surpluses of the corporate sector.) So something else had to be found. That turned out to be investment in residential housing and higher household spending. Happily for central banks, at least in the short run, the fall in global real interest rates was what Hyman Minsky called a 'displacement' event – the beginning of a runaway credit boom. House-price rises set these credit booms in motion, above all in the US, but also in a number of other high-income and emerging countries in the western, southern and eastern periphery of Europe with elastic credit. So central banks had something to build upon.

Financial Deregulation

Central banks were pouring petrol on the flames, because they wanted a blaze. The increasingly liberalized financial sector was only too happy to burn. Its richly rewarded participants found the borrowers they needed among foolish and ill-informed households. They found the purchasers of the securities they created among foolish and ill-informed investors, some of whom even turned out to be perversely rewarded parts of their own organizations. Fraud and near fraud – not to mention massaging of the data to show a prettier picture than was justified (by the rating agencies, for example) – exploded. As a by-product, household borrowing and spending soared and the financial sector boomed. The result was not just too much debt, but debt of doubtful value and, no less, massively increased leverage in the financial sector: median leverage of UK banks, for example, rose from

20:1 to 50:1 between 2000 and 2007.[8] Regulators, politicians and the economists who advised them were either unaware of the full extent of the dangers or were unable or unwilling to act to reduce them, partly because they were captured by the interests of the regulated, partly because they were intimated or seduced, but, above all, more so because they were prey to the very same cognitive errors.

Crisis Mismanagement

This had many elements: lack of preparedness; lack of understanding of what was happening, particularly the multiple ramifications of contagion; political, intellectual and bureaucratic resistance to taking effective action soon enough; the unavoidable difficulties of handling a crisis that required cooperation across borders; and, particularly, the Eurozone's political and institutional lack of preparedness. In all, given the difficulties, the disaster was handled far better than it might have been. It did not become a plunge on the scale of the 1930s. The collapse was halted and turned around. But it still left deep scars: prolonged recessions and, at the time of writing (in 2014), failure to regain pre-crisis growth rates of either production or productivity.[9]

Post-Crisis Mismanagement

The shift to fiscal austerity in 2010 (see Figure 42) and the subsequent weak recovery left monetary policy as the principal tool with which to achieve recovery. In countries with cyclically adjusted current-account deficits and a desire for a cyclically adjusted balanced budget, the cyclically adjusted private-sector financial balance has had go into deficit: in other words, the private sector had to end up spending more than its income and so borrowing more. The way to make this happen was to restart the private-sector's credit machine. That is what the central banks have been trying to do. The belief that government borrowing is the illness for which private borrowing is the cure has survived all that has happened. The chances are good that reliance on this surprisingly durable piece of conventional wisdom will lead to another and still bigger crisis.

CONCLUSION

The kernel of the story, then, is one of the interaction between global macroeconomic forces and an increasingly fragile, liberalized financial system. But it would be wrong to see the causality as going one way. Into this complex set of relationships always come asset-price bubbles and both monetary and fiscal policies. The idea that, in such a world, the central bank can target prices of goods and services while assuming that credit and the financial sector, which both creates and deals in debt, will be stable, is hopelessly naive. This, moreover, is not the end of the story. It is easy to believe that the scale of the current rescue operation might lead to bigger crises down the road, as critics argue. Huge sums of liquid finance, nearly all of it preserved by support from taxpayers during the crisis, now move around the world, most of it managed by agents rewarded for achieving short-term gains.

WHAT IS THE LEGACY?

It is too soon to tell what difference the crises that began in 2007 will make to the world. That partly depends on whether the afflicted economies make a strong and balanced recovery. Unlikely though this seems, it is possible. Yet some legacies are already evident, as the Introduction has discussed.

The economic and financial costs of misbehaving financial systems are revealed to be huge. How big the costs of these crises will end up being is still unknowable. But, in the cases of the US and the UK, the fiscal costs are of roughly the same scale as a world war, while the present value of the economic costs could be even greater, since economies often recover more strongly after wars than after financial crises (see Chapter Eight above).[10] In crisis-hit Eurozone countries the costs would be greater. Obviously, some part of the pre-crisis GDP level was unsustainable. But, as argued in Chapter Eight, the view that such enormous losses were unavoidable is unconvincing. Policymakers had choices over how long they let aggregate demand falter and so over how bad the longer-term effects would be. Research at the International Monetary Fund has suggested, for example, that the more expansionary the immediate macroeconomic policies, the smaller are the long-term losses in output.[11]

Yet another legacy is the mountains of private debt, mostly generated before the crisis, and public debt, generated after it. The lower the prospective economic growth, the more policymakers will rely on those four horsemen of post-crisis apocalypse: austerity, inflation, (financial) repression and (debt) restructuring. Since the crisis itself has damaged animal spirits, the likelihood is that trend growth will have been lowered for this reason alone. Moreover, while policymakers may want to drive the economy via another credit boom, they may find it hard to do so, even in the short term.

As important as the legacy of debt are the monetary consequences. Central banks have become unprecedentedly active players in the economies of all high-income countries, not excluding the Eurozone, where the ECB has been the decisive actor. If the contemporary monetary system is a public-private partnership, it became much more public and much less private after the crisis. Moreover, the role of the central bank as a creator of money and its role in supporting the financial system has become widely known. What has been learned cannot be unlearned.

Again, the economies of the high-income countries are considerably smaller than they were expected to be in 2006, whereas the economies of emerging economies have continued to grow quickly. This shift has accelerated the transition in relative economic weight. Moreover, the high-income economies have not only become relatively smaller more quickly than expected, but, more importantly, have found their credibility as effective managers of their economic affairs grievously damaged.

Unavoidably, the crises have also bequeathed some big questions about finance and the world economy. One such set of questions is how far the financial system should be integrated across frontiers. Another set of questions is how to end the global savings glut and associated imbalances. China has grasped the urgency of this point; but Germany and possibly also Japan have not done so. An important implication of attempts at reform is the need to take a new view of global institutions, particularly the International Monetary Fund. The same need exists in the Eurozone. The attempt to resolve its problems by turning the Eurozone into a bigger Germany is going to prove unworkable. If this is not understood – and it is not, as yet, where it matters – further crises seem certain.

Finally, the crisis has destroyed much of the orthodoxy that dominated monetary and financial policy before it occurred. Naive confidence in the stability of a deregulated financial system has vanished, perhaps for a generation, except in particularly secluded corners of the academic world. Trust between the authorities and the financial system has collapsed. The result will be a more regulated financial system than during the glad morning of financial liberalization during the 1980s, 1990s and early 2000s. Unless something extraordinary happens (such as election of a 'Tea Party' President and Congress in the US), this seems unlikely to change. The new orthodoxy rests on the old inflation-targeting monetary policy, plus more financial regulation and macroprudential supervision (see Chapters Six and Seven). But this approach might well fail. If so, greater radicalism will be needed.

WHAT IS TO BE DONE?

The answers to this question come over two time dimensions – the shorter and the longer terms. They come in two linked categories – macroeconomic and financial. And they need to be assessed on a spectrum of alternatives. The discussion below considers four, along that spectrum: the first is 'new orthodoxy' – the post-crisis policy consensus in the high-income countries of North America and Europe; the second is 'liquidationism' – a return to nineteenth-century free-market capitalism; the third is 'beyond the new orthodoxy' – more radical ideas than those of the current orthodoxy, but within the broad framework of that approach; and the fourth is 'radical reconstruction', principally (though not solely) of the monetary system. What becomes clear is that the best way forward is a pragmatic amalgam of these apparently distinct approaches. None embodies all wisdom.

Short-Term Recovery of Crisis-Hit Economies

The immediate challenge has been to engineer a recovery in the crisis-hit countries, all of which have ended up far below trend levels of output and most of which were well below pre-crisis peak output levels in 2013. Achieving this involves fixing three (closely interconnected) things: the financial system; the overhang of private debt; and the inadequate demand. In some cases, notably in southern Europe, it has also been necessary to promote greater market flexibility. In neither the US nor the UK were these reforms so important, since supposed 'rigidities' were not a credible obstacle to recovery.

The post-crisis 'new orthodoxy' was to tighten fiscal policy once evidence of stabilization and some recovery emerged in 2010, and so rely on monetary policy. As argued in Chapter Eight, this policy has created significant dangers. It might not work well, given the debt overhang. If it worked, it might begin another unsustainable credit-cum-asset-price boom. Yet, for some reason, policymakers regarded this reliance on monetary policy as the cautious option, despite the obvious risks of relying predominantly on monetary policy and so on relaunching the credit cycle.

The new orthodoxy also included recapitalization of the financial sector and real, but modest, increases in capital requirements for banks. The financial sector and markets that have emerged from this approach are, however, in essence the same as the ones that went into the crisis. Banking has even been further concentrated in a remarkably small number of banks: the official list includes just twenty-nine globally significant international banks.[12] It is not clear that these are all 'too big to fail', but it is highly unlikely that such banks could be resolved smoothly in a significant crisis, partly because they are still too interconnected to fail. Moreover, these institutions remain the beneficiaries of significant explicit and implicit subsidies from central banks and governments.[13] The new orthodoxy also generally failed to bring about a rapid restructuring of private debt, outside the financial sector, though, particularly in the US, bankruptcy procedures resulted in significant reductions in household debt, after house prices crashed.

In the US, the new orthodoxy generated a recovery that was feeble by historical standards, but not too bad for an economy hit by a financial crisis, particularly one far too large to gain much from export-led economic growth. In other crisis-hit countries, the economic rewards were far slower in coming. The UK's austerity programme, launched in 2010, removed fiscal support for recovery and, together with the falling output of North Sea oil, adverse shifts in the terms of trade and rising domestic prices of imports, resulted in economic stagnation for a further three years. The outcome was far worse in crisis-hit parts of the Eurozone, where the approach taken was close to liquidationism (on which see further below).

In brief, the short-term record of the new orthodoxy was far from a catastrophe. But it could have done far better. In particular, it failed to provide adequate support for demand, partly because of premature fiscal tightening.

A widely promoted alternative to the new orthodoxy has been 'liquidationism' – reliance on the free market, without fiscal or monetary policy support. This approach has limited support among academic economists, but substantial support among active participants in financial markets, including some successful speculators. Friedrich Hayek recommended this approach in the 1930s, as, famously, did US Treasury Secretary Andrew Mellon. In 1933, Irving Fisher explained the dangers of debt deflation, which can lead to much misery and, at worst, the replacement of democracy by authoritarianism of the left or right.[14]

Under German influence, the Eurozone's policy doctrine borders on liquidationism, though the Eurozone's central bank has been relatively aggressive and some fiscal support has also been granted. As discussed in Chapter Nine, the chosen policies consist of fiscal austerity, asymmetric adjustment of competitiveness (with virtually all the adjustment falling on deficit countries), and limited assistance with recapitalization of banks in crisis-hit countries. The ECB is handcuffed by exaggerated fears of inflation, notably in Germany, and so is resistant to the idea of quantitative easing or other controversial policies, such as significantly negative interest rates.[15] Unfortunately, deflationary liquidationism is sure to be a part of the adjustment process in a currency union with ultra-low overall inflation. Thus, if inflation remains low in the competitive economies, deflation is needed in less competitive ones. Not surprisingly, therefore, the Eurozone's policies have generated deep and prolonged recessions in the crisis-hit countries.

How might policymakers go beyond the new orthodoxy, but in the opposite direction to liquidationists, in addressing the short-term challenges? The alternatives would consist of more aggressive fiscal and monetary policies, together with forced recapitalization of banks and far more rapid write-downs of doubtful debts. An important element of monetary policy would be temporarily higher inflation, aimed at generating negative real interest rates. Such policies would generate far stronger recoveries.

A yet more radical short-term alternative exists: helicopter money. In other words, the government would send money to taxpayers, financed by the central bank. When people deposit this new money in their bank, they would obtain a deposit and the bank would simultaneously obtain a deposit at the central bank. What would make this policy different from conventional quantitative easing is that the new reserves would be *permanent*. Otherwise, when the central bank wished to tighten, it would find monetary policy ineffective, because bank reserves were no longer scarce: it is the ability of the central bank to make reserves scarce that allows it to set short-term interest rates. The central bank would then have to offer interest rates on the new reserves instead. That would make such reserves more like standard short-term government borrowing.

To avoid this, the central bank needs to raise reserve requirements, in which case only reserves above that new requirement would be relevant to monetary policy. This would, of course, be a step in the direction of the Chicago Plan for 100 per cent reserve banking, discussed in Chapter Six. It would also be a tax on the banking system that would presumably be passed on to customers. Forcing people out of banks into other forms of saving better suited to bearing risks would be one of the aims of this policy.[16]

Some will argue that the time for focusing on short-term recovery has passed. This is wrong. Given the scale of the slumps, policy should seek to generate many years of above-trend growth, as argued in Chapter Eight. In the US, for example, it would take ten years of economic growth at 4 per cent to return the economy to its pre-crisis trend; in the UK, it would take close to 5 per cent growth over a decade to achieve the same thing. The risks of inflation would rise if expansionary policy were aggressive. But the ability to expand output might prove far greater than pessimists suppose: the long period of low or even no productivity growth suffered since the crisis might, with expansionary policies, be followed by a period of above-trend productivity growth.

In the cases of the US and the UK, GDP and GDP per head both went back above their pre-Great Depression trends in the post-Second World War period, despite the vast output losses of that time. Figure 49 shows that the US fully recovered its long-term trend level and rate of growth of GDP per head at purchasing power parity (which was 1.9 per cent a year from 1870 to 2007) after the Great Depression and the Second World War. Since the 2007–09 crisis, however, it has been below that rate. Figure 50 shows that the UK did far better than recover its growth trend after its desperately poor interwar performance. Trend growth of the UK's GDP per head was a mere 1 per cent a year from 1870 to 1950. From 1950 to 2007, it jumped to 2.3 per cent. Since 2007, the growth rate has looked more like the pre-Second World War trend. This had not changed by 2014, despite the recovery, since productivity growth remained worryingly absent.

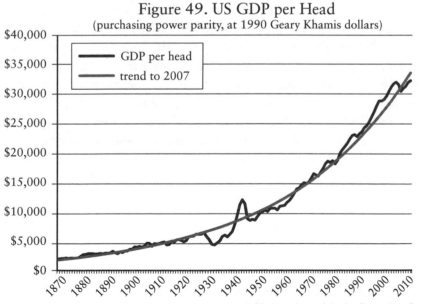

Figure 49. US GDP per Head
(purchasing power parity, at 1990 Geary Khamis dollars)

Source: Maddison project and the Conference Board

331

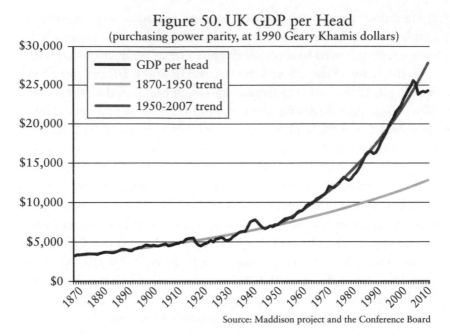

Figure 50. UK GDP per Head
(purchasing power parity, at 1990 Geary Khamis dollars)

Source: Maddison project and the Conference Board

Thus, even when financial crises cause huge recessions, financial crises need not leave permanent marks on the level of output, even though it will take a substantial number of years to return to the prior trend. But to achieve such a positive result would require fiscal and monetary policies of the type risked during the Second World War: huge fiscal deficits combined with monetary policies aimed at keeping both short- and long-term interest rates extremely low. That is beyond anybody's peacetime imagination, just as it was during the 1930s. As a result, it now looks as though crisis-hit economies might never regain pre-crisis trend levels of output or even their pre-crisis rates of economic growth.

Long-Term Health – Challenges to Crisis-Hit Economies

Putting the crisis securely behind the high-income economies is the immediate challenge. Then comes the search for healthy and sustainable economic growth.

The problems with the new orthodoxy become far more evident when we start looking at longer-term horizons. One obvious difficulty is that the application of today's orthodoxy would probably not have prevented the financial and economic crisis the world experienced after 2007. A core element of the new approach is macroprudential regulation (see Chapter Seven). Yet think about the following counterfactual. Suppose policymakers had indeed succeeded in raising the capital requirements on lenders, borrowers, or both during the early to middle years of the first decade of this century. Suppose, too, they had succeeded in reducing the scale of the asset-price bubbles, credit expansion, investment in construction and financial-sector leverage. They would then have slowed the rise in private spending and so generated a weaker economy, higher unemployment and lower inflation.

How would the policymakers have responded? Given their mandates, the most likely response of central banks would have been to lower interest rates still further, to encourage more borrowing, thereby undermining the efforts of the macroprudential regulators. This conflict between the macroprudential regulators and the monetary policymakers is precisely what one has seen in the UK in 2014. In other words, given the drivers of the savings glut – or, if one prefers, given chronic demand deficiency and so the threat of secular stagnation – internal balance (demand growing in line with potential output) would only occur in high-income countries (taken as a group) if credit and broad money grew significantly faster than nominal GDP. Under current conditions, the price of attaining macroeconomic equilibrium seems to be monetary and financial disequilibrium, unless some other radical change is made elsewhere in the world economy.

Other important longer-term elements in the new orthodoxy are higher capital requirements and worked-out resolution regimes for failing institutions. Both are important. The question, however, is whether either has been taken to a point of workability. My answer is that capital requirements are still too low (as noted in Chapter Seven); there is still too much reliance on inherently fallible risk-weighting, which is highly vulnerable to gaming by insiders; and the ability of the authorities to resolve systemically significant institutions in a crisis remains uncertain (see Chapter Seven). Nevertheless, a combination of macroprudential policies with somewhat higher equity requirements and the other changes should make the financial sector and the economy at least somewhat more resilient.

Supporters of free markets would insist that the answer is to rule out any form of 'bailout' and let the chips fall where they may. Such is the influence of this position that, in the US at least, another TARP ('troubled asset relief program') seems worryingly unlikely even if it were at some point essential. The disillusionment with a rescue that restored profitability to finance, but not a vibrant economy to ordinary people, is understandably influential, though the rage ignores the damage to ordinary people that would have been inflicted by a financial meltdown. Some even argue that there should be no central bank able to act as lender of last resort.

The logic behind the 'no bailout' position is that it would make everybody more prudent. There are, however, difficulties with this position. Among these is the fact that financial crises are not necessarily the product of expectations of a rescue. Almost certainly more important are false beliefs about the uncertain future – the belief in the middle of the last decade, for example, that house prices would rise forever, that the securitized financial assets discussed in Chapters One and Four would always find willing buyers and that crucial funding markets would always remain liquid. Of course, the existence of insurance creates a degree of rational carelessness about such risks, which is why it must always come with substantial risk of loss and regulatory oversight.

As important, the chain of bankruptcies triggered by an unchecked financial crisis harms the innocent along with the guilty and sound parts of the economy with the unsound. It was such secondary effects – mass bank failures, collapse of the money supply, soaring real rates of interest and debt deflation – that turned the post-1929 stock-market crash into the Great Depression. In the same way that we have fire services and fire standards, to prevent a fire in one building from becoming another Great Fire of London, so we now have regulatory standards, central banks and, in extreme cases, government-financed backstops, to prevent the failure of a few institutions from turning into another Great Depression.

Moreover, rescue facilities, particularly if limited in scope, should not encourage excessive financial imprudence, because those who make bad decisions still suffer harsh penalties to their finances, their reputations, or, more often, both. Yet liquidationism is still quite correct on one thing: *shareholders should never be rescued*. There should also be a clear order of conversion of debt into equity in a well-defined resolution regime that allows financial institutions to continue to function. Only in extreme circumstances should a government rescue be contemplated. But, in democracies, governments will always respond to the public's desire for basic security. Outright collapse of the core financial system cannot be permitted.

If pure liquidationism is unnecessary, unworkable and unbearable, the new orthodoxy is also insufficient. Additional steps are needed in six areas.

The first is making the financial system even more resilient than under current plans, as Chapter Eight argues. The most important elements of such reform are higher capital requirements and more bail-inable debt. Fortunately, there is a trade-off: the higher the financial institution's equity capital, the less necessary bail-inable debt would be. If, for example, the leverage of a bank were not to exceed, say, four to one, the need for bail-inable debt might disappear, greatly simplifying the regulatory task. Also important is proper funding of regulatory bodies and investigators of criminal misbehaviour. This is not just a matter of guarding against malfeasance before the event. It is also a matter of giving the population at large a sense of justice after it. If the guilty go unpunished, it becomes far more politically difficult to do what is needed to rescue the innocent.

The second area is de-leveraging the economy. The simplest way would be to eliminate the tax-deductibility of interest. Some argue that this would reduce levels of real activity, since a great many people are unwilling to take equity risks. If so, an alternative would be to make a standard tax deduction for the cost of equity. In that case, the tax treatment of debt and equity would be more equal. A properly constructed tax on land value would also help. This would not only be just, since it would appropriate to society gains that are generated by the investments of others, including the state, not by the effort of the individual beneficiary; it would also play a powerful role in ameliorating the speculation in land values that lies at the heart of each and every property-related credit boom.

The third area is wider reform of corporate taxation and governance, to reduce the accumulations of excess savings. Incentives to accumulate financial claims inside the corporation are quite likely (though not certain) to lead to an increase in the excess of desired savings over investment – a big problem during a global savings glut. One solution would be to abolish corporation tax and attribute all corporate income to shareholders. This would encourage higher distributions of profits. Alternatively, shareholders could offset corporation tax against their own individual tax payments, as was done in the Advance Corporation Tax system of the UK, prior to 1997. It would also be possible to raise corporation tax while increasing investment incentives. Again, the effect would be to encourage distribution of any profits over and above those needed for investment. In addition to these changes, as Andrew Smithers has argued, there is a powerful case for attacking the bonus culture, which leads management to under-invest in capital goods and over-invest in share buybacks.[17]

The fourth area is changes in financial contracts. The idea would be to create debt contracts that automatically adjust to circumstances. Index-linked debt is an example: the nominal value depends on the rate of inflation. Similarly, the nominal value of mortgage debt could be indexed to house prices: if house prices rose above a certain amount, lenders would share in the gain and similarly, if house prices fell, lenders would share in the losses. Such contracts might be an attractive way for investors to gain from rising house prices without having to put together portfolios of houses. They would also reduce the need for foreclosures.

The fifth area is income redistribution. Rapidly rising inequality is one reason why rapid credit growth is needed to generate adequate demand in high-income countries. If so, income could be redistributed through the tax system to people who would actually spend it. The French economist, Thomas Piketty, recommends substantially higher taxes on very high incomes as well as a global wealth tax, beyond the land tax alone. This is unquestionably too ambitious. But movement in these directions is desirable and should even be possible.[18] Not least, that would be a way to force the winners from globalization and technological innovation to provide some compensation to the losers.

The final area consists of policies aimed at raising the longer-term rate of economic growth. Obvious policies to consider are: support for scientific research; support for research and development; support for relevant education; greater incentives for investment in the private sector; tax reform; willingness to use the public-sector balance sheet in order to raise investment, particularly in infrastructure; and development of new financial institutions designed to support small and medium-sized businesses. Perhaps the most important area of financial innovation is public-private partnerships in national or regional development banks. Perhaps the most important area of tax reform is a shift from taxes on effort (that is work) to taxes on 'bads' (such as pollution, including carbon emissions) and taxes on wealth, particularly but certainly not exclusively on land.

What I have called 'beyond the new orthodoxy', while highly desirable, also remains within the context of the current conventional wisdom. The ideal way to go beyond it, at the national level, would be to adopt something closer to the Chicago Plan or similar radical monetary proposals for safe deposits and direct creation of money by the central bank. In other words, the monetary system would be built around 100 per cent backing for standard deposits. Meanwhile, other intermediation would be done either on a mark-to-market basis or with substantial equity requirements. Investors would have to accept substantial risk if they desired high returns. It would remain important to avoid the emergence of a shadow banking system able to destabilize economies. Thus, it would be crucial to curb excessive credit creation and maturity mismatches outside the banking system. That would continue to require regulatory oversight. But if the payment system were unquestionably safe, regulators might be able to be more relaxed than in the past about failure elsewhere.

Long-Term Health – Challenges for the Eurozone

Now turn to the challenges specific to the Eurozone. The crisis has raised questions about the longer-term institutional preconditions for a workable currency union.

In accordance with the views of Germany, the reformed Eurozone is designed as a system for imposing discipline upon wayward countries: it is a 'discipline union'. As currently designed, management of the Eurozone eviscerates national economic sovereignty over almost all important areas of economic policy, but rejects notions of collective insurance, at least in principle.[19] In essence, then, member countries are free to do precisely as they are told. The Eurozone has achieved an almost complete separation of responsibility for deciding policy from political accountability for its consequences. The tension between the desire of people for a say in how they are governed and the reality of how power is exercised in the Eurozone surely guarantees a huge political crisis at some point in the future.

Moreover, these external disciplines are also bound to be of varying effectiveness, since some countries are so much more equal than others. It is unlikely, for example, that the envisaged discipline would work on France, let alone Germany, should either get into serious difficulties with private debt, public debt, or, more likely, both. That might also happen. As Piketty notes, 'Germany was the country that, more than any other, drowned its public debt in inflation in the twentieth century.'[20] Currently, a return to those bygone ways seems inconceivable. But, particularly in view of the rapid ageing of the German population and the low birth rates, it is not inconceivable that some large negative economic shock could make inflation seem less undesirable at some point in the future even to Germans.

In the history of the Eurozone, a liquidationist alternative existed, to which a number of commentators, especially in Germany, return. It is the 'no-bailout' concept, enshrined in the original Maastricht Treaty. In practice, however, the financial, economic and political pressure for bailouts became overwhelming once the crisis hit. Such bailouts have come in two ways: open support from member governments and the IMF; and much larger and more tacit programmes of support from the ECB.

The option of a complete refusal to rescue countries or banks that fell into trouble would have created waves of defaults and almost certainly a break-up of the Eurozone. The creditor countries did not want the Eurozone to break up: that would have created costly adjustment problems for themselves – big losses for their own banks and huge losses of export competitiveness. It was far less embarrassing and less damaging to bail out their overexposed lenders indirectly, not to mention sustain the existence of the Eurozone, via support for the debtors. Exposed bankers were obviously enthusiastic about this rescue. Moreover, emergency support was also a way to ensure (or seek to ensure) that the cost would be borne by the hapless taxpayers of crisis-hit countries. Meanwhile, governments of crisis-hit countries were prepared to promise almost anything to avoid sovereign, banking or sovereign-cum-banking defaults. This was partly for good reason, given the huge primary fiscal deficits and current-account deficits bequeathed initially by the crisis: to be cut off from financing overnight would have imposed huge adjustment costs. Thus, extreme liquidationism failed. The situation in future will not be different.

Yet in some ways liquidationism, alas, also succeeded. Crisis-hit members are caught in an extreme demand shortage: their governments have to tighten their fiscal position, while the private sector is dependent on borrowing from banks no longer able to gain ready access to foreign funds. The countries are forced to follow the German model of the early to mid-2000s, by moving towards an external surplus, but in less auspicious external circumstances. This requires a big improvement in competitiveness, driven by wage suppression and rising productivity or, more bluntly, mass unemployment. The standard tools of liquidationism – depressions, mass bankruptcy and mass unemployment – are needed to deliver this outcome.

The Eurozone might even be described as structurally liquidationist. It is easy to understand why people argue that one should let the medicine work, unchecked, however bad the side effects. It is, like chemotherapy, a cure that comes close to killing the patient. But this liquidationism is also tempered, in practice, making its results slower and the treatment not quite as brutal as it would otherwise be. Yet did member countries really bargain for such a 'liquidationism light'?

Might it then be possible to temper the liquidationism, while also avoiding the onerous limits on sovereign discretion of the Eurozone's new orthodoxy? Yes. The most important requirement of all is a far more symmetrical adjustment – what one might call an 'adjustment union'. Thus, after a crisis, inflation would rise in the surplus countries, offsetting the falling inflation of countries in external deficit. The way to achieve this would be for the ECB to embrace unconventional measures, such as quantitative easing, negative interest rates, and even temporarily higher inflation targets. QE could be done by purchasing bonds of all Eurozone governments, in proportion to their share in the Eurozone economy or in the capital of the ECB.[21]

Another requirement is still better insurance against economic disaster. The ECB is doing some of this job by providing insurance for sovereigns, though the workability of its OMT programme in support of sovereign bond markets is still unknown, since it has not (yet) been tried. The advantage of greater formal insurance for banks or sovereigns – via joint backing of deposit-insurance funds, backup funds for bank recapitalization, or even a measure of shared-bond issuance – is that this would limit the scale of the catastrophes that afflict crisis-hit countries. The disadvantage is that such mechanisms delay needed adjustment. Permanent subsidization of uncompetitive economies would certainly be a dreadful outcome. The Eurozone might then turn much of the northern Mediterranean into something like the Italian Mezzogiorno. The challenge is instead to devise effective mechanisms for emergency support, while promoting adjustment in competitiveness rather than preventing it.

A final element should be conscious promotion of equity flows, rather than lending and, in particular, bank lending, across borders, inside the Eurozone. In the absence of a true banking union, in which banks operate symmetrically across the entire Eurozone, bank lending should be actively discouraged and equity flows encouraged.

For the Eurozone, radical reconstruction would mean moving in one of two opposite directions (though one could imagine both happening for different countries).

One direction would be a move towards federal union. The banking system would then have a federal backstop and access to safe, federally issued debt – eurobonds of some kind. There would be a shared fiscal system and a shared treasury. It need not be large, but it would be large enough to provide insurance for the banking sector and for member states. Yet such a federal state was impossible at the time of the negotiation of the Maastricht Treaty in 1990 and 1991. The sense of mutual responsibility needed to create such a federation appears, if anything, even more absent today.

The alternative radical direction would be the opposite one:

towards a degree of disintegration. This would mean abandoning the idea that capital-market integration is always desirable or even, for some members, giving up the euro itself. Given the inability to create and sustain a Eurozone-wide financial system with a Eurozone-wide fiscal backstop, a logical alternative would be to segment the financial system and so permit national governments and/or national central banks to impose controls on capital flows. By accident more than design, the exchange controls adopted by Cyprus after its banking crisis would show the way. It is particularly important to curb cross-border funding of banks as part of country-oriented macroprudential regulation. Of course, this would be a violation of the explicit goals of the Eurozone. But attempting to achieve this has not worked too well. It might be more sensible to accept that even inside a currency union, finance should be domestically focused and managed. Of course, the logical extreme of such a course is a break-up of the Eurozone itself, notwithstanding all the risks.

In brief, under German influence, the Eurozone has sought to introduce a combination of more discipline upon sovereigns – a 'discipline union' – with liquidationism, but a liquidationism only imposed on the crisis-hit countries. This is an undesirable and possibly even unworkable solution, which has imposed huge costs on the peoples of some member countries. Something different has to be tried. Far and away the most important change would be a move towards more symmetrical adjustment – a proper 'adjustment union', in other words. The ECB should work to achieve that by trying far harder to sustain Eurozone inflation at 2 per cent at the least, if not higher. It is worth noting, after all, that West German and subsequently German inflation averaged close to 3 per cent even under the Bundesbank. It is also essential to provide a bigger and better temporary backstop for crisis-hit countries and banks than is now envisaged, though permanent subsidization of weak economies would be a disaster. Finally, losses need to be borne by creditors as well as debtors. The former are just as guilty as the latter.

A truly federal union, though the logical complement to a currency union, is unavailable. A sensible alternative therefore would be partial segmentation of the financial sector, with much more emphasis on cross-border equity flows and far less on the integration of banking.

Controls on cross-border debt flow, especially banking flows, might even be viewed as necessary conditions for survival of the Eurozone rather than, as now, be deemed incompatible with it. Should such controls and a bigger safety net be ruled out, then, some time after the crisis is over, consideration might be given to a partial break-up of what has proved an enormously costly arrangement. Maybe some of the creditor countries should leave first.

Long-Term Health – Global Challenges

Now turn to the twin global challenges. The first issue is the future of globalized finance. The second is the future of global capital flows or, more broadly, of the balance between demand and supply at both national and global levels.

The aim of the new orthodoxy is to preserve a globally integrated economy, including an integrated global financial system, while recognizing the threats to stability created by such a globalized economy.

In the case of finance, the attempt to contain some of the adverse consequences of integration is driven by risks to fiscal solvency and, more importantly, to domestic economic stability. In response to such fears, proposals for ring-fencing domestic banking from global finance make powerful sense. This is particularly true for countries that are host to banking systems with huge assets and liabilities relative to domestic banking and the domestic economy. This might be called the 'Iceland trap'. But it was also relevant to the Netherlands, Switzerland and the UK. A similar concern is raised by reliance on short-term foreign funding, rather than domestic deposits, which was important for Ireland, Spain and the UK.

Macroprudential policy is designed to ensure domestic financial and macroeconomic stability, regardless of what happens in the world economy. Thus, in these important respects, the reaction to the crisis has, quite properly, been one of dis-integration. This reflects the obvious truth that *unless regulation and the supply of fiscal backstops is to be much more global, finance should be far less so*. Would anything important be lost in the process of diminishing the global integration of banking? Not obviously. At the same time, global agreement on regulatory standards is designed to preserve as much of the integrated global finance of the pre-crisis era as possible. Again, there has been some success with this approach. The result of all this effort is a complex balance between national responsibility and global finance. Not surprisingly, almost everybody is dissatisfied.

The global outcome on macroeconomics is also evolutionary. The resources of the International Monetary Fund were increased in response to the crises, but they remain only a little over 10 per cent of the stock of global foreign-currency reserves.[22] The need for countries that do not produce a reserve currency to insure themselves, via reserve accumulations, remains strong and so is the urge to limit current-account deficits. Again, the so-called 'mutual assessment programme' of the G-20 leading economies may have had some influence on securing a better balanced global adjustment process, but it is a small step towards a more rational net flow of capital.[23]

Again, liquidationists offer an alternative to the new orthodoxy: eliminate controls on cross-border finance, abolish international financial organizations, and go back on to gold. Many in this camp would also abolish fractional reserve banking. This would reduce backing of bank deposits to the supply of gold and increases in the supply of money to whatever mining would produce.

To understand how absurd this is, note that the global stock of bank deposits amounted to $54tn at the end of 2010, while the value of the world's total stock of gold, including jewellery, at prices at the end of 2013 was about $6tn.[24] Full gold backing of the broad money supply would require at least a tenfold rise in prices. This would redistribute global wealth in favour of gold speculators and miners. Why would anybody want to do that? Moreover, this assumes that jewellery would be converted into monetary gold. Otherwise, the price would need to be more than $20,000 a troy ounce. Realistically, gold backing of bank deposits is infeasible. A more plausible possibility would just be gold backing of notes. But the more limited the backing of the money supply, the greater becomes the risk of uncontainable panics. Backing for banks would have to come for some form of government liability. This would then become a 'gold exchange' standard, which proved highly unstable after the First World War.

The international gold standard is just a particularly rigid form of fixed exchange-rate arrangement. If one wants to understand the problems of such arrangements, in modern circumstances, one need merely look at what happened in the 1920s and 1930s and more recently in the Eurozone. Fixed exchange rates are a recipe for instability. For small open economies with flexible labour markets, such as Hong Kong or the Baltic states, this may be better than the instability generated by floating exchange rates. For larger economies the idea that the exchange rate should dictate monetary policy is less sensible. It is also inconceivable that the US would follow such a rule: it did not do so after creation of the Federal Reserve in 1913, even though the dollar was notionally tied to gold until 1971. In brief, the idea that the world will go back to gold-backed money or the international gold-exchange standard is a fantasy. It will not happen and, given the disasters it created after the First World War, it should not either.

There are two other directions in which the world economy might go. The first is towards far greater segmentation of the world's financial system. This would be a consequence of varying national preferences about the sort of financial system each country (or group of countries) wanted. Imagine, for example, that a country decided to adopt far higher capital requirements or far more onerous restrictions on the payment of bonuses than others. It is likely, at least in the short to medium run, that this would lead to 'regulatory arbitrage' – attempts to get round the rules by going offshore or in other ways. The authorities would surely respond by seeking to restrict access of foreign-based finance to the domestic market. That, in turn, would lead to segmentation of the global financial markets.

In such a world, investment banking and particularly trading in global markets might become the prerogative of banks whose home authorities have confidence in their ability to regulate and back them wherever they operate. A consequence would surely be a decline in global market liquidity. But it can also be argued that market liquidity is a dangerous illusion: an illusion because it is sure to disappear when it is most needed; dangerous, too, because confidence in the ability to dispose of unwanted assets encourages inadequate research by investors into the quality of assets they are buying, over-reliance on rating agencies, excessive confidence in risk models, over-extended agency chains, and so markets whose liquidity is built upon pervasive ignorance.

Global financial integration has value, not least because it allows investors to diversify their risks more widely and businesses to obtain their funding more cheaply. But it does not have an overriding value, particularly if it generates wasteful spending or increased economic instability. The same is true for flows of capital. Over the period prior to the crisis, capital flowed in huge net quantities from countries that generated vast surpluses – China, Germany and others – to countries that, it turned out, could not use it productively. The result was excess, waste and crises. Much of the flow of surplus funds was the result of deliberate interventions in foreign-exchange markets and consequent accumulations of foreign-exchange reserves. Yet transferring the excess saving of the Chinese into the wasteful consumption of Americans made no sense. Generating a huge financial crisis as a result was worse than senseless.

John Maynard Keynes stressed the concern that huge current-account surpluses might prove incompatible with macroeconomic stability in the years leading up to and then at the Bretton Woods conference in the summer of 1944, which laid the ground for the post-war international monetary system.[25] But the US, the dominant surplus country of the time, ensured that next to no constraints were imposed on the surplus countries.[26] The same has effectively been true inside the Eurozone: as is normally the case, adjustment is imposed solely on deficit countries. The US, as issuer of the world's reserve currency, is not forced to adjust in the same way, since it faces no constraint on financing: the rest of the world will accept the dollars it creates.

It is possible to imagine mechanisms that would force symmetrical adjustment, beyond more robust 'naming and shaming' by the IMF or other outside entities. Countries might impose tariffs or other trade measures on exports from surplus countries. Alternatively, they might tax foreign holdings of domestic assets, particularly government bonds. Finally, they might intervene in currency markets. But all such ideas run into substantial difficulties. First, what would be the trigger for such action? Would it be estimates of exchange-rate undervaluation, the scale of current-account surpluses, or the size of reserve accumulations? Second, who would determine that what was happening was unacceptable? Would it be an international organization – the

IMF or the World Trade Organization – or would it be the affected country or countries? Third, who would ensure that the action taken was proportionate, in scale or duration? Fourth, would it be possible to obtain the acquiescence of powerful surplus countries, particularly China? Fifth, what could be done within a currency union? This would really not be at all easy.

If the IMF had far bigger resources available to support countries in temporary difficulties, emerging and developing countries would not need to accumulate such huge reserves. Such insurance might encourage countries to accept larger current-account deficits, particularly ones that have already accumulated large reserves. Alternatively, the swap arrangements among central banks might be extended to a greater number of qualified recipients, including more central banks in emerging economies.

A still more radical approach would be to encourage net capital outflow from high-income countries, in order to finance greater investment in low-income ones.[27] Governments in the former might have to insure some of the risks. There would be losses. But they might still be smaller than those incurred in importing what turned out to be wasted foreign capital. Finally, if attempts to rebalance global accounts on a durable basis failed, it might be necessary for high-income countries to accept large fiscal deficits as a counterpart of higher public investment. Provided the investment brought sufficiently high returns, this should also be a stable solution.

There exist two more radical proposals that go partly in opposite directions. They are also parallel to the most radical alternatives for the Eurozone, which consist of either moving to a federal union or breaking the Eurozone up, in whole or in part. In the global case, the most radical outcomes would be the creation of a global money, to replace the national moneys (principally the dollar) currently used as anchors of the system, or a partial break-up of the open world economy.

Justin Lin, the Chinese former chief economist of the World Bank, argues that the expected move from dominance of the US dollar as a reserve currency to a multi-currency system, with the euro and the yuan playing a bigger part, is just as likely to prove destabilizing as stabilizing.[28] True, competition among currencies should impose greater discipline on the Federal Reserve's monetary policies. But sudden swings in preferences among different currencies might generate substantial instability. Professor Lin's suggestion, which harks back to the plans for Bancor, a global currency Keynes proposed at the Bretton Woods conference in 1944, is for a new global currency that he calls 'paper gold' or 'p-gold'. P-gold would, Mr Lin suggests, be produced according to some rule, possibly a constant rate of growth, as suggested by Milton Friedman.

The creation of the new currency and issuing central bank would, suggests Mr Lin, be governed by an international treaty. Crucially, national currencies would have fixed, but adjustable, pegs against p-gold. The well-known trilemma – that a country cannot simultaneously enjoy monetary policy freedom, absence of exchange controls and fixed exchange rates – means that countries would then either lose monetary-policy freedom (except when they choose to adjust their pegs) or have to impose exchange controls. But experience with adjustable-peg currency systems, in the absence of tight exchange controls, shows they can be highly destabilizing: that was the lesson of the crises in the exchange-rate mechanism of the European Monetary System in the early 1990s and again of the Asian crisis of 1997–98.

An additional disadvantage of this proposal is that from time to time panic would shift liquidity preferences dramatically. The envisaged treaty-bound monetary rule would then either impose a massive shortage of safe global liquidity or the issuance would have to rise, to accommodate the crisis-led increase in demand. But that would mean the creation of what amounts to a global central bank. There is no possibility of agreement on such an arrangement in the absence of some kind of a world government. If it were agreed, the world would have created many of the difficulties of the Eurozone.

For such reasons, many – probably, the vast majority – of countries would reject the plan, certainly including the US and the Eurozone. If it were accepted, there would also need to be pervasive exchange controls. Ironically, that would then lead to the same outcome, indirectly, as the other possible path for reform of the global financial system: towards limits on financial integration. This would free countries to adopt the monetary and financial systems they prefer or pursue the monetary policies they want. Such disintegration might still seem unthinkable. Yet the world might be no more than one or at most two huge crises away from such a radical deconstruction of globalized finance. The financial opening of the past three decades might yet go into reverse.

The evolutionary approach being taken to reform of the global financial and monetary systems is unlikely to prevent further crises. Further financial disintegration and greater discipline over global imbalances will almost certainly be needed. Beyond that, there exist radical ideas for new global currency arrangements that would also provide more discipline. Yet there is no chance of their being adopted. If so, the obvious alternative is to give up on full global financial integration. In the context of the current global monetary system, which largely reflects continued national sovereignty, financial integration has proved highly destabilizing. It might have to be sharply curtailed.

THE CHALLENGE OF RADICAL REFORM

The world is not going to go back to a nineteenth-century free market. The ultra-limited state is unacceptable to universal-suffrage democracies even if one believed it desirable. I do not: provision of social insurance and public consumption is a legitimate function of a wealthy state. The world is, instead, going to try the limited reforms of what I have called the new orthodoxy. The question is how far it should go beyond this. That partly depends on what sort of recovery emerges. But it also depends on how much risk societies will be prepared to take.

Some argue that we do not need to protect ourselves even against huge global crises if they only occur every eighty years or so. But that is far too insouciant. For decades after the Great Depression, finance was caged by extreme caution and tight regulations. The global system we know today began to emerge at most forty years ago. Since then, it has generated huge credit booms and massive crises, culminating in the advanced economy financial crisis that began in 2007. It seems a good bet that this will continue, if not firmly and powerfully checked, until governments are no longer able to prevent some kind of fiscal or monetary collapse. Thus, the insouciant position – that we should largely let the pre-crisis way of running the world economy and the financial system continue – is grotesquely dangerous.

We also know it is possible to run economies without financial crises: that is what happened between 1950 and the mid-1970s in high-income countries. The reason there were not crises is simple: finance was caged. The advanced economies also did very well at that time, though that was partly because of the exceptional opportunities afforded by the technologies and markets first developed in the 1920s, 1930s and 1940s. We do not know how much we would lose if we made a bigger effort to curb finance and, in particular, to separate more fully the core monetary system from our risk-taking financial system, as radical proposals suggest. The chances are that the economic losses would be small, if not actually negative. The social and political losses (and gains) are even harder to determine. But they, too, might be modest or, even more likely, highly negative. The evidence suggests that more finance equals more development, but only up to a point. Today's high-income economies seem to be well beyond that point: leveraging up existing assets is just not a particularly valuable thing to do: it creates fragility, but little, if any, real new wealth.

What I call the new orthodoxy goes in the right direction, but not far enough. This approach – an attempt to get a bigger recovery now, followed by far bigger reforms of the financial system and of the management of the global and Eurozone economies – is the least we need. That means more aggressive use of fiscal policy and radical monetary policies in the short run. It also means far more equity capital in financial institutions, as Anat Admati of Stanford University and Martin Hellwig of the Max Planck Institute argue (see Chapter Seven).[29] It should also mean more symmetrical adjustment in the Eurozone and a more balanced global monetary system, buttressed by stronger insurance mechanisms. Is this going to happen? Very unlikely, is the answer. But it should. It is the least we need to do to lower the probability of still bigger crises in future.

The ideas of the Chicago Plan for monetary and financial reform, or similar radical rearrangements, are, as Mervyn King argues, also intellectually compelling:

Another, more fundamental, example [of reform] would be to divorce the payment system from risky lending activity – that is to prevent fractional reserve banking ... In essence these proposals recognise that if banks undertake risky activities then it is highly dangerous to allow such 'gambling' to take place on the same balance sheet as is used to support the payments system, and other crucial parts of the financial infrastructure. And eliminating fractional reserve banking explicitly recognises that the pretence that risk-free deposits can be supported by risky assets is alchemy. If there is a need for genuinely safe deposits the only way they can be provided, while ensuring costs and benefits are fully aligned, is to insist such deposits do not coexist with risky assets.[30]

A system that is based, as today, on the ability of profit-seeking institutions to create money as a by-product of often grotesquely irresponsible lending is irretrievably unstable. The monetary system is not the only reason stability destabilizes, as Minsky argued, but it is probably the most important: far too much credit and money are created in good times and then far too little in bad times. The complex public-private partnership that underpins today's monetary and payment systems also forces public institutions to stand behind the irresponsibility and even malfeasance of private ones. It is little wonder bankers are irresponsible! They know that bank debt has a good chance of being treated as if it were public debt. Indeed, in several crisis-hit countries, bank debt has been treated as more sacrosanct than sovereign debt. Ordinary taxpayers are being forced to suffer in order to save a banking system that has brought them only excess and ruin. This is intolerable: indeed, a form of debt-slavery. (Just ask the Irish.) Beyond these direct fiscal effects are the vast fiscal and economic costs of the busts. No industry should have the capacity to inflict economic costs that may even surpass those of a world war. Happily, it is possible to imagine a system based on full government-creation of transactions money, along with a number of different legal and institutional treatments of the public's investments. The latter would be backed by assets that are explicitly risky. Those risks would then be clearly borne by final investors, not ludicrously undercapitalized intermediaries.

Today, nobody has the nerve to try such a radical scheme. But it would be wonderful if some countries dared to experiment with such a reform of today's inherently unstable financial and monetary systems. Indeed, the need for more experimentation and more diversity of experience seems to be one of the big lessons of past failures. Too many countries are being forced to adopt much the same arrangements under the pressure of orthodoxies imposed by global institutions under the control of a limited number of hegemonic powers. That should end.

WHY THIS MATTERS

Why, finally, does this matter? The answer is that financial crises do more than impose huge costs: they have bigger and more insidious effects.

We face big challenges in maintaining the supply of global public goods as the world integrates. But these challenges will not be managed successfully if we do not first overcome the legacy of the crisis. Moreover, all this must be done at a time of transition in global power and responsibility from a world dominated by Western powers to one in which new powers have arisen.

Inevitably, such crises also help undermine belief that a globalizing economy is of benefit to the vast majority of people. They make people anxious and angry and rightly so. Angry and anxious people are not open to the world. They want to hide in their caves, together with similarly angry people. That is what happened in the 1930s. Financial crises are the events most likely to bring the world back there.

Equally inevitably, crises undermine confidence in the elites. In democratic societies, a tacit bargain exists between elites and the rest of society. The latter say to the former: we will accept your power, prestige and prosperity, but only if we prosper too. A huge crisis dissolves that bargain. The elites come to be seen as incompetent, rapacious, or, in this case, both. The political results may come slowly. But come they will.

Here then are three huge failures of the Western elites.[31]

First, the economic, financial, intellectual and political elites misunderstood the consequences of headlong financial liberalization. Lulled by fantasies of self-stabilizing financial markets, they not only permitted but encouraged a huge and, for the financial sector, profitable bet on debt. The policy-making elite failed to appreciate the risks of a systemic breakdown. The financial elite was discredited by both its behaviour and its need to be rescued. The intellectual elite was discredited by its failure to anticipate a crisis or agree on what to do after it had struck. The political elite was discredited by their willingness to finance the rescue, however essential it was. The decline in confidence in these elites is even worse if the methods used to rescue the economy then make the parts of the elite most associated with the crisis richer than before. This undermines the sense of fairness that underpins the political economy of capitalism: there has to remain a belief that success is earned, not stolen or handed over on a platter.

Second, the past three decades have seen the emergence of a globalized economic and financial elite that has become ever more detached from the countries that produced them. In the process, the glue that binds democracy – the notion of citizenship – has weakened. The narrow distribution of the gains of economic growth risks exacerbating this development.

Third, in creating the euro, the Europeans took their project beyond the mundane into something far more important. The economic troubles of crisis-hit economies are evident: huge recessions, extraordinarily high unemployment, mass emigration and heavy debt overhangs. The constitutional disorder that has resulted remains insufficiently emphasized. Within the Eurozone, power is now concentrated in the hands of the governments of the creditor countries, principally Germany, and a trio of unelected bureaucracies – the European Commission, the European Central Bank and the International Monetary Fund. The peoples of adversely affected countries have no influence upon them. The politicians notionally accountable to them are powerless. This divorce between accountability and power strikes at the heart of democratic governance.

The loss of confidence in the competence and probity of elites inevitably reduces trust in democratic legitimacy. People feel even more than before that the country is not being governed for them, but for a narrow segment of well-connected insiders who reap most of the gains and, when things go wrong, are not just shielded from loss but impose massive costs on everybody else. This creates outraged populism, on both the left and the right. Yet willingness to accept shared sacrifice is likely to be still more important in the years ahead than it was before the crisis. The economies of the Western world are poorer than they imagined ten years ago. They must look forward to a long period of retrenchment. Making that both be and appear fair matters.

Every effort must be made to restore economies to growth, on both the demand and supply sides. Every effort must be made, too, to ensure that a similar crisis will not recur without eliminating those aspects of an open world economy and integrated finance that are of benefit. This will require more radicalism than most recognize. We must not only learn the lessons about how the world economy went awry. We must also act upon them. If we do not, next time a big crisis arrives even our open world economy could end in the fire.

Notes

ACKNOWLEDGEMENTS

1. The lecture, delivered on 17 October 2012, was subsequently published as 'Lessons from the Global Financial Crisis', *Insights: Melbourne Business and Economics*, vol. 13, April 2013.
2. Douglas A. Irwin and Kevin H. O'Rourke, 'Coping with Shocks and Shifts: The Multilateral Trading System in Historical Perspective', National Bureau of Economic Research Working Paper No. 1759, November 2011, www.nber.org.

PREFACE: WHY I WROTE THIS BOOK

1. Hyman P. Minsky, *Inflation, Recession and Economic Policy* (Brighton: Wheatsheaf, 1982), p. xi.
2. Martin Wolf, *Fixing Global Finance* (Baltimore and London: Johns Hopkins University Press and Yale University Press, 2008 and 2010).
3. Martin Wolf, *Why Globalization Works* (New Haven and London: Yale University Press, 2004), ch. 13.
4. The 'great moderation' was coined in 2002 by James H. Stock of Harvard and Mark Watson of Princeton as a way of describing the reduced volatility of US output. See 'Has the Business Cycle Changed and Why?', in Mark Gertler and Kenneth Rogoff (eds), *NBER Macroeconomics Annual 2002*, vol. 17 (Boston: MIT Press, 2003) http://www.nber.org/chapters/c11075.pdf, p. 162. Pride goes before a fall!
5. George Soros, *The New Paradigm for Financial Markets: The Credit Crisis of 2008 and What it Means* (New York: Public Affairs, 2008).
6. The post-Keynesian school derives from the work of John Maynard Keynes, but rejects attempts to incorporate his work within today's dominant school of neoclassical economics. The Austrian school derives

from the work of pre-Second World War Austrian economists, particularly Ludwig von Mises and Friedrich Hayek, but is now most influential in the US. Thus, 'Austrian' refers to a set of staunchly free-market ideas, not to the nationality of the believers.

7. Nouriel Roubini and Stephen Mihm, *Crisis Economics: A Crash Course in the Future of Finance* (London: Penguin, 2011), ch. 1. For 'white swan' and 'black swan' events, see Nassim Nicholas Taleb, *The Black Swan: The Impact of the Highly Improbable* (New York: Random House, 2007).

8. For a succinct discussion of Minsky's views of big government and central banks, see Hyman P. Minsky, 'Can "It" Happen Again? A Reprise' (1982), Hyman P. Minsky Archive, Paper 155. http://digitalcommons.bard.edu/hm_archive/155.

9. The preface to *Why Globalization Works* discusses my intellectual history. See ibid., pp. ix – xviii.

10. On the frequency of financial crises since 1980, see Carmen M. Reinhart and Kenneth S. Rogoff, *This Time is Different: Eight Centuries of Financial Folly* (Princeton and Oxford: Princeton University Press, 2009) pp. 73–5.

11. Daron Acemoglu offers an optimistic view of these developments, which I largely share, in 'The World our Grandchildren will Inherit: The Rights Revolution and Beyond', National Bureau of Economic Research Working Paper 17994, Cambridge, MA, April 2012, www.nber.org.

12. 'Federalism before a Fall', *Financial Times* (3 December 1991).

13. This is a theme of Raghuram Rajan's thought-provoking book, *Fault Lines: How Hidden Fractures still Threaten the World Economy* (Princeton and Oxford: Princeton University Press, 2010), especially ch. 1.

14. Isaiah Berlin, 'Two Concepts of Liberty', in Isaiah Berlin, *Four Essays on Liberty* (Oxford: Oxford University Press, 1969).

15. Albert O. Hirschmann, *Exit, Voice, and Loyalty: Responses to Decline in Firms, Organizations, and States* (Cambridge, MA: Harvard University Press, 1970).

16. On the English individualist tradition, see Alan Macfarlane, *The Origins of English Individualism: Family, Property and Social Transition* (Oxford: Blackwell, 1978).

17. In a splendid book, *Economics After the Crisis: Ends and Means* (Cambridge, MA, and London: MIT Press, 2012), p. 72, Lord (Adair) Turner argues that 'Economic freedom on both the consumption side and the production side – not only the right to choose what to consume but also the right to set up a new company, to work for oneself, and to compete

with new ideas – should be recognized as a desirable objective in and of itself, not because of any prosperity dividend it delivers.'

18. Friedrich Hayek put this point in the opposite way: 'whoever has sole control of the means must also determine which ends are to be served'. See Friedrich Hayek, *The Road to Serfdom* (Chicago: Chicago University Press, 1944), pp. 68–9.

INTRODUCTION: 'WE'RE NOT IN KANSAS ANY MORE'

1. A version of this chapter's discussion of the legacy of the financial crisis appears in 'Afterword: How the Financial Crises Have Changed the World', in Robert C. Feenstra and Alan M. Taylor, eds, *Globalization in an Age of Crisis: Multilateral Economic Cooperation in the Twenty-First Century* (Chicago: University of Chicago Press, 2013).

2. Gordon Brown, 'Speech to the Labour Party Conference in Brighton', 27 September 2004, http://news.bbc.co.uk/1/hi/uk_politics/3694046.stm.

3. Ben Bernanke, 'The Great Moderation', 20 February 2004, http://www.federalreserve.gov/boarddocs/speeches/2004/20040220/default.htm.

4. James H. Stock and Mark W. Watson coined the term 'great moderation' in 'Has the Business Cycle Changed and Why?', in Mark Gertler and Kenneth Rogoff, eds, *NBER Macroeconomic Annual 2012*, vol. 17 (Cambridge, MA: MIT Press, 2003), http://www.nber.org/chapters/c11075.pdf.

5. Bernanke, 'The Great Moderation'.

6. Foremost among the economists whose views were widely ignored were the late Hyman Minsky and Charles Kindleberger. See, for example, Hyman P. Minsky, *Stabilizing an Unstable Economy* (New Haven: Yale University Press, 1986), and Charles P. Kindleberger and Robert Z. Aliber, *Manias, Panics and Crashes: A History of Financial Crises*, 6th edn (London: Palgrave Macmillan, 2011).

7. See Carmen M. Reinhart and Kenneth S. Rogoff, *This Time is Different: Eight Centuries of Financial Folly* (Princeton and Oxford: Princeton University Press, 2009), pp. 231–2.

8. International Monetary Fund, 'Currency Composition of Official Foreign Currency Reserves (COFER)', 30 December 2013, http://www.imf.org/External/np/sta/cofer/eng/index.htm, and Sovereign Wealth Fund Institute, 'Sovereign Wealth Fund Rankings', http://www.swfinstitute.org/fund-rankings/.

9. The role of the global imbalances in the crisis was the theme of Martin Wolf, *Fixing Global Finance* (Baltimore and London: Johns Hopkins University Press, 2008 and 2010), especially ch. 8 of the revised edition.

See also Òscar Jordà, Moritz Schularick and Alan M. Taylor, 'Financial Crises, Credit Booms and External Imbalances', National Bureau of Economic Research Working Paper 16567, December 2010, www.nber.org, and Alan M. Taylor, 'The Great Leveraging', National Bureau of Economic Research Working Paper 18290, August 2012, www.nber.org.

10. Adair Turner, 'Financial Risk and Regulation: Do we Need More Europe or Less?', 27 April 2012, Financial Services Authority, http://www.fsa. gov.uk/library/communication/speeches/2012/0427-at.shtml.

11. Another example of 'de-globalization' is the proposed ring-fencing of domestic retail banking from global investment banking proposed by the UK's Independent Commission on Banking, of which I was a member. This was set up by the incoming coalition government under the chairmanship of Sir John Vickers. See Independent Commission on Banking, Final Report: Recommendations, September 2011, London, http://bankingcommission.s3.amazonaws.com/wp-content/uploads/2010/ 07/ICB-Final-Report.pdf, ch. 3.

PART I. THE SHOCKS

Prologue

1. No precise definitions of recessions and depressions (and so of the difference between them) exist. There exists a popular US convention that two quarters of negative growth define a recession. But the National Bureau of Economic Research, the authoritative body responsible for measuring recessions, merely states 'A recession is a period between a peak and a trough, and an expansion is a period between a trough and a peak. During a recession, a significant decline in economic activity spreads across the economy and can last from a few months to more than a year' (http://www.nber.org/cycles/recessions.html). Depressions are also recessions. But in a depression, the slump in activity is exceptionally deep and prolonged. Recessions are frequent events. Depressions (or slumps) are relatively rare.

1. From Crisis to Austerity

1. Robert E. Lucas, '"Macroeconomic Priorities", Presidential Address to the American Economic Association', 4 January 2003, http://pages.stern. nyu.edu/~dbackus/Taxes/Lucas%20priorities%20AER%2003.pdf.

2. Hank Paulson, *On the Brink: Inside the Race to Stop the Collapse of the Global Financial System* (New York and London: Business Plus and Headline, 2010), pp. 435–6.

3. Anatole Kaletsky, *Capitalism 4.0: The Birth of a New Economy* (London: Bloomsbury, 2010), pp. 147–8.

4. The literature on what happened in the crisis is now enormous. For detailed accounts of the US crisis, I would particularly recommend Andrew Ross Sorkin, *Too Big to Fail: Inside the Battle to Save Wall Street* (London: Penguin, 2010), and Alan S. Blinder, *After the Music Stopped: The Financial Crisis, the Response, and the Work Ahead* (New York: Penguin 2013). Robert Skidelsky provides an excellent short-hand account of the crisis in *Keynes: The Return of the Master* (London: Allen Lane, 2009), ch. 1. I also recommend Thomas Ferguson and Robert Johnson, 'Too Big to Bail: The "Paulson Put," Presidential Politics, and the Global Financial Meltdown', *International Journal of Political Economy*, vol. 38, no. 2 (Summer 2009), pp. 5–45. For a wider perspective, see Joseph Stiglitz: *Freefall: Free Markets and the Sinking of the Global Economy* (New York: W. W. Norton 2010), and Nouriel Roubini and Stephen Mihm, *Crisis Economics: A Crash Course in the Future of Finance* (London: Penguin Books, 2010 and 2011). For memoirs of those directly engaged in managing the crisis, see Paulson, *On the Brink*, and Alistair Darling, *Back from the Brink: 1,000 Days at Number 11* (London: Atlantic Books, 2011).

5. Martin Wolf, 'Session 3 (Round Table) Financial Globalisation, Growth and Asset Prices', in *International Symposium: Globalisation, Inflation and Monetary Policy*, Banque de France, March 2008, http://www.banque-france.fr/fileadmin/user_upload/banque_de_france/Economie-et-Statistiques/La_recherche/GB/session3b.pdf.

6. Richard Beales, Paul J. Davies, Chris Flood, Krishna Guha, Richard Milne and Gillian Tett, 'ECB Injects Euros 95bn to Aid Markets', *Financial Times*, 10 August 2007.

7. The International Monetary Fund's *Global Financial Stability Report* for April 2006 stated, baldly and boldly: 'There is growing recognition that the dispersion of credit risk by banks to a broader and more diverse set of investors, rather than warehousing such risk on their balance sheets, has helped make the banking and overall financial system more resilient.' See *Global Financial Stability Report* (Washington DC: International Monetary Fund, 2006), p. 51.

8. On IKB, see http://en.wikipedia.org/wiki/IKB_Deutsche_Industriebank,

on the eight Norwegian municipalities, see http://en.wikipedia.org/wiki/ Terra_Securities_scandal, and on Narvik, in particular, which lost $18 million in August 2007, see http://en.wikipedia.org/wiki/Narvik.

9. Skidelsky, *Keynes*, p. 8, and Tom Braithwaite and Chris Tighe, 'Patient Queues in Very British Bank Run', *Financial Times*, 14 September 2007.

10. Paul McCulley invented the term 'Shadow Banking System' for intermediation via money-market funds, special investment vehicles (SIVs), conduits and hedge funds. The system was unregulated. But it carried out the classic banking functions of financing long-term, relatively risky and illiquid assets from short-term, relatively safe and liquid liabilities.

11. Francesco Guerrera and Henny Sender, 'JP Morgan Buys Bear Stearns for $2 a Share', *Financial Times*, 16 March 2008.

12. Ben White, 'Buoyant Bear Stearns Shrugs Off Subprime Woes', *Financial Times*, 16 March 2007.

13. Martin Wolf, 'The Rescue of Bear Stearns Marks Liberalisation's Limit', *Financial Times*, 25 March 2008.

14. Paulson, *On the Brink*, p. 170, and Krishna Guha, Chris Giles, Saskia Scholtes and Joanna Chung, 'US Takes Control of Fannie and Freddie', *Financial Times*, 8 September 2008.

15. Paulson, *On the Brink*, pp. 208–22. As Mr Blinder makes clear, it is simply unclear, even now, why the US Treasury Secretary allowed Lehman to fail. The probability is that he did so not because there was no alternative, but because he could not bear becoming known forever as 'Mr Bailout'. See Blinder, *After the Music Stopped*, p. 123.

16. Paulson, *On the Brink*, p. 220. See also Evelyn Rusli, 'The Universal Appeal of BofA', Forbes.com, 15 September 2008, http://archive.is/ w503.

17. Blinder, *After the Music Stopped*, pp. 229–31, and 'Fed in $85bn AIG Rescue Deal', *Financial Times*, 17 September 2008.

18. Paulson, *On the Brink*, p. 230.

19. Paul Davies and Michael Mackenzie, 'Money Fund Sector Shocked as Reserve Breaks the Buck', *Financial Times*, 18 September 2012.

20. On the administration in the UK, see http://www.pwc.co.uk/business-recovery/administrations/lehman/lehman-faq.jhtml.

21. House of Commons Treasury Committee, 'Evidence on 24th June 2009', *Banking Crisis: Regulation and Supervision*, 14th Report of Session 2008–09 (London: The Stationery Office, 31 July 2009), Ev32.

22. *Ibid.*, p. 230.

23. Francesco Guerrera, Henny Sender, Michael Mackenzie, Krishna Guha, James Politi and Daniel Dombey, 'Fears Emerge over $700bn Rescue', *Financial Times*, 22 September 2008.

24. Henny Sender, Julie MacIntosh and Francesco Guerrera, 'WaMu Taken Over by US Regulators', *Financial Times*, 26 September 2012.

25. Francesco Guerrera and James Politi, 'Wells Set to Grab Wachovia after Citi Pulls Out', *Financial Times*, 10 October 2012.

26. Darling, *Back from the Brink*, p. 124.

27. Maggie Urry, 'Government to Push Lloyds-HBOS Deal Through', *Financial Times*, 18 September 2008.

28. Jane Croft, Kate Burgess and George Parker, 'B&B Set to be Taken into Public Ownership', *Financial Times*, 29 September 2008.

29. See Roubini and Mihm, *Crisis Economics*, p. 19. Investors who bought 'on margin' – that is, by borrowing from their brokers – have to put up more of their own money as the price of the assets they bought falls. This forces them to sell assets, causing a downward movement in prices that triggers yet more 'margin calls'.

30. See Guillermo A. Calvo, 'Capital Flows and Capital-Market Crises: The Simple Economics of Sudden Stops', *Journal of Applied Economics*, vol. 1, no. 1 (November 1998), pp. 35–54.

31. While the European Central Bank did stand behind the banks of these countries as a lender of last resort, it definitely did not stand behind their public debt.

32. John B. Taylor, 'The Financial Crisis and the Policy Response: An Empirical Analysis of What Went Wrong', National Bureau of Economic Research Working Paper 14631, January 2009, www.nber.org.

33. Ferguson and Johnson note that 'prices of credit default swaps on the four largest American banks, controlling some 40 per cent of all deposits, for example, all rose like rockets before falling back when Paulson, Bernanke and Geithner reversed course two days later and once again embraced single payer by bailing out AIG. The same holds for credit default swaps of Goldman Sachs and Morgan Stanley, the two most important remaining investment banks ... Another excellent general indicator of stress, the "option adjusted" spread on broad investment grade debt – what banks had to pay to raise new capital – also shows a sharp rise as Lehman gave up the ghost.' See Ferguson and Johnson, 'Too Big to Bail', p. 23.

34. See http://en.wikipedia.org/wiki/LIBOR%E2%80%93OIS_spread.

35. Paulson, *On the Brink*, p. 173.

36. The source is the Federal Reserve, http://www.federalreserve.gov/datadownload/.
37. Darling, *Back from the Brink*, p. 160.
38. *Ibid.*
39. Paulson, *On the Brink*, p. 265.
40. Krishna Guha, 'Action to Address "root" Causes, *Financial Times*, 15 October 2008.
41. Paulson, *On the Brink*, pp. 349–50.
42. Piergiorgio Alessandri and Andrew Haldane, 'Banking on the State', November 2009, http://www.bankofengland.co.uk/publications/Pages/speeches/2009/409.aspx, p. 23. In the case of the US, Mr Haldane listed $3.8tn in money creation and $0.2tn in 'collateral swaps', both from the Federal Reserve. He also listed $2.1tn in 'guarantees', $3.7tn in 'insurance' and $0.7tn in 'capital infusions' (from the TARP), all of which came from the government. The total came to $10.5tn.
43. International Monetary Fund, *Fiscal Monitor*, April 2012, www.imf.org, Table 7.
44. Quantitative easing was first used by the Bank of Japan in 2001. See http://en.wikipedia.org/wiki/Quantitative_easing.
45. Bank for International Settlements, *83rd Annual Report 2013*, Basel, 23 June 2013, http://www.bis.org/publ/arpdf/ar2013e.pdf, Figure VI. 3, p. 69.
46. Fiscal data are from the IMF's *World Economic Outlook* database, except where otherwise indicated.
47. Data on discretionary fiscal stimulus are taken from IMF, *Fiscal Monitor*, November 2010, www.imf.org, Box 1.1. The data exclude discretionary tightening. So they are likely to exaggerate the net effect of discretionary policy on deficits.
48. Carmen Reinhart and Kenneth Rogoff, *This Time is Different: Eight Centuries of Financial Folly* (Princeton and Oxford: Princeton University Press, 2009), p. 231. See also Table 14.1.
49. The countries affected by banking crises (with dates of their crises in parentheses) were: Malaysia (1997), Mexico (1994), Japan (1992), Norway (1987), Philippines (1997), South Korea (1997), Sweden (1991), Thailand (1997), Spain (1977), Indonesia (1997), Chile (1980), Finland (1991) and Colombia (1998). *Ibid.*, p. 232.
50. Paul Krugman, *End this Depression Now!* (New York: W. W. Norton, 2012), especially ch. 8.

51. Barry Eichengreen and Kevin O'Rourke, 'A Tale of Two Depressions Redux', 6 March 2012, http://www.voxeu.org/article/tale-two-depressions-redux.

52. For a superb discussion of the policy blunders that led to and then sustained the Great Depression, see Liaquat Ahmed, *Lords of Finance: The Bankers Who Broke the World* (London: Heinemann, 2009). For seminal economic analyses of the Great Depression (seminal in part because of the role of the author in the Great Recession), see Ben S. Bernanke, *Essays on the Great Depression* (Princeton: Princeton University Press, 2000). See also Nicholas Crafts and Peter Fearndon, *The Great Depression of the 1930s: Lessons for Today* (Oxford: Oxford University Press, 2013).

53. Niall Ferguson, 'Our Great Recession', *The New York Times*, 28 February 2009, http://www.nytimes.com/2009/03/01/opinion/01ferguson.html?_r=0.

54. Alan Taylor, 'When is the Time for Austerity?', 20 July 2013, http://www.voxeu.org/article/when-time-austerity, provides a compelling analysis of the high cost of fiscal austerity in the UK. See also Martin Wolf, 'How Austerity has Failed', *New York Review of Books*, 11 July 2013, http://www.nybooks.com/articles/archives/2013/jul/11/how-austerity-has-failed. Amartya Sen has also criticized the shift to austerity cogently, particularly in Europe. See, for example, 'Austerity is Undermining Europe's Grand Vision', *The Guardian*, 3 July 2010, http://www.theguardian.com/commentisfree/2012/jul/03/austerity-europe-grand-vision-unity.

55. Karl Brenke, Ulf Rinne, Klaus F. Zimmermann, 'Short-Time Work: The German Answer to the Great Recession', IZA Discussion Paper 5780, June 2011, http://ftp.iza.org/dp5780.pdf.

56. See Government Commission of the German Corporate Governance Code, 'German Corporate Governance Code (as amended on 18 June 2009), http://www.corporate-governance-code.de/eng/kodex/1.html.

57. Reinhart and Rogoff, *This Time is Different*, p. 224. Note that these data are for annual GDP per head at purchasing power parity, rather than GDP. The difference should not be large for these high-income countries with relatively slowly growing populations. The exception would be the US, where GDP per head fell somewhat faster than GDP. The countries in the comparisons for unemployment and GDP (with the dates of the crises in parentheses) were: Malaysia (1997), Indonesia (1997), Japan (1992), Thailand (1997), Philippines (1997), Hong Kong (1997), Norway (1987), South Korea (1997), Argentina (2001), Sweden

(1991), Spain (1977), Colombia (1998), Finland (1991) and US (1929). See Figs. 14.3 and 14.4, *Ibid.*, pp. 229–30.

58. Alan M. Taylor, 'The Great Leveraging', Working Paper 18290, National Bureau of Economic Research, August 2012, www.nber.org, p. 32.

59. Charles Roxborough et al., 'Debt and Deleveraging: Uneven Progress on the Path to Growth', updated research, McKinsey Global Institute, January 2012, http://www.mckinsey.com/insights/mgi/research/financial_markets/uneven_progress_on_the_path_to_growth, p. 3.

60. Martin Wolf, 'Mind the Gap: Perils of Forecasting Output', *Financial Times*, 9 December 2011.

61. Irving Fisher, 'The Debt-Deflation Theory of Great Depressions', *Econometrica* (1933).

62. For a full account of the first arrow of Abenomics, see 'Transcript of Interview with Haruhiko Kuroda, Governor of the Bank of Japan', *Financial Times*, 3 January 2014, http://www.ft.com/cms/s/0/f1e46c46-7472-11e3-9125-00144feabdco.html?siteedition=uk.

63. See Olivier Blanchard, Giovanni Dell'Ariccia and Paolo Mauro, 'Rethinking Macroeconomic Policy', IMF Staff Position Note, 12 February 2010, SPN/10/03, http://www.imf.org/external/pubs/ft/spn/2010/spn1003.pdf.

64. Keynes introduced this phrase in his classic book, *The General Theory of Employment, Interest and Money* (London: Macmillan, 1936).

65. Richard Koo, *The Holy Grail of Macroeconomics: Lessons from Japan's Great Recession* (Singapore: John Wiley, 2008).

66. 'Leaders' Statement: The Pittsburgh Summit', http://www.ft.com/cms/s/0/5378959c-aa1d-11de-a3ce-00144feabdco.html.

67. 'The G-20 Toronto Summit Declaration', 26–27 June 2010, http://www.g20.utoronto.ca/2010/to-communique.html.

68. Paul Samuelson, *Economics*, first edition (New York: McGraw-Hill, 1948).

69. Martin Wolf, 'The Toxic Legacy of the Greek Crisis', *Financial Times*, 18 June 2013, http://www.ft.com/cms/s/0/b31dd248-d785-11e2-a26a-00144feab7de.html.

2. The Crisis in the Eurozone

1. *Financial Times*, 5 September 2011.

2. Tony Barber, 'Greece Rapped for Understating Deficit', *Financial Times*, 20 October 2009.

3. European Commission, *Economic Forecast Autumn 2008*, 6/2008, http://ec.europa.eu/economy_finance/publications/publication13290_en.pdf.

4. 'Highlights – Eurogroup Finance Ministers' Meeting', Reuters, 19 October 2009, iahttp://www.reuters.com/article/2009/10/19/eurogroup-idUSLJ6461320091019.

5. Organisation for Economic Co-operation and Development, *Economic Outlook 94*, Statistics and Projections, Government Net Lending, as a Percentage of GDP, http://stats.oecd.org/BrandedView.aspx?oecd_bv_id=eo-data-en&doi=data-00676-en.

6. Joseph E. Stiglitz, *Freefall: Free Markets and the Sinking of the Global Economy* (London: Allen Lane, 2010).

7. See 'Basel I', http://en.wikipedia.org/wiki/Basel_I. Basel II, which was intended to replace Basel I, was published in 2004. It was subsequently replaced, in light of the crisis, by Basel III, which was agreed in 2010–11 and then modified in 2013. Collectively, these agreements on regulation are known as the Basel Accords (see http://en.wikipedia.org/wiki/Basel_Accords).

8. 'Statement by IMF Managing Director Dominique Strauss-Kahn on Greece', http://www.imf.org/external/np/sec/pr/2010/pr10168.htm.

9. 'IMF Executive Board Approves €30 Billion Stand-by Arrangement for Greece', Press Release No. 10/187, 9 May 2010, www.imf.org.

10. Dominique Strauss-Kahn resigned his position at the IMF on 18 May 2011, after allegations that he sexually assaulted a hotel maid in New York on 14 May. See 'IMF Managing Director Dominique Strauss-Kahn Resigns', Press Release No. 11/187, 18 May 2011, http://www.imf.org/external/np/sec/pr/2011/pr11187.htm, and 'IMF Chief Dominique Strauss-Kahn Quits over Sex Charge', http://www.bbc.co.uk/news/world-13450783.

11. 'IMF Reaches Staff-level Agreement with Greece on €30bn Stand-by Arrangement', Press Release No. 10/176, 2 May 2010, www.imf.org.

12. David Oakley, Mary Watkins and Kerin Hope, 'Greece Launches Debt Swap Offer', *Financial Times*, 24 February 2012.

13. On the European Financial Stabilization Mechanism, see http://ec.europa.eu/economy_finance/eu_borrower/efsm/index_en.htm. On the European Financial Stability Facility, see http://www.efsf.europa.eu/about/index.htm.

14. 'IMF Executive Board Approves €22.5 Billion Extended Arrangement for Ireland', 16 December 2010, Press Release No. 10/496, www.imf.org.

15. Lina Saigol and Janie Smyth, 'Ireland Posed to Exit EU Bailout', 13 December 2013, http://www.ft.com/cms/s/o/f896ba08-63e7-11e3-b70d-00144feabdco.html#slideo.
16. 'IMF Executive Board Approves a €26 Billion Extended Arrangement for Portugal', Press Release No. 11/190, 20 May 2011, www.imf.org.
17. See European Central Bank, 'The European Stability Mechanism,' *ECB Monthly Bulletin*, July 2011, http://www.ecb.int/pub/pdf/other/art2_mb201107en_pp71-84en.pdf.
18. 'IMF Executive Board Approves €1bn Arrangement under Extended Fund Facility for Cyprus', Press Release No. 13/175, 15 May 2013, http://www.imf.org/external/np/sec/pr/2013/pr13175.htm.
19. Jan Strupczeswki and Julien Toyer, 'Eurozone Agrees to Lend Spain up to 100bn Euros', 10 June 2012, Reuters, http://uk.reuters.com/article/2012/06/10/uk-Eurozone-idUKBRE85805E2012061.
20. See, for example, Barry Eichengreen, 'The Euro: Love it or Leave it?', 4 May 2010, http://www.voxeu.org/article/eurozone-breakup-would-trigger-mother-all-financial-crises. See also Martin Wolf, 'A Permanent Precedent', *Financial Times*, 17 May 2012, http://www.ft.com/cms/s/o/614df5de-9ffe-11e1-94ba-00144feabdco.html.
21. The term '*Ordoliberalism*' was coined by Hero Möller in 1950. It was named after the name of the journal *ORDO – Jahrbuch für die Ordnung von Wirtschaft und Gesellschaft* (The Ordo Yearbook of Economic and Social Order). 'Ordo' is the Latin word for 'order'.
22. On *Ordoliberalism*, see http://en.wikipedia.org/wiki/Ordoliberalism.
23. Charlemagne, 'The Driver and the Passenger', *The Economist*, 15 October 2011, http://www.economist.com/node/21532283.
24. Ralph Atkins, 'ECB Unveils New Support for Banks', *Financial Times*, 8 December 2012.
25. See, on the LTRO, International Monetary Fund, 'Euro Area Policies: 2012 Article IV Consultation', IMF Country Report No. 12/181, July 2012, www.imf.org, Box 5, p. 18.
26. 'Speech by Mario Draghi, President of the European Central Bank, at the Global Investment Conference in London', 26 July 2012, http://www.ecb.int/press/key/date/2012/html/sp120726.en.html.
27. 'Introductory Statement to Press Conference', 6 September 2012, http://www.ecb.int/press/pressconf/2012/html/is120906.en.html, and 'Technical Features of Outright Monetary Transactions', 6 September 2012, http://www.ecb.int/press/pr/date/2012/html/pr120906_1.en.html.
28. 'A necessary condition for Outright Monetary Transactions is strict and effective conditionality attached to an appropriate European Financial

Stability Facility/European Stability Mechanism (EFSF/ESM) pro-gramme. Such programmes can take the form of a full EFSF/ESM macroeconomic adjustment programme or a precautionary programme (Enhanced Conditions Credit Line), provided that they include the possibility of EFSF/ESM primary market purchases. The involvement of the IMF shall also be sought for the design of the country-specific conditionality and the monitoring of such a programme.' 'Technical Features of Outright Monetary Transactions', 6 September 2012, http://www.ecb.int/press/pr/date/2012/html/pr120906_1.en.html.

29. See Wolfgang Munchau, 'Germany's Constitutional Court has Strengthened the Eurosceptics', *Financial Times*, 9 February 2014, http://www.ft.com/cms/s/0/8a64e3ac-8f25-11e3-be85-00144feab7de.html.

30. 'Euro Area Policies: 2013 Article IV Consultation', IMF Country Report No. 13/231, July 2013, http://www.imf.org/external/pubs/ft/scr/2013/cr13231.pdf, Box 1, p. 8.

31. Paul de Grauwe, 'Panic-driven Austerity in the Eurozone and its Implications', 21 February 2013, http://www.voxeu.org/article/panic-driven-austerity-Eurozone-and-its-implications. See also de Grauwe, 'The Governance of a Fragile Eurozone', CEPS Working Documents, *Economic Policy*, 4 May 2011, http://www.ceps.eu/book/governance-fragile-Eurozone, and Martin Wolf, 'Be Bold Mario, Put Out that Fire', *Financial Times*, 25 October 2011, http://www.ft.com/cms/s/0/bd60ab78-fe6e-11e0-bac4-00144feabdc0.html.

32. Silvia Merler and Jean Pisani-Ferry, 'Sudden Stops in the Euro Area', Bruegel Policy Contribution Issue 2012/06, March 2012, www.bruegel.org, p. 1.

33. Zsolt Darvas, 'Intra-Euro Rebalancing is Inevitable, but Insufficient', Bruegel Policy Contribution Issue 2012/15, August 2012, www.bruegel.org, Table 1.

34. IMF, 'Euro Area Policies: 2013 Article IV Consultation', p. 8 and Box 2.

35. Merler and Pisani-Ferry, 'Sudden Stops in the Euro Area', Fig. 4 and p. 7.

36. TARGET stands for 'Trans-European Automated Real-time Gross Settlement Express Transfer'.

37. Hans-Werner Sinn of CESifo, in Munich, has played an important role in bringing the implications of the imbalances in the TARGET 2 system to the world's attention. See Hans-Werner Sinn and Timo Wollmershaeuser, 'Target Loans, Current Account Balances and Capital Flows: The ECB's Rescue Facility', National Bureau of Economic Research Working Paper 17626, November 2011, www.nber.org.

38. These data were prepared for the International Monetary Fund's Article IV surveillance of the Eurozone.

39. Cited in Merler and Pisani-Ferry, 'Sudden Stops in the Euro Area', p. 3. See Peter M. Garber, 'Notes on the Role of TARGET in a Stage III Crisis', National Bureau of Economic Research Working Paper 6619, June 1998, www.nber.org, especially p. 19.

40. IMF, 'Euro Area Policies 2012', pp. 4–5.

41. IMF, 'Euro Area Policies 2013', pp. 8–12.

42. *Ibid.*, p. 5.

43. 'About EFSF', http://www.efsf.europa.eu/about/index.htm.

44. 'European Financial Stabilisation Mechanism', http://ec.europa.eu/economy_finance/eu_borrower/efsm/index_en.htm.

45. See European Stability Mechanism, http://www.esm.europa.eu.

46. The Group of Twenty agreed in April 2009 to increase borrowed resources available to the IMF (complementing its quota resources) by up to $500 billion (which tripled the total pre-crisis lending resources of about $250 billion). In April 2010 the Executive Board duly adopted a proposal for expanded and more flexible 'New Arrangements to Borrow' (NAB), under which the NAB grew to about SDR 367.5 billion (about $560 billion). In December 2011 euro area member countries committed themselves to providing additional funds of up to €150 billion (about $200 billion). The 14th General Review of Quotas, approved in December 2010, will double the IMF's permanent resources to SDR 476.8 billion (about $737 billion). There will be a rollback in the NAB credit arrangements to SDR 182 billion, which will become effective when participants pay for these quota increases. In addition, in 2009, the membership agreed to make a general allocation of special drawing rights (SDRs), equivalent to $250 billion, resulting in a near tenfold increase in SDRs. See International Monetary Fund, 'IMF's Response to the Global Economic Crisis', 19 September 2013, http://www.imf.org/external/np/exr/facts/changing.htm.

47. International Monetary Fund, 'Greece: Ex Post Evaluation of Exceptional Access under the 2010 Stand-by Arrangement', 20 May 2013, http://www.imf.org/external/pubs/ft/scr/2013/cr13156.pdf.

48. Mark Rutte and Jan Kees de Jager, 'Expulsion from the Eurozone Has to Be the Final Penalty', *Financial Times*, 8 September 2011.

49. On Greek exit, or 'Grexit' as it came to be called, see http://en.wikipedia.org/wiki/Greece_withdrawal_from_the_Eurozone.

50. The Fiscal Compact (formally, the 'Treaty on Stability, Coordination and Governance in the Economic and Monetary Union', also referred to

as TSCG or, more plainly, the Fiscal Stability Treaty) is an intergovern-mental treaty, introduced as a new stricter version of the previous Stability and Growth Pact. The treaty was signed on 2 March 2012 by all member states of the EU, except the Czech Republic and the UK.

The treaty entered into force on 1 January 2013. Member states bound by the fiscal provisions of the treaty are required to have enacted, within one year of its entering into force, an 'implementation law' establishing a self-correcting mechanism, guided by the surveillance of an independent fiscal advisory council.

The treaty defines a balanced budget as a general government budget deficit less than 3 per cent of gross domestic product (GDP), in line with the Maastricht Treaty provisions, and a structural (or cyclically adjusted) deficit of less than 1 per cent of GDP, provided the debt to GDP ratio is significantly below 60 per cent. Otherwise, it should be below 0.5 per cent of GDP. The treaty also contains a direct copy of the 'debt brake' criteria outlined in the Stability and Growth Pact, which defines the rate at which debt levels above the limit of 60 per cent of GDP shall decrease.

See 'European Fiscal Compact', http://en.wikipedia.org/wiki/European_Fiscal_Compact, and 'Treaty on Stability, Coordination and Governance in the Economic and Monetary Union', http://european-council.europa.eu/media/639235/stootscg26_en12.pdf.

51. Walter Bagehot, 'Essay on Edward Gibbon' (1856), in *The Works and Life of Walter Bagehot*, Mrs Russell Barrington (ed.) (London: Longmans, Green, 1915) vol. 2 (Historical and Financial Essays), p. 83, http://rosenfels.org/pll-v5/pdf/Bagehot_1451-02_EBk_v5.pdf.

52. Paul de Grauwe, 'Governance of a Fragile Eurozone', 4 May 2011, http://www.ceps.eu/book/governance-fragile-Eurozone.

53. Paul de Grauwe, 'Managing a Fragile Eurozone', 10 May 2011, http://www.voxeu.org/article/managing-fragile-Eurozone.

54. In practice, the ECB's actions would be limited, but this is because of the political constraints on a multi-national central bank. So de Grauwe's point stands.

55. All member states agree fiscal targets with the European Commission. But countries with weak creditworthiness have to take them particularly seriously, since they might need help, in which case the targets would become conditions for assistance. See 'EU Economic Governance', http://ec.europa.eu/economy_finance/economic_governance/.

56. Larry Siedentop, *Democracy in Europe* (London: Allen Lane, 2001), p. 119.

3. Brave New World

1. Jonathan Wheatley, 'Brazil's Mantega Sees "International Currency War"', *Financial Times*, 27 September 2010.

2. In this chapter I have followed the definitions used by the staff of the International Monetary Fund in 'Resilience in Emerging Market and Developing Economies: Will it Last?', *World Economic Outlook*, October 2012, ch. 4. This defines advanced or, in my parlance, 'high-income' countries, as members of the Organization for Economic Co-operation and Development prior to 1990, with the exception of Turkey, which is treated as an emerging country. Developing countries are defined as the fifty-one low-income countries eligible for concessional loans from the Fund. The remainder are emerging economies. (See note 11 below.)

3. The semi-logarithmic trend line fitted to China's GDP data from the IMF's *World Economic Outlook* database has the extraordinarily high R-squared of 0.9986 – that is, effectively one. This means the deviations from the 10 per cent growth rate were negligible over the 1980–2012 period. It is a staggering growth performance. Obviously, there are also some questions about the reliability of these data.

4. The view that China's growth will slow to 6–7 per cent in coming years is well laid out by Ruchir Sharma of Morgan Stanley Investment Management. See *Breakout Nations: In Pursuit of the Next Economic Miracles* (London: W. W. Norton and Allen Lane, 2012), ch. 2.

5. Michael Pettis, *Avoiding the Fall: China's Economic Restructuring* (Washington DC: Carnegie Endowment for International Peace, 2013), presents a relatively pessimistic perspective on the challenges ahead.

6. These data are taken from the IMF's *World Economic Outlook* database.

7. Growth of the world economy at purchasing-power parity tends to be substantially higher than growth at market exchange rates, because the faster-growing economies are poorer, while the PPP adjustment makes the economies of poorer countries relatively bigger. (It does so because it adjusts upwards the prices of non-tradeable goods and, predominantly, services towards a common international level.) But the difference between growth at market and PPP exchange rates is relatively small among countries of roughly similar real GDP per head. Thus the expansions of the regions of the world economy shown in Figure 20 is probably quite close to what they would be at market exchange rates.

8. This section draws heavily on the IMF's *World Economic Outlook*, October 2012.

9. *Ibid.*, p. 129.

10. The 'median' is the observation in the middle of a distribution of outcomes. So, if country A grows by 6 per cent, country B grows by 2 per cent and country C grows by 1 per cent, median growth is 2 per cent (i.e. B's growth), while mean (average) growth is 3 per cent.

11. All economies, other than Australia, Austria, Belgium, Canada, Denmark, Finland, France, Germany, Greece, Ireland, Italy, Japan, Netherlands, New Zealand, Norway, Portugal, Spain, Sweden, Switzerland, the UK and the US, are 'emerging and developing economies'. 'Low-income countries' are defined as the fifty-one economies currently eligible for concessional IMF loans. The remaining sixty-nine countries in the group of 'emerging and developing economies' are considered to be 'emerging economies'. See *World Economic Outlook*, October 2012, p. 132 and Table 4.3.

12. *Ibid.*, Fig. 4.6.

13. *Ibid.*, pp. 131–2.

14. *Ibid.*, p. 132.

15. This is the conclusion of the study by Lawrence Edwards and Robert Z. Lawrence, *Rising Tide: Is Growth in Emerging Economies Good for the United States?* (Washington DC: Peterson Institute for International Economics, 2013). See, especially, ch. 10.

16. This was the central argument of my book, *Fixing Global Finance* (Baltimore and London: Johns Hopkins University Press and Yale University Press, 2008 and 2010).

17. Surjit Bhalla, *Devaluing to Prosperity: Misaligned Currencies and their Growth Consequences* (Washington DC: Peterson Institute for International Economics, 2012, and New Delhi: Oxford University Press, 2013).

18. In testimony to the Joint Economic Committee of Congress on 22 May, the Fed Chairman said that the Federal Open Markets Committee 'expects a highly accommodative stance of monetary policy to remain appropriate for a considerable time after the asset purchase program ends and the economic recovery strengthens'. But, in response to a question from Representative Kevin Brady, the committee chairman, Bernanke said the FOMC could consider reducing bond purchases within 'the next few meetings' if officials see signs of sustained improvement in the labour market. See 'Bernanke's Tapering Talk Backfires amid Bond Yield Surge', http://www.bloomberg.com/news/2013-06-13/bernanke-s-tapering-talk-backfires-amid-bond-yield-surge.html.

19. Press Release dated 18 December 2013, http://www.federalreserve.gov/newsevents/press/monetary/20131218a.htm.

20. See IMF, *World Economic Outlook*, October 2013, Fig. 1.10, p. 10.
21. Hyun Song Shin, 'The Second Phase of Global Liquidity and its Impact on Emerging Economies', 7 November 2013, Keynote Address at the Federal Reserve Bank of San Francisco, *Asia Economic Policy Conference*, 3–5 November 2013, http://www.princeton.edu/~hsshin/www/FRBSF_2013.pdf.
22. *Ibid.*, p. 11.
23. These data are from the IMF's *World Economy Database*, April 2013.
24. IMF, 'Emerging Markets: Where Are They and Where Are They Headed?', October 2013, unpublished.
25. See David Lipton, 'Emerging Markets in Transition', 8 October 2013, http://www.imf.org/external/np/msc/2013/am/lipton.pdf.
26. These data are taken from the IMF's online *World Economic Outlook* database.

PART II. THE SHIFTS

Prologue

1. See Robert H. Frank and Philip J. Cook, *The Winner-Take-All Society: Why the Few at the Top Get So Much More than the Rest of Us* (London and New York: Penguin, 1996).

4. How Finance Became Fragile

1. Ben Bernanke, 'The Housing Market and Subprime Lending', http://www.federalreserve.gov/newsevents/speech/bernanke20070605a.htm.
2. Michiyo Nakamoto and David Wighton, 'Citigroup Chief Stays Bullish on Buy-outs' *Financial Times*, 9 July 2007, http://www.ft.com/cms/s/0/80e2987a-2e50-11dc-821c-0000779fd2ac.html.
3. http://www.goodreads.com/author/quotes/756.Warren_Buffett.
4. Paul Volcker, 'Remarks by Paul A. Volcker at a Luncheon of the Economic Club of New York', New York, 8 April 2008, http://blogs.denverpost.com/lewis/files/2008/04/volckernyeconclubspeech04-08-2008.pdf.
5. Simon Bowers, 'Wall Street Banks in $70bn Staff Payout', *The Guardian*, 17 October 2008.
6. Gary B. Gorton, *Misunderstanding Financial Crises: Why we Don't See them Coming* (Oxford: Oxford University Press, 2012), ch. 9.

7. International Monetary Fund, *Global Financial Stability Report*, April 2006, p. 51. See also Adair Turner, *The Turner Review: A Regulatory Response to the Global Banking Crisis*, March 2009, Financial Services Authority, London, http://www.fsa.gov.uk/pubs/other/turner_review.pdf, p. 42.

8. Raghuram Rajan, 'Has Financial Development Made the World Riskier?', August 2005, pp. 313–69, http://www.kansascityfed.org/publicat/sympos/2005/pdf/rajan2005.pdf.

9. *Ibid.*, pp. 359–60.

10. Alistair Milne, *The Fall of the House of Credit: What Went Wrong in Banking and What Can be Done to Repair the Damage* (Cambridge: Cambridge University Press, 2009), p. 26.

11. The argument made here is similar to one advanced by Adair Turner, in a speech delivered at the South African Reserve Bank on 2 November 2012. See Turner, 'Monetary and Financial Stability: Lessons from the Crisis and from Classic Economics Texts', FSA, London, November 2012, http://www.fsa.gov.uk/static/pubs/speeches/1102-at.pdf.

12. Milne, *The Fall of the House of Credit*, p. 26.

13. Gorton, *Misunderstanding Financial Crises*, pp. 5–6.

14. Walter Bagehot, *Lombard Street: A Description of the Money Market*, 1873, http://www.gutenberg.org/ebooks/4359.

15. Between 1781 and 1836, three successive attempts were made to create a central bank in the US: The Bank of North America (1881, but not a federally chartered bank; The First Bank of the United States (1791–1811); and The Second Bank of the United States (1816–36). After the failure to renew the charter of the last, the US operated without a central bank until 1913. See 'History of Central Banking in the United States', http://en.wikipedia.org/wiki/History_of_central_banking_in_the_United_States#Bank_of_North_America.

16. See, on this, Piergiorgio Alessandri and Andrew Haldane, 'Banking on the State', November 2009, http://www.bankofengland.co.uk/archive/Documents/historicpubs/speeches/2009/speech409.pdf, p. 3.

17. See, for example, Gretchen Morgenson and Joshua Rosner, *Reckless Endangerment: How Outsized Ambition, Greed and Corruption Led to Economic Armageddon* (New York: Times Books, 2011).

18. In economic parlance, they are 'endogenous', not 'exogenous'.

19. Hyman Minsky, 'The Modeling of Financial Instability: An Introduction', in *Modeling and Simulation 5*, Proceedings of the Fifth Annual Pittsburgh Conference, 1974, Instrument Society of America, pp. 267–73.

20. John Cassidy, 'The Minsky Moment', *The New Yorker*, 4 February 2008, www.newyorker.com/talk/comment/2008/02/04/080204taco_talk_cassidy. See also 'Five Steps of a Bubble', Investopedia, 2 June 2010, http://www.investopedia.com/articles/stocks/10/5-steps-of-a-bubble.asp.

21. John Kenneth Galbraith, *The Great Crash of 1929* (Boston and New York: Mariner, 1997) p. 133.

22. See Bethany McLean and Joe Nocera, *All the Devils are Here: The Hidden History of the Financial Crisis* (London: Penguin, 2010) p. 129.

23. The term 'NINJA loan' was invented by Charles R. Morris. It was derived from the term 'NINA' (no-income, no-asset) loan used in the US mortgage industry. See *The Two Trillion Dollar Meltdown: Easy Money, High Rollers and the Great Credit Crash* (Philadelphia: Public Affairs, 2008).

24. A far more complete discussion of many of the topics addressed in this section is contained in Alan Blinder, *After the Music Stopped: The Financial Crisis, the Response, and the Work Ahead* (London: Penguin, 2013), Pt. II.

25. Turner, *The Turner Review*, pp. 32–5.

26. Haldane, Brennan and Madouros, Figure 19.

27. See Independent Commission on Banking, Fig. 5.5, and Ben Broadbent, 'Deleveraging', 15 March 2012, http://www.bankofengland.co.uk/publications/Documents/speeches/2012/speech553.pdf, Figure 3.

28. Broadbent, 'Deleveraging', p. 4.

29. George Akerloff, 'The Market for Lemons: Quality Uncertainty and the Market Mechanism', *Quarterly Journal of Economics*, vol. 84, no. 3 (1970), pp. 488–500.

30. Derivative transactions include a variety of financial contracts, including structured debt obligations, swaps, futures, options, caps, floors, collars, forwards, and various combinations of these. See http://en.wikipedia.org/wiki/Derivative_(finance).

31. See Nassim Nicholas Taleb, *Fooled by Randomness: The Hidden Role of Chance in Life and the Markets* (London: Penguin, 2004).

32. Thus, the 'exercise value' of an option to buy a stock at $100 a share is zero if the value of the share remains below $100 and has a value of only $10 if the market price of the share rises to $110. The 'time value' of the unexpired option will be positive, however, even if the exercise value is zero, since the option offers insurance against the possibility that the share price might rise above $100 before the option expires.

33. See data at http://www.bis.org/statistics/derstats.htm.

34. See 'Shadow Banking System', http://en.wikipedia.org/wiki/Shadow_banking_system#cite_note-22. For a definition of the shadow banking system, see Zoltan Pozsar, Tobias Adrian, Adam Ashcraft, Hayley Boesky, 'Shadow Banking', Staff Report No. 458, July 2010, revised February 2012, http://www.newyorkfed.org/research/staff_reports/sr458.html, especially p. 26.
35. In a repo, there is an agreement to sell and repurchase an asset, the price differential reflecting the interest rate. See http://en.wikipedia.org/wiki/Repurchase_agreement.
36. The literature on the new financial system is copious. Broad analyses are contained in Adair Turner, *The Turner Review*, Section 1.1. Even more important is the *Financial Crisis Inquiry Report* from the National Commission on the Causes of the Financial and Economic Crisis in the United States, http://www.gpo.gov/fdsys/pkg/GPO-FCIC/pdf/GPO-FCIC.pdf, January 2011, particularly ch. 2. On the specific and important challenge of the network-intensive nature of a market-based financial system, see Andrew Haldane, 'Rethinking the Financial Network', Bank of England, April 2009, http://www.bankofengland.co.uk/publications/Documents/speeches/2009/speech386.pdf. For a good popular account of the malign behaviour both permitted and encouraged by the new financial system, see, in particular, McLean and Nocera, *All the Devils are Here*.
37. See Turner, *The Turner Review*, Exhibit 1.10, p. 18.
38. See *Financial Crisis Inquiry Report*, p. xx. Shadow banking is defined to include commercial paper and other short-term borrowing (bankers' acceptances), repo, net securities loaned, liabilities of issuers of asset-backed securities, and assets of money-market mutual funds.
39. *Ibid.*, Fig. 2.1, p. 32.
40. Perry Mehrling, *The New Lombard Street: How the Fed Became the Dealer of Last Resort* (Princeton and Oxford: Princeton University Press, 2011), p. 123.
41. See Manmohan Singh and Peter Stella, 'Money and Collateral', WP/12/95, International Monetary Fund, April 2012, http://www.imf.org/external/pubs/ft/wp/2012/wp1295.pdf, p. 3.
42. Anat Admati and Martin Hellwig, *The Bankers' New Clothes: What's Wrong with Banking and What to Do about It* (Princeton and Oxford: Princeton University Press, 2013), especially chs. 2 and 3.
43. Michael S. Gibson, 'Understanding the Risk of Synthetic CDOs', July 2004, http://www.federalreserve.gov/pubs/feds/2004/200436/200436pap.pdf.

44. On the failure of risk-management and, in particular, value-at-risk models, see Hyun Song Shin, *Risk and Liquidity*, Clarendon Lectures in Finance (Oxford: Oxford University Press, 2010). The difficulty, in fact, was not only that the presumed distributions of outcomes were wrong. The assumption that the shape of the distribution could be known was itself wrong. So, too, was the assumption that the nature of the risks could themselves be known. This is a world of fundamental uncertainty, not of measurable risk. Similarly, the problem with the evidence is not only that it was too limited, but that it must be too limited, since the economic system is constantly changing.

45. Independent Commission on Bank, Final Report: Recommendations, September 2011, https://hmt-sanctions.s3.amazonaws.com/ICB %20final%20report/ICB%2520Final%2520Report%5B1%5D.pdf, Fig. 4.3.

46. Peter Thal Larsen, 'Goldman Pays the Price of Being Big', *Financial Times*, 13 August 2007.

47. In a reflexive relationship, the cause and the effect affect each other. So here the panic violates the risk models, which exacerbates the panic. See George Soros, *The Alchemy of Finance: Reading the Mind of the Market* (Hoboken: John Wiley and Son, 2003).

48. The standard deviation is the square root of the variance of a distribution, which is itself a measure of the dispersion of outcome. See http://en.wikipedia.org/wiki/Standard_deviation.

49. Kevin Dowd, John Cotter, Chris Humphrey and Margaret Woods, 'How Unlucky is 25-Sigma?', Centre for Risk & Insurance Studies, Nottingham University Business School, CRIS Discussion Paper Series – 2008.III, 24 March 2008, http://www.nottingham.ac.uk/business/cris/papers/2008-3.pdf.

50. See Andrew G. Haldane and Vasileios Maduros, 'The Dog and the Frisbee', 31 August 2012, paper given at the Federal Reserve Bank of Kansas City's 36th economic policy symposium, 'The Changing Policy Landscape', Jackson Hole, Wyoming http://www.bankofengland.co.uk/publications/Documents/speeches/2012/speech596.pdf. Mr Haldane's big point is that the world is not characterized by calculable risk, but by uncertainty. In this sort of world, robustness comes from simple rules, not sophisticated ones. Risk-weighting of assets is a good example of a complex set of rules that failed.

51. Independent Commission on Banking, Final Report, Fig. 5.4. The median is the position of the institution in the middle of the distribution of the leverage of all institutions.

52. Bank of England, *Financial Stability Report*, April 2007, http://www. bankofengland.co.uk/publications/Documents/fsr/2007/fsrfull0704. pdf, p. 10.

53. *Ibid.*, p. 5.

54. Andrew Haldane, Simon Brennan and Vasileios Madouros, 'What Is the Contribution of the Financial Sector: Miracle or Mirage?', in Adair Turner et al., *The Future of Finance: The LSE Report* (London: London School of Economics and Political Science, 2010), http://harr123et.files. wordpress.com/2010/07/futureoffinance5.pdf, p. 100 and Table 4.

55. See the *Financial Crisis Inquiry Report*, pp. 61–4.

56. *Ibid.*, p. 64.

57. Lucien A. Bebchuk and Holger Spamann, 'Regulating Bankers' Pay', *Georgetown Law Journal*, vol. 98, no. 2, http://papers.ssrn.com/sol3/ papers.cfm?abstract_id=1410072, p. 248. See also Raguram Rajan, 'Bankers' Pay is Deeply Flawed', *Financial Times*, 9 January 2008, and Martin Wolf, 'Why and How should we Regulate Pay in the Financial Sector?', in Turner et al., *The Future of Finance*, ch. 9.

58. Adair Turner, *The Turner Review: A Regulatory Response to the Global Banking Crisis*, Financial Services Authority, London. March 2009, http://www.fsa.gov.uk/pubs/other/turner_review.pdf, p. 39.

59. 'Greenspan Concedes to "Flaw" in his Market Ideology', 23 October 2008, http://www.bloomberg.com/apps/news?pid=newsarchive&sid= ah5qh9Up4rIg.

60. Andrew G. Haldane, 'The $100bn Question', Bank of England, March 2010, http://www.bankofengland.co.uk/publications/Documents/speeches/ 2010/speech433.pdf, p. 4. The figures are in 2009 prices.

61. *Ibid.*, p. 5.

62. *Financial Crisis Inquiry Report*, p. 96.

63. Turner, *The Turner Review*, p. 87.

64. See Danièle Nouy, 'Is Sovereign Risk Properly Addressed by Financial Regulation', Banque de France, Financial Stability Review, No. 16, April 2012, http://www.banque-france.fr/fileadmin/user_upload/banque_de_ france/publications/Revue_de_la_stabilite_financiere/2012/rsf-avril-2012/FSR16-article-09.pdf.

65. See *Financial Crisis Inquiry Report*, p. 444.

66. Blinder, *After the Music Stopped*, rebuts Wallison on p. 117.

67. These were three of the four Republican nominees to the Commission. Mr Wallison was the fourth. See *Financial Crisis Inquiry Report*, p. 415.

68. See David Min, 'Faulty Conclusions Based on Shoddy Foundations',

Center for American Progress, February 2011, http://www.american-progress.org/wp-content/uploads/issues/2011/02/pdf/pinto.pdf, Mike Konczal, 'Peter Wallison Discusses Fannie and Freddie for the American Spectator, or: Where are the Fact Checkers?', 18 May 2011, http://rortybomb.wordpress.com/2011/05/18/peter-wallison-discusses-fannie-and-freddie-for-the-american-spectator-or-where-are-the-fact-checkers, and *Financial Crisis Inquiry Report*, p. 219.

69. See McLean and Nocera, *All the Devils are Here*, p. 184.

70. See *Financial Crisis Inquiry Report*, p. xxvii.

71. Mark Gertler, 'Commentary: Whither Monetary and Financial Stability? The Implications of Evolving Policy Regimes', Federal Reserve Bank of Kansas City symposium on 'Monetary Policy and Uncertainty: Adapting to a Changing Economy', 28–30 August 2003, http://www.kansascityfed.org/publicat/sympos/2003/pdf/Gertler2003.pdf.

72. Bagehot, *Lombard Street*.

73. Anatole Kaletsky, *Capitalism 4.0: The Birth of a New Economy* (London: Bloomsbury, 2010), p. 136.

74. Thornton was the first person to present a rigorous theory of the lender of last resort. See Thomas M. Humphrey and Robert E. Keleher, 'The Lender of Last Resort: A Historical Perspective', *Cato Journal*, vol. 4, no. 1 (Spring/Summer 1984), pp. 275–321, http://object.cato.org/sites/cato.org/files/serials/files/cato-journal/1984/5/cj4n1-12.pdf.

75. Ian Davis of McKinsey may have been the first to use the term 'the new normal' in print. See 'The New Normal', *McKinsey Quarterly*, March 2009, http://www.mckinsey.com/insights/strategy/the_new_normal. Mohamed El-Erian of PIMCO was also an early user of the term. See Steven Goldberg, 'Investing in the New Normal,' 19 October 2010, http://www.kiplinger.com/article/investing/T041-C007-S001-investing-in-the-new-normal.html?topic_id=43.

5. How the World Economy Shifted

1. A. E. Housman, *Last Poems*, *XXXV*, http://www.chiark.greenend.org.uk/~martinh/poems/complete_housman.html#LPxxxv.

2. Interview with Dr Rudi Dornbusch, Frontline, http://www.pbs.org/wgbh/pages/frontline/shows/mexico/interviews/dornbusch.html.

3. Michiyo Nakamoto and David Wighton, 'Citigroup Chief Stays Bullish on Buy-outs' *Financial Times*, 9 July 2007, http://www.ft.com/cms/s/0/80e2987a-2e50-11dc-821c-0000779fd2ac.html.

4. Martin Wolf, *Fixing Global Finance* (Baltimore and London: Johns Hopkins University Press and Yale University Press, 2010), especially ch. 8.

5. Herbert Stein, 'Herb Stein's Unfamiliar Quotations: On Money, Madness, and Making Mistakes', in *Slate*, 16 May 1997, www.slate.com.

6. See Michael Dooley and Peter Garber, 'Global Imbalances and the Crisis: A Solution in Search of a Problem', 21 March 2009, www.voxeu.org.

7. *Ibid.*

8. 'The Global Saving Glut and the U. S. Current Account Deficit', Remarks by Governor Ben S. Bernanke at the Sandridge Lecture, Virginia Association of Economists, Richmond, Virginia, 10 March 2005.

9. Michael Pettis, *The Great Rebalancing: Trade, Conflict, and the Perilous Road Ahead for the World Economy* (Princeton and Oxford: Princeton University Press, 2013), p. 2.

10. This is no more than the simple IS-LM analysis of standard textbooks. It originates with a classic article by Sir John Hicks: J. R. Hicks, 'Mr Keynes and the "Classics", a Suggested Interpretation', *Econometrica*, vol. 5, no. 2, April 1937.

11. See Figure 3 above for the feeble economic response of the crisis-hit economies.

12. See Daniel Alpert, *The Age of Oversupply: Overcoming the Greatest Challenge to the Global Economy* (New York and London: Portfolio Penguin, 2013). Mr Alpert's book has a broadly similar analytical perspective to this one.

13. 'Natural Rate of Unemployment', http://en.wikipedia.org/wiki/Natural_rate_of_unemployment.

14. In standard Keynesian analysis, real and nominal interest rates are the same, because inflation is assumed to be zero. In the real world, they are different. The interest rate relevant to the idea of a savings glut is the real rate (that is, the one after expected inflation). The interest rate set by the central bank is the nominal rate (usually very short term). The relationship between real and nominal rates will be discussed further below.

15. I owe this brilliant description of the post-crisis state of the high-income economies to David Levy. See David Levy, 'The Contained Depression: 2008 – (2018?): What It Is, Why It Happened, How It Will Play Out, and What Will Follow', April 2012, The Jerome Levy Forecasting Center, http://levyforecast.com/jlwp/wp-content/uploads/2012/04/The-Contained-Depression-April-2012.pdf.

16. Mark Easton, 'The Great Myth of Urban Britain', 28 June 2012, http://www.bbc.co.uk/news/uk-18623096.

17. The behavioural economist, Robert Shiller, understood the dynamics of the housing-market excess better than most, including most economists. See Robert Shiller, *The Subprime Solution: How Today's Financial Crisis Happened, and What to Do about It* (Princeton: Princeton University Press, 2008).

18. Data come from the International Monetary Fund's World Economic Outlook database, http://www.imf.org/external/pubs/ft/weo/2013/01/weodata/index.aspx.

19. Peter Temin and David Vines, *The Leaderless Economy: Why the World Economic System Fell Apart and How to Fix It* (Princeton and Oxford: Princeton University Press, 2013), ch. 4, especially pp. 142–3.

20. *Ibid.*

21. On the reasons for China's huge savings in the 2000s, see Justin Yifu Lin, *Against the Consensus: Reflections on the Great Recession* (Cambridge: Cambridge University Press, 2013), ch. 5.

22. Pettis, *The Great Rebalancing*, p. 34.

23. Raghuram Rajan, *Fault Lines: How Hidden Fractures Still Threaten the World Economy* (Princeton and Oxford: Princeton University Press, 2010), ch. 2.

24. Pettis, *The Great Rebalancing*, p. 53.

25. See, on this strategy, Moritz Schularick, 'Touching the Brakes after the Crash: A Historical View of Reserve Accumulation and Financial Integration', *Global Economy Journal*, vol. 9, Issue 4 (2009), http://www.jfki.fu-berlin.de/faculty/economics/team/Ehemalige_Mitarbeiter_innen/schularick/A_Historical_View_of_Reserve_Accumulation_and_Financial_Integration.pdf?1376087666.

26. Rajan, *Fault Lines*, p. 10.

27. Between February 1999 and February 2004, Japan's foreign-currency reserves increased by $472bn.

28. Ben Bernanke, 'Deflation: Making Sure "It" Doesn't Happen Here', 21 November 2002, http://www.federalreserve.gov/boarddocs/speeches/2002/20021121/.

29. Pettis, *The Great Rebalancing*, pp. 174–7.

30. International Monetary Fund, 'Currency Composition of Official Foreign Exchange Reserves (COFER)', 28 June 2013, http://www.imf.org/external/np/sta/cofer/eng/index.htm.

31. Pettis, *The Great Rebalancing*, p. 16.

32. On the role of the Federal Reserve after the First World War, see Liaquat Ahamed, *Lords of Finance: The Bankers who Broke the World* (New York: Penguin, 2009).

33. My thinking on sectoral financial balances has been much influenced by the work of the late Wynne Godley. See, for a full elaboration, Wynne Godley and Marc Lavoie, *Monetary Economics: An Integrated Approach to Credit, Money, Income, Production, and Wealth* (Basingstoke: Palgrave Macmillan, 2007).

34. On the role of rising inequality in the US, see Temin and Vines, *The Leaderless Economy*, pp. 128–32, and Rajan, *Fault Lines*, ch. 1.

35. Rajan, *Fault Lines*, p. 8.

36. Congressional Budget Office, 'Trends in the Distribution of Household Incomes between 1979 and 2007', October 2011, http://www.cbo.gov/sites/default/files/cbofiles/attachments/10-25-HouseholdIncome.pdf, p. 3.

37. Claudio Borio, 'Global Imbalances and the Financial Crisis: Link or no Link?', BIS Working Paper No. 346, May 2011, http://www.bis.org/publ/work346.pdf.

38. *Ibid.*, Graph 5, p. 14.

39. See Adair Turner, 'Escaping the Debt Addiction: Monetary and Macro-Prudential Policy in the Post-Crisis World', 10 February 2014, pp. 12–18, http://ineteconomics.org/sites/inet.civicactions.net/files/Frankfurt%20Escaping%20the%20debt%20addiction%2010%20FEB.pdf.

40. Dirk J. Bezemer of Groningen University argues that 'flow of funds' models, with their attention to the shifting balances between income and expenditure, the size of the financial sector's balance sheet and the stock of financial liabilities, particularly of households, did far better than conventional general-equilibrium, 'Walrasian' models in forecasting the crisis. Indeed the latter, which exclude credit, are useless for forecasting such crises. See Bezemer, '"No One Saw This Coming": Understanding Financial Crisis through Accounting Models', 16 June 2009, Munich Personal RePEc Archive, http://mpra.ub.uni-muenchen.de/15892.

41. Jagdish Bhagwati, 'We Need to Guard against Destructive Creation', *Financial Times*, London, 16 October 2008, www.ft.com.

42. Lloyd Blankfein, 'Remarks to the Council of Institutional Investors', April 2009, http://www2.goldmansachs.com/ideas/public-policy/lcb-speech-to-cii.html.

43. Anton Brender and Florence Pisani, *Global Imbalances and the Collapse of Globalised Finance* (Brussels: Centre for European Policy Studies, 2010).

44. See Andrew Smithers and Stephen Wright, 'Stock Markets and Central Bankers – The Economic Consequences of Alan Greenspan', *World Economics* 3(1) (2002), pp. 101–24; Claudio Borio and William White, 'Whither Monetary and Financial Stability? The Implications of Evolving Policy Regimes', Federal Reserve Bank of Kansas City symposium on 'Monetary Policy and Uncertainty: Adapting to a Changing Economy', 28–30 August 2003, www.kansascityfed.org/publicat/sympos/2003/pdf/Boriowhite2003.pdf; and Richard Duncan, *The New Depression: The Breakdown of the Paper Money Economy* (Singapore: John Wiley & Sons, 2012).

45. John B. Taylor, *Getting off Track: How Government Actions and Interventions Caused, Prolonged and Worsened the Financial Crisis* (Stanford: Hoover Institution Press, 2009), ch. 1.

46. Claudio Borio, 'Global Imbalances and the Financial Crisis'.

47. Justin Yifu Lin, *Against the Consensus*.

48. *Ibid.*, ch. 7.

49. Duncan, *The New Depression*, p. 29.

50. Taylor, *Getting Off Track*, pp. 3–6.

51. Borio, 'Global Imbalances and the Financial Crisis', and William White, 'Ultra Easy Monetary Policy and the Law of Unintended Consequences', Federal Reserve Bank of Dallas, Globalization and Monetary Policy Institute, Working Paper No. 126, August 2012, http://dallasfed.org/assets/documents/institute/wpapers/2012/0126.pdf.

52. Pettis, *The Great Rebalancing*, p. 128.

53. See Emmanuel Saez and Thomas Piketty, 'Why the 1% Should Pay Tax at 80%', 24 October 2013, http://www.theguardian.com/commentisfree/2013/oct/24/1percent-pay-tax-rate-80percent.

54. See Lawrence Summers, 'Why Stagnation might Prove to be the New Normal', 15 December 2013, *Financial Times*, http://www.ft.com/cms/s/2/87cb15ea-5d1a-11e3-a558-00144feabdco.html. On Alvin Hansen, see http://en.wikipedia.org/wiki/Alvin_Hansen.

55. See http://en.wikipedia.org/wiki/Sovereign_wealth_fund#Size_of_SWFs and http://www.swfinstitute.org/fund-rankings/.

56. See Kenneth Rogoff, 'Globalization and Global Deflation', Paper prepared for the Federal Reserve Bank of Kansas City conference on 'Monetary Policy and Uncertainty: Adapting to a Changing Economy',

Jackson Hole, Wyoming, 29 August 2003, https://www.imf.org/external/np/speeches/2003/082903.htm.

57. See 'Moore's Law', http://en.wikipedia.org/wiki/Moore's_law.

58. On the forces driving inequality and their consequences, see Organisation for Economic Co-operation and Development, *Divided We Stand: Why Inequality Keeps Rising* (Paris: OECD, 2011), Joseph Stiglitz, *The Price of Inequality: How Today's Divided Society Endangers our Future* (New York and London: Norton, 2012), and Thomas Piketty, *Capital in the Twenty-First Century* (Cambridge, MA, and London, England, 2014).

59. See, in particular, a remarkable paper by Christoph Lakner and Branco Milanovic of the World Bank, 'Global Income Distribution: From the Fall of the Berlin Wall to the Great Recession', World Bank Research Working Paper 6719, December 2013, http://www-wds.worldbank.org/external/default/WDSContentServer/IW3P/IB/2013/12/11/000158349_20131211100152/Rendered/PDF/WPS6719.pdf.

60. See Organisation for Economic Co-operation and Development, *Divided We Stand*.

61. Stiglitz, *The Price of Inequality*, especially ch. 2.

62. Rajan, *Fault Lines*, ch. 1.

PART III. THE SOLUTIONS

6. Orthodoxy Overthrown

1. 'Speech by the Chancellor of the Exchequer, the Rt. Hon. Gordon Brown MP, at the Mansion House, London', 21 June 2006, http://www.ft.com/cms/s/0/00a235ba-015d-11db-af16-0000779e2340.html.

2. http://www.telegraph.co.uk/news/uknews/theroyalfamily/3386353/The-Queen-asks-why-no-one-saw-the-credit-crunch-coming.html.

3. Alan Greenspan, 'Testimony of Dr Alan Greenspan to the House of Representatives Committee of Government Oversight and Reform', 23 October 2008, http://www.clipsandcomment.com/2008/10/23/text-alan-greenspan-testimony-congress-october-23.

4. Walter Bagehot, *Lombard Street: A Description of the Money Market* (London: Henry S. King and Co., 1873), p. 11.

5. Letter to Her Majesty the Queen, 22 July 2009, http://media.ft.com/cms/3e3b6ca8-7a08-11de-b86f-00144feabdco.pdf.

6. The NEC, founded under President William Jefferson Clinton, is distinct from the Council of Economic Advisers, founded in 1946 under President Harry Truman.

7. Lawrence Summers and Martin Wolf, 'A Conversation on New Economic Thinking', Bretton Woods Conference, Institute for New Economic Thinking, 8 April 2011, http://ineteconomics.org/video/bretton-woods/larry-summers-and-martin-wolf-new-economic-thinking.

8. Ben Bernanke, Chairman of the Federal Reserve, also stressed the intellectual debt of central bankers to the journalist, Walter Bagehot, in a lecture on the Federal Reserve's response to the crisis. See Bernanke, 'The Federal Reserve's Response to the Financial Crisis', Lecture 3, George Washington University School of Business, 27 March 2012, http://www.federalreserve.gov/newsevents/lectures/federal-reserve-response-to-the-financial-crisis.htm.

9. http://rwer.wordpress.com/2013/02/19/robert-lucas-on-the-slump.

10. Adair Turner, 'Monetary and Financial Stability: Lessons from the Crisis and from Classic Economics Texts', Financial Services Authority, London, 2 November 2012, http://www.fsa.gov.uk/static/pubs/speeches/1102-at.pdf.

11. See Willem Buiter, 'The Unfortunate Uselessness of Most State of the Art Academic Macroeconomics', 3 March 2009, http://blogs.ft.com/maverecon/2009/03/the-unfortunate-uselessness-of-most-state-of-the-art-academic-monetary-economics.

12. See, for example, the capital-asset pricing model, http://www.investopedia.com/terms/c/capm.asp.

13. Felix Martin, *Money: The Unauthorised Biography* (London: Bodley Head, 2013).

14. Michael McLeay, Amar Radia and Ryland Thomas, 'Money Creation in the Modern Economy', *Bank of England Quarterly Bulletin* (2014), Q1, p. 14, http://www.bankofengland.co.uk/publications/Documents/quarterlybulletin/2014/qb14q102.pdf. See also Stuart Berry, Richard Harrison, Ryland Thomas and Iain de Weymarn, 'Interpreting Movements in Broad Money', *Bank of England Quarterly Bulletin* (2007), Q3, p. 377, http://www.bankofengland.co.uk/publications/Documents/quarterlybulletin/qb070302.pdf, and Josh Ryan-Collins, Tony Greenham, Richard Werner and Andrew Jackson, 'What Do Banks Do?', *Where Does Money Come From?* (London: New Economics Foundation, 2011), ch. 2.

15. See James Tobin, 'Commercial Banks as Creators of "Money"', Cowles Foundation Paper 205, Reprinted from Dean Carson (ed.), *Banking and Monetary Studies, for the Comptroller of the Currency, U. S. Treasury, Richard D. Irwin*, 1963, http://cowles.econ.yale.edu/P/cm/m21/m21-01.pdf.

16. 'Moneyness', as defined here, means the perfect substitutability of deposits for cash. A vast range of other assets are exchangeable for cash or even easily turned into cash (and so highly liquid), but they are not money, because their price in terms of cash is not fixed and they cannot be used as a means of payment.

17. Ben Bernanke, 'The Federal Reserve's Response to the Financial Crisis', Lecture 4, George Washington University School of Business, 29 March 2012, http://www.federalreserve.gov/newsevents/lectures/federal-reserve-response-to-the-financial-crisis.htm.

18. Mr Bernanke taught at the Stanford Graduate School of Business from 1979 until 1985 and went on to become a tenured professor at Princeton University. He has written seminal academic work on the Great Depression.

19. Bernanke, 'The Federal Reserve's Response to the Financial Crisis'.

20. *Ibid.*

21. The Federal Reserve has a dual mandate: maximum employment and stable prices. While it currently takes inflation-targeting quite seriously, it is not as obsessed with this one objective as the ECB, which has an overriding objective of 'price stability'. This is partly a matter of law. It is also partly a matter of national and institutional culture. The Bank of Japan operated without an inflation target until early 2013, when one was agreed with the government. Prior to that, the Bank of Japan argued that it could not achieve higher inflation with monetary policy. The Bank of England has an inflation target, but has, in practice, been prepared to consider activity levels as well, as has been shown by its willingness to accept overshooting of the target over many years, after the crisis of 2008–09.

22. Macroprudential policy is supposed to provide for the system as a whole what traditional prudential regulation provides for individual institutions. See Committee on the Global Financial System, 'Macroprudential Instruments and Frameworks: A Stocktaking of Issues and Experiences', CGFS Papers No. 38, May 2010, http://www.bis.org/publ/cgfs38.pdf.

23. See on this Thomas Aubrey, *Profiting from Monetary Policy: Investing through the Business Cycle* (Basingstoke: Palgrave Macmillan, 2013), especially chs. 3 and 4.

24. 'Knut Wicksell', http://en.wikipedia.org/wiki/Knut_Wicksell.

25. Michael Woodford, *Interest and Prices: Foundations of a Theory of Monetary Policy* (Princeton and Oxford: Princeton University Press, 2003).

26. Aubrey, *Profiting from Monetary Policy*, is an interesting attempt to apply Wicksell's ideas to the analysis of contemporary monetary conditions.
27. Claudio Borio and Piti Disyatat, 'Global Imbalances and the Financial Crisis: Link or no Link?', BIS Working Papers No. 346, May 2011, p. 24, http://www.bis.org/publ/work346.htm.
28. *Ibid.*, pp. 24–7.
29. William White, 'Ultra Easy Monetary Policy and the Law of Unintended Consequences', September 2012, http://www.dallasfed.org/assets/documents/institute/wpapers/2012/0126.pdf.
30. In an interesting paper, Thomas Laubach and John C. Williams of the Federal Reserve argue that, in an optimal growth model, the real rate of interest is determined by the long-run real rate of economic growth. But the long-run natural rate will vary with the potential rate of economic growth, which itself seems to be highly variable. Moreover, this estimate of the long-run natural rate is not necessarily the rate that generates price stability, as Wicksell assumed, in the presence of large short- to medium-run shocks. In fact, we have seen consistently large divergences between the real rate of interest on safe debt and the rate of growth of the world economy, probably because of the huge transitory shock of globalization and the rise of emerging economies on the world stage. See Laubach and Williams, 'Measuring the Natural Rate of Interest', Board of Governors of the Federal Reserve System, November 2001, http://www.federalreserve.gov/pubs/feds/2001/200156/200156pap.pdf.
31. See 'Austrian School', http://en.wikipedia.org/wiki/Austrian_School.
32. Jesús Huerta de Soto, *The Austrian School: Market Order and Entrepreneurial Creativity* (Cheltenham and Northampton, MA: Edward Elgar, 2008), provides a good introduction to the School. See especially chapters 5 and 6 for the contributions of Ludwig von Mises and Friedrich Hayek to monetary economics.
33. *Ibid.*, pp. 65–6.
34. Aubrey, *Profiting from Monetary Policy*, pp. 76–88, presents an interesting discussion of Austrian business-cycle theory.
35. *Ibid.*, pp. 79–81.
36. *Ibid.*, p. 84.
37. According to Herbert Hoover, US president from 1928 to 1932, Mellon advised the US to 'liquidate labor, liquidate stocks, liquidate farmers, liquidate real estate ... it will purge the rottenness out of the system. High costs of living and high living will come down. People will work harder, live a more moral life. Values will be adjusted, and enterprising

people will pick up from less competent people.' http://en.wikipedia.org/wiki/Andrew_W._Mellon.

38. See Paul Krugman, 'The Stimulus Tragedy', *The New York Times*, 20 February 2014, http://www.nytimes.com/2014/02/21/opinion/krugman-the-stimulus-tragedy.html?ref=paulkrugman.

39. A fractional reserve banking system with a reserve in inelastic supply will be highly unstable. In the absence of nineteenth-century politics – a limited franchise dominated by the wealthy, complete faith in the free market and a small state – the temptation to break the link, in order to create new reserves, will be overwhelming. Yet Brendan Brown has proposed a modern form of the gold standard, with strict monetary base control. See Brown, *The Global Curse of the Federal Reserve: How Investors can Survive and Profit from Monetary Chaos* (Basingstoke: Palgrave Macmillan, 2013).

40. Jaromir Benes and Michael Kumhof, 'The Chicago Plan Revisited', pp. 17–19, WP/12/202. International Monetary Fund. August 2012. http://www.imf.org/external/pubs/ft/wp/2012/wp12202.pdf.

41. *Ibid.*, p. 7.

42. Hyman Minsky, 'Financial Instability and the Decline (?) of Banking: Future Policy Implications', Working Paper No. 127, October 1994, The Jerome Levy Research Institute of Bard College, http://www.levyinstitute.org/pubs/wp127.pdf.

43. Laurence Kotlikoff, *Jimmy Stewart is Dead: Ending the World's Ongoing Financial Plague with Limited Purpose Banking* (Hoboken, NJ: John Wiley & Sons, 2010).

44. James Robertson, *Future Money: Breakdown or Breakthrough?* (Devon: Green Books, 2012), especially ch. 3.

45. See Andrew Jackson and Ben Dyson, *Modernising Money: Why our Monetary System is Broken and How it can be Fixed* (London: Positive Money, 2013).

46. M2 consists of (1) currency outside the US Treasury, Federal Reserve Banks, and the vaults of depository institutions; (2) travellers' checks of non-bank issuers; (3) demand deposits; (4) other checkable deposits (OCDs), which consist primarily of negotiable order of withdrawal (NOW) accounts at depository institutions and credit-union share-draft accounts; (5) savings deposits (which include money-market deposit accounts, or MMDAs); (6) small-denomination time deposits (time deposits in amounts of less than $100,000); and (7) balances in retail money-market mutual funds (MMMFs). Definitions are available at http://research.stlouisfed.org/fred2.

47. http://en.wikipedia.org/wiki/Pushing_on_a_string.

48. See, among many other things, Hyman P. Minsky, *Stabilizing an Unstable Economy* (New Haven: Yale University Press, 1986), and 'Financial Instability and the Decline (?) of Banking: Future Policy Implications', Working Paper No. 127, October 1994, The Jerome Levy Research Institute of Bard College, http://www.levyinstitute.org/pubs/wp127.pdf.

49. See 'Chartalism', http://en.wikipedia.org/wiki/Chartalism.

50. Adam Smith, *An Inquiry into the Nature and Causes of the Wealth of Nations* (1776), Bk. V, ch. 3, paragraph 82, http://www.econlib.org/library/Smith/smWN22.html#B.V, Ch. 3, Of Public Debts.

51. Georg Friedrich Knapp, *The State Theory of Money* (London: Macmillan, 1924).

52. Abba P. Lerner, 'Money as a Creature of the State', Papers and Proceedings of the Fifty-Ninth Annual Meeting of the American Economic Association, *American Economic Review*, vol. 37, no. 2 (May 1947), pp. 312–17.

53. Cited in Matthew Forstater, 'Functional Finance and Full Employment: Lessons from Lerner for Today', Working Paper No. 272, The Jerome Levy Economics Institute, July 1999.

54. See, in particular, L. Randall Wray, *Modern Monetary Theory: A Primer on Macroeconomics for Sovereign Monetary Systems* (London: Palgrave Macmillan, 2012), and Warren Mosler, *Seven Deadly Innocent Frauds of Economic Policy* (Valance, 2010). See also the writings of Bill Mitchell, http://bilbo.economicoutlook.net/blog, Warren Mosler, http://moslereconomics.com, and L. Randall Wray, http://www.economonitor.com/blog/author/rwray.

55. See Paul Sheard, 'Repeat After Me: Banks Cannot and Do Not "Lend Out" Reserves', 13 August 2013, http://www.standardandpoors.com/spf/upload/Ratings_US/Repeat_After_Me_8_14_13.pdf.

7. Fixing Finance

1. 'Communiqué', Meeting of Finance Ministers and Central Bank Governors, Busan, Republic of Korea, 5 June 2010, http://www.ft.com/cms/422d6406-7093-11df-96ab-00144feabdco.pdf.

2. *Financial Times*, 22 August 2013, http://www.ft.com/cms/s/0/6fea2b90-09bf-11e3-ad07-00144feabdco.html.

3. 'Declaration on Strengthening the Financial System', London Summit, 2 April 2009, http://www.mofa.go.jp/policy/economy/g20_summit/2009-1/annex2.html.

4. On Basel III, see http://en.wikipedia.org/wiki/Basel_III.

5. On Basel I, see http://en.wikipedia.org/wiki/Basel_I.

6. On Basel II, see http://en.wikipedia.org/wiki/Basel_II.

7. Basel Committee on Banking Supervision, 'Basel III: A Global Regulatory Framework for More Resilient Banks and Banking Systems', December 2010 (revised June 2011), http://www.bis.org/publ/bcbs189.pdf. See also Independent Commission on Banking, *Final Report: Recommendations*, London, September 2011, p. 84, https://hmt-sanctions.s3.amazonaws.com/ICB%20final%20report/ICB%2520Final%2520 Report%5B1%5D.pdf.

8. On Basel III and US implementation, see Daniel K. Tarullo, 'Statement by Daniel K. Tarullo, Board of Governors of the Federal Reserve System before the Committee on Banking, Housing, and Urban Affairs, US Senate', Washington DC, 11 July 2013, http://www.federalreserve.gov/newsevents/testimony/tarullo20130711a.htm and Board of Governors of the Federal Reserve Board, 'Agencies Adopt Enhanced Supplementary Leverage Ratio Final Rule and Issue Supplementary Leverage Ratio Notice of Proposed Rulemaking', 8 April 2014, http://www.federalreserve.gov/newsevents/press/bcreg/20140408a.htm.

9. On the leverage ratio, see Basel Committee on Banking Supervision, 'Consultative Document: Revised Basel III Leverage Ratio Framework and Disclosure Requirements', June 2013, http://www.bis.org/publ/bcbs251.pdf. It is worth noting that differences in accounting standards make it impossible to compare leverage ratios strictly.

10. See Financial Stability Board, 'Implementing the FSB Key Attributes of Effective Resolution Regimes – How Far have we Come?', PLEN/2013/55, 15 April 2013.

11. Tarullo, 'Statement', pp. 8–10.

12. Simon Wong, 'Some Banks' Pay Reform may Show the Way', *Financial Times*, 13 March 2011, http://www.ft.com/cms/s/0/578024fa-4c21-11e0-82df-00144feab49a.html.

13. Federal Deposit Insurance Company, 'Guidance on Sound Incentive Compensation Policies', http://www.fdic.gov/regulations/laws/rules/-5000-5350.html.

14. 'EU Bank Bonus Rules Approved', *Financial Times*, 13 March 2013, http://www.ft.com/cms/s/0/ca5becf0-91ae-11e2-b4c9-00144feabdc0.html?siteedition=uk.

15. Report of the Parliamentary Commission on Banking Standards, *Changing Banking for Good. Volume 1: Summary, and Conclusions and Recommendations*, 12 June 2013, p. 10. http://www.parliament.uk/

business/committees/committees-a-z/joint-select/professional-standards-in-the-banking-industry/news/changing-banking-for-good-report.

16. Tarullo, 'Statement', p. 11.

17. See Independent Commission on Banking, *Final Report*.

18. Independent Commission on Banking, *Interim Report: Consultation on Reform Options*, April 2011, http://s3-eu-west-1.amazonaws.com/htcdn/Interim-Report-110411.pdf, Fig. 2.2.

19. See EU Single Market, 'Banking Structural Reform (follow up to the Liikanen report)', http://ec.europa.eu/internal_market/bank/structural-reform/index_en.htm.

20. Erkki Liikanen, 'The Case for Structural Reforms of Banking after the Crisis', Brussels, 2 October 2012, http://www.suomenpankki.fi/en/suomen_pankki/ajankohtaista/puheet/Pages/puhe_el_hleg.aspx.

21. High-level Expert Group on reforming the structure of the EU banking sector, chaired by Erkki Liikanen, *Final Report*, Brussels, 2 October 2012, http://ec.europa.eu/internal_market/bank/docs/high-level_expert_group/report_en.pdf.

22. Andrew G. Haldane and Vasileios Madouros, 'The Dog and the Frisbee', http://www.bankofengland.co.uk/publications/Documents/speeches/2012/speech596.pdf, pp. 10–11.

23. In this section, I have drawn on an excellent paper by Charles A. E. Goodhart, 'The Optimal Financial Structure', Special Paper 20, LSE Financial Markets Group Paper Series, March 2013, http://www.lse.ac.uk/fmg/workingPapers/specialPapers/PDF/SP220.pdf.

24. *Ibid.*, p. 5.

25. See Jaromir Benes and Michael Kumhof, 'The Chicago Plan Revisited', WP/12/202, International Monetary Fund, August 2012, http://www.imf.org/external/pubs/ft/wp/2012/wp12202.pdf, and Laurence Kotlikoff, *Jimmy Stewart is Dead: Ending the World's Ongoing Financial Plague with Limited Purpose Banking* (Hoboken, NJ: John Wiley & Sons, 2010).

26. See, for example, James Robertson, *Future Money: Breakdown or Breakthrough?* (Devon: Green Books, 2012).

27. The arguments in this section draw heavily on Anat Admati and Martin Hellwig, *The Bankers' New Clothes: What's Wrong with Banking and What to Do about It* (Princeton and Oxford: Princeton University Press, 2013).

28. See '2008-11 Icelandic Financial Crisis', http://en.wikipedia.org/wiki/2008%E2%80%9311_Icelandic_financial_crisis. This default created

huge friction with the governments of the Netherlands and the UK, where many of the cheated foreign creditors lived.

29. See http://en.wikipedia.org/wiki/Modigliani%E2%80%93Miller_theorem.

30. Admati and Hellwig, *The Bankers' New Clothes*, pp. 44–5.

31. Independent Commission on Banking, *Interim Report*, Fig. 2.1, p. 18.

32. See Andrew G. Haldane, 'Control Rights (and Wrongs)', Wincott Annual Memorial Lecture, 24 October 2011, http://www.bankofengland.co.uk/publications/Documents/speeches/2011/speech525.pdf.

33. See David Miles, Jing Yang and Gilberto Marcheggiano, 'Optimal Bank Capital', External MPC Unit, Discussion Paper No. 31: revised and expanded version, April 2011, http://citeseerx.ist.psu.edu/viewdoc/download;jsessionid=DA5FA4A3231E2B8A6263D1A4035C469A?-doi=10.1.1.193.8030&rep=rep1&type=pdf.

34. Haldane and Madouros, 'The Dog and the Frisbee', p. 13.

35. 'Inching Towards World-Wide Accord on Bank Rules', *Wall Street Journal*, 30 August 2010.

36. Miles et al., 'Optimal Bank Capital', p. 18.

37. See Independent Commission on Banking, *Final Report*, Figure 3.4, p. 51.

38. See Stephen G. Cecchetti and Enisse Kharroubi, 'Reassessing the Impact of Finance on Growth', BIS Working Papers No. 381, July 2012, http://www.bis.org/publ/work381.pdf.

39. Alan Greenspan, 'Regulators Must Risk More, and Intervene Less', The A-List, ft.com, 26 July 2011, http://blogs.ft.com/the-a-list/2011/07/26/buffers-against-risk-carry-a-cost-to-society.

40. Basel Committee on Banking Supervision, 'An Assessment of the Long-Term Economic Impact of Stronger Capital and Liquidity Requirements', August 2010, http://www.bis.org/publ/bcbs173.pdf.

41. Admati and Hellwig, *The Bankers' New Clothes*, p. 211.

42. Goodhart, 'The Optimal Financial Structure', p. 5.

43. Admati and Hellwig, *The Bankers' New Clothes*, p. 187.

44. These Equity Recourse Notes (ERNs) are just a more sophisticated version of the Contingent Convertible (CoCo) bonds that are already being issued (Christopher Thomson, 'Coco Bond "avalanche" Expected from EU Banks', *Financial Times*, 25 November 2013, http://www.ft.com/cms/s/0/a169e4f8-55e6-11e3-96f5-00144feabdc0.html). On ERNs, see Jeremy Bulow, Jacob Goldfield and Paul Klemperer, 'Market-based Capital Regulation' 29 August 2013, http://www.voxeu.org/article/market-based-bank-capital-regulation.

45. Peter Sands, 'In Banking too much Simplicity can be Dangerous', *Financial Times*, 26 August 2013, http://www.ft.com/cms/s/0/15ba8044-f46a-11e2-a62e-00144feabdc0.html.
46. Haldane and Madouros, 'The Dog and the Frisbee', p. 22.
47. Alan Greenspan has reached a similar conclusion on the need for more capital. See *The Map and the Territory: Risk, Human Nature, and the Future of Forecasting* (London: Allen Lane, 2013).
48. Ben Bernanke made just this argument in 2002. See 'Asset Price "Bubbles" and Monetary Policy', 15 October 20012, http://www.federalreserve.gov/boarddocs/speeches/2002/20021015. Alan Greenspan had the same view.
49. On macroprudential policy, see, among many other writings, Stijn Claessens, Swati Gosh and Roxana Mihet, 'Macro-Prudential Policies to Mitigate Financial System Vulnerabilities', 12 November 2012, http://macrofinance.nipfp.org.in/PDF/JIMFPr_Claessens_NIPFP-DEA-JIMF_Conference_December_2012.pdf; Enrico Perotti, 'A Blueprint for Macroprudential Policy in the Banking Union', 16 December 2012, http://www.voxeu.org/article/blueprint-macroprudential-policy-banking-union; Otaviano Canuto and Matheus Cavallari, 'Integrating Monetary Policy and Macroprudential Regulation', 21 May 2013, http://www.voxeu.org/article/integrating-monetary-policy-and-macroprudential-regulation; and 'Macro-Prudential and Micro-Prudential Regulation', ch. 2, The Warwick Commission on International Financial Reform, *In Praise of Unlevel Playing Fields*, Report of the Second Warwick Commission, University of Warwick, 2009, http://www2.warwick.ac.uk/research/warwickcommission/financialreform/report/chapter_2.pdf.

8. The Long Journey Ahead

1. 'G20 Toronto Summit Declaration', 27 June 2010, http://www.washingtonpost.com/wp-dyn/content/article/2010/06/27/AR2010062702887_2.html?sid=ST2010062604320.
2. David Cameron, Speech, 7 March 2013, http://www.conservatives.com/News/Speeches/2013/03/Prime_Ministers_Speech_on_The_Economy.aspx.
3. Under these assumptions, the present value of the loss of GDP would be 17 per cent of the pre-crisis trend level of GDP forever.

4. This is the argument of Paul Krugman's *End this Depression Now* (New York: W. W. Norton, 2012). For a sceptical discussion of the argument that the UK's pre-crisis level of output was unsustainable, see Martin Wolf, 'How the Financial Crisis Changed Our World', 2013 Wincott Memorial Lecture, http://www.wincott.co.uk/lectures/2013.html.

5. International Monetary Fund, 'The Dog that didn't Bark: Has Inflation been Muzzled or was it just Sleeping?', *World Economic Outlook*, ch. 3, Washington DC, April 2013, http://www.imf.org/external/pubs/ft/weo/2013/01/pdf/text.pdf.

6. Mark Blyth, *Austerity: The History of a Dangerous Idea* (New York: Oxford University Press, 2013), provides a splendid account of the turn to austerity.

7. An important empirical paper by Moritz Schularick of the Free University in Berlin and Alan Taylor of the University of California, Davis, describes such disasters as 'credit booms gone wrong'. See Schularick and Taylor, 'Credit Booms Gone Bust: Monetary Policy, Leverage Cycles and Financial Crises, 1870–2008', National Bureau of Economic Research, Working Paper 15512, November 2009, www.nber.org.

8. Simon Wren-Lewis, 'The Two Arguments why the Zero Lower Bound Matters', *Mainly Macro*, 12 July 2013, http://mainlymacro.blogspot.it/2013/07/the-two-arguments-why-zero-lower-bound.html.

9. John Williams, 'A Defense of Moderation in Monetary Policy', Federal Reserve Bank of San Francisco Working Paper 2013-15, Abstract, July 2013, http://www.frbsf.org/economic-research/files/wp2013-15.pdf.

10. See, for example, William White, 'Ultra Easy Monetary Policy and the Law of Unintended Consequences', September 2012, http://www.dallasfed.org/assets/documents/institute/wpapers/2012/0126.pdf, and Raghuram Rajan, 'A Step in the Dark: Unconventional Monetary Policy after the Crisis', Andrew Crockett Memorial Lecture, Bank for International Settlement, 23 June 2013, http://www.bis.org/events/agm2013/sp130623.pdf.

11. See Allan H. Meltzer, 'When Inflation Doves Cry', Project Syndicate, 13 August 2013, http://www.project-syndicate.org/commentary/why-us-inflation-remains-low-by-allan-h--meltzer.

12. Paul Sheard, 'Repeat After Me: Banks Cannot and Do Not "Lend Out" Reserves', Standard & Poor's, 13 August 2013, http://www.standardandpoors.com/spf/upload/Ratings_US/Repeat_After_Me_8_14_13.pdf.

13. A controversial discussion of this issue was contained in the International Monetary Fund's *World Economic Outlook* for October 2012.

See 'Are we Underestimating Short-Term Fiscal Multipliers?', Box 1.1, pp. 41–3. See also Paul Krugman, http://krugman.blogs.nytimes. com/2013/08/31/the-arithmetic-of-fantasy-fiscal-policy.

14. J. Bradford de Long and Lawrence H. Summers, 'Fiscal Policy in a Depressed Economy', *Brookings Papers on Economic Activity* (Spring 2012), pp. 233–97.

15. The most prominent economists to believe that recessions are due entirely to real phenomena are those who believe in 'real business cycles'. See http://en.wikipedia.org/wiki/Real_business_cycle_theory.

16. Alberto Alesina and Silvia Ardagna, 'Large Changes in Fiscal Policy: Taxes versus Spending', *Tax Policy and the Economy*, vol. 24, ed. Jeffrey R. Brown (Cambridge, MA: National Bureau of Economic Research).

17. http://krugman.blogs.nytimes.com/2013/03/19/cogan-taylor-and-the-confidence-fairy/.

18. See Jaime Guajardo, Daniel Leigh, and Andrea Pescatori, 'Expansionary Austerity: New International Evidence', International Monetary Fund Working Paper, WP/11/158, July 2011, http://www.imf.org/external/ pubs/ft/wp/2011/wp11158.pdf, and 'Will it Hurt: Macroeconomic Effects of Fiscal Consolidation', ch. 3, *World Economic Outlook*, October 2012, http://www.imf.org/external/pubs/ft/weo/2010/02/pdf/c3. pdf.

19. Guajardo et al., 'Expansionary Austerity', p. 29.

20. Roberto Perotti, 'Rethinking Macro Policy II', International Monetary Fund, 16–17 April 2013, http://www.imf.org/external/np/seminars/ eng/2013/macro2/pdf/rp.pdf. See also Arjun Jayadev and Mike Konczal, 'The Boom Not The Slump: The Right Time For Austerity', The Roosevelt Institute, 23 August 2010, http://www.rooseveltinstitute.org/ sites/all/files/not_the_time_for_austerity.pdf, and Iyanatul Islam and Anis Chowdhury, 'Revisiting the Evidence on Expansionary Fiscal Austerity: Alesina's Hour?', 28 February 2012, http://www.voxeu.org/ debates/commentaries/revisiting-evidence-expansionary-fiscal-austerity-alesina-s-hour.

21. Alan Taylor, 'When is the Time for Austerity?', 20 July 2013, *Vox*, http:// www.voxeu.org/article/when-time-austerity.

22. These arguments were developed in Martin Wolf, 'How Austerity has Failed', *The New York Review of Books*, vol. LX, no. 12, 11 July–4 August 2013, pp. 20–22, http://www.nybooks.com/articles/archives/2013/jul/11/ how-austerity-has-failed/?pagination=false.

23. Carmen M. Reinhart and Kenneth Rogoff, 'Growth in a Time of Debt', National Bureau of Economic Research Working Paper No. 15639, January 2010, www.nber.org.

24. Thomas Herndon, Michael Ash and Robert Pollin, 'Does High Public Debt Consistently Stifle Economic Growth? A Critique of Reinhart and Rogoff', 15 April 2013, http://www.peri.umass.edu/fileadmin/pdf/working_papers/working_papers_301-350/WP322.pdf.

25. International Monetary Fund, *World Economic Outlook*, April 2013, Fig. 1.1.2.

26. See Paul Krugman, 'Conventional Wisdom', 27 May 2010, *New York Times*, http://krugman.blogs.nytimes.com/2010/05/27/conventional-madness. See also Bank for International Settlements, *83rd BIS Annual Report 2012/2013*, 23 June 2013, http://www.bis.org/publ/arpdf/ar2013e.htm.

27. See on this Martin Wolf, 'The Role of Fiscal Deficits in De-leveraging', 25 July 2012, http://blogs.ft.com/martin-wolf-exchange/2012/07/25/getting-out-of-debt-by-adding-debt.

28. Robert Kuttner, *Debtors' Prison: The Politics of Austerity Versus Possibility* (New York: Alfred A. Knopf, 2013), p. 206.

29. McKinsey Global Institute, *Debt and De-leveraging: Uneven Progress on the Road to Growth*, January 2012, http://www.mckinsey.com/insights/global_capital_markets/uneven_progress_on_the_path_to_growth.

30. Irving Fisher, 'The Debt-Deflation Theory of Great Depressions', *Econometrica*, vol. 1, no. 4 (October 1933), pp. 337–57, http://fraser.stlouisfed.org/docs/meltzer/fisdeb33.pdf.

31. Stephen King, chief economist of HSBC, has written a book with these characteristics: *When the Money Runs Out: The End of Western Affluence* (New Haven and London: Yale University Press, 2013).

32. See Robert Arnott and Denis Chaves, 'A New "New Normal" in Demography and Economic Growth', 27 August 2013, http://www.indexuniverse.com/docs/magazine/2/2013_229.pdf.

33. See International Monetary Fund, *Fiscal Adjustment in an Uncertain World, Fiscal Monitor*, April 2013, Fig. 2, p. 6.

34. See Robert Gordon, 'Is U. S. Economic Growth Over? Faltering Innovation Confronts the Six Headwinds', National Bureau of Economic Research Working Paper No. 18315, August 2012, www.nber.org; Tyler Cowen, *The Great Stagnation: How America Ate All the Low-Hanging Fruit of Modern History, Got Sick, and Will (Eventually) Feel Better* (London: Dutton/Penguin, 2011).

35. Erik Brynjolfsson and Andrew McAfee, *The Second Machine Age: Work, Progress and Prosperity in a Time of Brilliant Technologies* (New York and London: W. W. Norton, 2014), and *Race Against the Machine: How the Digital Revolution is Accelerating Innovation, Driving Employment and the Economy* (Lexington, MA: Digital Frontier Press, 2011).

36. See Mariana Mazzucato, *The Entrepreneurial State: Debunking Public vs Private Myths in Risk and Innovation* (London: Anthem Press, 2013).

37. See Lawrence Summers, 'Why Stagnation might Prove to be the New Normal', 15 December 2013, *Financial Times*, http://www.ft.com/cms/s/2/87cb15ea-5d1a-11e3-a558-00144feabdco.html.

38. Daniel Alpert, *The Age of Oversupply: Overcoming the Greatest Challenge to the Global Economy* (New York and London: Portfolio Penguin, 2013).

39. See also the analysis in ch. 5 above.

40. Joseph E. Stiglitz, *The Price of Inequality: How Today's Divided Society Endangers our Future* (New York and London: Norton, 2012), p. 85.

41. James K. Galbraith, *Inequality and Instability: A Study of the World Economy just before the Great Crisis* (Oxford and New York: Oxford University Press, 2012), p. 290.

42. Raghuram Rajan, 'A Step in the Dark: Unconventional Monetary Policy after the Crisis', Andrew Crockett Memorial Lecture, Bank for International Settlement, 23 June 2013, http://www.bis.org/events/agm2013/sp130623.pdf, pp. 3–4.

43. See Jeffrey D. Sachs, *The Price of Civilization: Reawakening American Virtue and Prosperity* (New York: Random House, 2011).

44. See Andrew Smithers, *The Road to Recovery: How and Why Economic Policy Must Change* (London: Wiley, 1013), especially ch. 3.

45. This is the theme of Michael Pettis, *The Great Rebalancing: Trade, Conflict, and the Perilous Road ahead for the World Economy* (Princeton and Oxford: Princeton University Press, 2013).

46. Full employment is extremely hard to measure. But the evidence from actual inflation rates in the main high-income economies suggests that even in early 2104 it would have been possible to expand demand and output without raising inflation. This also indicates that current rates of unemployment are above the NAIRU – the 'non-accelerating-inflation rate of unemployment'. Inflation would probably have been still lower if expectations had not been so well anchored by central-bank commitments to their inflation targets.

47. See Luis A. V. Catão and Gian Maria Milesi-Feretti, 'External Liabilities and Crisis Risk', 4 September 2013, http://www.voxeu.org/article/external-liabilities-and-crisis-risk.
48. International Monetary Fund, 'The G20 Mutual Assessment Process (MAP)', http://www.imf.org/external/np/exr/facts/g2omap.htm.
49. See *Report of the Commission of Experts of the President of the United Nations General Assembly on Reforms of the International Monetary and Financial System*, United Nations Conference on the World Financial and Economic Crisis and its Impact upon Development, 24–26 June 2009, New York, http://www.un.org/ga/president/63/interactive/financialcrisis/PreliminaryReport210509.pdf, p. 93.
50. Adair Turner, 'Debt, Money and Mephistopheles: How do we Get out of this Mess?', Cass Business School, 6 February 2013, http://www.fsa.gov.uk/static/pubs/speeches/0206-at.pdf.
51. *Ibid.*, p. 3.
52. Ben Bernanke, 'Some Thoughts on Monetary Policy in Japan', 31 May 2003, http://www.federalreserve.gov/boarddocs/speeches/2003/20030531. The suggestion by John Maynard Keynes comes from *The General Theory of Employment, Interest and Money* (London: Macmillan, 1936), Bk. 3, ch. 10, p. 129.

9. Mending a Bad Marriage

1. 'Interview with Jean-Claude Trichet, President of the ECB, and *Libération*, conducted by Jean Quatremer', Thursday, 8 July 2010, http://www.ecb.europa.eu/press/key/date/2010/html/sp100713.en.html.
2. Committee for the Study of Economic and Monetary Union, 'Report on Economic and Monetary Union in the European Community', 1989, http://ec.europa.eu/economy_finance/publications/publication6161_en.pdf.
3. Kevin H. O'Rourke and Alan M. Taylor, 'Cross of Euros', *Journal of Economic Perspectives*, vol. 27, no. 3 (Summer 2013), pp. 184–5.
4. On Brüning, see http://en.wikipedia.org/wiki/Heinrich_Br%C3%BCning.
5. O'Rourke and Taylor, 'Cross of Euros', Fig. 1, p. 175.
6. European Central Bank, 'Monetary Policy', http://www.ecb.europa.eu/mopo/html/index.en.html.
7. Reza Moghadam, Ranjit Tela and Pelin Berkmen of the International Monetary Fund's European Department provided a devastating critique of ECB policy and the cost of low inflation in 'Euro Area – "Deflation"

versus "Lowflation"', IMFdirect, 4 March 2014, http://blog-imfdirect. imf.org/2014/03/04/euro-area-deflation-versus-lowflation.

8. Zsolt Darvas, 'The Euro Area's Tightrope Walk: Debt and Competitive-ness in Italy and Spain', Bruegel Policy Contribution Issue 2013/11, September 2013, www.bruegel.org.

9. Stefan Wagstyl and Claire Jones, 'German Court Refers ECB Bond-Buying Programme to European Justice', 7 February 2014, *Financial Times*, http://www.ft.com/cms/s/0/3feab440-8fd5-11e3-aee9-00144feab7de.html. See also Paul de Grauwe, 'Why the ECJ Should Reject the German Constitutional Court's Ruling', 11 March 2014, *Social Europe Journal*, http://www.social-europe.eu/2014/03/german-constitutional-court.

10. O'Rourke and Taylor, 'Cross of Euros', p. 176.

11. This section draws from Martin Wolf, 'Why the Baltic States are no Model', *Financial Times*, 30 April 2013, http://www.ft.com/cms/s/0/090bd38e-b0c7-11e2-80f9-00144feabdco.html.

12. Olivier Blanchard, 'Lessons from Latvia', 11 June 2013, http://blog-imfdirect.imf.org/2012/06/11/lessons-from-latvia.

13. This section draws from Martin Wolf, 'The German Model is not for Export', *Financial Times*, 7 May 2013, http://www.ft.com/cms/s/0/aacd1be0-b637-11e2-93ba-00144feabdco.html.

14. See http://ec.europa.eu/economy_finance/economic_governance/macro-economic_imbalance_procedure/index_en.htm.

15. Soros calls for Germany to 'lead or leave euro', http://www.bbc.com/news/19537693.

16. See Paul de Grauwe and Yuemei Ji, 2013, 'Panic-Driven Austerity in the Eurozone and its Implications', 21 February 2013, http://www.voxeu. org/article/panic-driven-austerity-Eurozone-and-its-implications. See also Martin Wolf, 'Be Bold, Mario, Put Out that Fire', *Financial Times*, 25 October 2011, www.ft.com.

17. Alex Barker 'Marathon Talks Seal EU Banking Union', *Financial Times*, 20 March 2014, http://www.ft.com/cms/s/0/adfe7be4-b04e-11e3-8058-00144feab7de.html.

18. See http://en.wikipedia.org/wiki/European_Fiscal_Compact.

CONCLUSION: FIRE NEXT TIME

1. I have taken the chapter's title from that of a magnificent book (New York: Dial, 1963) by the American author, James Baldwin. He took it

from the lines of an African-American spiritual: 'God gave Noah the rainbow sign, no more water but fire next time.'

2. John Maynard Keynes, *Tract on Monetary Reform* (London: Macmillan, 1923), p. 80.

3. Mervyn King, 'Banking from Bagehot to Basel, and Back Again', 25 October 2010, The Second Bagehot Lecture, Buttonwood Gathering, New York City, http://www.bankofengland.co.uk/publications/Documents/speeches/2010/speech455.pdf, p. 18.

4. Luc Laeven and Fabian Valencia, 'Systemic Crises Database: An Update', International Monetary Fund Working Paper, WP/12/163, June 2102, http://www.imf.org/external/pubs/ft/wp/2012/wp12163.pdf.

5. This proposition is supported by Thomas Piketty, *Capital in the Twenty-First Century*, trans. Arthur Goldhammer (Cambridge, MA, and London: Harvard University Press, 2014).

6. For a detailed discussion of the evolution of real interest rates, see International Monetary Fund, *World Economic Outlook*, April 2014, ch. 3, http://www.imf.org/external/Pubs/ft/weo/2014/01/.

7. See the speech by Lawrence H. Summers at the 14th IMF Annual Research Conference in Honor of Stanley Fischer, 18 November 2013, http://larrysummers.com/imf-fourteenth-annual-research-conference-in-honor-of-stanley-fischer/. See also 'Why Stagnation Might Prove to Be the New Normal', *Financial Times*, 15 December 2013, http://www.ft.com/cms/s/2/87cb15ea-5d1a-11e3-a558-00144feabdco.html.

8. Independent Commission on Banking, *Interim Report: Consultation on Reform Options* (London, April 2011), http://s3-eu-west-1.amazonaws.com/htcdn/Interim-Report-110411.pdf), Fig. 2.1, p. 18.

9. Tim Geithner, former US treasury secretary, provides an informative and revealing account of the management of the crisis in *Stress Tests: Reflections on Financial Crises* (New York: Crown Publishers, 2014).

10. This conclusion was reached by assuming the reduction in economic output in 2013 – relative to the 1980–2007 trend – is permanent, the economy subsequently returns to the pre-crisis trend in GDP per head, and future incomes can be discounted at a real rate of interest of 3 per cent.

11. Abdul Abiad, Ravi Balakrishnan, Petya Koeva Brooks, Daniel Leigh, and Irina Tytell, 'What's the Damage? Medium-Term Output Dynamics After Banking Crises', WP/09/245, International Monetary Fund, November 2009.

12. See Financial Stability Board, '2013 Update of Group of Globally Systemically Important Banks (G-SIBs)', 11 November 2013, https://www.financialstabilityboard.org/publications/r_131111.pdf, Annex 1.

13. See International Monetary Fund, Global Financial Stability Report, April 2014, ch. 3, http://www.imf.org/External/Pubs/FT/GFSR/2014/01/index.htm.

14. Irving Fisher, 'The Debt-Deflation Theory of Great Depressions', *Econometrica*, 1(4), pp. 337–57, October 1933, http://fraser.stlouisfed.org/docs/meltzer/fisdeb33.pdf.

15. On the risks of low inflation or even deflation in the Eurozone, see Reza Moghadam, Ranjit Tela and Pelin Berkmen, 'Euro Area – "Deflation" Versus "Lowflation"', 24 March 2014, IMFdirect, http://blog-imfdirect.imf.org/2014/03/04/euro-area-deflation-versus-lowflation.

16. A fully worked out plan for such a reform is in Andrew Jackson and Ben Dyson, *Modernising Money: Why our Monetary System is Broken and How it Can be Fixed* (London: Positive Money, 2013).

17. See Andrew Smithers, *The Road to Recovery: How and Why Economic Policy Must Change* (London: Wiley, 2013).

18. See Piketty, *Capital in the Twenty-First Century*, Part Four.

19. For elements of the new Eurozone policy system, see 'Stability and Growth Pact', http://ec.europa.eu/economy_finance/economic_governance/sgp/index_en.htm; 'Macroeconomic Imbalance Procedure', http://ec.europa.eu/economy_finance/economic_governance/macroeconomic_imbalance_procedure/index_en.htm; 'Treaty on Stability, Co-ordination and Governance' (also known as the Fiscal Compact), http://european-council.europa.eu/media/639235/stootscg26_en12.pdf; 'European Semester', http://ec.europa.eu/europe2020/making-it-happen; 'Euro Plus Pact', http://ec.europa.eu/europe2020/pdf/euro_plus_pact_background_december_2011_en.pdf; and 'European Stability Mechanism', http://www.esm.europa.eu/index.htm; 'European Financial Supervision', http://ec.europa.eu/internal_market/finances/committees; and 'Banking Union', http://ec.europa.eu/internal_market/finances/banking-union.

20. Piketty, *Capital in the Twenty-First Century*, p. 142.

21. For shares in the ECB's capital, see http://www.ecb.europa.eu/ecb/orga/capital/html/index.en.html.

22. As of 24 September 2013, total resources of the IMF were $1,360bn, consisting of US $360bn in member-country quotas (as of 9 June 2013) and $1tn in other resources. See 'The IMF at a Glance', 24 September 2013, http://www.imf.org/external/np/exr/facts/glance.htm. At the end of the second quarter of 2013, total foreign-currency reserves amounted to $11,138bn. See 'The Currency Composition of Official Foreign Currency Reserves (COFER)', 30 September 2013, http://www.imf.org/External/np/sta/cofer/eng/index.htm.

23. International Monetary Fund, 'The G20 Mutual Assessment Process (MAP)', 26 September 2013, http://www.imf.org/external/np/exr/facts/g20map.htm.

24. For global deposits in 2010, see *Mapping Global Capital Markets 2011*, Exhibit 11, p. 23, August 2011, McKinsey Global Institute, http://www.mckinsey.com/insights/global_capital_markets/mapping_global_capital_markets_2011. For the stock of gold, estimated at 120,000–140,000 tonnes, see 'How much Gold is There?' http://www.bullionmark.com.au/how-much-gold-is-there. About a quarter of this total is held by governments as reserves. Another sixth is held by individuals as gold coins or bullion. The rest is held as jewellery. The gold price was $42,750 per tonne on 27 December 2013.

25. For an excellent account of efforts to discipline surplus countries, see John Williamson, 'Getting Surplus Countries to Adjust', Policy Brief PB11-01, January 2011, Peterson Institute for International Economics, http://www.iie.com/publications/pb/pb11-01.pdf.

26. The articles establishing the IMF included a 'scarce currency clause', which permitted discrimination against a country's exports if the IMF ran out of its currency. In practice the clause has proved useless, because the constraint has never been actual shortage of the relevant currency. See http://www.oxfordreference.com/view/10.1093/oi/authority.20110803100444615.

27. This is the recommendation of Justin Yifu Lin, former chief economist of the World Bank. See *Against the Consensus: Reflections on the Great Recession* (Cambridge: Cambridge University Press, 2013), Pt. II.

28. *Ibid.*, Pt. IV.

29. See Anat Admati and Martin Hellwig, *The Bankers' New Clothes: What's Wrong with Banking and What to Do about It* (Princeton and Oxford: Princeton University Press, 2013).

30. Mervyn King, 'Banking from Bagehot to Basel, and Back Again', pp. 16–17.

31. This is drawn from Martin Wolf, 'Failing Elites Threaten our Future', *Financial Times*, 14 January 2014, http://www.ft.com/cms/s/0/cfc1eb1c-76d8-11e3-807e-00144feabdco.html.

References

Abiad, Abdul, Ravi Balakrishnan, Petya Koeva Brooks, Daniel Leigh and Irina Tytell. 'What's the Damage? Medium-Term Output Dynamics After Banking Crises', WP/09/245, International Monetary Fund, Washington DC, November 2009.

Acemoglu, Daron. 'The World our Grandchildren will Inherit: The Rights Revolution and Beyond', National Bureau of Economic Research Working Paper 17994, April 2012. www.nber.org.

Admati, Anat and Martin Hellwig. *The Bankers' New Clothes: What's Wrong with Banking and What to Do about It* (Princeton: Princeton University Press, 2013).

Ahamed, Liaquat. *Lords of Finance: The Bankers who Broke the World* (New York: Penguin, 2009).

Akerloff, George. 'The Market for Lemons: Quality Uncertainty and the Market Mechanism', *Quarterly Journal of Economics*, vol. 84, no. 3 (1970), pp. 488–500.

Alesina, Alberto and Silvia Ardagna. 'Large Changes in Fiscal Policy: Taxes versus Spending', *Tax Policy and the Economy*, vol. 24 (2010), ed. Jeffrey R. Brown (Cambridge, MA: National Bureau of Economic Research). http://www.nber.org/chapters/c11970.pdf?new_window=1.

Alessandri, Piergiorgio and Andrew Haldane. 'Banking on the State', November 2009. http://www.bankofengland.co.uk/publications/Pages/speeches/2009/409.aspx.

Alpert, Daniel. *The Age of Oversupply: Overcoming the Greatest Challenge to the Global Economy* (New York and London: Portfolio Penguin, 2013).

Arnott, Robert and Denis Chaves. 'A New "New Normal" in Demography and Economic Growth', 27 August 2013. http://www.indexuniverse.com/docs/magazine/2/2013_229.pdf.

Atkins, Ralph. 'ECB Unveils New Support for Banks', *Financial Times*, 8 December 2012. www.ft.com.

Aubrey, Thomas. *Profiting from Monetary Policy: Investing through the Business Cycle* (Basingstoke: Palgrave Macmillan, 2013).

Bagehot, Walter. 'Essay on Edward Gibbon' (1856), *The Works and Life of Walter Bagehot*, ed. Mrs Russell Barrington, vol. 2 (*Historical and Financial Essays*). http://rosenfels.org/pll-v5/pdf/Bagehot_1451–02_EBk_v5.pdf.

Bagehot, Walter. *Lombard Street: A Description of the Money Market* (1873). http://www.gutenberg.org/ebooks/4359.

Bank for International Settlements. *83nd Annual Report*, Basel, 23 June 2013. http://www.bis.org/publ/arpdf/ar2013e.pdf.

Bank of England. *Financial Stability Report*, April 2007. http://www.bankofengland.co.uk/publications/Documents/fsr/2007/fsrfull0704.pdf.

Bank of England. 'The Funding for Lending Scheme', *Quarterly Bulletin*, Q4, (2012). http://www.bankofengland.co.uk/publications/Documents/quarterlybulletin/qb120401.pdf

Barber, Tony. 'Greece Rapped for Understating Deficit', *Financial Times*, 20 October 2009. www.ft.com.

Barker, Alex. 'Marathon Talks Seal EU Banking Union', *Financial Times*, 20 March 2014. http://www.ft.com/cms/s/0/adfe7be4-b04e-11e3-8058-00144feab7de.html.

Basel Committee on Banking Supervision. 'An Assessment of the Long-Term Economic Impact of Stronger Capital and Liquidity Requirements', August 2010. http://www.bis.org/publ/bcbs173.pdf.

Basel Committee on Banking Supervision. 'Basel III: A Global Regulatory Framework for More Resilient Banks and Banking Systems', December 2010 (rev. June 2011). http://www.bis.org/publ/bcbs189.pdf.

Basel Committee on Banking Supervision. 'Consultative Document: Revised Basel III Leverage Ratio Framework and Disclosure Requirements', June 2013. http://www.bis.org/publ/bcbs251.pdf.

Beales, Richard Paul J. Davies, Chris Flood, Krishna Guha, Richard Milne and Gillian Tett. 'ECB Injects Euros 95bn to Aid Markets', *Financial Times*, 10 August 2007. www.ft.com.

Bebchuk, Lucien A. and Holger Spamann. 'Regulating Bankers' Pay', *Georgetown Law Journal*, vol. 98, no. 2 (2010), pp. 247–87. http://papers.ssrn.com/sol3/papers.cfm?abstract_id=1410072.

Benes, Jaromir and Michael Kumhof. 'The Chicago Plan Revisited', WP/12/202. International Monetary Fund. August 2012. http://www.imf.org/external/pubs/ft/wp/2012/wp12202.pdf.

Berlin, Isaiah. 'Two Concepts of Liberty', in *Four Essays on Liberty* (Oxford: Oxford University Press, 1969).

Bernanke, Ben. *Essays on the Great Depression* (Princeton: Princeton University Press, 2000).

Bernanke, Ben. 'Asset Price "Bubbles" and Monetary Policy', 15 October 2002. http://www.federalreserve.gov/boarddocs/speeches/2002/20021015.

Bernanke, Ben. 'Deflation: Making Sure "It" Doesn't Happen Here', 21 November 2002. http://www.federalreserve.gov/boarddocs/speeches/2002/20021121.

Bernanke, Ben. 'Some Thoughts on Monetary Policy in Japan', 31 May 2003. http://www.federalreserve.gov/boarddocs/speeches/2003/20030531.

Bernanke, Ben. 'The Great Moderation', 20 February 2004. http://www.federalreserve.gov/boarddocs/speeches/2004/20040220/default.htm.

Bernanke, Ben. 'The Global Saving Glut and the U.S. Current Account Deficit', Remarks by Governor Ben S. Bernanke at the Sandridge Lecture, Virginia Association of Economists, Richmond, Virginia, 10 March 2005. http://www.federalreserve.gov/boarddocs/speeches/2005/200503102.

Bernanke, Ben. 'The Housing Market and Subprime Lending', 5 June 2007. http://www.federalreserve.gov/newsevents/speech/bernanke20070605a.htm.

Bernanke, Ben. 'The Federal Reserve's Response to the Financial Crisis, Lectures 3 & 4', George Washington University School of Business, 27 and 29 March 2012. http://www.federalreserve.gov/newsevents/lectures/federal-reserve-response-to-the-financial-crisis.htm.

Berry, Stuart, Richard Harrison, Ryland Thomas and Iain de Weymarn. 'Interpreting Movements in Broad Money', *Bank of England Quarterly Bulletin* (2007), Q3. http://www.bankofengland.co.uk/publications/Documents/quarterlybulletin/qb070302.pdf.

Bezemer, Dirk J. '"No One Saw This Coming": Understanding Financial Crisis through Accounting Models', 16 June 2009, Munich Personal RePEc Archive, http://mpra.ub.uni-muenchen.de/15892.

Bhalla, Surjit. *Devaluing to Prosperity: Misaligned Currencies and their Growth Consequences* (Washington DC: Peterson Institute for International Economics, 2012; New Delhi: Oxford University Press, 2013).

Blanchard, Olivier, Giovanni Dell'Ariccia and Paolo Mauro. 'Rethinking Macroeconomic Policy', IMF Staff Position Note 10/03, 12 February 2010. http://www.imf.org/external/pubs/ft/spn/2010/spn1003.pdf.

Blanchard, Olivier. 'Lessons from Latvia', 11 June 2013. http://blog-imfdirect.imf.org/2012/06/11/lessons-from-latvia.

Blankfein, Lloyd. 'Remarks to the Council of Institutional Investors', April 2009. http://www2.goldmansachs.com/ideas/public-policy/lcb-speech-to-cii.html.

Blinder, Alan S. *After the Music Stopped: The Financial Crisis, the Response, and the Work Ahead* (New York: Penguin, 2013).

Blyth, Mark. *Austerity: The History of a Dangerous Idea* (New York: Oxford University Press, 2013).

Board of Governors of the Federal Reserve Board. 'Agencies Adopt Enhanced Supplementary Leverage Ratio Final Rule and Issue Supplementary Leverage Ratio Notice of Proposed Rulemaking', 8 April 2014. http://www.federalreserve.gov/newsevents/press/bcreg/20140408a.htm.

Borio, Claudio. 'Global Imbalances and the Financial Crisis: Link or no Link?', BIS Working Papers No. 346, May 2011. http://www.bis.org/publ/work346.pdf.

Borio, Claudio and William White. 'Whither Monetary and Financial Stability? The Implications of Evolving Policy Regimes', Federal Reserve Bank of Kansas City symposium on 'Monetary Policy and Uncertainty: Adapting to a Changing Economy', 28–30 August 2003. www.kansascityfed.org/publicat/sympos/2003/pdf/Boriowhite2003.pdf.

Braithwaite, Tom and Chris Tighe. 'Patient Queues in Very British Bank Run', *Financial Times*, 14 September 2007. www.ft.com.

Bowers, Simon. 'Wall Street Banks in $70bn Staff Payout', *The Guardian*, 17 October 2008. http://www.theguardian.com/business/2008/oct/17/executivesalaries-banking.

Brender, Anton and Florence Pisani. *Global Imbalances and the Collapse of Globalised Finance* (Brussels: Centre for European Policy Studies, 2010).

Brenke, Karl, Ulf Rinne and Klaus F. Zimmermann. 'Short-Time Work: The German Answer to the Great Recession', IZA Discussion Paper 5780, June 2011, http://ftp.iza.org/dp5780.pdf.

British Academy. 'Letter Sent to The Queen on 22 July 2009'. http://www.britac.ac.uk/events/archive/forum-economy.cfm.

Broadbent, Ben. 'Deleveraging', 15 March 2012. http://www.bankofengland.co.uk/publications/Documents/speeches/2012/speech553.pdf.

Brown, Brendan. *The Global Curse of the Federal Reserve: How Investors can Survive and Profit from Monetary Chaos* (Basingstoke: Palgrave Macmillan, 2013).

Brown, Gordon. 'Speech to the Labour Party Conference in Brighton', 27 September 2004. http://news.bbc.co.uk/1/hi/uk_politics/3694046.stm.

Brown, Gordon, 'Speech by the Chancellor of the Exchequer, the Rt. Hon. Gordon Brown MP, at the Mansion House, London', 21 June 2006. http://www.ft.com/cms/s/0/00a235ba-015d-11db-af16-0000779e2340.html.

Brynjolfsson, Erik and Andrew McAfee. *Race Against the Machine: How the Digital Revolution is Accelerating Innovation, Driving Employment and the Economy* (Lexington, MA: Digital Frontier Press, 2011).

Brynjolfsson, Erik and Andrew McAfee. *The Second Machine Age: Work, Progress and Prosperity in a Time of Brilliant Technologies* (New York and London: W. W. Norton, 2014).

Buffett, Warren. 'Goodreads'. http://www.goodreads.com/author/quotes/756. Warren_Buffett.

Buiter, Willem. 'The Unfortunate Uselessness of Most State of the Art Academic Macroeconomics', 3 March 2009. http://blogs.ft.com/maverecon/2009/03/the-unfortunate-uselessness-of-most-state-of-the-art-academic-monetary-economics.

Bulow, Jeremy, Jacob Goldfield and Paul Klemperer. 'Market-Based Capital Regulation', 29 August 2013. http://www.voxeu.org/article/market-based-bank-capital-regulation.

Calvo, Guillermo. 'Capital Flows and Capital-Market Crises: The Simple Economics of Sudden Stops', *Journal of Applied Economics*, vol. 1, no. 1 (November 1998), pp. 35–54.

Cameron, David. Speech, 7 March 2013. http://www.conservatives.com/News/Speeches/2013/03/Prime_Ministers_Speech_on_The_Economy.aspx.

Canuto, Otaviano and Matheus Cavallari. 'Integrating Monetary Policy and Macroprudential Regulation', 21 May 2013. http://www.voxeu.org/article/integrating-monetary-policy-and-macroprudential-regulation.

Cassidy, John. 'The Minsky Moment', *The New Yorker*. 4 February 2008. http://www.newyorker.com/talk/comment/2008/02/04/080204taco_talk_cassidy.

Cassidy, John. *How Markets Fail: The Logic of Economic Calamities* (London: Penguin, 2009).

Catão, Luis A. V. and Gian Maria Milesi-Feretti. 'External Liabilities and Crisis Risk', 4 September 2013. http://www.voxeu.org/article/external-liabilities-and-crisis-risk.

Cecchetti, Stephen G. and Enisse Kharroubi. 'Reassessing the Impact of Finance on Growth', BIS Working Papers No. 381, July 2012. http://www.bis.org/publ/work381.pdf.

Chaffin, Joshua. 'EU Bank Bonus Rules Approved', *Financial Times*, 13 March 2013. http://www.ft.com/cms/s/0/ca5becf0-91ae-11e2-b4c9-00144feabdco.html?siteedition=uk.

Claessens, Stijn, Swati Gosh and Roxana Mihet. 'Macro-Prudential Policies to Mitigate Financial System Vulnerabilities', 12 November 2012. http://macrofinance.nipfp.org.in/PDF/JIMFPr_Claessens_NIPFP-DEA-JIMF_Conference_December_2012.pdf.

Committee for the Study of Economic and Monetary Union. 'Report on Economic and Monetary Union in the European Community', 1989. http://ec.europa.eu/economy_finance/publications/publication6161_en.pdf.

Committee on the Global Financial System. 'Macroprudential Instruments and Frameworks: A Stocktaking of Issues and Experiences', CGFS Papers No. 38, May 2010. http://www.bis.org/publ/cgfs38.pdf.

Congressional Budget Office. 'Trends in the Distribution of Household Incomes between 1979 and 2007', October 2011. http://www.cbo.gov/sites/default/files/cbofiles/attachments/10-25-HouseholdIncome.pdf.

Cowen, Tyler. *The Great Stagnation: How America Ate All the Low-Hanging Fruit of Modern History, Got Sick, and Will (Eventually) Feel Better* (New York: Dutton, 2011).

Crafts, Nicholas and Peter Fearndon. *The Great Depression of the 1930s: Lessons for Today* (Oxford: Oxford University Press, 2013).

Croft, Jane, Kate Burgess and George Parker. 'B&B Set to be Taken into Public Ownership', *Financial Times*, 29 September 2008.

Darling, Alistair. *Back from the Brink: 1,000 Days at Number 11* (London: Atlantic Books, 2011).

Darvas, Zsolt. 'Intra-Euro Rebalancing is Inevitable, but Insufficient', Bruegel Policy Contribution Issue 2012/15, August 2012. www.bruegel.org.

Darvas, Zsolt. 'The Euro Area's Tightrope Walk: Debt and Competitiveness in Italy and Spain', Bruegel Policy Contribution Issue 2013/11, September 2013. www.bruegel.org.

Davies, Paul and Michael Mackenzie. 'Money Fund Sector Shocked as Reserve Breaks the Buck', *Financial Times*, 18 September 2012. www.ft.com.

Davis, Ian. 'The New Normal', *McKinsey Quarterly* (March 2009). http://www.mckinsey.com/insights/strategy/the_new_normal.

Davis, Polk. 'Basel III Leverage Ratio: U. S. Proposes American Add-On; Basel Committee Proposes Important Denominator Changes', 13 July 2013. http://www.davispolk.com/sites/default/files/files/Publication/7a0a4791-d6cb-4248-8ff0-3f8968a19dab/Preview/PublicationAttachment/55dacc73-e480-42a3-9524-425fb2ffca3a/07.19.13.Basel.3.Leverage.pdf.

De Grauwe, Paul. 'The Governance of a Fragile Eurozone', CEPS Working Documents, *Economic Policy*, 4 May 2011. http://www.ceps.eu/book/governance-fragile-eurozone.

De Grauwe, Paul. 'Managing a Fragile Eurozone', 10 May 2011. http://www.voxeu.org/article/managing–fragile–eurozone.

De Grauwe, Paul. 'Why the ECJ Should Reject the German Constitutional Court's Ruling', 11 March 2014. *Social Europe Journal*. http://www.social-europe.eu/2014/03/german-constitutional-court.

De Grauwe, Paul and Yuemei Ji. 'Panic-Driven Austerity in the Eurozone and its Implications', 21 February 2013. http://www.voxeu.org/article/panic–driven–austerity–eurozone–and–its–implications.

De Long, J. Bradford and Lawrence H. Summers. 'Fiscal Policy in a Depressed Economy', *Brookings Papers on Economic Activity* (Spring 2012), pp. 233–97. http://www.brookings.edu/~/media/Projects/BPEA/Spring%202012/2012a_DeLong.pdf.

Dooley, Michael and Peter Garber. 'Global Imbalances and the Crisis: A Solution in Search of a Problem', 21 March 2009. www.voxeu.org.

Dowd, Kevin, John Cotter, Chris Humphrey and Margaret Woods. 'How Unlucky is 25-Sigma?', Centre for Risk & Insurance Studies, Nottingham University Business School, CRIS Discussion Paper Series – 2008.III, 24 March 2008. http://www.nottingham.ac.uk/business/cris/papers/2008-3.pdf.

Duncan, Richard. *The New Depression: The Breakdown of the Paper Money Economy* (Singapore: John Wiley & Sons, 2012).

Easton, Mark. 'The Great Myth of Urban Britain', 28 June 2012. http://www.bbc.co.uk/news/uk-18623096.

Edwards, Lawrence and Robert Z. Lawrence. *Rising Tide: Is Growth in Emerging Economies Good for the United States?* (Washington DC: Peterson Institute for International Economics, 2013).

Eichengreen, Barry. 'The Euro: Love it or Leave it?', 4 May 2010. http://www.voxeu.org/article/eurozone-breakup-would-trigger-mother-all-financial-crises.

Eichengreen, Barry and Kevin O'Rourke. 'A Tale of Two Depressions Redux', 6 March 2012. www.voxeu.org/article/tale-two-depressions-redux.

European Central Bank. 'Monetary Policy', http://www.ecb.europa.eu/mopo/html/index.en.html.

European Central Bank. 'The European Stability Mechanism', *ECB Monthly Bulletin* (July 2011). http://www.ecb.int/pub/pdf/other/art2_mb201107en_pp71–84en.pdf.

European Central Bank. 'Speech by Mario Draghi, President of the European Central Bank, at the Global Investment Conference in London', 26 July 2012. http://www.ecb.int/press/key/date/2012/html/sp120726.en.html.

European Central Bank. 'Introductory Statement to Press Conference', 6 September 2012. http://www.ecb.int/press/pressconf/2012/html/is120906.en.html.

European Central Bank. 'Technical Features of Outright Monetary Transactions', 6 September 2012. http://www.ecb.int/press/pr/date/2012/html/pr120906_1.en.html.

European Commission. *Economic Forecast Autumn 2008*, 6/2008. http://ec.europa.eu/economy_finance/publications/publication13290_en.pdf.

European Commission. 'Banking Structural Reform (follow-up to the Liikanen Report)'. http://ec.europa.eu/internal_market/bank/structural-reform/index_en.htm.

European Commission. 'Banking Union'. http://ec.europa.eu/internal_market/finances/banking-union.

European Commission. 'European Financial Stabilisation Mechanism'. http://ec.europa.eu/economy_finance/eu_borrower/efsm/index_en.htm.

European Commission. 'Euro Plus Pact'. http://ec.europa.eu/europe2020/pdf/euro_plus_pact_background_december_2011_en.pdf.

European Commission. 'European Financial Supervision'. http://ec.europa.eu/internal_market/finances/committees.

European Commission. 'European Semester'. http://ec.europa.eu/europe2020/making-it-happen.

European Commission. 'European Stability Mechanism'. http://www.esm.europa.eu.

European Commission. 'Macroeconomic Imbalance Procedure'. http://ec.europa.eu/economy_finance/economic_governance/macroeconomic_imbalance_procedure/index_en.htm.

European Commission. 'Stability and Growth Pact'. http://ec.europa.eu/economy_finance/economic_governance/sgp/index_en.htm.

European Commission. 'Treaty on Stability, Coordination and Governance in the Economic and Monetary Union'. http://european-council.europa.eu/media/639235/stootscg26_en12.pdf.

Federal Deposit Insurance Company. 'Guidance on Sound Incentive Compensation Policies', 16 September 2013. http://www.fdic.gov/regulations/laws/rules/5000-5350.html.

Feenstra, Robert C. and Alan M. Taylor, eds. *Globalization in an Age of Crisis: Multilateral Economic Cooperation in the Twenty-First Century* (Chicago: University of Chicago Press, 2013).

Ferguson, Niall. 'Our Great Recession', *The New York Times*, 28 February 2009. http://www.nytimes.com/2009/03/01/opinion/01ferguson.html?_r=0.

Ferguson, Thomas and Robert Johnson. 'Too Big to Bail: The "Paulson Put", Presidential Politics, and the Global Financial Meltdown', *International Journal of Political Economy*, vol. 38, no. 2 (Summer 2009), pp. 5–45.

Finance Ministers and Central Bank Governors. 'Communiqué', Busan, Republic of Korea, 5 June 2010. http://www.ft.com/cms/422d6406-7093-11df-96ab-00144feabdco.pdf.

Financial Stability Board. 'Implementing the FSB Key Attributes of Effective Resolution Regimes – How Far have we Come?', PLEN/2013/55, 15 April 2013.

Financial Stability Board. '2013 Update of Group of Global Systemically Important Banks (G-SIBs)', 2013. https://www.financialstabilityboard. org/publications/r_131111.pdf.

Fisher, Irving. 'The Debt-Deflation Theory of Great Depressions', *Econometrica*, vol. 1, no. 4 (October 1933), pp. 337–57. http://fraser.stlouisfed.org/docs/meltzer/fisdeb33.pdf.

Forstater, Matthew. Functional Finance and Full Employment: Lessons from Lerner for Today', Working Paper No. 272, The Jerome Levy Economics Institute, July 1999.

Fox, Justin. *The Myth of the Rational Market: A History of Risk, Reward, and Delusion on Wall Street* (New York: HarperCollins, 2009).

Frank, Robert H. and Philip J. Cook. *The Winner-Take-All Society: Why the Few at the Top Get So Much More than the Rest of Us* (London and New York: Penguin, 1996).

Frydman, Roman and Michael D. Goldberg. *Beyond Mechanical Markets: Asset Price Swings, Risk, and the Role of the State* (Princeton, NJ: Princeton University Press, 2011).

Galbraith, James K. *Inequality and Instability: A Study of the World Economy Just Before the Great Crisis* (Oxford and New York: Oxford University Press, 2012).

Galbraith, John Kenneth. *The Great Crash of 1929* (Boston and New York: Mariner, 1997).

Garber, Peter M. 'Notes on the Role of TARGET in a Stage III Crisis', National Bureau of Economic Research Working Paper No. 6619, June 1998. www.nber.org.

Geithner, Tim. *Stress Tests: Reflections on Financial Crises* (New York: Crown Publishers, 2014).

Gertler, Mark. 'Commentary: Whither Monetary and Financial Stability? The Implications of Evolving Policy Regimes', Federal Reserve Bank of Kansas City symposium on 'Monetary Policy and Uncertainty: Adapting to a Changing Economy', 28–30 August 2003. http://www.kansascityfed.org/publicat/sympos/2003/pdf/Gertler2003.pdf.

Gibson, Michael S. 'Understanding the Risk of Synthetic CDOs', July 2004. http://www.federalreserve.gov/pubs/feds/2004/200436/200436pap.pdf.

Godley, Wynne and Marc Lavoie. *Monetary Economics: An Integrated Approach to Credit, Money, Income, Production, and Wealth* (Basingstoke: Palgrave Macmillan, 2007).

Goldberg, Steven. 'Investing in the New Normal', October 2010. http://www.kiplinger.com/article/investing/T041-C007-S001-investing-in-the-new-normal.html?topic_id=43.

Goodhart, Charles A. E. 'The Optimal Financial Structure', Special Paper 20, LSE Financial Markets Group Paper Series, March 2013. http://www.lse. ac.uk/fmg/workingPapers/specialPapers/PDF/SP220.pdf.

Gordon, Robert. 'Is U. S. Economic Growth Over? Faltering Innovation Confronts the Six Headwinds', National Bureau of Economic Research Working Paper No. 18315, August 2012. www.nber.org.

Gorton, Gary B. *Misunderstanding Financial Crises: Why we Don't See them Coming* (Oxford: Oxford University Press, 2012).

Government Commission of the German Corporate Governance Code. 'German Corporate Governance Code (as amended 18 June 2009)', 2009. http://www.corporate – governance – code.de/eng/kodex/1.html.

Gov.uk. 'Help to Buy: Home Ownership Schemes', 2013. https://www.gov. uk/affordable-home-ownership-schemes/help-to-buy-equity-loans.

Greenspan, Alan. 'Testimony of Dr Alan Greenspan to the House of Representatives Committee of Government Oversight and Reform', 23 October 2008. http://www.clipsandcomment.com/2008/10/23/text-alan-greenspan-testimony-congress-october-23.

Greenspan, Alan. 'Regulators must Risk More, and Intervene Less', 26 July 2011.ft.com.http://blogs.ft.com/the-a-list/2011/07/26/buffers-against-risk-carry-a-cost-to-society.

Greenspan, Alan. *The Map and the Territory: Risk, Human Nature, and the Future of Forecasting* (London: Allen Lane, 2013).

Greetham, Trevor. 'Rising Household Debt Threatens UK Recovery', *Financial Times*, 2 September 2013. http://www.ft.com/cms/s/0/9825ad6a-0bda-11e3-8f77-00144feabdco.html?siteedition=uk.

Group of 20. 'Declaration on Strengthening the Financial System', London Summit, 2 April 2009. http://www.mofa.go.jp/policy/economy/g20_summit/2009-1/annex2.html.

Group of 20. 'G20 Toronto Summit Declaration', 27 June 2010. http://www. washingtonpost.com/wp-dyn/content/article/2010/06/27/AR201006270 2887_2.html?sid=ST2010062604320.

Guajardo, Jaime, Daniel Leigh and Andrea Pescatori. 'Expansionary Austerity: New International Evidence', International Monetary Fund Working Paper. WP/11/158, July 2011. http://www.imf.org/external/pubs/ft/wp/2011/wp11158.pdf.

Greetham, Trevor. 'Rising Household Debt Threatens UK Recovery', *Financial Times*, 2 September 2013. http://www.ft.com/cms/s/0/9825ad6a-0bda-11e3-8f77-00144feabdco.html?siteedition=uk.

Guerrera, Francesco and Henny Sender. 'JP Morgan Buys Bear Stearns for $2 a Share', *Financial Times*, 16 March 2008. www.ft.com.

Guerrera, Francesco, Henny Sender, Michael Mackenzie, Krishna Guha, James Politi and Daniel Dombey. 'Fears Emerge over $700bn Rescue', *Financial Times*, 22 September 2008. www.ft.com.

Guha, Krishna. 'Action to Address "Root" Causes', *Financial Times*, 15 October 2008. www.ft.com.

Guha, Krishna, Aline van Duyn, Michael Mackenzie and Francesco Guerrera. 'Fed in $85bn AIG Rescue Deal', *Financial Times*, 17 September 2008. www.ft.com.

Guha, Krishna, Chris Giles, Saskia Scholtes and Joanna Chung, 'US Takes Control of Fannie and Freddie', *Financial Times*, 8 September 2008. www.ft.com.

Haldane, Andrew G. 'Rethinking the Financial Network', Bank of England, April 2009. http://www.bankofengland.co.uk/publications/Documents/speeches/2009/speech386.pdf.

Haldane, Andrew G. 'The $100bn Question', Bank of England, March 2010. http://www.bankofengland.co.uk/publications/Documents/speeches/2010/speech433.pdf.

Haldane, Andrew G. 'Control Rights (and Wrongs)', Wincott Annual Memorial Lecture, 24 October 2011. http://www.bankofengland.co.uk/publications/Documents/speeches/2011/speech525.pdf.

Haldane, Andrew G. and Vasileios Maduros. 'The Dog and the Frisbee', Paper given at the Federal Reserve Bank of Kansas City's 36th Economic Policy Symposium, 'The Changing Policy Landscape', Jackson Hole, Wyoming, 31 August 2012. http://www.bankofengland.co.uk/publications/Documents/speeches/2012/speech596.pdf.

Haldane, Andrew G., Simon Brennan and Vasileios Madouros. 'What is the Contribution of the Financial Sector: Miracle or Mirage?', in Adair Turner et al., *The Future of Finance: The LSE Report* (London: London School of Economics and Political Science, 2010). http://harr123et.files.wordpress.com/2010/07/futureoffinance-chapter21.pdf, Figure 19.

Hayek, Friedrich. *The Road to Serfdom*, (Chicago: Chicago University Press, 1944).

Herndon, Thomas, Michael Ash and Robert Pollin. 'Does High Public Debt Consistently Stifle Economic Growth? A Critique of Reinhart and Rogoff', 15 April 2013. http://www.peri.umass.edu/fileadmin/pdf/working_papers/working_papers_301-350/WP322.pdf.

Hicks, John R. 'Mr Keynes and the "Classics": A Suggested Interpretation', *Econometrica*, vol. 5, no. 2 (April 1937).

High-level Expert Group on reforming the structure of the EU banking sector, chaired by Erkki Liikanen. *Final Report*, Brussels, 2 October 2012.

http://ec.europa.eu/internal_market/bank/docs/high-level_expert_group/report_en.pdf.

Hirschmann, Albert O. *Exit, Voice, and Loyalty: Responses to Decline in Firms, Organizations, and States* (Cambridge, MA: Harvard University Press, 1970).

House of Commons Treasury Committee. 'Evidence on 24th June 2009', *Banking Crisis: Regulation and Supervision*, 14th Report of Session 2008–09. (London: The Stationery Office, 31 July 2009).

Housman, A. E., *Last Poems*, XXXV http://www.chiark.greenend.org.uk/~martinh/poems/complete_housman.html#LPxxxv.

Huerta de Soto, Jesús. *The Austrian School: Market Order and Entrepreneurial Creativity* (Cheltenham and Northampton, MA: Edward Elgar, 2008).

Humphrey, Thomas M. and Robert E. Keleher. 'The Lender of Last Resort: A Historical Perspective', *Cato Journal*, vol. 4, No. 1 (Spring/Summer 1984) pp. 275–321. http://object.cato.org/sites/cato.org/files/serials/files/cato-journal/1984/5/cj4n1-12.pdf.

Independent Commission on Banking. *Interim Report: Consultation on Reform Options*, April 2011. http://s3-eu-west-1.amazonaws.com/htcdn/Interim-Report-110411.pdf.

Independent Commission on Banking. *Final Report: Recommendations*, London, September 2011. https://hmt-sanctions.s3.amazonaws.com/ICB%20final%20report/ICB%2520Final%2520Report%5B1%5D.pdf.

Institute for New Economic Thinking. 'Why Did So Many Economists Fail to Predict the Global Financial Crisis, and So Many Policymakers Mishandle It – While Some Saw It All Coming?'. http://ineteconomics.org/financial-crisis-blinders.

International Monetary Fund, 'Statement by IMF Managing Director Dominique Strauss-Kahn on Greece', 23 April 2010. http://www.imf.org/external/np/sec/pr/2010/pr10168.htm.

International Monetary Fund, 'IMF Reaches Staff-level Agreement with Greece on €30bn Stand-by Arrangement', Press Release No. 10/176, 2 May 2010. www.imf.org.

International Monetary Fund. 'IMF Executive Board Approves €30 Billion Stand-by Arrangement for Greece', Press Release No. 10/187, 9 May 2010. www.imf.org.

International Monetary Fund. 'IMF Executive Board Approves €22.5 Billion Extended Arrangement for Ireland', Press Release No. 10/496, 16 December 2010. www.imf.org.

International Monetary Fund. 'IMF Managing Director Dominique Strauss-Kahn Resigns', Press Release No. 11/187, 18 May 2011. http://www.imf.org/external/np/sec/pr/2011/pr11187.htm.

International Monetary Fund. 'IMF Executive Board Approves an €26 Billion Extended Arrangement for Portugal', Press Release No. 11/190, 20 May 2011. http://www.imf.org/external/np/sec/pr/2011/pr11190.htm.

International Monetary Fund. 'Euro Area Policies: 2012 Article IV Consultation', IMF Country Report No. 12/181, July 2012. www.imf.org.

International Monetary Fund. 'IMF Executive Board Approves €1bn Arrangement under Extended Fund Facility for Cyprus', Press Release No. 13/175, 15 May 2013. www.imf.org.

International Monetary Fund. 'Greece: Ex-Post Evaluation of Exceptional Access under the 2010 Stand-by Arrangement', 20 May 2013. http://www.imf.org/external/pubs/ft/scr/2013/cr13156.pdf.

International Monetary Fund. 'Euro Area Policies: 2013 Article IV Consultation', IMF Country Report No. 13/231, July 2013. http://www.imf.org/external/pubs/ft/scr/2013/cr13231.pdf.

International Monetary Fund. 'IMF's Response to the Global Economic Crisis', 19 September 2013. http://www.imf.org/external/np/exr/facts/changing.htm.

International Monetary Fund. 'The IMF at a Glance', 24 September 2013. http://www.imf.org/external/np/exr/facts/glance.htm.

International Monetary Fund. 'The G20 Mutual Assessment Process (MAP)', 26 September 2013. http://www.imf.org/external/np/exr/facts/g20map.htm.

International Monetary Fund. 'Emerging Markets: Where Are They and Where Are They Headed?', October 2013, unpublished.

International Monetary Fund. 'Currency Composition of Official Foreign Exchange Reserves (COFER)'. 30 December 2013. http://www.imf.org/external/np/sta/cofer/eng/index.htm.

International Monetary Fund, *Fiscal Monitor*, Various Issues. www.imf.org.

International Monetary Fund. *Global Financial Stability Report*. Various issues. www.imf.org.

International Monetary Fund. *World Economic Outlook*. Various issues. www.imf.org.

Investopedia. 'Five Steps of a Bubble', 2 June 2010. http://www.investopedia.com/articles/stocks/10/5-steps-of-a-bubble.asp.

Islam, Iyanatul and Anis Chowdhury. 'Revisiting the Evidence on Expansionary Fiscal Austerity: Alesina's Hour?', 28 February 2012. http://www.voxeu.org/debates/commentaries/revisiting-evidence-expansionary-fiscal-austerity-alesina-s-hour.

Jackson, Andrew and Ben Dyson. *Modernising Money: Why our Monetary System is Broken and How it Can be Fixed* (London: Positive Money, 2013).

Jayadev, Arjun and Mike Konczal. 'The Boom Not The Slump: The Right Time For Austerity', The Roosevelt Institute, 23 August 2010. http://www. rooseveltinstitute.org/sites/all/files/not_the_time_for_austerity.pdf.

Jordà, Òscar, Moritz Schularick and Alan M. Taylor. 'Financial Crises, Credit Booms and External Imbalances', National Bureau of Economic Research Working Paper No. 16567, December 2010. www.nber.org.

Kaletsky, Anatole. *Capitalism 4.0: The Birth of a New Economy* (London: Bloomsbury, 2010).

Kay, John. *The Truth about Markets: Why Some Nations are Rich but Most Remain Poor* (London: Penguin, 2004).

Keating, Frank. 'There Is Such a Thing as Having Too Much Capital', *Financial Times*, 22 August 2013. http://www.ft.com/cms/s/0/6fea2b90-09bf-11e3-ad07-00144feabdco.html.

Keynes, John Maynard. *Tract on Monetary Reform* (London: Macmillan, 1923).

Keynes, John Maynard. *The General Theory of Employment, Interest and Money* (London: Macmillan, 1936).

Kindleberger, Charles P. and Robert Z. Aliber. *Manias, Panics and Crashes: A History of Financial Crises*, 6th edn (London: Palgrave Macmillan, 2011).

King, Mervyn. 'Banking from Bagehot to Basel, and Back Again', 25 October 2010, The Second Bagehot Lecture, Buttonwood Gathering, New York City, http://www.bankofengland.co.uk/publications/Documents/speeches/2010/speech455.pdf.

King, Stephen. *When the Money Runs Out: The End of Western Affluence* (New Haven and London: Yale University Press, 2013).

Knapp, Georg Friedrich. *The State Theory of Money* (London: Macmillan, 1924).

Konczal, Mike. 'Peter Wallison Discusses Fannie and Freddie for the American Spectator, or: Where are the Fact Checkers?', May 2011. http:// rortybomb.wordpress.com/2011/05/18/peter-wallison-discusses-fannie-and-freddie-for-the-american-spectator-or-where-are-the-fact-checkers.

Koo, Richard. *The Holy Grail of Macroeconomics: Lessons from Japan's Great Recession* (Singapore: John Wiley, 2008).

Kotlikoff, Laurence. *Jimmy Stewart is Dead: Ending the World's Ongoing Financial Plague with Limited Purpose Banking* (Hoboken, NJ: John Wiley & Sons, 2010).

Krugman, Paul. *End this Depression Now!* (New York: W. W. Norton, 2012).

Krugman, Paul. 'Conventional Wisdom', *The New York Times*, 27 May 2010. http://krugman.blogs.nytimes.com/2010/05/27/conventional-madness.

Krugman, Paul. 'Cogan, Taylor, and the Confidence Fairy', *The New York Times*, 19 March 2013. http://krugman.blogs.nytimes.com/2013/03/19/cogan-taylor-and-the-confidence-fairy.

Krugman, Paul. 'The Stimulus Tragedy', *The New York Times*, 20 February 2014. http://www.nytimes.com/2014/02/21/opinion/krugman-the-stimulus-tragedy.html?ref=paulkrugman.

Kuttner, Robert. *Debtors' Prison: The Politics of Austerity Versus Possibility* (New York: Alfred A. Knopf, 2013).

Laeven, Luc and Fabian Valencia. 'Systemic Banking Crises: A New Database', International Monetary Fund WP/08/224, 2008. www.imf.org.

Lakner, Christoph and Branco Milanovic. 'Global Income Distribution: From the Fall of the Berlin Wall to the Great Recession', World Bank Research Working Paper No. 6719, December 2013. http://www-wds.worldbank.org/external/default/WDSContentServer/IW3P/IB/2013/12/11/000158349_20131211100152/Rendered/PDF/WPS6719.pdf.

Lanman, Scott and Steve Matthews. 'Greenspan Concedes to "Flaw" in his Market Ideology', 23 October 2008. http://www.bloomberg.com/apps/news?pid=newsarchive&sid=ah5qh9Up4rIg.

Larsen, Peter Thal, 'Goldman Pays the Price of Being Big', *Financial Times*, 13 (August 2007), www.ft.com.

Laubach, Thomas and John C. Williams. 'Measuring the Natural Rate of Interest', Board of Governors of the Federal Reserve System, November 2001. http://www.federalreserve.gov/pubs/feds/2001/200156/200156pap.pdf.

Lerner, Abba P. 'Money as a Creature of the State', Papers and Proceedings of the Fifty-Ninth Annual Meeting of the American Economic Association, *American Economic Review*, vol. 37, no. 2 (May 1947), pp. 312–17.

Letter to Her Majesty the Queen, 22 July 2009, http://media.ft.com/cms/-3e3b6ca8-7a08-11de-b86f-00144feabdco.pdf.

Levy, David. 'The Contained Depression: 2008 – (2018?): What It Is, Why It Happened, How It Will Play Out, and What Will Follow', April 2012, The Jerome Levy Forecasting Center. http://levyforecast.com/jlwp/wp-content/uploads/2012/04/The-Contained-Depression-April-2012.pdf.

Liikanen, Erkki. 'The Case for Structural Reforms of Banking after the Crisis', Brussels, 2 October 2012 http://www.suomenpankki.fi/en/suomen_pankki/ajankohtaista/puheet/Pages/puhe_el_hleg.aspx.

Lin, Justin Yifu. *Against the Consensus: Reflections on the Great Recession* (Cambridge: Cambridge University Press, 2013).

Lipton, David. 'Emerging Markets in Transition', 8 October 2013 http://www.imf.org/external/np/msc/2013/am/lipton.pdf.

Lucas, Robert E. 'Macroeconomic Priorities', Presidential Address to the American Economic Association', 4 January 2003. http://pages.stern.nyu.edu/~dbackus/Taxes/Lucas%20priorities%20AER%2003.pdf.

McKinsey Global Institute. *Mapping Global Capital Markets 2011*, August 2011. http://www.mckinsey.com/insights/global_capital_markets/mapping_global_capital_markets_2011

McKinsey Global Institute. *Debt and Deleveraging: Uneven Progress on the Road to Growth*. January 2012. http://www.mckinsey.com/insights/global_capital_markets/uneven_progress_on_the_path_to_growth.

McLean, Bethany and Joe Nocera, 2010. *All the Devils are Here: The Hidden History of the Financial Crisis* (London and New York: Portfolio Penguin, 2010).

McLeay, Michael, Amar Radia and Ryland Thomas. 'Money Creation in the Modern Economy', *Bank of England Quarterly Bulletin*, Q1 (2014), pp. 14–27. http://www.bankofengland.co.uk/publications/Documents/quarterlybulletin/2014/qb14q102.pdf.

Macfarlane, Alan. *The Origins of English Individualism: Family, Property and Social Transition* (Oxford: Blackwell, 1978).

Martin, Felix. *Money: The Unauthorised Biography* (London: Bodley Head, 2013).

Mazzucato, Mariana. *The Entrepreneurial State: Debunking Public vs Private Myths in Risk and Innovation* (London: Anthem Press, 2013).

Mehrling, Perry. *The New Lombard Street: How the Fed Became the Dealer of Last Resort* (Princeton and Oxford: Princeton University Press, 2011).

Meltzer, Allan H. 'When Inflation Doves Cry', Project Syndicate, 13 August 2013. http://www.project-syndicate.org/commentary/why-us-inflation-remains-low-by-allan-h-meltzer.

Merler, Sylvia and Jean Pisani-Ferry. 'Sudden Stops in the Euro Area', Bruegel Policy Contribution 2012/06, March 2012. www.bruegel.org.

Miles, David, Jing Yang and Gilberto Marcheggiano. 'Optimal Bank Capital', External MPC Unit. Discussion Paper No. 31: revised and expanded version, April 2011. http://citeseerx.ist.psu.edu/viewdoc/download;jsessionid=DA5FA4A3231E2B8A6263D1A4035C469A?doi=10.1.1.193.8030&rep=rep1&type=pdf.

Milne, Alistair. *The Fall of the House of Credit: What Went Wrong in Banking and What Can Be Done to Repair the Damage* (Cambridge: Cambridge University Press, 2009).

Min, David. 'Faulty Conclusions Based on Shoddy Foundations', Center for American Progress, February 2011. http://www.americanprogress.org/wp–content/uploads/issues/2011/02/pdf/pinto.pdf.

Minsky, Hyman P. 'The Modeling of Financial Instability: An Introduction', in *Modeling and Simulation 5*, Proceedings of the Fifth Annual Pittsburgh Conference. Instrument Society of America (1974), pp. 267–73.

Minsky, Hyman P. 'Can 'It' Happen Again? A Reprise', Introduction to Minsky, *Can 'It' Happen Again? Essays on Instability and Finance* (Armonk: M. E. Sharpe, 1982), also in *Challenge*, July-August 1982, Hyman P. Minsky Archive, Paper 155. http://digitalcommons.bard.edu/hm_archive/155.

Minsky, Hyman P. *Inflation, Recession and Economic Policy* (Brighton: Wheatsheaf, 1982).

Minsky, Hyman P. *Stabilizing an Unstable Economy* (New Haven: Yale University Press, 1986).

Minsky, Hyman P. 'Financial Instability and the Decline (?) of Banking: Future Policy Implications', Working Paper No. 127, October 1994. The Jerome Levy Research Institute of Bard College. http://www.levyinstitute.org/pubs/wp127.pdf.

Moghadam, Reza, Ranjit Tela and Pelin Berkmen. 'Euro Area – "Deflation" versus "Lowflation"'. IMFdirect, 4 March 2014. http://blog-imfdirect.imf.org/20.14/03/04/euro-area-deflation-versus-lowflation.

Morgenson, Gretchen and Joshua Rosner. *Reckless Endangerment: How Outsized Ambition, Greed and Corruption Led to Economic Armageddon* (New York: Times Books, 2011).

Morris, Charles R. *The Two Trillion Dollar Meltdown: Easy Money, High Rollers and the Great Credit Crash* (Philadelphia: Public Affairs, 2008).

Mosler, Warren. *Seven Deadly Innocent Frauds of Economic Policy* (Valance, 2010).

Munchau, Wolfgang. 'Germany's Constitutional Court has Strengthened the Eurosceptics', *Financial Times*, 9 February 2014. http://www.ft.com/cms/s/0/8a64e3ac-8f25-11e3-be85-00144feab7de.html.

Nakamoto, Michiyo and David Wighton. 'Citigroup Chief Stays Bullish on Buy-Outs', *Financial Times*, 9 July 2009. http://www.ft.com/cms/s/0/80e2987a-2e50–11dc-821c-0000779fd2ac.html.

National Commission on the Causes of the Financial and Economic Crisis in the United States. *Financial Crisis Inquiry Report*, January 2011. http://www.gpo.gov/fdsys/pkg/GPO-FCIC/pdf/GPO-FCIC.pdf.

Nouy, Danièle. 'Is Sovereign Risk Properly Addressed by Financial Regulation?', Banque de France, *Financial Stability Review*, no. 16 (April 2012). http://www.banque-france.fr/fileadmin/user_upload/banque_de_france/

publications/Revue_de_la_stabilite_financiere/2012/rsf-avril-2012/FSR16-article-09.pdf.

Oakley, David, Mary Watkins and Kerin Hope 'Greece Launches Debt Swap Offer', *Financial Times*, 24 February 2012. www.ft.com.

Organisation for Economic Co-operation and Development. *Divided We Stand: Why Inequality Keeps Rising* (Paris: Organisation for Economic Co-operation and Development, 2011).

Organisation for Economic Co-operation and Development. *Economic Outlook*, various issues (Paris: Organisation for Economic Co-operation and Development, 2013).

O'Rourke, Kevin H. and Alan M. Taylor. 'Cross of Euros', *Journal of Economic Perspectives*, vol. 27, No. 3 (Summer 2013), pp. 167–92.

Paletta, Damian. 'Inching Toward World-Wide Accord on Bank Rules', *The Wall Street Journal* 30 August 2010. http://online.wsj.com/news/articles/SB10001424052748703418004575455822415872894..

Parliamentary Commission on Banking Standards. *Changing Banking for Good: Volume 1. Summary, and Conclusions and Recommendations*, 12 June 2013. http://www.parliament.uk/business/committees/committees-a-z/joint-select/professional-standards-in-the-banking-industry/news/changing-anking-for-good-report.

Paulson, Hank. *On the Brink: Inside the Race to Stop the Collapse of the Global Financial System* (New York and London: Business Plus and Headline, 2010).

Perotti, Enrico. 'A Blueprint for Macroprudential Policy in the Banking Union', 16 December 2012. http://www.voxeu.org/article/blueprint-macroprudential-policy-banking-union.

Perotti, Roberto. 'Rethinking Macro Policy II', International Monetary Fund, 16–17 April 2013. http://www.imf.org/external/np/seminars/eng/2013/macro2/pdf/rp.pdf.

Pettis, Michael. *Avoiding the Fall: China's Economic Restructuring* (Washington DC: Carnegie Endowment for International Peace, 2013).

Pettis, Michael. *The Great Rebalancing: Trade, Conflict, and the Perilous Road ahead for the World Economy* (Princeton and Oxford: Princeton University Press, 2013).

Pierce, Andrew. 'The Queen Asks Why No One Saw the Credit Crunch Coming', *The Daily Telegraph*, 5 November 2008. http://www.telegraph.co.uk/news/uknews/theroyalfamily/3386353/The-Queen-asks-why-no-one-saw-the-credit-crunch-coming.html.

Piketty, Thomas. *Capital in the Twenty-First Century*, trans. Arthur Goldhammer (Cambridge, MA, and London: Harvard University Press, 2014).

Portes, Jonathan. 'Recessions and Recoveries: An Historical Perspective', (updated to 7 August 2012). http://notthetreasuryview.blogspot.it/2012/04/recessions-and-recoveries-historical.html.

Pozsar, Zoltan, Tobias Adrian, Adam Ashcraft and Hayley Boesky. 'Shadow Banking', Staff Report No. 458, July 2010, revised February 2012. http://www.newyorkfed.org/research/staff_reports/sr458.html.

Rajan, Raghuram. 'Has Financial Development Made the World Riskier?', August 2005. http://www.kansascityfed.org/publicat/sympos/2005/pdf/rajan2005.pdf.

Rajan, Raghuram. 'Bankers' Pay is Deeply Flawed', *Financial Times*, 9 January 2008.

Rajan, Raghuram. *Fault Lines: How Hidden Fractures Still Threaten the World Economy* (Princeton and Oxford: Princeton University Press, 2010).

Rajan, Raghuram. 'A Step in the Dark: Unconventional Monetary Policy after the Crisis', Andrew Crockett Memorial Lecture, Bank for International Settlement, 23 June 2013. http://www.bis.org/events/agm2013/sp130623.pdf.

Reinhart, Carmen M. and Kenneth S. Rogoff. *This Time is Different: Eight Centuries of Financial Folly* (Princeton and Oxford: Princeton University Press, 2009).

Reinhart, Carmen M. and Kenneth S. Rogoff. 'Growth in a Time of Debt', National Bureau of Economic Research Working Paper No. 15639, January 2010. www.nber.org.

Report of the Parliamentary Commission on Banking Standards. *Changing Banking for Good: Volume 1. Summary, and Conclusions and Recommendations*, 12 June 2013. http://www.parliament.uk/business/committees/committees-a-z/joint-select/professional-standards-in-the-banking-industry/news/changing-banking-for-good-report.

Robertson, James. *Future Money: Breakdown or Breakthrough?* (Devon: Green Books, 2012).

Rogoff, Kenneth. 'Globalization and Global Deflation'. Paper prepared for the Federal Reserve Bank of Kansas City conference on 'Monetary Policy and Uncertainty: Adapting to a Changing Economy', Jackson Hole, WY, 29 August 2003. https://www.imf.org/external/np/speeches/2003/082903.htm.

Roubini, Nouriel and Stephen Mihm. *Crisis Economics: A Crash Course in the Future of Finance* (London: Penguin, 2011).

Rusli, Evelyn. 'The Universal Appeal of BofA', Forbes.com, 15 September 2003 http://archive.is/w503.

Rutte, Mark and Jan Kees de Jager. 'Expulsion from the Eurozone Has to Be the Final Penalty', *Financial Times* 8 September 2011. www.ft.com.

Ryan-Collins, Josh, Tony Greenham, Richard Werner and Andrew Jackson. *Where Does Money Come From?* (London: New Economics Foundation, 2011).

Sachs, Jeffrey D. *The Price of Civilization: Reawakening American Virtue and Prosperity* (New York: Random House, 2011).

Saez, Emmanuel and Thomas Piketty. 'Why the 1% should Pay Tax at 80%', 24 October 2013. http://www.theguardian.com/commentisfree/2013/oct/24/1percent-pay-tax-rate-80percent.

Saigol, Lina and Janie Smyth. 'Ireland Poised to Exit EU Bailout', *Financial Times*, 13 December 2013. www.ft.com

Samuelson, Paul. *Economics*, first edition (New York: McGraw-Hill, 1948).

Sands, Peter. 'In Banking Too Much Simplicity Can Be Dangerous', *Financial Times*, 26 August 2013. http://www.ft.com/cms/s/0/15ba8044-f46a-11e2-a62e-00144feabdco.html.

Schularick, Moritz. 'Touching the Brakes after the Crash: A Historical View of Reserve Accumulation and Financial Integration', *Global Economy Journal*, vol. 9, no. 4 (2009). http://www.jfki.fu-berlin.de/faculty/economics/team/Ehemalige_Mitarbeiter_innen/schularick/A_Historical_View_of_Reserve_Accumulation_and_Financial_Integration.pdf?1376087666.

Schularick, Moritz and Alan Taylor. 'Credit Booms Gone Bust: Monetary Policy, Leverage Cycles and Financial Crises, 1870–2008', National Bureau of Economic Research. Working Paper No. 15512. November 2009. www.nber.org.

Sen, Amartya. 'Austerity is Undermining Europe's Grand Vision', *The Guardian*, 3 July 2010. http://www.theguardian.com/commentisfree/2012/jul/03/austerity-europe-grand-vision-unity.

Sharma, Ruchir. *Breakout Nations: In Pursuit of the Next Economic Miracles* (London: W. W. Norton and Allen Lane, 2012).

Sheard, Paul. 'Repeat After Me: Banks Cannot and Do Not "Lend Out" Reserves', 13 August 2013. http://www.standardandpoors.com/spf/upload/Ratings_US/Repeat_After_Me_8_14_13.pdf.

Shiller, Robert. *The Subprime Solution: How Today's Financial Crisis Happened, and What to Do about It* (Princeton: Princeton University Press, 2008).

Shin, Hyun Song. *Risk and Liquidity*, Clarendon Lectures in Finance (Oxford: Oxford University Press, 2010).

Shin, Hyun Song. 'The Second Phase of Global Liquidity and its Impact on Emerging Economies', 7 November 2013. http://www.frbsf.org/economic-research/events/2013/november/asia-economic-policy-conference/program/files/The-Second-Phase-of-Global-Liquidity-and-Its-Impact-on-Emerging-Economies.pdf.

Siedentop, Larry. *Democracy in Europe* (London: Allen Lane, 2001).

Singh, Manmohan and Peter Stella. 'Money and Collateral', WP/12/95, International Monetary Fund, April 2012. http://www.imf.org/external/pubs/ft/wp/2012/wp1295.pdf.

Sinn, Hans-Werner and Timo Wollmershaeuser. 'Target Loans, Current Account Balances and Capital Flows: The ECB's Rescue Facility', National Bureau of Economic Research Working Paper No. 17626, November 2011. www.nber.org.

Skidelsky, Robert. *Keynes: The Return of the Master* (London: Allen Lane, 2009).

Smith, Adam. *An Inquiry into the Nature and Causes of the Wealth of Nations*, Book V, Chapter 3 (1776). http://www.econlib.org/library/Smith/smWN22.html#B.V, Ch. 3, Of Public Debts.

Smithers, Andrew. *The Road to Recovery: How and Why Economic Policy Must Change* (London: Wiley, 2013).

Smithers, Andrew and Stephen Wright. 'Stock Markets and Central Bankers – The Economic Consequences of Alan Greenspan', *World Economics*, vol. 3, no. 1 (2002), pp. 101–24.

Sorkin, Andrew Ross. *Too Big to Fail: Inside the Battle to Save Wall Street* (London: Penguin, 2010).

Soros, George. *The Alchemy of Finance: Reading the Mind of the Market* (Hoboken: John Wiley, 2003).

Soros, George. *The New Paradigm for Financial Markets: The Credit Crisis of 2008 and What it Means* (New York: PublicAffairs, 2008).

Sovereign Wealth Fund Institute, 'Sovereign Wealth Fund Rankings'. http://www.swfinstitute.org/fund-rankings.

Stein, Herbert. 'Herb Stein's Unfamiliar Quotations: On Money, Madness, and Making Mistakes', *Slate*, 16 May 1997. www.slate.com.

Stiglitz, Joseph E. *Freefall: Free Markets and the Sinking of the Global Economy* (New York: W. W. Norton, 2010).

Stiglitz, Joseph E. *The Price of Inequality: How Today's Divided Society Endangers our Future* (New York and London: W. W. Norton, 2012).

Stock, James H. and Mark W. Watson. 'Has the Business Cycle Changed and Why?', in Mark Gertler and Kenneth Rogoff, eds., *NBER Macroeconomic Annual 20012*, vol. 17 (Cambridge, MA: MIT Press, 2003). http://www.nber.org/chapters/c11075.pdf.

Strupczeswki, Jan and Julien Toyer. 'Eurozone Agrees to Lend Spain up to 100bn Euros', Reuters, 10 June 2012. http://uk.reuters.com/article/2012/06/10/uk-Eurozone-idUKBRE85805E2012061.

Summers, Lawrence. Speech at the 14th IMF Annual Research Conference in Honor of Stanley Fischer, 18 November 2013. http://larrysummers.com/imf-fourteenth-annual-research-conference-in-honor-of-stanley-fischer.

Summers, Lawrence. 'Why Stagnation Might Prove to Be the New Normal', 15 December 2013, *Financial Times*. http://www.ft.com/cms/s/2/87cb15ea-5d1a-11e3-a558-00144feabdco.html.

Summers, Lawrence and Martin Wolf. 'A Conversation on New Economic Thinking', Bretton Woods Conference, Institute for New Economic Thinking, 8 April 2011. http://ineteconomics.org/video/bretton-woods/larry-summers-and-martin-wolf-new-economic-thinking.

Taleb, Nassim Nicholas. *Fooled by Randomness: The Hidden Role of Chance in Life and the Markets* (London: Penguin, 2004).

Taleb, Nassim Nicholas. *The Black Swan: The Impact of the Highly Improbable* (New York: Random House, 2007).

Tarullo, Daniel K. 'Statement by Daniel K. Tarullo, Member, Board of Governors of the Federal Reserve System before the Committee on Banking, Housing, and Urban Affairs, US Senate', Washington DC, 11 July 2013. http://www.federalreserve.gov/newsevents/testimony/tarullo20130711a.htm.

Taylor, Alan M. 'The Great Leveraging', National Bureau of Economic Research Working Paper No. 18290, August 2012. www.nber.org.

Taylor, Alan M. 'When is the Time for Austerity?', 20 July 2013. http://www.voxeu.org/article/when-time-austerity.

Taylor, John B. 'The Financial Crisis and the Policy Response: An Empirical Analysis of What Went Wrong', National Bureau of Economic Research Working Paper 14631, January 2009. www.nber.org.

Taylor, John B. *Getting off Track: How Government Actions and Interventions Caused, Prolonged and Worsened the Financial Crisis* (Stanford: Hoover Institution Press, 2009).

Temin, Peter and David Vines. *The Leaderless Economy: Why the World Economic System Fell Apart and How to Fix it* (Princeton and Oxford: Princeton University Press, 2013).

Thomson, Christopher. 'Coco Bond "Avalanche" Expected from EU Banks', *Financial Times*, 25 November 2013. http://www.ft.com/cms/s/0/a169e4f8-55e6-11e3-96f5-00144feabdco.html.

Tobin, James. 'Commercial Banks as Creators of "Money"', Cowles Foundation Paper 205. Reprinted from Dean Carson (ed.), *Banking and Monetary Studies, for the Comptroller of the Currency, U. S. Treasury, Richard D. Irwin* (1963). http://cowles.econ.yale.edu/P/cm/m21/m21-01.pdf.

Trichet, Jean-Claude. 'Interview with Jean-Claude Trichet, President of the ECB, and *Libération*, Conducted by Jean Quatremer', European Central

Bank, 8 July 2010. http://www.ecb.europa.eu/press/key/date/2010/html/sp100713.en.html.

Turner, Adair. *The Turner Review: A Regulatory Response to the Global Banking Crisis*, Financial Services Authority, London, March 2009. http://www.fsa.gov.uk/pubs/other/turner_review.pdf.

Turner, Adair. 'Financial Risk and Regulation: Do We Need More Europe or Less?', Financial Services Authority, London, 27 April 2012. http://www.fsa.gov.uk/library/communication/speeches/2012/0427-at.shtml.

Turner, Adair. 'Monetary and Financial Stability: Lessons from the Crisis and from Classic Economics Texts', Financial Services Authority, London, 2 November 2012. http://www.fsa.gov.uk/static/pubs/speeches/1102-at.pdf.

Turner, Adair. *Economics After the Crisis: Ends and Means* (Cambridge, MA, and London: MIT Press, 2012).

Turner, Adair. 'Debt, Money and Mephistopheles: How Do we Get out of this Mess?', Cass Business School, 6 February 2013. http://www.fsa.gov.uk/static/pubs/speeches/0206-at.pdf.

Turner, Adair. 'Escaping the Debt Addiction: Monetary and Macro-Prudential Policy in the Post-Crisis World', 10 February 2014. http://ineteconomics.org/sites/inet.civicactions.net/files/Frankfurt%20Escaping%20the%20debt%20addiction%2010%20FEB.pdf.

Turner, Adair et al. *The Future of Finance: The LSE Report* (London: London School of Economics and Political Science, 2010). http://harr123et.files.wordpress.com/2010/07/futureoffinance5.pdf.

United Nations Conference on the World Financial and Economic Crisis and its Impact upon Development. Report of the Commission of Experts of the President of the United Nations General Assembly on Reforms of the International Monetary and Financial System, 24–26 June 2009, New York. http://www.un.org/ga/president/63/interactive/financialcrisis/PreliminaryReport210509.pdf.

Urry, Maggie. 'Government to Push Lloyds-HBOS Deal Through', *Financial Times*, 18 September 2008.

Volcker, Paul. 'Remarks by Paul A. Volcker at a Luncheon of the Economic Club of New York', 8 April 2012. http://blogs.denverpost.com/lewis/files/2008/04/volckernyeconclubspeech04-08-2008.pdf.

Wagstyl, Stefan and Claire Jones. 'German Court Refers ECB Bond-Buying Programme to European Justice', 7 February 2014. http://www.ft.com/cms/s/0/3feab440-8fd5-11e3-aee9-00144feab7de.html.

Warwick Commission on International Financial Reform. 'Macro-Prudential and Micro-Prudential Regulation', ch. 2, *In Praise of Unlevel Playing Fields*, 2009, The Report of the Second Warwick Commission, University of Warwick. http://www2.warwick.ac.uk/research/warwickcommission/financialreform/report/chapter_2.pdf.

Weiler, Jonathan. 'Why the Tea Party is a Fraud', *Huffington Post*, 15 April 2010. http://www.huffingtonpost.com/jonathan-weiler/why-the-tea-party-is-a-fr_b_539550.html

Wheatley, Jonathan. 'Brazil's Mantega Sees "International Currency War"', *Financial Times*, 27 September 2010. www.ft.com.

White, Ben. 'Buoyant Bear Stearns Shrugs Off Subprime Woes', *Financial Times*, 16 March 2007.

White, William. 'Ultra Easy Monetary Policy and the Law of Unintended Consequences', September 2012. http://www.dallasfed.org/assets/documents/institute/wpapers/2012/0126.pdf.

Williams, John. 'A Defense of Moderation in Monetary Policy', Federal Reserve Bank of San Francisco, Working Paper 2013–15. http://www.frbsf.org/economic-research/files/wp2013-15.pdf.

Williamson, John. 'Getting Surplus Countries to Adjust', Policy Brief PB11-01, January 2011, Peterson Institute for International Economics. http://www.iie.com/publications/pb/pb11-01.pdf.

Wolf, Martin. 'Federalism before a Fall', *Financial Times*, 3 December 1991.

Wolf, Martin. *Why Globalization Works* (New Haven and London: Yale University Press, 2004).

Wolf, Martin. 'Session 3 (Round Table) Financial Globalisation, Growth and Asset Prices', *International Symposium: Globalisation, Inflation and Monetary Policy*, Banque de France, March 2008. http://www.banque-france.fr/fileadmin/user_upload/banque_de_france/Economie-et-Statistiques/La_recherche/GB/session3b.pdf.

Wolf, Martin. 'The Rescue of Bear Stearns Marks Liberalisation's Limit', *Financial Times*, 25 March 2008).

Wolf, Martin. *Fixing Global Finance* (Baltimore and London: Johns Hopkins University Press and Yale University Press, 2008 and 2010).

Wolf, Martin. 'Why and How should we Regulate Pay in the Financial Sector?', in Adair Turner et al., *The Future of Finance: The LSE Report* (London: London School of Economics and Political Science, 2010).

Wolf, Martin. 'Be Bold, Mario, Put Out that Fire', *Financial Times*, 25 October 2011. http://www.ft.com/cms/s/0/bd60ab78-fe6e-11e0-bac4-00144feabdco.html.

Wolf, Martin. 'Mind the Gap: Perils of Forecasting Output', *Financial Times*, 9 December 2011.

Wolf, Martin. 'A Permanent Precedent', *Financial Times*, 17 May 2012. http://www.ft.com/cms/s/0/614df5de-9ffe-11e1-94ba-00144feabdco.html.

Wolf, Martin. 'The Role of Fiscal Deficits in Deleveraging', 25 July 2012. http://blogs.ft.com/martin-wolf-exchange/2012/07/25/getting-out-of-debt-by-adding-debt.

Wolf, Martin. 'Afterword: How the Financial Crises Have Changed the World', in Robert C. Feenstra and Alan M. Taylor, eds., *Globalization in an Age of Crisis: Multilateral Economic Cooperation in the Twenty-First Century* (Chicago: University of Chicago Press, 2013).

Wolf, Martin. 'How the Financial Crisis Changed Our World', Wincott Memorial Lecture, 2013. http://www.wincott.co.uk/lectures/2013.html.

Wolf, Martin. 'Lessons from the Global Financial Crisis', *Insight: Melbourne Business and Economics*, vol. 13 (April 2013).

Wolf, Martin. 'Why the Baltic States are No Model', *Financial Times*, 30 April 2013. http://www.ft.com/cms/s/0/090bd38e-b0c7-11e2-80f9-00144feabdco.html.

Wolf, Martin. 'The German Model is Not for Export', *Financial Times*, 7 May 2013. http://www.ft.com/cms/s/0/aacd1be0-b637-11e2-93ba-00144feabdco.html.

Wolf, Martin. 'The Toxic Legacy of the Greek Crisis', *Financial Times*, 18 June 2013. http://www.ft.com/cms/s/0/b31dd248-d785-11e2-a26a-00144feab7de.html.

Wolf, Martin. 'How Austerity Has Failed', *New York Review of Books*, 11 July 2013. http://www.nybooks.com/articles/archives/2013/jul/11/how-austerity-has-failed.

Wolf, Martin. 'Failing Elites Threaten our Future', *Financial Times*, 14 January 2014. http://www.ft.com/cms/s/0/cfc1eb1c-76d8-11e3-807e-00144feabdco.html.

Wong, Simon. 'Some Banks' Pay Reform may Show the Way', *Financial Times*, 13 March 2011. http://www.ft.com/cms/s/0/578024fa-4c21-11e0-82df-00144feab49a.html.

Woodford, Michael. *Interest and Prices: Foundations of a Theory of Monetary Policy* (Princeton and Oxford: Princeton University Press, 2003).

Wray, L. Randall. *Modern Monetary Theory: A Primer on Macroeconomics for Sovereign Monetary Systems* (London: Palgrave Macmillan, 2012).

Wren-Lewis, Simon. 'The Two Arguments Why the Zero Lower Bound Matters', *Mainly Macro*, 12 July 2013. http://mainlymacro.blogspot.it/2013/07/the-two-arguments-why-zero-lower-bound.html.

Zarlenga, Stephen A. *The Lost Science of Money: The Mythology of Money – the Story of Power* (New York: American Monetary Institute, 2002).

Index

comparisons with Spain, 81–4,
82*fig*, 83*fig*
current-account deficits, 280, 281
economic costs of crisis, 35,
260–1, 325
employment ratio in, 35*fig*
fiscal deficit in, 30, 30*fig*, 235–6,
268*fig*, 270, 283, 325
globalization of banking system,
126–7, 176, 228
gross debt of financial system
(2007), 129
growth of wholesale funding,
126, 138, 176
high marginal tax rates in
1970s, 183
house-price booms, 157, 157*fig*,
158, 187
ill-timed austerity policy, 34,
87–8, 268, 270–1, 328–9
Independent Commission on
Banking, 132, 227, 228,
230–1
index-linked gilts, 154, 155,
155*fig*, 156
interest rates, 29, 81, 153,
153*fig*, 154–6, 155*fig*,
175, 267–8, 270
leverage ratios in banks,
240, 323–4
macroprudential-monetary
conflict (2014), 333
as net capital importer, 99, 126
output forecasts (for 2017), 38
output gap (2013), 261,
264, 270
Parliamentary Commission on
Banking Standards, 229
post-crisis slump in, 38, 260–1,
269, 270, 328–9

pre-crisis growth trends, 259–60,
260*fig*, 261–2, 330, 331,
332*fig*
private debt in, 18, 126, 187,
273–4
public debt in, 28–9, 30, 81,
82–3, 82*fig*, 268–9
reliance on short-term foreign
funding, 342
ring-fencing of retail banking in,
230–31
risks of euro and, 290
securitized credit in, 126, 136
slow rate of de-leveraging in,
273–4
slow recovery in, 34, 270–1
as sovereign monetary area, 83,
84, 87–8, 311
sterling devaluations
(1949 and 1967), 67
structural surpluses in, 279–80,
280*fig*
unemployment in, 36
United States of America (USA)
ageing population in, 275
austerity policy in, 87–8, 268,
270–1
balance-sheet recession in, 40–1,
171
bank bailout in, 26–7
banking crisis in, 20–2, 23–5
Civil War, 67, 309
Community Reinvestment Act,
140–1
comparisons with Eurozone,
290–1, 308–10, 309*fig*, 311
Congressional Budget Office, 169
construction industry in, 34,
168, 262
corporate culture in, 34–5